CUCINA DEL SOLE

Also by Nancy Harmon Jenkins

THE ESSENTIAL MEDITERRANEAN

FLAVORS OF TUSCANY

FLAVORS OF PUGLIA

THE MEDITERRANEAN DIET COOKBOOK

THE BOAT BENEATH THE PYRAMID

WM

WILLIAM MORROW
An Imprint of HarperCollins*Publishers*

Nancy Harmon Jenkins

CUCINA DEL SOLE

A CELEBRATION OF SOUTHERN ITALIAN COOKING

HarperCollins books may be purchased for educational, business, or sales promotional use. For information please write: Special Markets Department, HarperCollins Publishers, 10 East 53rd Street, New York, NY 10022.

FIRST EDITION

Designed by Fritz Metsch

Library of Congress Cataloging-in-Publication Data

Jenkins, Nancy Harmon.
    Cucina del sole: a celebration of southern Italian cooking / Nancy Harmon Jenkins.— 1st ed.
        p. cm.
    Includes bibliographical references and index.
    ISBN: 978-0-06-072343-9
    ISBN-10: 0-06-072343-2
    1. Cookery, Italian—Southern style.   I. Title.

TX723.2.S65J44 2006
641.5945'7—dc22
                                                    2005057499

07 08 09 10 11   RRD   10 9 8 7 6 5 4 3 2

For Susan Friedland, with thanks

Contents

In Another Country: The Mezzogiorno d'Italia

We have deep roots in this warm soil of Italy,
which brought forth a goodly tithe of what is best
in our own lives, in our arts and aspirations.
—Norman Douglas, *In Old Calabria*

Norman Douglas, British writer, wit, and constant traveler, wrote the words above more than a century ago, after he had spent long months happily roaming on his own over the rugged terrain and along the half-deserted coastlines of the Italian South, through hapless villages, teeming cities, and the shattered remnants of ancient cultures, haunted relics of a time when the impoverished South had been the richest and most desirable part of the entire Italian peninsula. Among the arts that Douglas rather conspicuously failed to mention, however, except in what his close friend Elizabeth David described as "thundering denunciations," were the culinary arts.

Meandering alone or with a local guide along drove roads and forest trails, clambering over mountain fastnesses, wading through streams, examining ruins—classical, Byzantine, Norman, Baroque—with the eye of the connoisseur if not of the archaeologist, talking, questioning, ruminating on things read and spoken and done in times past, Douglas would arrive in a village late in the day, tired and hungry, only to find that the manageress of the chosen inn "met my suggestion about eatables with a look of blank astonishment.

"Was there nothing in the house, then? No cheese, or meat, or macaroni, or eggs—no wine to drink?

"'Nothing!' she replied. 'Why should you eat things at this hour? You must find them yourself, if you really want them. I might perhaps procure you some bread.'

"*Avis aux voyageurs,* as the French say."

If, a hundred years ago, in this impoverished and backward hinterland you could still discern the roots of European high culture, it was quite impossible for a person of Douglas's refined tastes to see any connection at all between European cuisine, high or low, and the foods and foodways of the Mezzogiorno. As late as 1959, when Ann Cornelisen wrote *Women of the Shadows,* in her village in Puglia, she said the butter was rancid, the pecorino cheese had "an indefinable flavor of old drains and sour rags," the meat was tough and expensive, and the fish, when it arrived, was "reduced to a few scaly midsections of unknown origin and some very suspect clams which annually brought hepatitis, typhoid, and most recently cholera."

So why on earth should I write a book about the food of the Mezzogiorno and why, above all, should I ask you to buy it, read it, cook from it?

Because the food of southern Italy, *pace* Douglas, Cornelisen, and dozens of others writing over the centuries, is actually and always has been exceptional, drawing deeply from that Mediterranean trinity of wheat, vines, and olive trees that have flourished here since time immemorial, adding to them the harvest of fruits and vegetables, legumes and greens, which thrive in this blessed climate, and enriching all that with a restricted but nonetheless indispensable yield from the abundance of the seas and the flocks in mountain pastures (sheep for the most part, but goats, pigs, and sometimes cattle too). But in the recent past (by recent, I mean the last two hundred years or so), poverty in the region has been so overwhelming as to obscure, especially to discriminating foreign visitors, the nature of what was always there.

It's important to understand that southern Italian poverty was not a poverty of resources or one that came about for the usual reasons—wars, plagues, natural calamities, crop failures of one sort or another. Instead it was a politically imposed poverty, the result of deliberate choices and policies put in place by regional and national governments.

The root cause of poverty in the Mezzogiorno was the result of a land distribution system that was more than inequitable, that kept the great majority of the population who worked the land—impoverished, illiterate, little more than serfs—in thrall to the small class who owned it. This landowning class, far more often than not, was made up of absentee aristocrats and petty nobility who lived in cities like Palermo and Napoli and were totally distanced from and indifferent to what was happening on their own lands, as long as the profits kept accruing. And they needn't be very large profits either. Anyone who doubts this should read, or reread, Giuseppe Tomasi di Lampedusa's brilliant novel of life in southern Italy (Sicily, to be specific), *Il gattopardo* (*The Leopard* in English), which, apart from being a superb example of the novelist's craft, is also an astute social document.

After the unification of Italy in 1861, the church and the bourgeoisie, working together, continued to impose a hands-off policy that left the Italian South permanently underdeveloped and an ongoing source of cheap labor for the United States, Canada, Argentina, Australia, and other countries to which poor southern Italians, those at least who could scrape together the pitiful funds necessary, fled from an intolerable situation. A permanent wound on the body politic left by these deliberate policies was distrust of the government in any form and a misplaced trust in the mafia in Sicily and similar criminal organizations that developed in other regions—the camorra in Napoli, the 'ndrangheta in Calabria.*

But times have changed.

It's almost impossible nowadays to credit the accounts of poverty and desperation from only a few decades past. Today, chefs of fancy North American restaurants and writers from our glossiest food and travel magazines flock to southern Italy and Sicily for instruction and inspiration. Tourists—even North American tourists, surely among the most timid travelers in the world—arrive by the planeload at Palermo, Naples, and, increasingly, Bari, fearlessly seeking out small, exclusive luxury hotels, complete with infinity pools and adjacent golf courses, and chic, well-appointed restaurants serving elegant updates of traditional dishes. Sicily, Campania, and Puglia are in the forefront of this quest, but Calabria and Basilicata are not far behind. Southern Italy, long the forgotten and despised stepchild of the more progressive Italian North, has arrived as a full-fledged destination for even the most demanding tastes.

How and why this has come about is far too long and complex a story to fit into the introduction to a recipe collection, but, briefly, two reasons, it seems to me, are at the core of the change, one internal and one external. The internal reason is the increasing—and still relative—prosperity of Italy's South, something that has been a long time coming. Prosperity began in the North within twenty years of the end of World War II, but it took a good half-century after that conflict for affluence to spread south, and even today, it has to be said, the region includes pockets of shocking poverty and some of the highest unemployment rates, especially among young people, in the European Union.

As for the external reason, it has little to do with what happens in Italy and more to do with modern consumers and their relentless pursuit of the novel and the fashionable. Whole industries have grown up to satisfy this pursuit, so it's not surprising that, after a surfeit of Rome, Florence, and Venice, the march of the fashionable has been drawn south, bringing in its wake construction, reconstruction, and—most important for southerners themselves—jobs. And the cuisine—or, I should say, the cuisines—of the Mezzogiorno have at last been recognized as a deeply rooted source for "what is best in our own lives," to use Douglas's words, and what is best on our tables.

Some of the food described in this book comes from just such fashionable hot spots. My own explorations over the years have led me happily to places where chefs and restaurateurs are firm in their adherence to local traditions, even as they have modified techniques and lightened flavors that would be too aggressive for modern tastes—people like Alfonso and Livia Iaccarino

---

*This is perforce a simplistic explanation of a complex social phenomenon. For a deeper analysis, see Denis Mack Smith's *A History of Sicily: Volume 2, Modern Sicily After 1713*. New York: 1968. Mack Smith discusses Sicily, but his analysis is valid for much of southern Italy.

at Alfonso 2000 in Campania, Dora and Angelo Ricci (and now their daughter Antonella and her husband, Vinobha Sookhar) at Fornello da Ricci in Puglia, Federico Valicenti at Luna Rossa in Basilicata, Ciccio Sultano at Il Duomo in southeastern Sicily, Gaetano Alia at the Locanda d'Alia in Calabria, and many, many other fine chefs. This is what Italians call *cucina di territorio,* by which they mean not just ingredients but also preparations that come strictly from the region and the traditions that have evolved there. In restaurants like these, you will not find white truffle oil or balsamic vinegar, but you might find an aged local vinegar or an oil infused with the crushed zest of a local citrus. You won't find basil-based pesto genovese, but you might find pesto from Trapani made with red tomatoes and pounded roasted almonds. And you certainly won't find the rich egg-based pastas of the Italian North, served in buttery sauces and dressed with a veil of grated parmigiano reggiano, but you will find instead, and just as satisfying, the handmade pastas of southern tradition, made with tasty durum wheat and often dressed, even in these notable restaurants, with the simplicity of garlic, olive oil, anchovies, and a pleasant scattering of crisp toasted bread crumbs.

But I have also sought out *cucina di territorio* from more old-fashioned and rather humble trattorias and osterias, places you might come across deep in the countryside or tucked into an alley in the centro storico of cities like Lecce, Foggia, Catania, and Trapani and in smaller provincial towns and villages too numerous to mention. And there is in this book, of course, food from individuals—cooks, yes, from peasant and aristocratic families alike, but also farmers, teachers, cheesemakers, winery and oil mill owners, producers of foodstuffs from pasta to tomato extract, bakers like Donato Caroppo in the village of Specchio Galone in Puglia, and the wives of all these too—for, apart from restaurants, it's the women, still, who do most of the cooking and preserve the traditions. And even in restaurants, it's often women who are in charge of the kitchen.

This book is about the foods and foodways of Campania, Calabria, Basilicata, Puglia, and Sicily, five regions that make up the bulk if not the entirety of what is conventionally called the Mezzogiorno* and that seem to me to be so closely related, so integrated in terms of cuisine, as to form almost a single cultural unit. Of course there are important differences among these regions, just as there are within each one: Sicily's food is often highly complex, Puglia's much simpler and straightforward; the urbane and self-confident pizzas of Napoli are altogether different from the rustic, bread-based country soups of Basilicata; Calabrese and Lucanian cooks rely on chilies to a degree that is unknown elsewhere, while in Puglia north and south, east and west, cooks are divided on the uses of garlic.

---

*The name, like the French Midi, used for the south of France, means "midday" or "noontime"; I have never seen a satisfactory explanation of why the southern part of a country should be named for the middle of the day, unless it's because the sun is strongest there and then.

But in the end, whether in the kitchen or at the table, all of these regions, and their subregions, are more alike than they are diverse, relying as they all do on bread and pasta made from hard durum wheat as the very foundation of the diet, olive oil—and to a lesser extent pork fat—as the principal cooking medium, and wine as the lubricant that makes it all go down. Butter is almost unknown, except in certain fancy desserts, most of which are derived from the French tradition. Like the bread, pasta is made from the simplest of ingredients—water, salt, and *semola di grano duro,* the gritty flour from durum wheat—the only distinction being the addition of leavening to make the bread rise. Except on feast days, meat is used more as a seasoning than as a primary ingredient. Seafood is as profuse in its variety as in its presentations. And everywhere the tomato is king, the eggplant is queen, and the courtiers—to stretch the metaphor past the breaking point—are made up of a whole series of greens, wild and cultivated, raw and cooked.

All over the world, even in our own fast-food nation, what people eat and how they prepare it is based on two big factors, environment and history. The more time I spend in the Italian South, the more I'm persuaded that what holds these five regions, and these five cuisines, together is a shared environment and a history that goes back thousands of years. It begins with the Mycenaean Greeks, intrepid *voyageurs* of the Mediterranean, whose ships penetrated the Adriatic and explored along the Ionian coasts of Sicily and the mainland back in the twelfth century B.C.E. Centuries later, in the territory that would come to be known as Magna Graecia, or Megara Hellas (Great Greece), Greek colonies flourished. (The word *colony* is really a misnomer, for Magna Graecia was made up of autonomous, often very rich, and quarrelsome small kingdoms and city-states that were quite independent of the mother country.) In Sicily alone, there were more Greeks than there were in Greece itself, and the Greeks of Syracusae, Crotona, Tarantum, Metapontum, Sybaris, sophisticated and luxury loving, looked askance at the rustics they had left behind back home. After the Roman centuries, Greek rule returned once more with the Byzantines, who dominated the old lands of Magna Graecia, off and on, for centuries, struggling against Goths, Vandals, Lombards, Normans, and the papacy until the ninth century, when Moslem Arabs and Berbers invaded and took over most of Sicily and parts of mainland southern Italy as well.

By the tenth century, most of southern Italy was in the hands of either Arabs or Normans, and Greek rule never returned. But for many southern Italians and Sicilians, Greek continued to be the common language for years, with their communities constantly reinforced by refugees from Balkan wars and politics, especially Albanian Christians who, though not Greek speaking, shared Orthodox beliefs and culture. To this day there are communities in the Italian South where the dialects commonly spoken are Griko among descendants of Greeks (five of them in Puglia alone) and Arberesh among Albanians. Greek monasteries flourished for centuries throughout much of the South, and Eastern rite churches, even though ruled from the Vatican, are still an important part of southern Italian culture.

I dwell on this age-old connection with Greece because I think the modern world sometimes forgets that many of the borders drawn so precisely on twentieth-century maps did not always exist and in any case are often meaningless when trying to piece out social and cultural entities. The Greek connection, ancient and ongoing, has had a profound effect on southern foods and foodways. The lavish use of olive oil, the flavors of the oil itself (rich and fruity, unlike the more astringent oils of the North), the way it's used not just for cooking but perhaps even more important as a garnish to make almost anything more savory, is one aspect of Greek influence. But when I taste certain favorite dishes—for instance, the puree of dried fava beans called variously *macco, maccu,* or, in Puglia, *'ncapriata*—I taste a link to Greece, just as I do when my teeth crunch on the hard, twice-baked, barley-meal biscuits called *frisedde* in the Salento and *paximadia* in Crete. In the early days of spring, countryfolk, many of them elderly, scour fields and roadsides for the wild greens—chicories, wild asparagus, and tassel hyacinth bulbs (*Muscari racemosum*), called *lampascione* in Italy and *volvous* in Greece—that are revered in both kitchens. And there are many, many other characteristics that link the two places and that make this Mezzogiorno often feel more like a part of the Aegean than of the West. I would even venture the theory, contrary to what most culinary historians say, that Greece had a guiding hand in the evolution of pasta here in southern Italy, and I have often thought that you could transport a country housewife from the Mezzogiorno straight into a Greek island kitchen and, language apart, she'd have no trouble at all putting together a tasty meal.

But almost as important as the Greeks in their impact on southern Italian cooking were the Arabs—who were called Saracens when they were menacing raiding parties and, more politely but less correctly, Moors when they settled down and established themselves on the northern coast of the Mediterranean. Sicily was most heavily influenced by this Arab (and Berber) Moslem culture, which persisted on the island for several centuries. But other parts of the South also bear unmistakable traces of the Arab presence.

It's not hard to tease out Arab influences on the cuisine of the Mezzogiorno, but tough to determine whether they were a direct result of Arab rule or came later with the Spanish, who themselves were under compelling Arab dominance during the more than six hundred years that various Arab and Berber regimes ruled Spain. The famous heritage breed of sheep, for instance, called charmingly *gentile da Puglia,* whose milk is responsible for the finest pecorino cheeses from Calabria and Basilicata, are descendants, remotely, of a Berber breed that was brought to Spain, where they became Spanish merinos, renowned for their wool, and were then transported to southern Italy under the Spanish regnum. A hardy breed, they were well suited to travel the long, dusty drove roads or tratturi that connected summer pastures in the high Abruzzi hills to winter grazing in the lowland plains around Foggia.

Techniques, too, seem linked to the Arabs. Certainly a valid argument can be made that deep-fat frying in olive oil, practiced with such expertise in the Mezzogiorno, is inherited from the Arab kitchen, but possibly transmitted by the Spanish, or by the Jews, both of whom share a similar proficiency.

Whether directly or through Spain, however, it is clear that Arabs were responsible for many new products, the most important of which were rice and sugar. Arab farmers introduced the cultivation of sugarcane in Sicily and Calabria, and quite possibly—though there's no contemporary evidence for it—Arab sweetmakers further developed the art of using sugar in confectionery. Even today Sicilian sweets are far more elegant and ornate than in other parts of the South, whether we're talking about elaborate constructions like cassata with its green and white icing and jewellike candied fruits or almond-studded torrone or the delightful marzipan confections called *frutti della Martorana* that come in such amazing variety—apples, cherries, bananas, prickly pears, half-peeled roasted chestnuts, and so on. (The most elaborate and convincing I ever saw was in a shop in Siracusa where the marzipan was in the shape of a tangerine, half peeled and with a few segments detached, all the white filaments of the fruit reproduced in almond paste and colored to look like the real thing.) It's tempting to see this flamboyance as a first cousin once removed to the elaborate, nutty, syrup-drenched pastries one finds glittering in glass cases in shops in Beirut and Cairo.

Along with new products, and of broader consequence, Arab farmers also introduced new agricultural technologies to the Italian South. It is sometimes said that the Arabs "invented" irrigation—they didn't, of course, for farmers have been watering their crops since agriculture began. But new kinds of irrigation systems, adopted from farther east, along with more advanced understanding of the value and methods of crop rotation, seem to have given renewed energy and impetus to southern Italian agriculture.

The final great impact on southern Italian food and cuisine came after 1492 with the introduction of new foods from the Americas, especially—do I need to point this out?—the tomato, without which the food of the South, as we know it today, could hardly be said to exist. As in most parts of the world where it was a newly arrived exotic, the tomato had a rocky road to success. The first real recipe using tomatoes was not published until 1692—significantly enough, in Naples. *Lo scalco alla moderna* ("the modern steward") was written by Antonio Latini, who was—and this is also significant—chef and steward to the Spanish governor of Naples, and he claims his sauce is *alla spagnuola,* in the Spanish style. From that Spanish sauce to Napoli's quintessential *pizza alla marinara* is a mere step or two in time. Here's the recipe, as translated into English by Rudolf Grewe:

> Take half a dozen tomatoes that are ripe, and put them to roast in the embers, and when they are scorched, remove the skin diligently, and mince them finely with a knife. Add onions, minced finely, to discretion; hot chili peppers, also minced finely; and thyme in a small amount. After mixing everything together, adjust it with a little salt, oil, and vinegar. It is a very tasty sauce, both for boiled dishes or anything else.

Indeed!

Let me offer another quote, this time from an early-nineteenth-century Neapolitan writer, that says a lot about the southern Italian kitchen:

> *I primi elementi della buona Cucina sono le provvisioni; queste debbono essere di ottima qualità, buone e salubri; . . . l'erbe siano colte nello stesso giorno: gli ovi più freschi, che sia possibile; i frutti maturi a perfezione, i vini sinceri e non tanto aspri. La manipolazione di tutto ciò sia semplice, e naturale, il brodo non molto carico di carne, i sughi senza tanto lardo prosciutto e butirro, il sale, il pepe, le droghe e ogni altro condimento di questo genere in pochissima quantità.*

> The first elements of good cuisine are the provisions; these must be of the best quality, both fine and salubrious; . . . the greens should be harvested the same day: the eggs should be the freshest possible; the fruits perfectly ripened, the wines undoctored and not too rough. The manipulation of all this should be simple, and natural, the broth not overly meaty, the sauces without too much fat, prosciutto and butter, the salt, the pepper, the spices and every other condiment of this nature in the smallest quantities.

The words might be those of any modern Italian—or French or North American or British—chef, one of those written up with breathless enthusiasm in the food pages of magazines and newspapers. In fact, they were set down nearly two hundred years ago by Ippolito Cavalcanti, Duke of Buonvicino, a Neapolitan aristocrat and bon vivant whose goal was to provide a manual of practical culinary theory. *Cucina teorico-pratica*, he called his book, which he published in 1837. The book went through ten editions, the final one in 1910, but Cavalcanti's recipes are as fresh and lively and interesting for today's cooks as ever they were a century or more ago. (Several recipes in this book are interpretations of Cavalcanti's own.)

Even in the nineteenth century, however, his ideas about simple, natural ingredients were not revolutionary, at least not in southern Italy. The theory that food should be as fresh as possible, prepared simply to bring out the natural goodness of products, has been dear to southern cooks and cookery writers since time immemorial. Here's a recipe for ribbon-fish that may well be the earliest recipe ever set down in the entire Mediterranean. It was composed by a Sicilian Greek, Mithaecus, who was probably a chef and probably lived in the late fifth or early fourth century B.C.E.: "Gut, discard the head, rinse and fillet; add cheese and oil."*

You can't get much simpler than that.

In the final analysis, that's what the food of the South has always been about: the simplicity of natural ingredients combined effortlessly to enhance rather than conceal innate flavors and

*Translation by Andrew Dalby, *Siren Feasts,* 1996, page 110.

textures and the simplicity of easy, straightforward, uncomplicated techniques. Of course, there are preparations—some of them in this book—that belie this, but even pasta, once you've made it two or three times, loses its daunting nature and becomes something normal, natural, everyday, as it is throughout the Mezzogiorno: take a half a pound of flour, take a couple of eggs if you will, take a little water and a pinch of salt, mix them to a dough, knead it, roll it out, and cut it into the shapes you want.

This, I believe, is the major reason the cuisine of southern Italy has such enormous appeal for modern cooks and diners. It's the kind of food we want to eat right now. I would leave it to social psychologists to winkle out the possible connections between the increasing, anxiety-making complexity of modern life and the simple, earth-based flavors of this cuisine, which grows out of the exigencies of busy hardworking people, whether countryfolk or city dwellers, professional chefs or home cooks, people who don't have the time or inclination to fiddle with complex sauces. An added appeal is that it is one of the world's most healthful ways of eating, a contention that has been proved over and over again by nutritional scientists examining the health benefits of the traditional Mediterranean diet—and there's no better example of the traditional Mediterranean diet than right here in the south of Italy.

In the recipes that follow, the reader-cook will find many attributed to a specific region or a place or even to an individual cook, others that are more generally derived, possibly from a number of different sources and many different places in southern Italy. But even in the rare but happy cases when I've received an actual written recipe from the hands of the cook herself, I haven't always stuck by it. That's because I, or the women who've helped me with the testing, have concluded that the recipe can be improved by adding more of this or less of that, cutting down on cooking times, raising oven temperatures, adjusting the recipe in the thousands of little ways that cooks all over the world have always done.

This raises, however, the vexed question of authenticity. My own time-tested belief is that in a practice, an art if you will, as dynamic, as ephemeral, and as individualistic as cooking, authenticity is pretty much in the eye of the beholder. You know, almost instinctively, when something rings of authenticity and even more instinctively when it does not. Anyone who has talked with southern Italian women—*especially* with women—about the way they cook or watched southern Italian cooks in operation knows that practices change from one community to the next, even from one household to the next, and even within a single family—all too often the source of dire domestic tension. One woman's authentic ragù, handed down from her nonna and her bisnonna since time immemorial, is another woman's bastardized sauce undeserving of the very name. Rather than offering the reader-cook dozens of slightly different recipes for traditional dishes like that, I have sometimes combined what seem to be the best of many ideas and put them together in a way that, I hope, is true to the originals. But if your nonna made her ragù differently, by all means, stick with tradition.

Notes on Some Ingredients

As far as ingredients for southern Italian cooking are concerned, North Americans are fortunate to have Italian and Italian-American grocers, bakers, pastrymakers, and other food purveyors still close to hand, good sources for authentic cheeses, olive oils, salumi, and other ingredients like rice, dried borlotti and fava beans, pickles and preserves, canned tomatoes, salted anchovies and capers—all the incredible and delicious variety that Italian cooks commonly expect to find in their larders. Many alternative grocers and health food stores, including the growing national chain of Whole Foods, also stock Italian ingredients, especially olive oil, pasta, nuts, grains, and beans. And for those who can't command a neighborhood shop, there are increasingly good mail-order sources, through catalogs and especially through the Internet. The sources at the back of this book include a number of suggestions for where to find various and specific ingredients.

EXTRA-VIRGIN OLIVE OIL is the single most important ingredient in southern Italian cooking. Nothing else will do. Refined olive oil (marketed as just plain "olive oil") is fine for deep-fat frying, but for all other purposes, whether cooking or garnishing, you will want the flavor impact of extra-virgin oil, pure and unrefined, from Italy or possibly from elsewhere in the Mediterranean. (Some very good extra-virgin oils from Greece and Spain are close in flavor to southern Italian oils and often are economically priced, especially when purchased in three- or five-liter tins.)

Legally to qualify as extra-virgin, an oil must be produced simply by mechanically extracting the juice of the olive without the use of chemical solvents; the oil, moreover, must have a free oleic fatty acid content of less than 1%* and must be judged to have "perfect" taste and aroma. Minimal processing in a centrifuge removes the natural vegetable water that is part of the extracted juice, and sometimes the oil is also filtered to clarify it. But that's it, the simplest process imaginable: crush the olives, squeeze out the juice, separate the vegetable water, and bottle the oil. Oils that fail to qualify as extra-virgin, because of unacceptable flavors and aromas, are refined, usually through chemical processes that strip them of flavor and aroma, then bottled with a small amount of extra-virgin added to give them some (but only a little) character.

Both extra-virgin and refined oils are high in valuable monounsaturated fat, the fat that lowers bad LDL cholesterol and raises or stabilizes good HDL cholesterol, but extra-virgin oil carries the added benefit of polyphenols and antioxidants that are absent from the refined oils, and those polyphenols, as well as being powerhouse fighters against various cancers and other

*The term *free oleic fatty acid* refers to a laboratory test that determines actual or potential rancidity in the oil. It does not mean that the oil tastes acid or sour.

chronic diseases, are responsible for the big flavors that extra-virgin oil adds to southern dishes.

There was a time not too long ago when it was hard to recommend a southern Italian oil, when most southern oils had to be refined to make them palatable. That time, thankfully, is past. The only secret to producing good oil is cleanliness and speed—cleanliness both in the harvest and in the frantoio, or oil mill, and speed because the longer the time between harvest and crushing, the more likely it is that the olives will start to turn rancid, and rancid olives produce nasty oil. In the last few decades southern producers have learned to clean up and speed up their methods such that exceptional oils from all over the South, but especially from Puglia and Sicily, are now starting to show up in North American markets.

Which one should you buy? The only way to tell is by experimenting, trying different oils, until you find one that pleases you. Some cooks like to keep one oil for cooking and another for garnishing, others use the same oil for both purposes, and still others may have a range of five or six or more oils to use depending on the occasion.

Time and again, I hear North American cooks say you can't cook with extra-virgin olive oil, that the flash point is too low. Nothing could be further from the truth, as cooks know well all over the Mezzogiorno (in fact, all over the Mediterranean), where they wouldn't think of cooking with anything else. Olive oil can be comfortably heated to 360°F, an ideal temperature for deep-fat frying, and even higher. The only commendable reason not to use extra-virgin oil in the kitchen is price, but there are enough lower-priced extra-virgins available to make that objection immaterial.

Unlike wine, extra-virgin oil does not improve with age; in fact, true oil mavens believe the best oil is consumed in the first six months after it has been pressed. Properly stored, olive oil will keep for several years, but, believe me, it doesn't get better. Probably the single most important bit of advice I can give you is to keep your olive oils away from heat and light, both of which will destroy the oil's character and lead eventually to rancidity. It's best to keep oil stored in a cool, dark place, but not in the refrigerator. You can keep a small amount by the stove for convenience, but the rest should be kept in a cool pantry cupboard. And never buy oil from a purveyor who displays it in a shop window—that's certain death to good oil.

OLIVES: Whether black (ripe) or green (unripe), olives are incredibly bitter when fresh off the tree—as anyone who's ever had the misfortune to eat one can readily attest. They must always be treated to make them edible, usually by soaking in some sort of brine, acid, or wood-ash solution to leach out the bitterness. Black olives can also be cured more simply by being layered in a basket with large quantities of salt; gradually, the olives shrivel and become sweet as they lose their bitter vegetable water, which drains through the basket. When done, these olives are rinsed, then rubbed lightly with oil, for which reason they're often called "oil-cured" olives.

You may find small, black, brine-cured Gaeta olives from southern Italy in supermarket deli sections, and occasionally also the enormous green olives called Bella di Cerignola, from Puglia. Don't feel restricted to Italian olives, however, as our shops and delis are full of a great variety of olives from all over the Mediterranean. Some recipes call specifically for black or green olives, but apart from that, most olives are suitable to use. If they've been further treated with herbs, garlic, or sometimes citrus, however, you may want to rinse them very briefly to get rid of any flavors that aren't called for in the dish you're making.

So-called "California-style" canned black olives (which may have nothing to do with California) should be avoided: green olives that have been artificially processed to make them black, they have a rubbery texture and almost no flavor. Equally to be avoided are jars of green olives that have been stuffed with pimientos, almonds, or anchovies. They belong, if anywhere, on the antipasto tray, but not in cooking.

LARD: Having said that extra-virgin olive oil is critical to producing southern Italian food with authentic flavors, I have to add lard, another fat that is important but much harder to find in North America. Lard is rendered pork fat,* called *strutto* or *sugna* in Italian. It is made by melting down the solid fat of the pig, which then becomes as soft and spreadable as butter, an excellent ingredient (as your grandmother knew if she wasn't Jewish) for producing tender pastry and also a superb medium for deep-fat frying. The problem is that most lard available in North American supermarkets has been processed with preservatives. To find good, pure lard you must go to butchers in German neighborhoods, like Philadelphia and the Pennsylvania German countryside, or Polish areas, such as around Chicago. (See Where to Find It, page 415.)

BREAD: It might seem curious to list bread as an ingredient, but a quick glance through the recipes in this book will show you that it is indeed part of many recipes, whether sliced, cubed, or grated into bread crumbs. There are good southern-style bread recipes starting on page 26 for those who'd like to make their own, but for those who lack the time or inclination, the best bread to use is what I call a "crusty, country-style loaf," a bread that has firm texture and the good nutty flavor of the wheat without a preponderance of sour, yeasty aromas. Most home bakers in southern Italy make their breads by the sourdough or old dough method, using dough put aside from a previous baking to start again with a fresh batch of flour. Be advised that a lot of the bread sold as sourdough in North America is made with dough that has been deliberately made sour by the addition of Lord-knows-what. Good, authentic sourdough bread should have a very slight tang to it, but it should never taste vinegary and never so sour that it conceals the flavor of the wheat.

---

*Lard is not at all the same thing as *lardo*. Lardo, which has received a lot of favorable press recently, is Italian for cured pork fatback—the fat is removed in strips and cured for several months in a mixture of salt, garlic, and aromatics. It is delicious, but it isn't lard.

Much of the bread used in southern Italy is made from *semola di grano duro,* hard durum wheat ground to a gritty texture, like what we call *semolina.* Carotenes naturally present in the wheat give the bread a beautiful golden color. You can sometimes find semolina bread at an artisanal bakery, but if necessary you can substitute any good white loaf made with wheat flour. (Do please keep in mind that *wheat* flour does not necessarily mean *whole wheat* flour. *All* flour, except rye, barley, or cornmeal, is made from wheat.) For bread to use in these recipes, white bread is more appropriate than whole wheat bread (which, in any case, is usually made with less than whole grains of wheat), as long as it has a good rustic texture.

CHEESES: The multitude of great cheeses from southern Italy and the complex and fascinating story of their evolution could easily fill a book of their own. Here I will simply outline some of the different types and mention a few outstanding examples. Not all of them are available in North American markets, but they are worth seeking out while traveling in the Mezzogiorno.

Several factors give a cheese distinctive flavors:

- The nature of the beast whose milk is used—cow, sheep (ewe), goat, buffalo, or a mixture of types.
- The pasture on which the animals have grazed. Roberto Rubino, southern Italy's great cheese authority and head of the Associazione Formaggi Sotto il Cielo, which promotes pasturing as a critical element in producing fine cheeses, has identified hundreds of different plants with quaint names—lengua pecorina, sulla (a clover), porraccio, ferla (an umbellifer)—on which sheep graze in the mountainous pastures of Basilicata and Calabria. Most high-quality cheese that actually originates in the South (there are cheeses made elsewhere with southern names—provolone is the best example) comes from pasture-fed animals. Cheese from stall-fed animals is inferior, experts agree, and cheese from silage fed animals is out of the question.
- The choice of rennet to coagulate the milk, whether vegetable rennet (from wild artichokes or cardoons or from the "milk" of the fig tree), which gives a sweeter-tasting cheese, or animal rennet (from the stomach of ruminants—calves, lambs, kids—who are still milking), which gives a sharper cheese.
- And, finally, the cheesemaker's own methods: whether or not to warm the milk, when to cut the curd, how to induce fermentation, how long to age and in what conditions, all the plethora of small adjustments that can produce distinctive cheeses.

All over Italy south of the Po Valley, sheep's milk cheese, called *pecorino,* is dominant, and the South is no different. The name comes from *pecora,* "sheep," and most sheep's milk cheeses are simply called *pecorino,* whether they are young or aged, fresh or hard. Within the generic term, cheeses are often given names to denote something special, even if it's just the area where they're made. A pecorino di Filiano or Moliterno comes from one of two towns in Basilicata that are famous for the high quality of their cheeses. A pecorino called *piacentinu* from Enna, high on a mountaintop in central Sicily, is flavored and brilliantly colored with saffron. *Tuma* is Sicilian for a very fresh, young, unsalted sheep's milk cheese, really just the unprocessed curds, not meant for aging; after the tuma is salted, it becomes *primosale* (first salt), which is also consumed when very young. *Canestrato* from Puglia (and other regions too) is a hard, aged pecorino, named for the reed baskets in which the cheese curds are set to drain and which stamp a pretty pattern on the outside of the cheese.

Many southern pecorino cheeses recall the ancient practice of transhumance, when great flocks of animals, often numbering in the thousands, were transported, herded back and forth along historic drove roads like grassy autostradas. Many of these tratturi date back to Roman times. They connect summer pastures high in the mountains with the winter grazing grounds along the coasts where the climate is milder; nowadays many of the tratturi have been preserved as hiking trails since trucks have replaced the long, quiet tramp of the shepherds. One reason for the high quality of Filiano pecorino, Roberto Rubino told me, is the use of goat's milk, up to 10 percent, mixed with the milk of gentile da Puglia sheep. For every ten sheep in a flock, shepherds always kept at least one goat—reluctant sheep would follow the more adventurous goats into less accessible pasture, and their milk, naturally, would be mixed with the sheep's milk to make the cheese.

Such blendings aside, 100-percent-goat's-milk cheeses are much less prevalent in southern Italy than they are, for instance, in southern France. Most of them come from mountainous Calabria and Basilicata. *Casieddu* is a prestigious Basilicata cheese, very hard to find, a soft, fresh cheese lightly flavored with nepeta or nepitella, a wild mint, while *caprino d'Aspromonte* is a goat's milk cheese made high in the wild Aspromonte region of Calabria and available either fresh or aged. It's hard enough to find these cheeses outside their region of origin in Italy, let alone in North America.

A surprising number of cow's milk cheeses are also made in the Mezzogiorno—surprising in part because it's often said that cows won't thrive in a hot climate. That may be (I'm no expert in animal husbandry), but local breeds of cattle are favored in places as far apart as Agerola, up on the steep slopes of the Salento peninsula south of Naples, where prized *provolone del Monaco,* made all or in part with the milk of agerolese cows, is aged in caves carved in the hillsides, and the stony plains around Ragusa in southeastern Sicily (actually south of the city of Tunis), where a type of caciocavallo called *ragusano,* formed into big bricks that can weigh up to 10 kilograms (22 pounds) and aged by hanging from ropes in vast barnlike warehouses, is made from the milk of local modicana cows.

Both *caciocavallo* and *provolone,* along with *provola, scamorza,* and a few lesser-known southern cow's milk cheeses, are made by an unusual method called *pasta filata* ("stretched curd"). Only one sheep's milk cheese, *vastedda del Belice* from Sicily, is made by this method, but the most famous pasta filata cheese of all, of course, is *mozzarella di bufala*.

There is a product called mozzarella that is widely available in North American stores and supermarkets. It is gummy, tasteless, and elastic and bears no resemblance whatsoever to the real thing. Why it is called mozzarella is a mystery. Real mozzarella is sold in whey or brine-filled containers; it comes in braids or balls of varying sizes, including some very small ones called *bocconcini* ("little mouthfuls") about the size of a walnut. The texture of the finished cheese is tender, the flavor is fresh and slightly tangy, and when you slice it, you will see the several layers created by stretching and folding the curd. The finest mozzarella is made from the milk of water buffalo (*mozzarella di bufala*) in and around Battipaglia, south of Naples, or Caserta to the north, and Neapolitans endlessly debate which area produces the best. Another kind of mozzarella, made with cow's milk, is more widely produced throughout the mainland South. Legally the cow's milk version should be called *fior di latte,* but almost everyone, in Italy and abroad, refers to it as *mozzarella di vacca,* or cow's milk mozzarella.

The curious process of making pasta filata cheeses probably has ancient roots in the Mezzogiorno. Whether fresh mozzarella or aged caciocavallo, the process is similar. Some authorities have suggested that it's a primitive sort of pasteurization, since the curd is worked in very, very hot water. The fresh milk is curdled in the usual way, but then, once the curds have formed and developed, they are softened in hot water and pulled, over and over again, to make a smooth, elastic (but not gummy) paste. For mozzarella the paste is shaped deftly into balls or braids, then tossed into a briny whey and sent to market. Naturally enough, the fresher the mozzarella is, the better it tastes; many southern Italians would refuse mozzarella that's more than a day old. On the other hand, we here in North America are lucky if we can get mozzarella that is two or three days old.

For pasta filata cheeses to be aged (scamorza, provolone, caciocavallo, etc.), the curd is allowed to firm up and ripen overnight, then it is sliced into long strips that are worked by the cheesemaker, over and over again, shaped and kneaded in water that is almost unbearably hot, until they reach the correct consistency when the cheese is shaped, molded, salted, and set aside to age.

Grated cheese plays an all-important role in Italian cuisine, and no less so in the South than elsewhere, a final flourish to accent the flavors of pasta, soups, and other dishes. For the most authentic southern flavors, aged pecorino, caciocavallo, and provolone from the region are the best choices, but they are not always easy to find. You could substitute a well-aged pecorino toscano or pecorino sardo, if available, but pecorino romano should be avoided as it has a very special and rather peculiar flavor. As a last resort, use parmigiano reggiano or its cheaper cousin grana padano, although both these cheeses, while utterly delicious in their own right, give a northern taste to southern dishes.

Ricotta is another cheese product, or rather by-product, that plays an enormously important role throughout the Italian kitchen. Ricotta (the name means "recooked") is made from whey left over after the initial cheesemaking; when the whey is reheated, sometimes with a little fresh milk added, the proteins that remain will coagulate and rise like blossoms of white cotton to the top of the simmering liquid. In the Mezzogiorno, naturally enough given the importance of sheep in the dairy, most ricotta is made from sheep's milk, and it is a rich and telling flavor indeed. Alas, in much of North America, we don't even have good cow's milk ricotta, let alone any made from sheep's or goat's milk. If you have access to local sheep's or goat's milk cheesemakers, and if you can persuade them that there is a good market for ricotta, you will be set for life with southern dishes. Otherwise, you will have to make do with commercial ricotta made from cow's milk. Do, however, avoid skim-milk ricotta. It doesn't save much in the way of fat or calories, and it loses a lot in flavor. One trick for success with ricotta: Before using it, drain it well for several hours in a fine-mesh sieve lined with cheesecloth. You may be surprised at the amount of liquid that comes out.

See Where to Find It, page 415, for suppliers of imported cheeses.

SALUMI: This is the generic Italian word for all types of cured, salted pork products, from prosciutto to salami to fresh sausages. Most of the salumi made in the Mezzogiorno is unavailable in the United States because of controls on the importation of meat products. In recipes that call for prosciutto, I substitute prosciutto di Parma or di San Daniele, both of which are available in North America. For any other sausage or cured pork, whether fresh or dry-cured, substitute good-quality American-made Italian-style sausages such as the first-rate examples from P. G. Molinari & Sons in San Francisco or from D'Angelo Brothers in Philadelphia (see Where to Find It, page 415).

If you travel in the Mezzogiorno, it's a good idea to spend some time seeking out local sausages and local methods of curing. Not all sausage is made with pork. In Puglia, for instance, *zampina* is a type of veal sausage, very long and thin, that is cut into shorter lengths and curled into pinwheels for grilling. Fresh pork sausages in Puglia are said to be best when prepared *al punto di coltello*, meaning hand-chopped with a big butcher's knife. *Luganega,* or *lucanica,* is an ancient name for a sausage that, on the authority of various Latin writers, originated in the territory of Lucania, as Basilicata was once called. (That certainly sounds reasonable, but I have to note that a popular Greek sausage is also called *loukanika.* In fact there are many sausages throughout the Mediterranean that are called some version of *lucanica.*) In Basilicata the long, thin sausage is usually flavored with fennel and red chili and sometimes lightly smoked at the beginning of the cure. *Soppressata* is another lightly spicy Basilicata sausage, with a fine texture from the use of lean cuts of pork mixed judiciously with fat.

Among the most unusual sausages from the Mezzogiorno is *'nduja,* a soft and spicy spreadable sausage from Calabria. Fiery with chilies and often used as a pizza topping or stirred into a minestrone, it is usually served simply spread on bread for a spuntino, or snack. Another is a soppressata made in and around the town of Gioi in the Cilento national park in Campania, with a strip of pork fat that runs through the center of the fine-textured sausage and gives it richness and aroma.

Pancetta is unsmoked, salt-cured bacon. It is widely available, especially in shops in Italian neighborhoods. Like bacon, pancetta may be stored in the refrigerator for ten days to two weeks or, well wrapped in foil, in a freezer for several months. Most recipes call for just a small amount, usually diced, and cooked as part of the soffrito that forms the basis of so many soups and sauces. If you can't find pancetta, use slab bacon, but blanch it in boiling water for 5 minutes or so to get rid of smoky flavors.

One more pork product that you'll find mentioned as an ingredient in bean and bean soup recipes is *cotenne* or *cotiche* (both words are used), pork rind that has been salted and cured and that lends a lot of flavor to dried legumes. Often this is available as a roll, secured with string and perhaps with a bay leaf and other aromatics tucked inside. You should be able to find cotenne or cotiche in Italian neighborhood groceries and butcher shops. Before using it, scald it briefly in boiling water to soften the skin, especially if the recipe calls for slicing it before adding it.

ANCHOVIES: Salt-packed whole anchovies are available from Italian neighborhood groceries by the ounce or in large cans. They last forever, it seems, though once a can has been opened, it is best kept refrigerated. (Keep the can well covered if you don't want anchovy-flavored butter.) To use salt-packed anchovies, rinse each whole little fish under running water to get rid of the salt, then split it down the middle into two fillets and discard the bony tail and backbone. Don't worry if you don't get every last little bone out—they are soft and easily digestible and, on top of that, a good source of calcium.

Oil-packed anchovies, especially those imported from Italy or Spain, are a good alternative; in fact, they are simply anchovies that have been salt-cured, then filleted and packed in oil.

An interesting by-product of the anchovy fishery along the coast of Campania is *colatura*, a clear golden liquid made by pouring off the liquid that is naturally exuded by anchovies during the curing process. In flavor colatura is somewhat like Vietnamese fish sauce (nuoc mam) but milder and sweeter, possibly the closest we moderns can come to the ancient Roman specialty garum. It's especially delicious stirred into pasta with a simple addition of chopped garlic and dried chilies.

SALT COD (BACCALÀ): All cod comes from the North Atlantic—or, rather, came from the North Atlantic before the stocks became so diminished. But because salted Atlantic cod has been such an important ingredient in the cooking of the Mezzogiorno, it is included here. It isn't always easy to get good salt cod in North America—avoid in any case the cute little wooden boxes from Nova Scotia filled with inferior bits of cod. Look for a fishmonger in a Greek, Portuguese, or Italian neighborhood who has thick, meaty, pure white sides of salt cod. The most flavorful still has the bones attached, but easier to use are the boneless fillets. Browne Trading in Portland, Maine, makes its own sides of salt cod and will ship all over the country (see Where to Find It, page 415).

CAPERS: Capers grow wild all over the Mediterranean, but some of the most prized of these odd little flower buds come from the Sicilian islands of Salina and Pantelleria. Technically part of Sicily, Pantelleria is way out in the Mediterranean, halfway to Tunisia. The unopened buds of caper flowers are carefully harvested and packed in salt to preserve them. Pugliese cooks prefer capers packed in vinegar or brine, but the flavor of salted capers is so superior that it seems a wonder anyone would use anything else. Salted capers should be rinsed thoroughly in a sieve to rid them of salt before using, and if you must use brined capers, it's a good idea to rinse them too, to get rid of their acid flavor.

BEANS AND LEGUMES: The most ubiquitous legume in the Mezzogiorno, and the staple food for countryfolk throughout the winter, is the fava bean, dried either with its skin on or with the skin removed. Skinned fava beans are easier to use and will dissolve nicely into a puree when simmered and stirred. Dried fava beans with the skin left on are perhaps easier to find in shops in North America. Fortunately, they don't take a lot of work to prepare (not nearly as much as skinning fresh fava beans, a practice that in any case I heartily disapprove of). Soak the beans overnight in water and in the morning, with the help of a little paring knife, you can quickly slit the skins and pop the beans right out.

Other legumes are used too—chickpeas (garbanzo beans) are common, as are ordinary dried beans like borlotti or cannellini, often named after the place where they are grown, like the tender fagioli di Sarconi from Basilicata. One special legume used in the Mezzogiorno, and in a few other places in Italy that cling to the oldest traditions, is the cicerchia, *Lathyrus sativa,* a type of vetch that is one of the most ancient elements of the Mediterranean diet.

CHILIES: Many Italian cuisines use a small amount of dried chili, called peperoncino, to season certain stews and bean dishes—always with the caution that it mustn't be too much, mustn't be too hot. Only Calabria and Basilicata are noted for the heat of their food, but, with few exceptions, the food is not so fiery after all, or at least not to someone accustomed to Thai or Mexican chilies. Condiments like hot chili–infused oil or the sausage mentioned earlier ('nduja) may take the roof off the mouths of unsuspecting diners, but the overall flavor profile of the cuisine is one of a pleasantly warm spice that suffuses dishes without calling great attention to itself. Dried chilies should be used with respect, always tasting as you add them, since they vary enormously in strength and heat.

Southern Italian cooks almost always use dried rather than fresh chilies. They may be added whole to a soup, stew, or sauce, in which case they will give a little bite but not a dominating heat. Or they may be broken in half, crumbled coarsely between the fingers, or crushed into flakes to extract more flavor. Like most spices, chilies keep better whole than they do crushed, flaked, or ground to a powder. Keep a jar of small whole chilies in the pantry and, when necessary, break one or more into smaller pieces, or grind in a mortar if a fine powder is what's required.

According to the Accademia Italiana del Peperoncino, Italian peperoncini have an average of 100 to 150 Scoville units (a measure of heat in peppers), while serrano chilies have 10,000 to 23,000 Scovilles, and Thai bird chilies have a massive 50,000 to 100,000 units. You should be aware that, with all chilies, most of the heat is in the seeds and white internal membranes. If you really can't tolerate spicy food, you should remove these bits before adding any chili to the pot.

Chilies vary more according to the soil and climate where they're grown almost than any other food plant that I know, so place is important in assessing chilies. The peperone di Senise, from the Sinni River valley in Basilicata, is a good example. It has exactly that most desirable quality, delicious flavor and enough heat to suffuse the palate with warmth but nothing that screams out a warning. It is available in the region—I have not seen it sold elsewhere—as crushed or stone-ground dried chili, but more interesting are the chilies dried whole on strings hanging from house balconies, like New Mexican ristras. In wintertime these whole chilies may be deep-fried to make crisp, crunchy *cruschi* that are served as an accompaniment, a contorno, to regional dishes of roast and braised lamb.

TOMATOES: On page 127, I have written about the quality of Neapolitan tomatoes, especially those grown in the mineral-rich volcanic soil below Vesuvius. But those are not the only delicious tomatoes in Italy, a country that abounds in the flavorful fruit. Pachino tomatoes, from the southernmost tip of Sicily, farther south even than the city of Tunis, are prized, especially small, deeply ridged costoluti and ciliegioni, like fat, succulent cherry tomatoes. Then there are *pomodori a pennula,* small cluster tomatoes, harvested when barely ripe and hung by the cluster in a dry, airy pantry to mature slowly as the sweet juices concentrate and the flavor deepens throughout the long months of winter. (I didn't believe it, the first time I heard about it, but in Puglia these fragrant tomatoes are a staple of the winter kitchen, lasting well into spring.)

Fortunately tomatoes can be preserved in many different ways, from the traditional farmhouse *pomarola* (page 129), to sun-dried whole tomatoes, to *pelati,** canned whole tomatoes that make an entirely acceptable substitute for fresh ones. Tomatoes, in fact, are one of the few vegetables that take well to canning. Like cooks in Italy, I don't hesitate to use canned tomatoes when good-quality fresh ones are not available. Do try out several different brands and find one

---

Pelati means "peeled," but in the culinary context it means any kind of canned whole tomatoes; ordinarily these are always peeled, but the genuine original San Marzanos have such a thin skin that they are canned skin and all. Still, they are called *pelati.*

that pleases you. One favorite, imported from the tomato fields below the slopes of Mt. Vesuvius, is called Il Miracolo di San Gennaro, "The Miracle of San Gennaro," Gennaro being the patron saint of Napoli (see Where to Find It, page 415). Another high-quality, and much less expensive, Italian brand is Academia di Barilla, while a California company, Muir Glen, makes a variety of tomato products from organically raised fruits. The last two brands are widely available in supermarkets and specialty food shops.

One special way of preserving the bright flavor of tomatoes is called *estratto di pomodoro* (or just *stratto*) in Sicily and *conserva di pomodoro* in Campania. It's a delicious confection, made in August when the sun is hottest, the air is driest, and the tomatoes are ripest. Plum tomatoes are cut in half, salted, and then exposed to the sun for several days on flat boards spread out in the *cortile,* the farmyard. Once the tomatoes have dried a little and concentrated their sweetness, they are put through a sieve or a special hand-cranked machine that reduces them to a puree. (In Sicily, the tomatoes may be cooked into a thick puree to begin with.) Then the puree itself is spread on clean boards or on terra-cotta platters made for the purpose and once more exposed to the sun. Each day the red sauce reduces and concentrates as the juices evaporate and the color turns slowly from bright red to a deep almost-mahogany color. While it dries it must be stirred patiently, two or three times a day, to mix the drier edges into the still-moist center. When the whole thing has reached the right density, it's transferred to terra-cotta jars and covered with a film of olive oil for storage. Made like this, tomato conserve or extract will keep for years.

Incidentally, it takes five kilos (eleven pounds) of tomatoes to make five hundred grams (one little pound) of conserva.

Stratto made in Sicily by olive-oil producer Lorenzo Piccione is available from Gustiamo.com, while that made by Sicilian pastry maker Maria Grammatico can be found through Manicaretti (see Where to Find It, page 415).

One other point about tomatoes that sometimes surprises North Americans: for most salads, Italians generally, not just in the South, prefer underripe tomatoes, so underripe that we might consider them too green to be eaten raw. The slightly acerbic flavor, they say, is preferable to the full sweetness of a ripe red tomato.

CELERY: Readers will notice that I often refer to "green celery" in lists of ingredients. Not just in the South but throughout Italy celery is used more as an aromatic, like parsley, than as a vegetable in its own right. Cooks seek out unblanched, rather tough, dark green celery for the superior flavor it lends, especially when chopped with onions, carrots, and other vegetables for the battuto that is the basis of most sauces and soups. Since we can't get that kind of celery, I look for the greenest celery in the produce section and use the tougher outside stalks rather than the tender hearts.

PANE, PIZZE, FOCACCE, ECC.

Breads, Pizzas, Savory Pies, Etc.

It could seem like a miracle, and yet it happens over and over again—every week or ten days on family farms, more frequently, sometimes even twice a day, in village and town bakeries across southern Italy. Wheat flour, often flour from the local hard durum wheat or *semola,* is mixed with water, a little salt, and some leavening made either from fresh yeast or from a piece of fermented dough ("sourdough") put aside from a previous baking. Kneaded, shaped, and put to rise, the loaves are thrust into the intense white heat of the oven chamber where they rise further, crack slightly on their surfaces, and turn a delicious golden brown, the color of the wheat fields just before the harvest when the treasured grains are fully ripe.

The simplicity of it all is what makes this process so appealing—simplicity and antiquity too, for bread like this has been made all over southern Italy, indeed all over the Mediterranean, since farmers first cultivated wheat along with its near-cousin barley. It would be difficult to over-emphasize the importance of bread in the Italian diet, especially the southern diet. It is considered food in an absolute sense, nourishment par excellence, so much so that often in times past, when people spoke of being without food, what they really meant was that, for one reason or another, they were without bread.

Nowadays, bread in the Italian South comes in an astonishing variety of shapes—rounds, rings, braids, buns, and massive loaves of ten or more kilos (twenty-two or more pounds). The basic dough may be mixed with something as simple as chopped black olives, or almonds, or it can be rolled out and filled with a complex stuffing like Sicilian *impanata di pesce spada,* with its combination of swordfish, zucchini, and raisins. The dough may be enriched with eggs, sugar, and olive oil, perhaps bits of cheese or candied fruit, to make any number of holiday breads for Christmas, Easter, and other canonical feasts. It may be stretched flat and covered with a savory topping to make focaccia or stretched even flatter and crowned with what seems like an infinite variety of ingredients to make pizza. And in a delicious departure from the oven, it can even be deep-fried, with or without a stuffing.

Miracle though it may be, there is no mystery to making bread. All it really takes is time—much of it spent waiting for the dough to rise, an exceptionally pleasant way to pass the time—and patience, a virtue well worth cultivating in this harried world we inhabit. In fact, for me, and for many other home bakers, making bread—mixing, kneading, waiting, and the patience required—is a way to withdraw from the hustle-bustle, to get in touch profoundly with a slow pace that allows time for meditation, for just being. There is a zen to breadmaking, but you don't come to it instantly. If you are not accustomed to making bread, allow yourself the luxury of time to enjoy the process. Truly, making bread is about process, far more than it's about the product that results. But the product has its own satisfactions.

A person could write an encyclopedia about the breads and savory pies from southern Italy, and that is not what I have tried to do here. Rather, I've given directions for a couple of very basic bread and pizza doughs, then a wide sampling of the variety of fantasy productions. As with most southern Italian recipes, once you've mastered the basic technique—which is no different, requires no greater skills, than any kind of breadmaking and is perhaps simpler than most—you should feel free to let your own fantasies take over, up to a point. The one unmistakable benchmark is the bread itself: whether it comes as a loaf, a pie casing, or a flat pizza, you should be able to taste the goodness of the bread. So that when someone bites into it, they'll say, perhaps with some surprise, "Hey, this is good! And you know what? You can really taste the bread."

Much of the bread in southern Italy is made, entirely or in part, from the flour of hard durum wheat (*Triticum turgidum* var. *durum*). One of the many remarkable properties of durum is that the kernel has a hard vitreous quality such that, when it is milled, it shatters like glass; bread wheat, soft wheat, *Triticum aestivum,* which is the wheat from which we get our all-purpose flour, crushes when milled to a soft powder. In Italy, the flour of durum wheat or grano duro is called *semola* when it is ground to a somewhat gritty texture and *semola rimacinata* or *farina di grano duro* or *semolina* when it is ground to a finer, more "floury" texture. Often the flour comes from special, locally grown wheats, heirloom varieties like "Senatore Capelli," a revered durum strain that was developed in the 1930s for both bread and pastamaking. Sicilian *grano rossello* is another heritage grain, so old it reminds us that Sicily was one of the bread baskets of the Roman Empire; *timiglia* or *tumminia,* grown around Castelvetrano in the southern part of the island, is used to make a fine local bread called *pane nero di Castelvetrano,* which earned accolades from the Slow Food movement. It is very good bread indeed, with lots of nutty wheat flavor and a pleasing creamy grayish-beige color, not really *nero* at all. More typically, durum wheat, because of its high carotene content, yields a buttery yellow flour and a correspondingly golden bread, so much so that you might suspect, wrongly, that eggs had been added to the bread dough.

There is some confusion between American and Italian terminology because what we call semolina and what Italians call *semolina* are two different things. In North America, semolina refers to the coarse-textured grind of durum wheat that Italians call *semola*. And what they call *semolina* or *semola rimacinata* is what we call durum flour. I prefer to use semola (American semolina) most of the time, but semola rimacinata (American durum flour or hard wheat flour) can also be used in the following recipes whenever semolina is called for. If you use the latter, you may find that you need less water to arrive at the right dough texture.

Another important point that needs clarification is a false distinction that has crept into our language between "white" bread and "wheat" bread. Unless it's called specifically by another name—rye bread or cornbread, for instance—white bread is *always* made of wheat flour, but wheat flour that has had a large proportion of the bran extracted during the milling process to yield a whiter flour. What shopkeepers and sandwich makers call "wheat" bread is made from whole wheat flour in which less of the bran and germ is extracted during milling. But in both cases, it's wheat flour for sure.

Italian flour terminology, apart from the distinction between durum wheat and regular bread wheat, is very different from our own. White refined flour is referred to as 0 (*zero*) or 00 (*doppio zero*), which refers not to the extraction rate but rather to the ash content. You can occasionally find Italian flour like this from North American mail-order and specialty foods sources, but I don't find it's worth the effort to get it. Since most high-quality refined flour in Italy is made from North American grain, why bother?

So what flour should you use in the following recipes? For a more authentic southern Italian bread dough, you will want to use either coarse-textured semolina or finer-milled durum flour or a combination of the two. But unless it's otherwise stated, you may also use unbleached all-purpose flour, all or in part, with results that will be almost as good if not quite so true to type. In some of the recipes, such as for pizza dough, I call for unbleached all-purpose flour with a little semolina added to give it texture. This will produce something closer to the Neapolitan original.

An excellent resource for flours of all kinds, along with baker's equipment and other types of ingredients, is the King Arthur Flour Company in Vermont. Its standard flours are available in shops and supermarkets throughout the Northeast, but it is worth consulting the mail order catalog, The Baker's Catalog (http://shop.bakerscatalogue.com), for a wider range, including semolina, durum flour, and an "Italian style" flour that compares well to the 00 flour mentioned above.

To mimic the effect of a wood-fired stone or masonry baker's oven, many home bakers, myself included, like to bake directly on a baking stone or pizza stone or on an oven shelf lined with ceramic baking tiles. If you do this, be sure to put the stone or tiles in a cold oven, then turn the heat on. (I have cracked a pizza stone by putting it cold into a very hot oven.) It will take a little more preheating to get the stone really hot, so if your oven normally preheats to the desired temperature in 5 minutes, give it at least an extra 15 minutes of preheating to get the stone thoroughly hot before baking.

Pane di Semola, Pane di Grano Duro

GOLDEN SEMOLINA BREAD

This recipe takes time, but most of it is spent waiting for the dough to rise, when you can be reading a book or doing something else entirely. Don't feel hidebound by the rising schedule—an hour or two more or less to fit the cook's convenience is not going to affect the outcome.

Like many Italian bread recipes, this begins with a biga, or starter dough. A series of long, slow rises at coolish temperatures helps to build flavor in the eventual bread; the cooler the temperature, the slower the fermentation or rise will be and the more flavor that will develop as a result. But only up to a point. Bread dough need not be refrigerated unless for some reason you must halt the process. If that happens, simply punch down the dough, cover the bowl tightly with plastic wrap to prevent drying, and put it in the refrigerator. Later you can bring it back to room temperature by kneading vigorously. If you live in a *very* hot climate (Arizona in the summertime, for instance), you may find that dough rises too quickly, in which case either set it to rise, away from drafts, in an air-conditioned room or, if you *must,* refrigerate it, keeping in mind that the whole process will be much, much slower if you do so.

For variety's sake, you may substitute 2 cups of barley flour or whole wheat flour for 2 cups of the semolina or durum flour in the recipe. In fact, you could make the following recipe using only regular all-purpose flour. It won't be semolina bread, but it will be pretty darned good bread anyway.

MAKES 4 TO 5 POUNDS OF BREAD: two 2- to 2½-pound loaves, or other quantities (1 loaf and 1 focaccia, 1 loaf and a couple of pizzas, for example), depending on how the dough is shaped

½ teaspoon dry yeast	7 to 8 cups semolina, durum flour, or a mixture	A little extra-virgin olive oil
1½ cups unbleached all-purpose flour	1 to 2 tablespoons sea salt	Small handful of semolina or cornmeal

First make the *biga* (starter): Mix the yeast with about a cup of water that is a little warmer than body temperature—up to 110°F if you are using a thermometer, though 10° more or less won't make much difference. Very hot or very cold water won't work. Set aside until the yeast dissolves and the water looks quite cloudy, 5 or 10 minutes.

Put the all-purpose flour in a large bowl, make a well in the center, and add the dissolved yeast. Use a wooden spoon to stir the flour into the liquid. In very dry weather, you may need to add more warm water, another ½ cup or so, to get the desired consistency, which should be like thick sour cream. Don't worry if there are lumps in the dough. Cover the bowl with plastic wrap or a damp towel and set aside in a cool place for 6 to 8 hours or overnight.

Once the starter is ready and has swollen to a puffy, bubbly mass, stir in a cup of warm water and 1½ cups of the semolina or durum flour. Mix well with a wooden spoon, adding more water if necessary—it should look like a rough and ragged slurry. Cover again and set aside in a cool place to rise several hours or overnight. This is the first rise.

At this point the dough, having risen again, may have separated, leaving liquid in the bottom of the bowl. Don't worry—it will all come together in the end. Have ready 5 cups of semolina or durum flour and 1½ cups warm water. Add the semolina and the water, a little of each at a time, to the dough in the bowl, mixing in each addition. Use a wooden spoon at first and later, as the dough starts to firm up, your hands. You may not need all the water or all the semolina—much depends on the relative humidity in your kitchen.

When the dough comes together well, spread another cup of semolina or durum flour on a bread board or wooden countertop and turn the dough out onto it. Sprinkle the dough with sea salt to taste and knead it vigorously for 10 to 15 minutes, gradually incorporating the flour on the board, until the dough loses its stickiness and has the texture of a baby's bottom or an earlobe.

This is the point at which to add, if you wish, any of the garnishes listed in the variations, kneading them thoroughly into the dough.

(If it is easier for you, you may also knead the dough using an electric mixer and a dough hook. Personally, although it saves time, I've never found this very satisfactory. The dough seems to get stickier and stickier and require greater amounts of flour—not a good thing.)

Rinse out and dry the bowl. Add about a teaspoon of oil to the bottom and turn the ball of dough in the bowl to coat it lightly with oil. Cover again with a damp cloth and set aside, at room temperature, to rise for 2 hours. This is the second rise.

Turn the dough out onto the bread board and punch it down. Now it's ready to shape, and here the possibilities are many—one very large round loaf or 2 or more smaller ones; you might also divide the dough in half and use half to make a loaf of bread and the other to make focaccia, sfincione, pizza, impanata, or any of the many other shaped, stuffed, and filled breads that follow.

To make one very large loaf, as bakers in Puglia do, punch down the dough and knead briefly. Scatter some semolina or cornmeal on the bread board to make it easier to shift the bread after it has risen. Pat the dough out on the board in a roughly oval shape. Cover lightly with a kitchen towel or plastic wrap and set aside to rise and double while you preheat the oven to 450°F. If you are using baking tiles or a baking stone—which I recommend for best results—

arrange them in the oven *before you turn it on* and preheat for at least 30 minutes to make sure the stones are heated thoroughly.

When the dough has doubled and the oven is hot, flip one end of the dough over the other end—slide your palm under the right side of the oval and turn it over the left side as if it were a big, doughy wallet. Do not slash the dough but transfer it to a baking sheet or, if you are baking directly on tiles, to a wooden peel, sprinkled with semolina or cornmeal. Shift it to the oven and bake for 15 minutes, then turn the heat down to 350°F and continue baking for 45 to 60 minutes longer, or until the bread is golden and crisp on top and rings hollow when you thump the bottom of it with a knuckle.

If you wish to make several smaller loaves, divide the dough, using a bench or dough scraper, into as many individual loaves as you wish—2 smaller loaves or 4 long baguettes or 10 or 12 individual rolls. Shape the loaves and set to rise, lightly covered, while you preheat the oven. Immediately before transferring the loaves to the oven, slash the tops of the breads with a very sharp knife or baker's razor. This allows the dough to expand quickly in the very hot oven. The smaller the loaf, obviously, the less time it will take to cook through, so keep an eye on it, especially for small rolls, which can be done in as little as 20 minutes.

Once the bread is done, transfer it to a rack and let cool.

To make focaccia with this dough, see page 37.

VARIATIONS

🌿 Add ¼ to ½ cup of any of the following to the bread dough before the second rise, kneading to distribute the added element throughout the dough:

> coarsely chopped black or green olives, well drained
> cubes of pecorino or caciocavallo cheese
> coarsely chopped walnuts, almonds, hazelnuts, or other nuts
> small dice of pancetta or prosciutto

🌿 Once the bread has been shaped into loaves, but before the final rise, spread a thick layer of sesame seeds or a mixture of sesame and fennel seeds on a bread board and roll the loaves in the seeds, pressing the seeds firmly into the surface of the loaf—this is a typically Sicilian treatment. About ¼ cup of seeds will be sufficient for a loaf made from half the dough recipe. (This is the bread to use for Pane Cunzato, which follows.)

Pane Cunzato may well be the mother of the Italian-American hero sandwich or grinder, a great favorite that was always available in Italian delicatessens and groceries when I was a child. In New Orleans, the muffoletta, with its distinctive olive salad, is a direct descendant of Pane Cunzato, no doubt brought by Sicilians who immigrated to that city in the early years of the last century. (Mary Simeti, an American long resident in Sicily, writes of muffolette made in her neighboring town of Alcamo as a Saturday night treat. The soft buns are bought hot at the bakery and taken home to fill with ricotta, anchovies, oregano, and olive oil—another take on Pane Cunzato.)

The purest expression of Pane Cunzato is made simply with olive oil, oregano, salt, and lots of black pepper, but more elaborate combinations are also possible. I haven't listed any salami or other cured pork sausage here, but if you wish, by all means include them, thinly sliced of course.

The most important part of this recipe is bread that is hot and fresh from the oven so that it fully absorbs all the added flavors.

6 or 8 freshly baked small sesame-coated breads made from ½ recipe Golden Semolina Bread (page 26)	Sea salt and freshly ground black pepper	12 anchovy fillets, chopped
	6 small ripe tomatoes, very thinly sliced	½ cup coarsely chopped pitted black olives, preferably salt-cured
¾ cup extra-virgin olive oil, preferably Sicilian	½ pound pecorino or caciocavallo, very thinly sliced	½ cup coarsely chopped pitted green olives
2 tablespoons dried oregano		

The bread used for Pane Cunzato should be fresh from the oven and so hot it's almost painful to slice or tear open; and indeed, it is better, if possible, to tear the bread in half rather than slicing it with a knife since the uneven surface of torn bread will absorb more oil. Douse each half of bread with an abundance of olive oil and a heavy sprinkling of oregano, salt, and pepper. Then on one half of each bread, arrange slices of tomato and/or cheese, as well as the anchovy bits and the olives. Top with the other half of the bread and press together lightly.

Pane Cunzato should be consumed, with a glass of wine, while still warm.

Pane di Patate

POTATO BREAD

This potato bread from Puglia probably evolved as a way of eking out a scarcity of flour with cheaper potatoes. It makes a deliciously moist and tasty bread that is also excellent for toast. Focaccia made with this dough (page 37) is superb and traditional around Bari. Use the recipe to make a couple of loaves of bread or, if you wish, a single loaf and a focaccia for an after-school (or after-work) snack or light supper, perhaps with one of the soups from pages 97 to 120.

MAKES ABOUT 3½ POUNDS OF DOUGH: 2 or 3 loaves of bread, or 1 focaccia and 1 loaf of bread, or 2 focaccias, 8 servings each

1 pound russet potatoes (2 medium to large potatoes)	5 to 6 cups unbleached all-purpose flour	Extra-virgin olive oil
½ teaspoon dry yeast	Sea salt	Small handful of semolina or cornmeal

Boil the potatoes, with their skins on, in lightly salted water to cover until they are tender all the way through—20 to 35 minutes, depending on size.

While the potatoes are cooking, dissolve the yeast in ½ cup warm water.

Drain the potatoes and set aside just until cool enough to handle, then peel them and thoroughly mash with a fork or a potato masher in a large bowl or put them through a vegetable mill. Add the dissolved yeast to the warm mashed potatoes and stir it in.

Now start adding 4½ to 5 cups of the flour and 1 cup of warm water, a little at a time—about 1 cup of flour, then about ¼ cup of water, kneading with a wooden spoon and then with your hands as the flour and water are absorbed. Use all the water, but you may not need to use all the flour—a lot depends on ambient humidity. When all the water has been incorporated and the dough has a nice elastic feel to it, spread ½ cup of the remaining flour on a bread board and start kneading the bread on the board. Knead for about 10 minutes, adding salt—about 2 teaspoons, more or less, according to taste. When the dough has a nice silky texture, shape it into a ball. Rinse out and dry the bowl. Smear about a teaspoon of olive oil around the bowl and transfer the ball, turning it to coat it lightly with the oil. Cover with plastic wrap and set in a warm place to rise for about 2 hours.

Punch the dough down and divide it in two with a bench or dough scraper. Shape the dough as desired:

- 2 round loaves to bake on a sheet pan or directly on baking tiles or stone
- 2 or 3 loaves to bake in lightly oiled rectangular baking pans, about 9 × 5 inches, to make sandwich bread
- 1 of either of the above and 1 focaccia (page 37)
- 2 focaccias

To make bread: Shape the dough into round loaves or in loaf pans. If baking round loaves on a sheet pan, scatter a little semolina or cornmeal over the sheet and set the breads on it. If using loaf pans, oil them very lightly, bottom and sides, with olive oil and set the dough halves in them, pushing the dough out to the edges of the pans. Cover the loaves lightly with a towel or plastic wrap and set aside in a warm place to rise for 30 to 40 minutes.

Preheat the oven to 450°F. If you're using tiles or a stone, arrange in the oven before you turn it on and preheat for at least 30 minutes to make sure the tiles are heated thoroughly.

Just before putting the loaves in the oven, slash the tops in 3 or 4 places with a very sharp knife or a baker's razor so that, when they are hit with the high heat of the oven, they will expand rapidly.

Bake at 450°F for 15 minutes, then turn the oven down to 350°F and bake for another 40 to 45 minutes, until the loaves are golden brown and crisp on top—check frequently during the last 15 minutes of baking to make sure they don't burn.

Remove from the oven and cool on a wire rack for 30 minutes before slicing.

Little round breads with black olives or bits of flavorful local ham embedded in the dough are a specialty of the Salento, the peninsula at the tip end of Puglia. At the Caroppo Bakery in the tiny hamlet of Specchia Gallone, baker Donato Caroppo deftly works with a dough so wet and viscous that it slips and slides in the baker's hands. As fast as Caroppo shapes the breads, he drops them onto a wooden peel and his assistant flips them onto the floor of the wood-fired oven to bake quickly.

Loose, wet doughs like these actually produce better bread than tighter doughs but they are devilishly hard to work with at home. The results are so terrific, however, that I encourage you to try. You may find that it's easier to work this dough with an electric mixer, using the bread hook attachment. You may, if you wish, bake the finished breads on a baking stone, but I find that this slippery dough is less problematic with a flat cookie sheet.

MAKES 6 PUCCIE

FOR THE BIGA	FOR THE BREAD	1 cup coarsely chopped black olives, very savory baked ham, finely slivered onion, minced flat-leaf parsley, or a mixture
1 teaspoon dry yeast	1 cup whole wheat flour	
1 cup unbleached all-purpose flour	3 to 4 cups semolina or durum flour	
	Extra-virgin olive oil	Cornmeal or semolina for the board
	Sea salt	

Make the biga at least 1 hour in advance. Sprinkle the yeast over a cup of warm (about 110°F) water and leave for a couple of minutes to dissolve, then stir in the cup of all-purpose flour and set aside at room temperature, covered with a damp cloth. (You may also make the biga a day in advance and keep it in a cool place overnight. If you must refrigerate, bring the biga back to room temperature before continuing with the bread.)

When ready to make the bread dough, transfer the biga to a large mixing bowl and add 1½ cups very warm water. Using a wooden spoon or your hands, break up the biga and mix it with the water to make a sloppy slurry. Add the whole wheat flour and 2½ to 3 cups semolina or durum flour. When the flours are well mixed in the watery biga, turn the dough out onto a lightly floured board and knead for 5 to 7 minutes, or until the dough is springy and soft and has lost its stickiness. Put a few drops of oil in the bottom of a clean, dry mixing bowl and turn the dough in the oil. Cover with a damp cloth and set aside for 2 to 3 hours to rise until more than doubled in bulk.

When ready to bake, set the oven at 450°F.

Punch the dough down in the bowl and add another cup of warm water to it. Add the sea salt—1 teaspoon should be plenty, but if you are not planning to add salty olives or ham, 1½ teaspoons will be better. Using your hands, mix the water with the dough to a sloppy slurry. If you have a mixer with a dough hook, use it to knead the water into the dough for 3 to 5 minutes, to make a viscous dough that is nonetheless smooth and satiny on its surface. If you do not have a dough hook, beat the water into the dough with a stiff, flat hand used like a paddle.

When the dough has reached the right texture, it will be more like a batter than a normal bread dough, and you will be able to feel the strands of gluten as you mix it with your hands. Add the garnish(es) and mix in with your hands, turning the dough over and over to mix as thoroughly as possible.

Have ready a large baking or cookie sheet with a little cornmeal or semolina sprinkled over it. You should also have a bowl of water in which to dip your hands to keep the dough from sticking. Wet your hands and take up as much dough as you can handle in two hands cupped together. Using an under-and-over motion with your hands, quickly form the dough into the shape of a bulky roll and drop it onto the sheet. Working quickly, continue with the rest of the dough—you should get 8 to 10 small breads out of this. As soon as all the breads are formed, transfer the sheet to the oven and bake for 45 minutes, turning the sheet around once during the cooking time to ensure even baking.

Remove from the oven and cool on a rack.

Casatiello di Pasqua o Pasquetta

A FESTIVE EASTER BREAD FROM NAPLES

Naples, like Palermo, its sister city in Sicily, has a strong aristocratic culinary tradition, the result of a long history as the capital of a wealthy (if often scandalously indolent) ruling class. Rich combinations of ingredients and elaborate techniques to fashion them are the hallmarks of this upper-class cuisine, often created by *monzù*, family chefs who were trained in French traditions and called themselves monzù, a corruption of the French monsieur. But the two cities also share an equally exuberant popular cuisine, not just the cuisine of street food vendors and tiny neighborhood restaurants, but also the dishes prepared in homes, however modest, for the important feast days, especially Christmas and Easter.

Casatiello is part of that tradition. Nowadays this famous Neapolitan treat is available year-round, but in the not-so-distant past—and by that I mean when I first went to Naples in the 1970s—casatiello was made only at Easter and quite specifically for Pasquetta, Little Easter, the Monday after Easter Sunday, which, like the day after Christmas, is a national holiday. In the South, families use Pasquetta as an excuse for a picnic in the countryside, and certain foods are de rigueur, among them this rich bread with a texture slightly reminiscent of brioche—although curiously made typically with lard, not butter. Some casatielli are plainer than others—I've seen a recipe for casatiello that is simply an ordinary bread dough into which extra yeast and lard are incorporated along with lots and lots of cracked black pepper. Others are far more elaborate, with three or four kinds of cheese, several sausages, and other types of cured pork. But whatever else is in the casatiello, there's always plenty of lard and plenty of black pepper.

For best results, casatiello should be prepared a day before serving. It is almost never eaten fresh from the oven, unless by exceptionally greedy children. Extra yeast gives the bread a high, puffy shape, best achieved by using a round cake pan 9 to 10 inches in diameter and 3 inches deep.

MAKES 1 CASATIELLO; 10 to 12 servings

FOR THE BIGA	1 tablespoon sugar	¼ cup coarsely grated pecorino sardo or pecorino toscano
1 cup whole milk	1 teaspoon salt	
1 tablespoon dry yeast	3 eggs, beaten	
2 cups unbleached all-purpose flour	About ⅓ cup pure pork lard, at room temperature	¼ cup coarsely grated parmigiano reggiano
FOR THE DOUGH	¼ pound pancetta, diced	¼ pound salami, diced (½ to ¾ cup)
3½ cups unbleached all-purpose flour, plus more for the board	2 teaspoons coarsely ground black pepper, or more to taste	⅓ cup diced provolone

To make the biga, heat the milk until it's hot. Transfer the milk to a medium bowl and when it's cool enough that you can hold your finger in the milk and count to 5, add the yeast, stirring with a wooden spoon to mix it in. When the yeast has dissolved, add the flour and stir to mix well. Don't worry if it's a little lumpy. Cover the bowl with plastic wrap and set aside to rise for several hours or overnight.

When you're ready to make the dough, toss the 3½ cups flour with the sugar and salt in a large mixing bowl. Make a well and stir in the beaten eggs, ½ cup warm (about 110°F) water, and a tablespoon of the lard. Add the biga and work the flour together with the other ingredients, first with a wooden spoon, then with your hands. When the dough holds together, turn it out onto a lightly floured board and knead until the dough is smooth and well mixed, with a nice elastic spring to it. Roll the dough out into a rectangle on the board. Smear another tablespoon of the lard all over the dough. Then, starting from one end, roll the dough up like a jelly roll and knead it 2 or 3 more times.

Shape the dough into a ball and place it in the rinsed-out mixing bowl. Cover with plastic wrap and set aside in a warm place to rise for 30 to 40 minutes, or until the dough has doubled.

While the dough is rising, sauté the pancetta in a skillet over medium-low heat, adding a teaspoon of lard or olive oil if necessary. Thoroughly brown the pancetta, then remove with a slotted spoon and drain on paper towels.

Smear 1 or 2 tablespoons of the lard all over the bottom and sides of a 9- or 10-inch round cake pan at least 3 inches deep and 9 to 10 inches in diameter.

Turn the risen dough out onto the lightly floured board. Add the black pepper and grated cheeses and knead them in well. Roll the dough into a rectangle once more. Spread with a tablespoon of lard and then strew the pancetta, salami, and diced provolone over the rectangle. Starting at a short end, roll the rectangle of dough like a jelly roll. Halfway through, smear the roll with another tablespoon of lard. Continue rolling until you have a tight cylinder. Pull the two ends together to make a fat circle. Set the dough in the prepared cake pan. Cover loosely with plastic wrap and set aside in a warm place to rise for 2 hours.

Preheat the oven to 400°F.

When the casatiello is fully risen, transfer it to the hot oven. Bake for 20 minutes, then reduce the heat to 325°F and bake for 45 to 55 minutes longer, or until the bread is thoroughly cooked and golden on top. Remove from the oven and let cool. Then transfer the bread to a paper bag, rolling the top to seal it, and set it aside until the next day to ripen before slicing and serving.

Focaccia and Potato Focaccia

The plainest, and possibly the best, focaccia is made on baking day with some of the bread dough that has been set aside for this purpose. Rolled out into a rectangle, the dough is topped with something simple and savory and popped into the hot oven for half an hour or so. It is a quick and easy way to feed hungry children who tend to congregate around the oven when the smell of baking bread becomes overwhelming.

Traditionally, focaccia was a hearth-baked bread. You can tell that from the name, which has the same root as *focolare,* the fireplace that was at the heart of every Italian country home. Later focaccia evolved as a way for bakers to gauge the heat of the wood-burning oven before putting in the full loaves of risen dough. And nowadays focaccia has become a delicious snack food in its own right, with a variety of toppings to please all tastes.

Focaccia, by one name or another, is known all over Italy. As you will see from the following recipes, the basic preparation, bread dough with a savory topping, goes by many other names including, confusingly, *pizza* and *sfincione.* On top of that, and even more confusing, many breads that don't at all fit the preceding description are also called *focaccia:* In Puglia, a focaccia is a double-crusted savory pie that is known elsewhere as *pizza rustica* or *torta* or *scaccia.* Not to put too fine a point on it, in a part of the world where the names of things change with the spoken dialect from one valley to another, often from one village to another, it's not surprising that something as elemental as bread-with-a-savory-topping should be known by many names.

The simplest focacce are often served as bread to accompany the meal, but more frequently they are offered as between-meal snacks, *spuntini* or merende. Sometimes a focaccia, cut into smaller pieces, is served as an antipasto, with a glass of wine or an aperitivo before lunch or dinner.

You may top focaccia with nothing more than olive oil, salt, and chopped rosemary or crumbled oregano; this is sometimes called *pizza bianca* (but see also the recipe for Pizza Bianca on page 49) and is baked in a sheet pan, cut into rectangles, and sold by the etto (100 grams) in city bakeries to schoolchildren, street workers, and others looking for a quick, healthful pick-me-up. A more elaborate focaccia will have added to the basic topping coarsely chopped tomatoes, olives, anchovies, and/or lots of garlic, but it will always look more informal, more thrown together, than the more deliberate topping of a pizza.

The following recipe, based on a focaccia known as *puddica* in Puglia, is a model. Feel free to play around with it, adding coarsely chopped pitted olives, chopped anchovy fillets, or other kinds of dried or fresh herbs. Like pizza, focaccia is best served piping hot, straight from the oven.

Make the bread dough ahead of time, through the second rise. Note that the Potato Bread recipe makes a smaller focaccia than the Golden Semolina Bread. Adjust quantities of topping ingredients accordingly.

MAKES 8 GENEROUS SERVINGS OR 16 SNACKS

½ recipe Golden Semolina Bread (page 26) or Potato Bread (page 30)	2 garlic cloves, thinly sliced or chopped	Coarse sea salt
10 to 12 cherry or grape tomatoes, halved	¼ to ⅓ cup extra-virgin olive oil	About 1 tablespoon dried oregano

Lightly oil a 12 × 18-inch baking sheet with sides at least ½ inch high. Roll the bread dough out on a lightly floured board until it more or less fits the pan—if the dough is very elastic, this may take some time and effort, but it will happen. Transfer the dough to the pan—it should be about ½ inch high—and use your fingers or the handle of a wooden spoon to dimple it all over with indentations. Press the tomato halves, cut side down, into the dough, then scatter the garlic over, pressing it lightly into the dough. Dribble the olive oil all over the top so that it puddles in the indentations, then sprinkle the surface liberally with coarse salt and oregano. Set aside, lightly covered with plastic wrap, to rise for 30 to 40 minutes.

While the dough is rising, preheat the oven to 450°F.

When the dough has risen, slide the focaccia pan into the preheated oven and bake for 5 minutes, then lower the heat to 350°F and continue baking for 30 minutes, or until the top is golden brown.

Transfer from the oven to a wire rack. The focaccia should be served immediately, piping hot.

To make Focaccia con Tonno (sometimes called *Pizza Bianca con Tonno*), substitute the following for the topping in the recipe, pressing the tuna and parsley lightly into the dough before topping with the seasonings and olive oil:

One 6-ounce can oil-packed tuna, drained and flaked	Sea salt and freshly ground black pepper	¼ cup extra-virgin olive oil, more or less
½ cup coarsely chopped flat-leaf parsley leaves	2 tablespoons capers, preferably salt-packed, rinsed, drained, and coarsely chopped	

Focaccia al Pomodoro e Ricotta

FOCACCIA WITH TOMATO AND RICOTTA TOPPING

Ricotta enriches the top of this focaccia, which comes from Puglia. The best tomatoes to use are fleshy ripe plum tomatoes, the bigger the better. Slicing them vertically makes what southern Italian cooks call *filetti di pomodoro,* tomato fillets.

Make the bread dough ahead of time, through the second rise.

MAKES 8 GENEROUS SERVINGS OR 16 SNACKS

3 large ripe plum tomatoes	¼ cup extra-virgin olive oil	1 tablespoon dried oregano
1 cup whole-milk ricotta	16 to 20 black or green olives, pitted	⅓ cup grated hard aged cheese: pecorino, caciocavallo, or parmigiano reggiano
½ recipe Golden Semolina Bread (page 26) or Potato Bread (page 30)	Coarse sea salt and freshly ground black pepper	

Bring a pot of water to a boil and dip each tomato in the boiling water for 12 to 15 seconds. Remove and peel, then slice each tomato lengthwise into long, thin strips, discarding most of the seeds.

Put the ricotta through the fine disk of a food mill or whirl it in a food processor for a few seconds to make it lighter and creamier.

Roll the dough out as described in the Basic Focaccia recipe (page 37). Dribble a tablespoon of olive oil over the top of the dough, then smear a thin layer of ricotta all over the top, leaving a narrow border around the edges. Stud the ricotta with the tomato strips and the olives, pressing them lightly into the ricotta. Dribble another 2 tablespoons of olive oil over the topping, then sprinkle with coarse salt, plenty of black pepper, and the oregano, crumbling the herb in your fingers. Sprinkle grated cheese over the top and dribble with the remaining tablespoon of olive oil.

Bake, as directed for Basic Focaccia. Remove from the oven and serve immediately.

Focaccia con le Tre Cipolle

THREE-ONION FOCACCIA

This focaccia, topped with a melting combination of red and yellow onions and leeks, is served as part of the antipasto at a delightful farmhouse-inn, Agriturismo Seliano, outside the ancient Greek city of Paestum in Campania. At the farmhouse dinner table, the focaccia is accompanied by big, round, whey-dripping balls of creamy mozzarella di bufala, made from the milk of water buffalo raised on the farm.

Instead of the following dough, you could use half the dough for either Golden Semolina Bread (page 26) or Potato Bread (page 30).

Rather than grating the cheese, use a vegetable peeler to sliver it, making what Italian cooks call *scaglie di formaggio,* or scales of cheese.

MAKES ABOUT 18 PIECES

FOR THE DOUGH

1 teaspoon dry yeast

4½ cups unbleached all-purpose flour

2 tablespoons sea salt

1 teaspoon extra-virgin olive oil

FOR THE TOPPING

¼ cup extra-virgin olive oil

1 pound red onions, halved and sliced (about 2 medium onions)

¾ pound yellow onions, halved and sliced (about 1½ medium onions)

Sea salt and freshly ground black pepper

½ pound leeks, trimmed (2 medium leeks)

1 tablespoon sugar

½ cup slivered hard aged cheese: pecorino, caciocavallo, parmigiano reggiano, or grana padano

First make the biga or starter: Combine the yeast with a cup of warm (110°F) water and set aside until the yeast has dissolved, 5 to 10 minutes. Combine the dissolved yeast with a cup of the flour in a large bowl. Mix together to a thick slurry, cover the bowl with plastic wrap, and set it aside to rise and develop flavor for at least 2 hours, or you may leave it in a cool place (not refrigerated) overnight.

When ready to continue with the dough, dissolve the sea salt in a cup of warm water. Mix about 3 cups of the remaining flour into the dough, adding the salty water in small increments— you may not need to use all the water. Knead the dough briefly in the bowl, then spread the remaining ½ cup of flour on a wooden board or countertop and turn the dough out onto the board. Knead for about 10 minutes, or until the dough is springy and elastic. Rinse out and dry the mixing bowl, add the teaspoon of oil to the bowl, then turn the ball of dough in the oil to coat it lightly. Cover the bowl with plastic wrap and set aside in a warm place to rise for at least 2 hours.

Meanwhile, make the topping: In a large saucepan, combine the ¼ cup olive oil with the onions, stirring to mix well. Set over low heat and cook very slowly, stirring from time to time, until the onions have reduced to a soft and rather creamy mass, about 30 minutes. As the onions cook down, add at least a tablespoon of salt and lots of black pepper.

Rinse the leeks, cut them in half lengthwise, and slice very thinly. When the onions are thoroughly reduced, stir the leeks and sugar into the mass, raise the heat to medium, and cook for 15 minutes longer. The onions will start to brown slightly as you do this.

Preheat the oven to 400°F. Lightly oil a baking sheet about 12 × 18 inches.

Punch down the dough and roll it out in a rough rectangle about 12 × 18 inches and not more than ½ inch thick. Set the dough on the oiled baking sheet and and use your fingers or the handle of a wooden spoon to dimple it all over with shallow indentations, then spoon the onion topping all over the top of the dough, smoothing it right out to the edges. Cover the top of the onions with the scales of cheese.

Transfer to the preheated oven and bake 30 to 40 minutes, or until the crust is brown and the top is slightly crisp and starting to brown while the cheese has melted.

Remove from the oven, cut into squares, and serve immediately.

Pizza Rianata Trapanese

TRAPANI-STYLE FOCACCIA

Despite the name, this really is a focaccia, but in the province of Trapani on Sicily's west coast, it's called *pizza rianata,* and in other parts of Sicily *sfincione,* and a sfincione is really a Sicilian focaccia. (Confused? So am I!) *Pizza rianata* literally means "pizza with oregano"—but there's much more to this, as you will see.

Fontina and asiago, made from cow's milk in northern Italy, are not found in the South, but they are as close as many of us can come in North America—in flavor and, more important, texture—to the kind of young pecorino (sheep's milk) cheeses that would be used for pizza rianata in Trapani. If you happen to come across a Sicilian pecorino that's less than three months old, by all means use it instead; I also occasionally find young cow's milk cheeses at my farmer's market that work well with this.

Note the egg, which makes the dough richer than most.

MAKES 8 TO 12 SERVINGS as an antipasto or part of a light lunch

FOR THE DOUGH	FOR THE TOPPING	
1 teaspoon dry yeast	12 anchovy fillets, coarsely chopped	Freshly ground black pepper
3 cups unbleached all-purpose flour, plus more for the board	1/4 cup extra-virgin olive oil	1/2 pound cheese, such as young pecorino, fontina, or asiago, thinly sliced
1 cup semolina	4 garlic cloves, chopped	1/2 cup dry bread crumbs
Sea salt	One 28-ounce can plum tomatoes, drained and chopped	1/2 cup grated aged cheese: pecorino, caciocavallo, or ricotta salata
2 tablespoons extra-virgin olive oil	3/4 cup chopped flat-leaf parsley	1 tablespoon dried oregano
1 egg		

To make the dough, add the yeast to 1/2 cup warm (110°F) water and set aside to dissolve.

Combine the flour, semolina, and salt to taste in a large bowl. Make a well in the center and pour in the dissolved yeast. Add the oil and mix, adding in another 1/4 cup warm water. Add the egg and continue mixing, adding more water, a tablespoon at a time, up to 1/4 cup in all. Turn the dough out onto a lightly floured board and knead for about 10 minutes, or until the dough is silky smooth and has lost any tackiness. Form the dough into a ball, dust it with flour, and set it in the rinsed-out and dried bowl. Cover with plastic wrap and set aside in a warm place to rise until doubled—about 30 minutes.

While the dough is rising, make the topping. Combine the anchovy fillets and 1 tablespoon of the olive oil in a sauté pan and cook gently, crushing the anchovies into the oil with a fork. Stir in the garlic, then add the chopped tomatoes and parsley. Bring to a simmer and cook, stirring frequently, until the sauce has thickened and reduced to $1\frac{1}{2}$ to $1\frac{3}{4}$ cups. Remove from the heat, stir in lots of black pepper, and set aside.

Use a small amount of olive oil to oil the bottom and sides of a 12 × 18-inch baking sheet. Turn the dough out onto a lightly floured board, punch it down, and roll it out to fit the oiled pan. Set the dough in the pan, then spread the tomato sauce all over, leaving a $\frac{1}{4}$-inch border around the edges.

Layer the sliced cheese over the tomato sauce, then sprinkle with bread crumbs and grated cheese. Add the oregano, crumbling it in your fingers, and then dribble the remaining olive oil over the top. Cover lightly with plastic wrap and set aside in a warm place to rise for about 30 minutes.

Preheat the oven to 400°F. Bake the focaccia for 20 to 30 minutes, or until the crust is golden and the top is sizzling. Remove from the oven and let rest for 4 or 5 minutes, then slice and serve immediately.

Pizza and Calzone

We make a lot of fuss about pizza but really it is nothing more than a flatbread, traditionally made, like focaccia, from a simple bread dough, a portion of which was set aside on baking day to make a quick, easy, nourishing treat for eating out of hand. Either Golden Semolina Bread (page 26) or Potato Bread (page 30) could be used to make pizza—you'll need about a pound of dough to make a single 12- to 14-inch pizza or enough to make 8 slices—four servings if that's all you're serving, with a salad or a bowl of soup to go with it. As with focaccia, you could divide either of those bread doughs in half, using one half to make a loaf of bread and the other half for a couple of pizzas.

Or just follow the recipe for Basic Dough for Pizza or Calzone that follows. Note that this pizza dough is made with all-purpose flour, which is closest to the type of flour (in Italian it's called *00* or *doppio zero*) used in the best pizzerie in Naples.

A good pizza is judged by its crust, not by what's on top of it. The dough, in fact, is the defining ingredient—not whether it's thin or thick, which is a function of personal preference, but how tasty and chewy and tender it is. As with pasta, the idea is that the topping or the sauce is there to enhance the basic wheat flavors of the pizza dough or pasta. But the key word is digestibility: Pizza must never rest heavy on the stomach.

An indigestible pizza is one made with improperly raised dough that hasn't been cooked sufficiently: Pizza should be slowly raised and quickly cooked, rather than vice versa. The best pizzaiuoli swear by a minimum of twenty-four hours of rising time—and many claim forty-eight or even seventy-two hours is better, while a two- to three-hour rise is considered unacceptably speedy. Modern American flours are very strong and springy, but that's not always a good thing since they will rise rapidly if the temperature is not kept low. Long slow rise at a cool temperature, then, is the key to good pizza as much as it is to good bread.

The other factor in producing great pizza is a very hot oven, not so easy in North American home kitchens. You'll want to preheat your oven to the highest possible baking temperature, preferably with a pizza stone, a baking stone, or terra-cotta oven tiles to simulate the kind of wood-burning masonry ovens used in Napoli. The clay in the stone or tiles pulls moisture from the dough and helps produce a crisp crust. Be sure to put the stone or tiles in a *cold* oven and preheat them for at least 30 to 45 minutes before putting in the pizza. (Even if the oven temperature registers a high heat more quickly, the clay inserts may not be hot all the way through.) With the oven set at 550°F, you should be able to bake a pizza in five to seven minutes. (This is a lot longer than the sixty to ninety seconds of a Neapolitan pizzeria, but it's the best we can do under the circumstances.)

Finally, don't pile on the topping. If the point of a good pizza is the crust, then you don't want to obscure that crisp texture and good yeasty, bready flavor by heaping a refrigerator full of extra ingredients on top. In Napoli, one, two, or a maximim of three ingredients are considered sufficient for most pizzas—tomato sauce or ripe fresh tomatoes, a little cheese, and maybe a few anchovies or sliced or crumbled sausage (never the two together) or a sprinkle of fresh herbs. Pizza should be a snack or a light meal, with the emphasis on light, not an opportunity to gorge on rich and greasy combinations.

When I first went to Italy almost half a century ago, it was difficult to find pizza north of Naples, but just as pizza has conquered the world, so has it conquered northern Italy, and it's now considered not just street food or snack food but a full-fledged meal in itself. Young Italians (and even some old ones!) go out to a pizzeria in the same way North Americans do, and even, sometimes, buy takeout pizza to carry home. No Domino's yet, but it may be just around the next corner.

Pizza in Napoli

Napoli is the birthplace of pizza, although flatbreads, baked on the hearth or on the floor of the oven, have been around for as long as bread itself. No one disputes that pizza, modern pizza, and especially pizza with a topping that includes tomato sauce, is a Neapolitan invention. Even though the humble pie has spread all over the known world, it is still to Naples that one turns to find out how a real pizza should be made.

I couldn't possibly tell you how many pizzerie there are in Naples (eighty by one count, more than five hundred by another, with others ranging everywhere in between)—so much depends on how you define the term. But far and away the most authentic, for my money at least, is a not quite hole-in-the-wall called da Michele, located in the spirited Tribunali district of Spaccanapoli, right in the pulsing heart of old Napoli.

There's nothing flashy about the place, nothing apart from lines of people waiting to get in that indicates this is something special. A red-lettered sign over the door reads "PIZZERIA," while next to it hangs the familiar round Coca-Cola symbol. Da Michele is distinguished solely by austerity: Its plain, white-tiled décor gives new meaning to the word unassuming, while the menu, if you can call it that, is equally plain—pizza Margherita, pizza marinara, calzone e basta. Nothing more. And it has been that way since the original Michele Condurro opened his establishment back in the mid–nineteenth century. (Until recently, Michele's three grandsons continued the tradition, but now that they are in their eighties, yet another generation has taken over and, I've been told, the pizzeria is now run by Alfonso Cucciniello, husband of a Condurro daughter.)

There is something deeply pleasing to me in this kind of continuity, this kind of purity. Luigi Condurro, one of the three grandsons, was the chief pizzaiolo when I first discovered da Michele back in the 1980s. He explained to me the manner in which the pizza was made, unchanged since his grandfather's day, with a dough made from 00 flour and a starter put by the day before, shaped by hand, dressed with sugna, or lard, with a topping of tomato sauce, pummarola made solely from San Marzano tomatoes (see page 127) grown in the mineral-dense soil of the volcanic plain below Vesuvius. Then the decision is made: Marinara or Margherita? A scattering of oregano and slivers of raw garlic? Or a patriotic distribution of red sauce, green basil, and white mozzarella, a pizza that was "invented" in the late nineteenth century and named in honor of united Italy's first queen, Margherita di Savoia?

"Mozzarella di bufala?" I asked in all innocence the first time.

"Macchè, mozzarella di bufala!" Luigi scoffed. "If you use buffalo mozzarella, you'll have wet dough and a pizza swimming in milk. We use cow's milk mozzarella, *fior di latte* it's called, from Agerola up in the mountains on the Sorrento Peninsula."

Making pizza at da Michele is a rapid-fire operation that sometimes moves so fast you can't believe your eyes. The dough is slapped into shape on a worktable, quickly dressed, then dropped onto a wooden peel that slides it into the ever-burning wood-fired oven in a corner of the room. The pizzaiolo watches it intently. Sometimes he throws in a handful of sawdust to raise the temperature just before the pizza goes in—it should be very hot, up to 900°F, or hot enough to fire pottery; sometimes he shifts it slightly from one side of the domed oven to another to take advantage of different levels of heat. But it's all over in less than a minute and a half, and the steaming pizza emerges like Vesuvius itself, the crust crisp-blistered and smoky, the sauce bubbling like red lava, and is skated onto a marble-topped table where the customer awaits what is probably the best pizza he or she will ever consume.

Basic Dough for Pizza or Calzone

The best pizza dough, like the best bread dough, is made with a long slow period of rising—a good six to twelve hours for the biga, followed by another six to twelve hours for the dough itself. Obviously it's not always possible to do this. If you're in a hurry, you can also make the dough relatively quickly, letting the biga rise for just thirty minutes and giving the dough itself an hour or so. But when you have the luxury of thinking ahead and using the long, slow technique, I think you will find the quality of the dough improved immeasurably.

Many pizzaioli scorn the use of olive oil in the dough; others swear by it. Try it both ways and see which you prefer.

If you wish, substitute a cup of whole wheat flour for a cup of the all-purpose flour.

MAKES 1½ TO 2 POUNDS OF DOUGH, enough for two 12- to 14-inch round or free-form pizzas, 6 to 8 servings each, or 8 to 12 small calzone

½ teaspoon dry yeast 3½ cups unbleached all-purpose flour	1½ teaspoons sea salt ½ cup semolina	1 tablespoon extra-virgin olive oil (optional), plus a little more for the bowl and the baking pan

Make the biga: Sprinkle the yeast over a cup of warm water in a bowl. When the yeast has dissolved, add about a cup of the all-purpose flour. Stir just until blended, but don't fret about getting rid of all the lumps. Cover the bowl with plastic wrap and set aside for at least 30 minutes and up to 6 hours or overnight to let the flavors develop.

When ready to continue, add the salt to ½ cup of hot water and set aside to cool slightly.

Set aside ½ cup of all-purpose flour to use on the bread board. Add the remaining all-purpose flour and the semolina to the biga and stir to mix, stirring in a tablespoon of olive oil if you wish. (If you wish to add a teaspoon of vinegar to correct the pH of your water [see page 53], you should do so now.) Add half the salt water and stir it in, then as much of the remaining salt water as necessary to make the dough sufficiently soft and ready to knead. You may need as little as ½ cup or as much as a full cup of liquid—much depends on ambient humidity.

Use the reserved ½ cup of flour to dust a bread board lightly. Turn the dough out onto the board and knead for 10 minutes, gradually incorporating more flour—but only if it seems necessary; otherwise, use just enough flour on the board to keep the dough from sticking. Knead until you have a nice, springy, elastic dough that has lost its tackiness.

Rinse and dry the bowl and smear the insides with a little olive oil. Shape the dough into a ball and sprinkle it with a light dusting of flour. Set it in the bowl, cover lightly with plastic wrap, and set aside in a warm place to rise for at least an hour, although letting the dough rise in a cool place overnight will yield a more complex flavor.

When ready to make pizza, punch the dough down and turn out onto a lightly floured board. Divide in half or into 8 smaller pieces, depending on what you wish to do with the dough. In any case, while you work with a piece of dough, keep the remaining dough lightly covered with a slightly damp towel so it doesn't dry out.

This is the simplest pizza imaginable. I like to serve it along with a bowl of some hearty bean or legume soup—true comfort food for a cold winter night. On the other hand, served on the porch alongside a crisp green salad, it's just as good to round off lunch on a hot summer day.

MAKES ONE 12- TO 14-INCH PIZZA

½ recipe Basic Dough for Pizza or Calzone (page 47)

Cornmeal or semolina for the peel

FOR THE TOPPING

2 tablespoons extra-virgin olive oil, more or less

Leaves from 2 fresh rosemary branches or ¼ cup coarsely chopped flat-leaf parsley

1 or 2 garlic cloves, coarsely chopped

2 tablespoons grated aged cheese: pecorino, caciocavallo, or parmigiano reggiano

1 tablespoon coarse sea salt, more or less

Preheat the oven to 450 to 550°F. If you are using a pizza stone, set it in the oven before you turn it on and preheat for at least 45 minutes to get the stone nice and hot before putting the pizza in the oven. If you are using a pizza pan, you need heat the oven only until the thermostat indicates that it has reached 450 to 550°F.

When ready to make pizza, punch the dough down and turn out on a lightly floured board. Knead the dough briefly. To relax the dough, pick it up and slam it against the board three-four-five times, then shape it into a ball on the lightly floured board and stretch it into a rough disk about 12 to 14 inches in diameter and less than ¼ inch thick. You may use a rolling pin to do this, although professional pizzaioli seldom do so, preferring to shape a rough circle of dough, then stretch it with their hands, turning it rapidly and pulling gently on the outer edge of the circle. (That business of spinning and tossing the circle of dough high overhead, once an attraction of American pizza parlors, requires a good deal of practice and, while impressive, is not the most efficient way to arrive at a satisfactory pizza.)

If you are using a wooden peel, sprinkle it heavily with semolina or cornmeal and stretch the dough circle over the peel. (If you are using a baking sheet, simply lay the circle of dough on the pan.) Dribble with a tablespoon of olive oil, then scatter the herbs and garlic over the pizza.

Taste the cheese: If it's too salty, you may not wish to add salt. Otherwise, scatter the grated cheese and salt over the surface and then dribble the remaining olive oil in a thin thread over the pizza.

When the oven is hot, slide the pizza with a brisk shake from the peel directly onto the pizza stone or simply transfer the pan to an oven rack. Bake for about 7 to 10 minutes, or until the pizza is golden and the oil is sizzling. Remove, slice, and serve immediately.

The classic Neapolitan pizza is said to have been designed for Margherita di Savoia, the first queen of united Italy, when she visited Naples in the late nineteenth century. Any food like this one, which combines red (tomatoes), white (mozzarella), and green (basil), the colors of the Italian flag, tends to receive a name that reflects Italian patriotism. Curiously, it's about the only thing in Italy that does.

Although buffalo-milk mozzarella, an exquisite product, is made very near Naples, most pizzaioli prefer mozzarella made from cow's milk, properly called *fior di latte*. The cow's milk version, they say, doesn't release liquid the way buffalo-milk mozzarella does. They would use mozzarella di bufala only when the cheese is more than twenty-four hours old. Since mozzarella di bufala available here is a good deal older than that, and since American-made mozzarella is from cow's milk anyway, you don't have to worry about it. Do not under any circumstances, however, use the tough, rubbery, plastic-wrapped cheese sold in American supermarkets as mozzarella. It bears little resemblance to the real thing.

MAKES ONE 12- TO 14-INCH PIZZA

½ recipe Basic Dough for Pizza or Calzone (page 47) **FOR THE TOPPING** ¾ cup Basic Tomato Sauce (page 125)	Sea salt and freshly ground black pepper 3 ounces mozzarella, preferably cow's milk (*fior di latte*), sliced or coarsely chopped	Dried oregano 3 or 4 fresh basil sprigs ¼ to ½ cup freshly grated aged pecorino or parmigiano reggiano Extra-virgin olive oil for the top

Roll or stretch out the pizza dough, following the directions on page 49. Preheat the oven to 450 to 550°F.

Bring the tomato sauce to a slow simmer, taste, and add salt and pepper if necessary, then spread the sauce over the rolled-out pizza dough, leaving a ¼- to ½-inch edge all around. Arrange the mozzarella slices over the tomato sauce and sprinkle with dried oregano to taste, rubbing it between your fingers.

Pull off 5 or 6 whole basil leaves and set aside for garnish. Sliver the rest of the basil and sprinkle it over the mozzarella. Add the grated cheese, dribble with olive oil, and transfer the pizza to the preheated oven, as described on page 50, to bake for 7 to 10 minutes, or until the crust is golden and the top is bubbling. Remove, garnish with the reserved basil leaves, then slice and serve immediately.

VARIATION

🌿 In the Cilento, south of Salerno along the coast of Campania, a similar pizza is made with the local slightly aged goat cheese. Except in a few small regions, goat cheese is not widely known in Italy. It gives a pleasantly different flavor. If you wish to try it, use about ¼ pound of firm goat cheese, grated or sliced, in place of the cheeses listed.

Tempest in a Pizza Oven, or How to Create an Official Legal Status for La Verace Pizza Napoletana

Maybe it's a result of persistent globalization, but in recent years Neapolitans, not otherwise known for observance of rules and regulations, have been agitating noisily for legal recognition for what they call *la verace pizza napoletana*. That is, "real" Neapolitan pizza, as opposed to all those fake *pizze napoletane* made in other parts of the world.

Neapolitans revere their pizza as a proud and unmistakable symbol of civic identity, but the fact is that Neapolitans themselves have carried the humble pie wherever they have gone in the world, from Buenos Aires to Brisbane, Bombay to Boston, and well beyond. Around the world, pizza has become as ubiquitous as McDonald's, possibly more so. Adopted by cultures and cuisines far from Naples, it has proven itself almost infinitely adaptable, from the ham and pineapple pizza of Hawaii to the chocolate pizza, spread with Nutella, sold in the *centro storico* of Rome, to the pizza depicted recently on an American food television network, a pizza barely discernible beneath a pile of clams, prosciutto, mushrooms, fresh tomatoes, tomato sauce (itself flavored with quantities of butter, basil, and chicken stock), salt, pepper, basil, and more than four cups of three different kinds of grated cheese, enough to make even an exuberant Neapolitan queasy.

So it was clear that something had to be done about all this, and in 2004 it was: The Italian government published an official decree setting a standard for Neapolitan pizza, called *specialità tradizionale garantita*, guaranteed traditional specialty. Henceforth, no one, at least no one in Italy, could legally call a pizza "Neapolitan" (or, for that matter, "marinara" or "margherita" or even "margherita extra") unless it was made according to Italian-decreed standards.

Can you really legislate a recipe for pizza? Well, in Italy, apparently you can. The regulations require that the pizza be worked by hand, without a rolling pin or, worse yet, an automatic pizza-maker.

They also call for some surprising ingredients—for instance, the dough is to be made from 00 (*doppio zero*) flour, which is softer than American all-purpose flour, and the cheese must be mozzarella di bufala DOP—guaranteed buffalo-milk mozzarella from the plains of Campania south of Naples, a product that most pizzaioli scorn.

But the ultimate qualification for a true Neapolitan pizza is the oven temperature. The new regulations demand that the pizza be baked in a high-temperature wood-fired oven—up to 900°F—for less than two minutes, exactly as it's always been done at da Michele (see page 45). A pizza cooked at this temperature is a miracle of flavor and texture, crisp yet chewy, recalling not so much crackers as truly the bread from which pizza evolved.

In fact, it was a displaced Neapolitan working for Academia Barilla, a study center for traditional Italian foods established by the Barilla pasta company in Parma, who taught me one or two valuable lessons. "Always dissolve the yeast in warm water," Evandro Taddei cautioned, "and always dissolve the salt in warm water too." Moreover, he added, whipping out a serious-looking dial, "be careful of the *piacca* of your water."

"The *piacca*?" Then I understood—the pH (*pee Acca* in Italian), the acid level of water. Most water in Italy, Taddei said, is too soft, too sweet, for a good, responsive dough. If you think that's a problem with your own tap water, take a tip from Taddei: Add a teaspoon of white vinegar to the bread or pizza dough to bring it to the right acidity.

Pizza alla Friarielle

PIZZA TOPPED WITH BITTER GREENS

This substantial pizza topping could also make a filling for a two-crust pie or for calzone (see page 56). Friarielle are an especially pungent variety of broccoli rabe widely available in Neapolitan markets during winter and, as far as I know, unknown in North America. But you can use almost any kind of bitter green, from broccoli rabe (sometimes called *rapini*) to lacinato ("black" or "dinosaur" or Tuscan) kale to turnip greens; even Chinese flowering broccoli is good in this treatment. If you don't like bitter greens (unimaginable, but some folks don't), you could make this with ordinary sweet green broccoli.

MAKES ONE 12- TO 14-INCH PIZZA

½ recipe Basic Dough for Pizza or Calzone (page 47)

1 pound broccoli rabe (rapini)

2 tablespoons extra-virgin olive oil, plus a little more for the top

2 garlic cloves, coarsely chopped

8 anchovy fillets

1 tablespoon capers, preferably salt-packed, rinsed and drained

1 tablespoon golden raisins, plumped in hot water and drained

1 tablespoon pine nuts

¼ cup coarsely chopped pitted black olives, preferably oil-cured

Sea salt and freshly ground black pepper

¼ pound fresh goat cheese, crumbled, or whole-milk ricotta

¼ cup grated aged pecorino or parmigiano reggiano

Have the pizza dough ready before you start to make the topping.

Pick over the broccoli rabe, discarding any yellow or wilted leaves. Rinse thoroughly and chop into inch-long pieces. Transfer to a saucepan and cook, covered, over medium-low heat in the water clinging to the greens until the broccoli rabe is tender. If necessary, add a tablespoon or two of boiling water during the cooking to keep the greens from scorching. Drain the greens in a colander, squeezing gently between your hands to get rid of excess water. Set aside.

Combine the olive oil and garlic in a medium sauté pan over medium-low heat and cook until the garlic is tender, about 3 minutes. Chop the anchovy fillets and add to the garlic, crushing the anchovies with a fork and dissolving them into the oil. Turn the drained greens into the anchovy-garlic oil, mixing well, then add the capers, raisins, pine nuts, and olives. Cook briefly, no more than 2 or 3 minutes, stirring to meld the flavors. Taste and add salt if needed and pepper, keeping in mind that the cheese will also add salt to the pizza.

Roll or stretch out the pizza dough, following the directions on page 49. Preheat the oven to 450 to 550°F.

Top the pizza crust with the greens and sprinkle on the two cheeses, then dribble with olive oil. Transfer the pizza to the preheated oven, as described on page 50, and bake for 15 to 20 minutes, or until the pizza crust is golden and the cheese on top is melting. Remove, slice, and serve immediately.

Calzone con Salsiccia e Ricotta

CHEESY SAUSAGE AND RICOTTA CALZONE

Classic calzone are simply pizzas in a different shape—folded over to make an envelope. The dough is the same as pizza dough, and anything that can go on top of a pizza can be put inside a calzone—even a simple margherita topping. It makes sense since the original way of eating pizza was to fold it *a portafoglio,* like a man's wallet, or *a libretto,* like a book, so you could consume it easily while standing at a pizzeria counter or walking along the street. From there, simple logic dictated closing up the edges to keep the insides from spilling out and—*ecco!*—un calzone, a word we might translate into English as "long-johns."

The following is a particularly delicious—and filling—filling, but keep in mind that you could also use this as a topping for a conventional pizza. Some cooks add a pinch of ground cinnamon—I don't, because I don't care for it, but you may, if you wish, add a little cinnamon with the black pepper.

MAKES 10 CALZONE, 5 TO 6 INCHES ACROSS

½ recipe Basic Dough for Pizza or Calzone (page 47)	¼ cup finely minced white onion	12 black olives, pitted and coarsely chopped
½ pound flavorful Italian-style fresh sausage	2 garlic cloves, finely minced	Freshly ground black pepper to taste
1 cup grated hard aged cheese: pecorino, caciocavallo, grana padano, or parmigiano reggiano	¼ cup finely minced flat-leaf parsley	2 tablespoons extra-virgin olive oil, plus a little more for the pan
2 teaspoons dried oregano	¼ cup finely minced fresh basil	½ cup whole-milk ricotta
	1 teaspoon crumbled dried red chili, or to taste	

Have the pizza dough ready before you make the filling.

Remove the casing from the sausage and transfer the meat to a bowl. Add all the other ingredients (except the dough) and mix thoroughly using your hands.

Divide the pizza dough into 10 pieces. While you're working on one piece, keep the others covered with plastic wrap or a damp towel. Preheat the oven to 400°F. Rub a baking sheet with a little olive oil.

Roll out a piece of dough to make a thin round, 7 or 8 inches in diameter. Spread 3 to 4 tablespoons of the meat-ricotta mixture on half of the round, leaving about a ½-inch border.

Dampen the edge with a little water and fold the other half over the filling. Roll or crimp the edges together to seal. As you finish each round, transfer it to the baking sheet.

When all the rounds are done, brush a little oil over the top of each one, paying special attention to the sealed edges. Transfer to the preheated oven and bake until the calzone are golden, 25 to 35 minutes, checking from time to time to make sure they are not getting too brown. When they are golden, remove and let rest for 7 or 8 minutes, then serve immediately.

VARIATION

For a party buffet or a bite to have with an aperitif before dinner, make smaller calzone, called *calzoncine.* They're quick and easy little bites, especially when friends are sitting around the kitchen table, sipping wine and noshing while you prepare the rest of the meal. Cut the rolled-out dough into 3- to 4-inch squares or circles (you should have enough dough for about twenty-four 3-inch calzoncine, eighteen 4-inch ones), whichever you prefer. Drop about a heaping teaspoon of filling into the middle of each dough square or round and fold it over to make a miniature calzone. They need less time in the oven—12 to 15 minutes—but they're best when hot, so time them accordingly.

Peppery Pork Calzone

Sun-dried tomatoes are preferred for this very tasty filling from Sicily, but if you must use canned plum tomatoes, drain them thoroughly, then chop and drain again; otherwise, the filling will be watery.

Primosale is a fresh white Sicilian sheep's milk cheese, not more than about two weeks old. Since it's hard to find in North America, I have substituted a young goat's milk cheese instead.

MAKES 10 CALZONE, 5 TO 6 INCHES ACROSS

½ recipe Basic Dough for Pizza or Calzone (page 47)

4 whole sun-dried tomatoes or canned plum tomatoes, chopped and well drained

3 small potatoes (about ¾ pound), peeled and diced

¼ cup extra-virgin olive oil

20 black olives, pitted and chopped (½ cup)

1 small onion, minced

1 garlic clove, minced

2 tablespoons minced flat-leaf parsley

½ pound ground lean pork or mixed pork and veal

1 tablespoon crushed dried red chili

Freshly ground black pepper

⅓ cup fresh white cheese, preferably sheep's milk, but if not available young goat's milk or cow's milk

⅓ cup coarsely grated aged pecorino or caciocavallo

Sea salt, if needed

Have the pizza dough ready before you make the filling. Cover the dried tomatoes in a bowl with very hot water. When the tomatoes are soft, after about 15 minutes, cut them into fine slivers. (You may also use canned plum tomatoes, drained, chopped, and drained again very thoroughly before being combined with the other ingredients.)

In a medium skillet over medium-low heat, combine the potato dice with 2 tablespoons of the olive oil. Cook, stirring frequently, until the potatoes are tender and starting to brown. Transfer the potatoes and the oil in which they cooked to a bowl and stir in the chopped olives, along with the onion, garlic, and parsley.

Mix the meat, chili, and lots of black pepper into the potatoes and add the tomato slivers. Stir in the two cheeses. To test for seasoning, sauté a little spoonful of the mixture, then add salt if necessary (the cheese may provide plenty of salt) or more pepper—the filling should be very peppery.

Fill and bake the calzone as described on pages 56 to 57.

Double-Crust Pies

The following savory pies are all double crusted. They go by many names, including *pizza, pitta, torta,* and, most confusingly, *sfinciune* and/or *focaccia,* depending on where in the South they are made. Many, perhaps most, of these savory pies are made with yeasted dough, but the modern trend is to use a pasta frolla, or short-crust pastry. If you wish, you may substitute the pasta frolla on page 68 for any of the yeasted doughs in these recipes.

A savory pie has many uses. It makes a delicious snack, elegant picnic fare, and a welcome part of an antipasto buffet, but it's also very good on its own as a first course or even served as the main dish along with a soup or salad. And while at their best hot from the oven, savory pies are almost as good as room-temperature leftovers the next day.

Pitta Chicculiata

TUNA AND TOMATO PIE

Apart from the dough, which should rise for at least a couple of hours, this pie from Calabria is easy to throw together with ingredients that most cooks will have on hand—canned tomatoes, tuna, capers, and so forth. It's spectacularly good as an antipasto, to serve guests with a glass of wine at the start of a meal, while you're still putting other courses together. But it's also delicious as a light, summery lunch, with a green salad on the side.

MAKES ONE 12-INCH PIE; 8 servings as an appetizer

FOR THE DOUGH

1 teaspoon dry yeast

2½ cups unbleached all-purpose flour

1½ cups semolina

2 egg yolks, beaten

1 tablespoon extra-virgin olive oil, plus a little more for the pan

FOR THE FILLING

1 tablespoon finely minced garlic (about 4 plump cloves)

¼ cup extra-virgin olive oil

One 28-ounce can whole tomatoes

6 anchovy fillets

2½ tablespoons capers, preferably salt-packed, rinsed and drained

½ cup pitted black olives

One 6-ounce can oil-packed tuna

¼ cup minced flat-leaf parsley

Sea salt and freshly ground black pepper

½ teaspoon dried oregano, crumbled (optional)

Pinch of crumbled dried red chili

Make a biga, or starter dough, by combining the yeast in a large bowl with 1 cup warm water. As soon as the yeast has dissolved, add a cup of the all-purpose flour and mix together with a wooden spoon. Cover with plastic wrap and leave at room temperature for several hours or overnight—until the biga is bubbly and slightly collapsed.

Set aside another ½ cup of the all-purpose flour to use for the board. Add 1 cup warm water to the biga and stir in all the remaining flour and the semolina. Stir with the wooden spoon to mix well.

Sprinkle some of the reserved flour on a wooden board and turn the dough out. Knead well, adding a little more reserved flour as necessary, until the dough is silky and has lost its stickiness. Return the dough to the rinsed-out and dried bowl, cover with plastic wrap, and set aside at room temperature to rise for about 1 hour, or until doubled.

Meanwhile, make the filling: Combine the garlic and oil in a skillet over gentle heat and cook until the garlic is soft but not brown. Add the tomatoes, with all their liquid, raise the heat, and cook rapidly to thicken the sauce, chopping the tomatoes coarsely with the side of a spoon.

Combine the anchovies, capers, and olives on a board and chop to a coarse paste. Add to the tomato sauce, along with the drained, flaked tuna. Add the parsley, salt and pepper to taste, and, if desired, oregano and/or chili. Cook, stirring occasionally, until the sauce is thick.

Punch down the risen dough. Remove about a spoonful of the beaten egg yolks and set aside to glaze the top of the pie. Stir the rest of the beaten eggs into the dough along with the oil, kneading to incorporate fully. Divide the dough into pieces, one slightly smaller than the other.

Lightly oil a 12-inch round pan, with low sides—like a pizza pan. Roll out the larger of the 2 pieces of dough on a lightly floured wooden board until it is large enough to cover the bottom and sides of the pan. Fit the dough into the pan and distribute the tomato sauce over the dough in an even layer no more than ½ inch thick. (You may not need to use all of the sauce; freeze or refrigerate any leftovers to use later as a pasta sauce.) Roll out the other piece of dough and use it to top the pie, pulling the edges together to seal completely. Mix a few drops of water into the reserved spoonful of egg yolk and use it to paint the top of the pie, especially where the edges come together. Prick the top of the pie all over with a fork and set aside to rise for 1 hour.

Preheat the oven to 400°F.

Set the pie in the oven and bake for 25 to 30 minutes, or until the top is golden and crisp. Remove and serve immediately or cool to room temperature before serving.

In Mola di Bari, north of Bari itself, *scalciaune* is the dialect word for calzone, which, as we've seen, in Puglia means a double-crust pie. A fresh cow's or sheep's milk cheese, not more than a day or two old, is called for in the traditional recipe, but in North America it's easier to find fresh young goat's milk cheese, which is what I've used here. If you do have access to fresh cow's or sheep's milk cheeses, by all means use them.

In the area around Bari, where this is a popular Lenten dish, it's made with an allium called *sponsale* or *cipolle porraie* (leek-onions), which are long, thin, and as white as leeks. If you can find very young, slender leeks, use them instead of the scallions in this pie. Just remember that you need enough to make 12 cups thinly sliced.

MAKES ONE 14-INCH PIE; 8 servings

1 teaspoon dry yeast	1 teaspoon sea salt	15 to 20 large black olives, pitted and coarsely chopped
4 cups unbleached all-purpose flour	3½ ounces fresh goat cheese or other young fresh cheese	Freshly ground black pepper
1 teaspoon sea salt	½ cup grated pecorino, such as pecorino toscano or pecorino sardo	
10 to 12 bunches of scallions		
About ¼ cup extra-virgin olive oil		

Add the yeast to 1 cup warm water and set aside to dissolve. Place 3 cups of the flour in a large mixing bowl and make a well in the middle. Pour the yeast mixture into the well and gradually mix the flour into the yeast, pulling it in from the sides. Add ½ cup more warm water to the dough and mix well, adding more warm water as necessary to make a soft, easily worked dough. Spread the remaining cup of flour out on a bread board and turn the dough out. Knead for 10 to 15 minutes, incorporating the salt as you knead. When the dough is soft, silky, and elastic, transfer it to the rinsed-out and dried bowl and set aside, covered with plastic wrap, to rise for 1 hour.

Meanwhile, make the filling: Trim the scallions and cut into 1-inch lengths—you should have about 12 cups. Place in a large skillet with 3 tablespoons of the olive oil and the salt, stirring to mix well. Set over medium-low heat and cook, covered, for 30 to 40 minutes, or until the scallions are tender and have given off a good deal of liquid. Uncover the pan, raise the heat, and boil down the liquid for about 5 minutes. Then drain the scallions, setting aside the liquid for later use. You should have about 3 cups of cooked scallions.

Transfer the drained scallions to a bowl and mix in the fresh cheese, grated cheese, olives, and abundant black pepper. If the mixture seems very stiff, mix in a tablespoon or so of the scallion-cooking liquid.

Preheat the oven to 400°F.

Punch down the dough and divide it in two, one half slightly larger than the other. Roll out the larger piece into a circle a little greater than 14 inches in diameter. Use a little of the remaining oil to rub over the bottom of a shallow 14-inch round pan—like a pizza pan. Spread the rolled-out dough over the pan, then spread the scallion filling over the dough. Now roll out the other piece of dough to fit the top. Roll the edges of the dough together, fluting them to seal. Rub the last of the oil over the top of the pie with your hands and slide it into the preheated oven. Bake for about 30 minutes, or until the top of the pie is golden.

Remove from the oven and serve immediately, or let cool slightly, but the pie is best when fresh from the oven.

Torta Rustica/Pizza Rustica

There's nothing rustic about this pie, which hails from Naples, hands-down one of the most urbane cities in the entire world. Traditionally made with bread dough, torta rustica is more often made nowadays with a *pasta frolla*, or short-crust pastry, which is easier to roll into a thin sheet. Even more than the pastry that encases it, however, what distinguishes a torta or pizza rustica is the rich filling, based on ricotta and eggs. (There are sweet versions, too, including the famous Neapolitan Easter pie, Pastiera di Grano, page 401, which includes candied fruits and grains of peeled wheat.)

Pizza rustica is almost obligatory at Easter, especially for Pasquetta, the "little Easter" on Easter Monday. Italian-Americans will recognize this as their beloved pizza gaina, another strong Easter tradition.

You can make this as a double-crust pie, but I prefer a lattice topping, which makes it lighter and more appealing. Have the salami and prosciutto cut into single thick slices, to make it easier to dice. If you can't find an aged sheep's milk cheese, use imported grana padano or parmigiano reggiano instead.

MAKES 8 SERVINGS

Pasta Frolla (page 68), shaped into 2 disks, one slightly larger than the other, refrigerated for at least 30 minutes	3 to 4 ounces Italian-style salami, diced small	1 cup grated pecorino sardo or other aged sheep's milk cheese
2¾ cups whole-milk ricotta, drained	3 to 4 ounces imported Italian prosciutto, diced small	Freshly ground black pepper
3 eggs, 1 separated	½ pound mozzarella, preferably buffalo-milk, diced	Crushed dried red chili
		2 tablespoons minced flat-leaf parsley

Preheat the oven to 375°F. Remove the pasta frolla disks from the refrigerator so that they will soften slightly before you roll them out.

Make the filling: Combine the ricotta, whole eggs and egg yolk in a food processor. Process briefly, just to combine the mixture and make it as smooth as possible. Turn it into a mixing bowl.

Stir the salami and prosciutto dice into the ricotta mixture. Drain the mozzarella on paper towels, finely dice it, then stir into the filling, along with the grated cheese and plenty of black pepper. Add red chili (peperoncino) to taste and the parsley.

Roll out the larger of the 2 pastry disks between 2 sheets of wax paper to fit a 10-inch quiche or pie dish that is about 1½ to 2 inches deep. Roll the crust as thin as you can, then transfer it to the pie dish, pressing the pastry into the sides of the disk. Use excess pastry to repair any cracks.

Turn the filling into the prepared pastry. Roll out the second disk as thin as you can and slice it into ½-inch-wide strips, then crisscross the strips over the filling to make a lattice topping. Seal and crimp the edges of the pie. Trim away any excess pastry.

Beat the egg white with 1 teaspoon of water, then paint the top lattice crust and around the edges of the pie. Transfer the pie to the preheated oven and bake for 55 to 65 minutes, or until the crust is crisp and brown and the filling is firm. Remove and let the pie rest for 30 minutes before serving.

VARIATIONS

🌿 Many other ingredients can be added to the basic ricotta-egg mixture for the filling, among them diced smoked provolone or other smoked cheese; diced cooked ham; Italian sausages (sweet or hot), crumbled and browned in a pan and then drained carefully; cooked greens, such as spinach or broccoli rabe, drained, chopped, and squeezed dry; roasted red peppers, peeled and diced; minced onion, sautéed in olive oil and drained thoroughly.

Pasticcio di Scarola con Pesce

CHRISTMAS PIE OF FISH AND GREENS

La Cantina del Triunfo is a sparkling, well-stocked wine shop in Naples, run by Tina Nicodemo and her husband, Carmelo. Most evenings, Tina turns the back room behind the wine collection into a restaurant, where she serves dinner. A superb cook as well as a passionate student of the rich culinary history of Naples, she is as quick to draw from her own inspiration as from a favorite cookbook—*Cucina Teorico-Pratica* by Ippolito Cavalcanti, Duca di Buonvicino, first published in 1837 and still in print, from which comes this recipe for a traditional savory Christmas pie. Cavalcanti's book includes not only the rich, French-influenced cuisine of his fellow aristocrats but also a whole series of recipes, written in Neapolitan dialect, from *la cucina popolana*, the cuisine of the people.

To bake this, you'll need a 10-inch round quiche pan or a pie pan with straight sides, about 1 inch deep, preferably with a removable bottom.

MAKES 8 TO 10 SERVINGS

FOR THE PASTRY

8 tablespoons (1 stick) unsalted butter

1¼ cups unbleached all-purpose flour

½ teaspoon sea salt

2 egg yolks

3 to 4 tablespoons ice water

FOR THE FILLING

1¼ cups dry white wine

½ teaspoon black peppercorns

2 fresh thyme sprigs

1 bay leaf

2 pounds haddock or cod fillets

2 tablespoons pine nuts

2 tablespoons golden raisins

1 medium onion, finely chopped

2 tablespoons extra-virgin olive oil

1 pound escarole, rinsed but not dried

2 tablespoons coarsely chopped pitted Gaeta olives

1 tablespoons capers, preferably salt-packed, rinsed and drained

Pinch of crushed dried red chili

Sea salt and freshly ground black pepper

1 egg yolk, mixed with 1 tablespoon water

Make the pastry: Cut the butter into the flour in a bowl until combined thoroughly. Add the salt and mix in the egg yolks with a fork, adding enough ice water to make a dough that comes together without being sticky. You may not need all the ice water. Transfer to a lightly floured board and knead briefly, then gather the dough into a ball and divide into 2 pieces, one slightly larger than the other. Shape into fat disks, wrap each disk in plastic, and refrigerate for at least 30 minutes.

Meanwhile make the filling: Combine 1 cup of the wine with 1 cup of water in a saucepan. Add the peppercorns, thyme, and bay leaf. Bring to a simmer over low heat. Add the fish and poach very gently, until the fish is just firm, about 5 minutes. Don't overcook; the fish will finish cooking in the pie. Remove from the cooking liquid with a slotted spoon and set aside.

In a small skillet, toast the pine nuts over medium-low heat, stirring constantly, until golden. Be careful, because pine nuts quickly turn from golden to dark brown. As soon as they start to turn, remove from the heat, transfer to a plate or bowl, and set aside.

In a small saucepan, bring the remaining wine to a boil, add the raisins, and remove from the heat, setting aside to steep.

Combine the chopped onion and olive oil in a saucepan large enough to hold all the escarole and set over low heat. Cook until the onions are softened but not brown, then add the rinsed escarole, raise the heat slightly, and cook until thoroughly wilted; add a couple of tablespoons of water if necessary to keep the greens from scorching. When they are wilted, drain and set aside until cool enough to handle, then squeeze the greens dry. Coarsely chop the escarole and transfer to a bowl, stirring in the olives, capers, and red chili.

(The recipe may be prepared to this point up to several days ahead, but if you must refrigerate these ingredients, leave time to bring them to room temperature before finishing the pie.)

Preheat the oven to 375°F. Remove the pastry disks from the refrigerator.

On a lightly floured board, roll out the larger piece to fit the bottom and sides of a 10-inch round baking dish or pie pan with straight sides—like a quiche pan. Fit the dough into the pan and up the sides, patting it in place.

Drain the raisins, discarding the wine, and stir them into the escarole along with the pine nuts. Flake the fish into big pieces and mix gently into the escarole. Add salt and black pepper to taste.

Roll out the pastry disk to fit the top of the pie. Fill the bottom of the pie with the fish mixture and cover with the second round of pastry, crimping the edges to seal it tightly.

Lightly brush the dough with the egg wash. Cut a few steam holes in the top and transfer the pie dish to the preheated oven. Bake for about 30 minutes, or until the top is golden brown. Remove from the oven and let cool for about 30 minutes before serving.

Sicilian Savory Pies

Sicilian cooks have a great repertoire of savory pies and a great number of names for them, including *scaccia, pastizzu* (a dialect word from the Italian *pasticcio,* which simply means "pie"), and *'mpanata* or *impanata*, a name that comes from the Spanish *empanada* and derives from the centuries when Sicily was ruled by Spain.

By long tradition these double-crust pies were always made from a yeasted bread dough. Nowadays, however, they're made almost as frequently with a pasta frolla or short-crust pastry dough, which is a good deal easier to manipulate. Although they can be very simple in their ingredients, the best are often flamboyant—and delicious—combinations of fruits (raisins and olives) and green herbs with meats or fish, pine nuts, onions sweetly stewed in olive oil, wine, or vinegar, the sort of savory mélanges we associate with the ancient world, to which have been added New World tomatoes and occasionally a hint or more of chili.

These are very old dishes indeed, similar to savory pies found all over the eastern Mediterranean and especially in the Greek Islands, which may have been their original home. Nowadays such pies are always baked in the oven, but once upon a time they were cooked on the hearth, with coals piled up around the rim of the pie dish and over the domed lid that covered it—"cooking between two fires," as this was called in many different languages.

I've also included here a most unusual "focaccia" from Ragusa in the southeastern corner of the island. Traditionally it's made with a yeasted bread dough folded and layered with its filling, which gets its prominent flavor from the local caciocavallo cheese called *ragusano.*

Pasta Frolla

SHORT-CRUST PASTRY FOR A SAVORY PIE

Don't be put off by the sugar and lemon zest in the recipe—the sugar is scarcely noticeable but, along with the lemon zest, gives a pleasant contrast to the savory fillings.

MAKES ENOUGH FOR 1 DOUBLE-CRUST PIE, 10 to 12 inches in diameter

2 cups unbleached all-purpose flour	2 tablespoons sugar	Grated zest of 1 lemon, preferably organic
½ cup pastry (cake) flour	6 ounces (1½ sticks) unsalted butter, cut into pieces	3 to 4 tablespoons very cold dry white wine
Pinch of sea salt	2 eggs, 1 separated	

Combine the flours, salt, and sugar in the bowl of an electric mixer, using the flat paddle attachment. With the mixer running at a slow speed, add the pieces of butter, a few at a time. When the butter has been absorbed, add, one after another, the whole egg, the white of the second egg, and the lemon zest, then start adding the very cold wine, a tablespoon at a time (you may not need all the wine). As soon as all the ingredients come together, gather them into a ball and knead on a lightly floured board very briefly, with just 2 or 3 strokes. Divide into 2 portions, one slightly larger than the other, and shape each portion into a thick disk. Wrap the disks in plastic and set in the refrigerator for an hour or so while you prepare the filling.

The yolk of the separated egg will be beaten with a teaspoon or so of water and used to paint the top of the pie before it's popped into the oven.

Impanata di Pesce Spada

SAVORY PIE OF SWORDFISH AND ZUCCHINI

If you don't have a good supply of swordfish, substitute haddock, halibut, or other white-meat fish, boned and cut into chunks.

MAKES 6 TO 8 SERVINGS

2 disks of Pasta Frolla (page 68), one slightly larger than the other, refrigerated for at least 30 minutes

1 medium onion, coarsely chopped

½ to ¾ cup extra-virgin olive oil

1 pound swordfish

Unbleached all-purpose flour

Sea salt and freshly ground black pepper

Pinch of ground dried red chili pepper

1 medium zucchini, grated on the large holes of a grater

⅓ cup chopped flat-leaf parsley

¼ cup golden raisins, soaked in hot water to plump and drained

¼ cup pine nuts

⅓ cup Basic Tomato Sauce (page 125)

Remove the pastry disks from the refrigerator.

Combine the chopped onion with ¼ cup olive oil in a heavy skillet over medium-low heat. Cook until the onion is soft but not brown, stirring frequently.

Meanwhile, cut the fish into bite-sized pieces. Put a cup of flour in a paper bag and add salt, black pepper, and red chili pepper to taste. Add the fish pieces and shake vigorously to coat with the flour mixture.

Transfer the cooked onion to a bowl with a slotted spoon. Add another ¼ to ½ cup olive oil to the skillet—enough to bring the oil up to about ¼ inch. Raise the heat to medium and, when the oil is hot, add the fish pieces, shaking them a little to rid them of excess flour. Fry until crisp and remove with a slotted spoon; drain briefly on a rack covered with paper towels, then transfer the fish to the bowl with the onion.

Add the grated zucchini, parsley, drained raisins, and pine nuts to the fish mixture, stirring to mix well, then stir in the tomato sauce. Set aside. (The pie filling may be made ahead but if refrigerated, bring it to room temperature before continuing with the recipe.)

Preheat the oven to 425°F.

Roll out the larger of the two Pasta Frolla disks in a circle large enough to fit the bottom and sides of a 10- to 12-inch round pan with straight sides, like a quiche pan. Set the pastry disk in the pan, pressing it firmly into the corners. Fill the pastry casing with the fish mixture, spreading it in an even layer.

Roll out the second (smaller) piece of Pasta Frolla to fit the top of the pie. Trim away any excess dough and crimp the edges of the top and bottom crusts together to seal firmly, folding to make a decorative edge. Brush the top crust all over with the egg wash made from the reserved yolk in the Pasta Frolla recipe. Use the tip of a sharp-pointed knife to pierce several small holes in the crust.

Set the pie dish on a sheet pan or cookie sheet and transfer to the preheated oven. Bake for 45 to 60 minutes, or until the top is golden. Remove and let the pie cool slightly before serving.

Impanata di Maiale Ragusana

PORK PIE FROM RAGUSA

In Ragusa, which could be called the pork capital of Sicily, the popular impanata gets stuffed with ground pork.

MAKES 6 TO 8 SERVINGS

2 disks of Pasta Frolla (page 68), one slightly larger than the other, refrigerated for at least 30 minutes

1 medium yellow onion, chopped

¼ cup extra-virgin olive oil

1 pound lean ground pork

⅓ cup coarsely chopped pitted black olives

2 tablespoons capers, preferably salt-packed, rinsed and drained

⅓ cup minced flat-leaf parsley

Sea salt and freshly ground black pepper

Ground dried red chili pepper

2 tablespoons dry red wine

½ cup Basic Tomato Sauce (page 125)

2 tablespoons fine dry bread crumbs

1 egg beaten with 1 tablespoon water for a wash

Remove the pastry disks from the refrigerator.

Combine the chopped onion with the olive oil in a heavy skillet over medium heat and cook until the onion is soft but not brown, stirring frequently. Transfer the cooked onion to a bowl with a slotted spoon. Add the pork to the skillet and raise the heat slightly. Cook, breaking the pork up with a fork, until it has all changed color but is not too brown. Transfer the cooked pork with a slotted spoon to the bowl with the onions. Add the olives, capers, and parsley and stir to mix well, then stir in salt, pepper, and red chili to taste. Finally, mix in the wine and tomato sauce. Set aside.

Preheat the oven to 425°F.

Roll out the larger pastry disk and fill the pie as described on page 70. Scatter bread crumbs over the top of the filling before rolling out and adding the top layer of pie crust. Crimp the edges together, cut vent holes in the top, and brush the top with the egg wash.

Set the pie on a baking sheet and transfer to the preheated oven. Bake for 30 to 40 minutes, or until the top is golden brown. Remove and set aside to cool slightly before serving. The pie may also be served at room temperature.

Impanata di Carne d'Agnello

CHILI-SPIKED LAMB PIE

MAKES 6 TO 8 SERVINGS

2 disks of Pasta Frolla (page 68), one slightly larger than the other, refrigerated for at least 30 minutes

1 pound lean boneless lamb leg or shoulder, cut into small pieces

Sea salt and freshly ground black pepper

Big pinch of crumbled or ground dried red chili

2 garlic cloves, chopped

⅓ cup chopped flat-leaf parsley

3 to 4 tablespoons minced fresh mint or basil leaves

¼ cup dry red wine

3 tablespoons extra-virgin olive oil

1 sweet red pepper, diced or thinly sliced

1 medium onion, halved and thinly sliced

12 black olives, pitted and halved

2 tablespoons fine dry bread crumbs

1 egg beaten with 1 tablespoon water for a wash

Remove the pastry disks from the refrigerator.

Combine the lamb in a bowl with salt, black pepper, and red chili to taste. Chop the garlic, parsley, and mint together and add to the lamb along with the red wine and 2 tablespoons of the olive oil. Stir to mix well, then cover the bowl with plastic wrap and set aside to marinate for several hours or overnight. (Refrigerate in warm weather.)

Add the remaining tablespoon of olive oil and the pepper and onion slices to a heavy skillet over medium-low heat. Cook, stirring frequently, until the vegetables are softened but not brown. Transfer the vegetables to a bowl.

Add the marinated lamb, with its juices, to the skillet, raise the heat to medium, and cook briefly, stirring frequently, just until the lamb has started to brown. Scrape the lamb with all its juices into the bowl with the vegetables and add the olives. Mix well, taste, and adjust seasoning.

Preheat the oven to 425°F.

Roll out the dough, fill the pie, brush with egg wash, and vent the pie as described on page 70. Scatter bread crumbs over the top of the filling before adding the top layer of pie crust.

Set the pie dish on a baking sheet and transfer to the preheated oven. Bake for 35 to 45 minutes, or until the top is golden brown. Remove and set aside for at least 15 minutes before serving. The pie may also be served at room temperature.

La Focaccia Ragusana

CHEESE PIE FROM RAGUSA

This is probably the most unusual focaccia of all, made up of layers of dough rolled out till almost as thin as filo; the difference, however, is that this is a yeasted dough, so it rises and puffs in a way that filo never does. It comes from Ragusa, a hill town in the southeastern corner of Sicily. Ragusano cooks, who fire their old-fashioned masonry ovens with olive branches or almond shells, say it's the finest way to show off Ragusa's prized caciocavallo cheese, called *ragusano* and made from the milk of the local dark-brown modicana cows, beautiful, gentle beasts. If you can find this delicious cheese (and it isn't easy in North America), by all means use it; but I have occasionally used a nicely aged asiago, which works almost as well. In any case, for the most authentic flavor you will definitely want a cow's milk cheese, preferably made from raw milk and aged for a couple of months at least.

MAKES 3 FOCACCE; 12 servings

½ teaspoon dry yeast	2 cups Basic Tomato Sauce (page 125)	Freshly ground black pepper
3 cups semolina, plus more for the board	¾ pound ragusano or other cheese (see headnote)	18 to 24 fresh basil leaves or 2 to 3 teaspoons dried oregano
Sea salt	½ cup finely grated hard aged cheese: pecorino sardo, parmigiano reggiano, or grana padano	
About ¼ cup extra-virgin olive oil		
All-purpose flour for the board		

First make the dough: Mix the yeast with 1 cup of very warm (120°F) water and set aside until the yeast is fully dissolved, about 5 minutes. Add 1 cup of the semolina to a large bowl and pour in the yeast mixture. Stir with a wooden spoon to mix well, but don't worry if the mixture is a little lumpy and looks more like porridge than bread dough. Cover with plastic wrap and set aside for 2 hours to ferment and develop.

When the surface of the starter dough is puffy and bubbly, add about a tablespoon of salt to ½ cup of very warm water and set aside to dissolve. Stir the remaining 2 cups of semolina into the starter dough, then add 2 tablespoons of the olive oil and stir to mix well. Add the salted water, a little at a time, stirring it in well after each addition. You may not need to use all of it—much depends on the humidity of the room in which you're working. Stir the water in with a wooden spoon, then with your hands. Finally, when you can handle the dough easily, spread about ½ cup of all-purpose flour on a bread board and turn the dough out. Knead for 5 to 10 minutes, or until the dough is soft and elastic and has lost much of its stickiness.

Rinse the bowl and dry it, then sprinkle a few drops of olive oil in the bottom. Add the dough to the bowl, turning it to cover with olive oil, then cover with plastic wrap and set aside to develop for 2 to 4 hours, or until the dough has doubled.

While the dough is rising, either use a vegetable peeler to shave the ragusano cheese into flakes or grate the cheese on the largest holes of a box grater. Set aside.

When ready to make the focaccia, separate the dough into 3 equal pieces. Coat the bottom of a baking sheet that will hold all 3 focacce with olive oil. Have ready the tomato sauce, cheeses, pepper, and basil. Spread a layer of semolina on the bread board and roll the dough out with a rolling pin to make a big oval a good 14 to 16 inches long and about 10 inches wide. Roll the dough as thin as you possibly can—less than ¹⁄₁₆ inch thick is ideal. Working quickly, spread a good ¼ cup of tomato sauce over the surface of the oval, then lay a handful of the shaved cheese down the middle and sprinkle with some of the grated cheese. Layer the basil leaves over the tomato sauce or sprinkle with oregano. Grind black pepper over all.

Fold the long left side of the oval in over the center of the dough, then fold the right side in on top of it, as if you were folding a letter. You will have a long rectangle. Paint the top surface with about 2 tablespoons of tomato sauce and scatter a little more grated cheese over it. Now fold the bottom of the rectangle to cover the middle part of the dough and, again, smooth a little tomato sauce and grated cheese on top. Then fold down the top of the rectangle to cover the sauce. At this point you will have a thick portfolio or envelope made of layers of dough, tomato sauce, and cheese. Transfer the portfolio to the oiled sheet and continue assembling the remaining 2 pieces of dough.

When all the dough has been shaped, dribble or paint a little oil over the top and set aside, lightly covered with plastic wrap, to rise for about 1 hour.

Preheat the oven to 425°F. Transfer the risen focacce to the oven and bake for 40 to 60 minutes, or until the crust is crisp and brown on top and cooked all the way through. Remove from the oven and serve immediately.

ANTIPASTI

Small Dishes
of Southern Italy

The word *antipasto* means "before the *pasto,* before the meal." An antipasto, then, is the opening to the meal, little savory bits and pieces of food, sometimes a selection of elaborately constructed dishes, sometimes as simple as thinly sliced, locally cured, and usually quite salty prosciutto with fresh and sweetly dripping slices of pink melon or green figs. An antipasto may be as effortless as a thin frittata, a flat omelet made to embrace a vegetable that's in season and particularly tasty at the moment—artichokes, trimmed to their tender hearts, in late winter, or thick slices of red and green peppers in summer. In any case, it's always rather small and intended to engage the hungry diner rather than to fill him up. In some parts of southern Italy an antipasto is actually called an *apristomaco,* a stomach-opener, a rather gastroenterological explanation but vivid nonetheless.

An antipasto can be a single preparation, even just a dish of garlicky olives mixed with bright bits of orange peel, or salty almonds, or a selection of locally cured hams, sausages, and other pork products, perhaps with a giardiniera of pickled vegetables to accompany them. In restaurants, the antipasto course may be a combination of several different dishes, and in some places, famed for their antipasti, there will be enough on the table to make up the balance of the meal. "You don't want to order anything else until you've had our antipasto," said the waitress at Agorà, a comfortable little tavern perched on the main square of Civita, an Albanian* town hidden in the hills behind Castrovillari in Calabria. "You may not want anything more," she added, and she was right as dish after dish came out of the kitchen, first cold plates and then hot dishes and the spicy sausages for which the Arbëreshë community is famed. Once the antipasto course was over and done with, there was little room for anything more than a palate-cleansing salad.

*Albanian, or Arbëreshë, communities are scattered over the deep south of Italy and in Sicily. Albanians began to arrive in the early fifteenth century, and they have continued to do so, often as the result of political, religious, or economic persecution, to the present day. Incredibly, they retain many of their ancient customs, including language, food culture, and, most important, their Greco-Byzantine religious rites.

It should be said, however, that meals in southern Italy, even restaurant meals, do not invariably begin with an antipasto. Indeed, antipasti usually mark the special nature of the meal to follow. It may be a Sunday or celebratory lunch in a private home or farmhouse, in which case the antipasti will be multiple but not necessarily elaborate since everything will have been prepared in the home kitchen. But the best place to see the full glory to which antipasti can aspire, if you can wangle an invitation, is at one of the long, elaborate banquets called *ricevimenti* in which southern Italian hoteliers delight. Held to commemorate baptisms, first communions, or, especially, weddings, these kinds of meals are an anthropologist's dream, displays of conspicuous consumption as elaborate as an Indian potlatch that go on for hours and hours of the most relentless feasting. And it all begins with a vast array of antipasti.

Merende, on the other hand, are a different kind of meal altogether, often scarcely a meal at all. For field workers, a merenda could be as simple as bread with a slice of prosciutto and a hefty swig of white wine in the middle of a hot morning's labors, while for children it's either a slice of pizza bianca (pizza with little more than oil, salt, and oregano or rosemary on top) or bread smeared with Nutella, the ubiquitous chocolate-hazelnut spread. The word *merenda* is often translated as "snack," and if by snack we mean something eaten quickly and casually between the canonical meals of the day, it is indeed that. But in Italy even snacks are canonical, and the time to partake is almost ritualistic: eleven o'clock in the morning, as a break between what is, by American standards, a strikingly meager breakfast of milky coffee and something sweet, and lunch, which rarely comes before 2:00 P.M. and is still often the main meal of the day.

So the merenda, too, has an important if restricted role to play in the daily round of food moments. One huge difference between a merenda and any other meal: The merenda can be, and often is, eaten while standing up and, more often than not, eaten out of hand. Otherwise, Italians in general, and southern Italians in particular, always take their meals while sitting down. The American habit of munching while strolling down the street is, along with our addiction to white running shoes in the city, what marks us as barbarians in Italian eyes.

How to fit all these antipasti and merende into a North American way of eating isn't difficult since many dishes that fit into this category, whether starter or snack, can become, on the one hand, part of—even the star of—a full-fledged meal or, on the other hand, the kind of small dish that Americans delight in for a little meal at any time of day, whether a light lunch or a quick supper. A lot of these dishes would even be appropriate for that all-American meal, brunch.

Don't feel constrained to serve only the dishes in this section as either antipasto or merenda. Many other recipes in the book, especially in the section on pizzas and savory pies as well as in the vegetable chapter, would be equally suitable. In fact, whether antipasto or merenda, as what sociologists call "a moment of consumption," the content is very much up to the imagination of the cook or provider.

Antipasto Misto

MIXED ANTIPASTO/SLICED MEATS

If you live near a well-supplied Italian grocery or delicatessen, like the ones in Boston's North End or South Philadelphia or parts of New Orleans not far from the French Quarter, your antipasto worries are at an end. Most likely, the owners of the place will claim a southern Italian heritage (except for the Italian deli I came across in Brooklyn's Carroll Gardens, an old Italian neighborhood where recent Russian immigrants had taken over one of the best-supplied local shops and were happily stretching curd to make mozzarella every morning) and will have an array of the kinds of fresh and cured pork products that are the pride of the region. It's a good idea to ask how and where the meat has been cured and an even better idea to request a little taste before you buy.

That said, to make up a platter for an antipasto misto, you will want at least two slices of each kind of cured pork for each person at the table. Include prosciutto by all means, but also look for salami flavored with fennel and/or black pepper, capocollo, soppressata, guanciale, mortadella, and pancetta, as well as anything else that may be a specialty of the shop.

Arrange all these meats nicely on a platter and then add to them either fresh fruits (melons and/or figs are favorites) or pickled vegetables (artichoke hearts and small spicy red peppers are ideal), perhaps some oil-packed sun-dried tomatoes, olives of course, both black and green, and some cubes of well-aged pecorino or caciocavallo cheese with a lot of pungent flavor. (I say "either/or" because it seems to me that you want either sweet fruity flavors with the salty meat or pungent, sharp flavors, but not both.) Add bread, of course, and perhaps from your own kitchen a little bowl of caponata (page 364) or some wedges of a very simple frittata (page 90). And that's it—except for the wine, which is the most important part and the reason, ultimately, for this array. With such a variety of flavors, I think a hearty red, an aglianico del Vulture from Basilicata, a Taurasi, also made from the aglianico grape, from Campania, or a nero d'Avola from Sicily would be a good choice.

Bottarga doesn't need a recipe so much as an explanation of what it is and how to serve it. Basically, bottarga is the salted, pressed, and dried roe of either tuna (bottarga di tonno) or gray mullet (bottarga di muggine). The former, which is produced in many parts of the Italian South (as well as in other places around the Mediterranean), is what you are most apt to encounter. The latter, bottarga di muggine, is native to Sardinia and rather more precious than bottarga di tonno, presumably because there's less of it. The entire roe sac is harvested intact, just as it is with caviar, then packed in salt to draw out all the moisture. Pressed very gently, it is dried in the sun for several days, an ancient technique that preserves the roe. When it has finished curing, bottarga di tonno looks like a firm, dark-colored brick or block, often coated with easily removable wax to keep it from drying out. It is quite expensive, but a little goes a long way. Buy it by the ounce, just as you would caviar. Like caviar, it is salty, fishy, and utterly delicious—addictive, as they say in the food magazines.

Bottarga is often grated over pasta (see the recipe on page 143), but to serve it as an antipasto, slice it in very, very thin shavings and arrange them on a plate. Dress with the finest extra-virgin olive oil, one that has quite a robust flavor, and freshly squeezed lemon juice. Serve with good crusty bread and unsalted butter, with a simple salad of arugula alongside. For a change, I like it with a flinty white wine from Friuli in the north of Italy, which seems to go better with the strong flavors of the bottarga than a fruitier wine from the South.

Cazzilli ("Crocchè" di Patate)

POTATO CROQUETTES

These are an enticing example of the kinds of crisply fried food served hot and fresh from *friggitorie*, fried food stands, all over Naples and Palermo. Called *cazzilli* in Sicily and *crocchè* (pronounced like croquet, the game) in Naples, where even street-food cooks have an abiding love for French terminology, they're really nothing more than potato puffs, deep-fried and served piping hot. Rapidly cooked in clean lard or olive oil, they are a miracle of texture and flavor, light, puffy, tender, and full of delicious surprises. They can be as simple as mashed potatoes, flavored with a little garlic, salt, and pepper, but the best are more elaborate, as in this recipe with its rich addition of chopped salami and cheese. The combination of finely grated and diced cheese yields surprising nuggets of melting cheese in the centers of the fritters.

Use a deep-frying or candy thermometer to be sure the oil is hot enough before frying.

MAKES 24 TO 30 CROQUETTES; 8 to 10 servings

2 pounds russet potatoes	¼ cup finely grated aged cheese: pecorino, caciocavallo, parmigiano reggiano, or grana padano	⅓ cup finely minced flat-leaf parsley
Sea salt		Freshly ground black pepper
3 eggs		1 cup fine dry bread crumbs
3 to 4 ounces salami, cut into small dice (½ cup)	½ cup diced aged cheese	Olive oil, preferably extra-virgin, for deep-fat frying

Preheat the oven to 425°F. Bake the potatoes until very tender, 30 to 45 minutes. Remove from the oven and, when cool enough to handle but still quite warm, peel the potatoes and puree with a vegetable mill or ricer. Immediately, while they are still warm, incorporate, one after another, 2 of the eggs, then the salami, cheeses, and parsley. Taste and add more salt, if necessary, and plenty of black pepper.

Beat the remaining egg with 1 tablespoon of water in a soup plate. Add the bread crumbs to another soup plate. Put about 1½ inches of olive oil into a saucepan and heat over medium heat to about 360°F (a small cube of bread will brown in about a minute).

While the oil is heating, shape the potato mixture into small round balls about 1½ inches in diameter. Roll them in the egg mixture, then in the bread crumbs, and drop each into the hot oil. Fry until golden and crisp all over, turning once. Transfer to a rack covered with paper towels to drain, then serve immediately.

CHICKPEA FRITTERS FROM PALERMO

Anyone familiar with panisses, the crisp, salty chickpea flour fritters from Nice in the south of France will immediately recognize their cousins in these panelle, a favorite street food of Palermo. Sicilian food writer Anna Tasca Lanza says they are examples of "port food," food that traveled from port to port all over the Mediterranean. And they are delicious. Sicilians often eat panelle in a sandwich as a midmorning merenda, but I prefer them as they come from the fryer, eaten out of hand and as addictive as potato chips.

MAKES ABOUT 70 PANELLE

1 quart cool water	2 tablespoons finely minced flat-leaf parsley or chopped fresh rosemary	Olive oil, preferably extra-virgin, for deep-fat frying
2 cups (½ pound) chickpea flour		Coarse sea salt for sprinkling
Sea salt and freshly ground black pepper		

Add the water to a saucepan set over medium heat. Gradually add the chickpea flour, a little at a time, stirring with a wire whisk to get rid of any lumps. By the time all the flour has been added, the water should be very hot but not yet boiling. Continue stirring, adding salt and pepper to taste. Once the porridge has come to a boil, turn the heat down to just barely simmering. Simmer about 20 minutes, stirring frequently, until the porridge is very dense but still pouring consistency.

Have ready a cookie sheet measuring about 12 x 18 inches. Stir the parsley into the porridge and pour it onto the cookie sheet. Use a spatula dipped in water to smooth it out to a consistent ⅛-inch thickness.

Let cool until quite firm. Cut into triangles, lozenges, or whatever shapes suit your fancy.

Heat about 2 inches of olive oil in a frying pan to about 360°F. Using tongs, drop the panelle into the oil, a few at a time, and fry until crisp and lightly golden, turning once. Drain on a rack covered with paper towels. Serve piping hot, sprinkled with coarse sea salt.

Pittule Pugliese

SAVORY FRITTERS FROM PUGLIA

Little fritters of bread dough stuffed with anchovies, black olives, capers, or a combination thereof are very tasty and welcome when served straight out of the frying pan with a glass of a robust Pugliese red such as a Salice Salentino or a Primitivo di Manduria.

This makes a very liquid dough—really more a batter than a conventional bread dough.

MAKES 50 TO 60 FRITTERS

1 teaspoon dry yeast	1 teaspoon sea salt	Olive oil, preferably extra-virgin, for deep-fat frying
2½ cups unbleached all-purpose flour plus 1 cup pastry flour	1 cup Pepone (Pepper Relish, page 342), or ¼ cup drained capers and ½ cup coarsely chopped pitted black olives	1 tablespoon capers, preferably salt-packed, rinsed and drained

Dissolve the yeast in ½ cup of warm water in a large mixing bowl. When the yeast is dissolved, stir in another cup of warm water and the flour, stirring with a wooden spoon or rubber spatula just enough to mix the dough without kneading it. Cover the bowl and set aside in a warm place to rise for 2 to 3 hours or until doubled in size.

When the dough has risen, dissolve the salt in 1 cup of warm water and add it, mixing it into the dough with your hands. The dough will look very raggedy at first but gradually will form a more creamy texture, though still lumpy. Using your hand as a paddle, beat the dough until it is smooth and uniform in texture and you can feel the strands of gluten developing. If the dough is too liquid to handle, beat in up to another ½ cup of flour; it should not be at all like bread dough—rather more like a batter, dense and creamy in consistency. When it is ready, you should be able to gather the dough in one hand and squeeze it to form a very loose and amorphous ball of dough on top of your fist. If you can't do that, the dough is too liquid and a little more flour should be added.

When the dough has reached the right consistency, beat in the Pepper Relish, or the capers and olives, or one of the alternatives suggested below. Whatever you choose to flavor the fritter batter, beat it in thoroughly and then set the bowl aside, lightly covered with a cloth, for the dough to rest for about 15 minutes.

Meanwhile, in a deep frying pan, heat about 1 inch of oil to 360°F. Drop the tablespoon of drained capers in the hot oil to fry—they give a sweet spiciness to the oil. Have a bowl of water ready in which to dip your hands. Wet your hands and take up a little batter in your left hand (assuming you are right-handed). Make a fist, squeezing the dough up into a small, shapeless blob above your thumb. Take this in your right hand, which you will have dipped in water, and carefully drop it into the hot oil. Proceed with the rest of the batter: You can do up to a dozen pittule at once, depending on the size of your pan. As soon as they are golden-brown on one side, turn and brown on the other. Then remove and drain on paper towels spread on a rack. Serve immediately, while still crisp and hot.

VARIATIONS

🌿 Any of the following may be added instead of the Pepper Relish or the caper-olive combination:

- Small pieces of steamed salt cod
- Small cauliflower pieces, steamed till just tender, then lightly salted
- A combination of: ¼ cup coarsely chopped pitted black olives; 4 anchovy fillets, coarsely chopped; 1 tablespoon capers, coarsely chopped; 1 small onion, finely minced; and crushed red pepper flakes to taste

🌿 Similar fritters are made in Campania, where they are called *zeppole* (not to be confused with sweet Zeppole di San Giuseppe, page 394). But in Campania, cooks often add about a pound of boiled, peeled, and riced russet potatoes to the batter, which makes fritters that are even crisper and crunchier than Pugliese Pittule.

Panzerotti Napoletane

NEAPOLITAN FRIED RAVIOLI

These little fried ravioli, filled with a tasty mix of ricotta and parsley, bits of smoked cheese, melting mozzarella, and diced ham or salami, are unsurpassable with a glass of lightly chilled wine before dinner. The pasta is unusual in that it is enriched not with eggs but with a lump of pure pork lard. Squeamish cooks may be surprised to learn that, according to the U.S. Department of Agriculture, pork lard has less cholesterol than butter. Good natural pork lard, without preservatives, is often available from German or Polish butchers, and many of them will supply it by mail order (see Where to Find It, page 415). Fortunately, lard keeps just about forever, so buy a couple of pounds and keep it on hand for when you make piecrusts or these panzerotti.

As with most ricotta recipes, you'll have better success if you drain the ricotta overnight in a fine-mesh sieve to get rid of the whey.

MAKES 45 TO 50 PANZEROTTI

FOR THE DOUGH	FOR THE FILLING	
2 tablespoons pure pork lard	1¼ cups well-drained whole-milk ricotta	½ cup very finely diced provola affumicata or other smoked cheese
2 cups unbleached all-purpose flour	1 egg	⅔ cup finely diced cow's milk mozzarella (*fior di latte*)
Big pinch of salt	¼ cup finely grated parmigiano reggiano	⅔ cup finely diced or chopped baked ham or salami
	1 cup finely minced flat-leaf parsley	Sea salt
	Freshly ground black pepper	Olive oil, preferably extra-virgin, for deep-fat frying

Make the dough by blending the lard into the flour in a mixing bowl. Add the salt and mix thoroughly. Now start adding warm water, ¼ cup at a time. You will need at least ½ cup and maybe as much as ¾ cup, depending on ambient humidity. When all the ingredients come together in a soft dough, turn it out of the bowl onto a board and knead briefly to amalgamate everything very thoroughly. When the dough is soft and smooth, shape it into a flattened ball and set it aside, covered with the mixing bowl or a lightly dampened cloth, for at least 30 minutes.

While the dough is resting, make the filling: Put the ricotta in a mixing bowl and beat with a hand beater or wire whisk until it is as smooth as yogurt. Beat in the egg and then the grated parmigiano. Use a spatula to fold in, one after the other, the parsley, plenty of black pepper, the provola, mozzarella, and ham. Taste the mixture and add salt if it seems necessary.

Divide the dough in half and keep the half you're not working with covered. Roll out half the dough into a broad circle as thin as you can make it—less than $1/16$ inch is fine. Using a wineglass or a cookie cutter 4 inches in diameter, cut out circles from the rolled-out dough. Into each circle, drop about a teaspoon of filling, slightly off center. Dip your finger in cool water and run it around the edge of the circle, then flip half the circle over to cover the filling and make a semicircle. Press the edges tightly together all the way around to make sure the filling cannot escape. Transfer to a kitchen towel lightly dusted with flour.

When all the dough is used up (you will have 45 to 50 panzerotti), heat about 2 inches of olive oil in a frying pan or deep skillet. If you are using a thermometer, which I recommend, heat the oil to 360°F. Otherwise, drop in a cube of bread; the oil is ready when the bread browns in about a minute. Drop 5 or 6 of the stuffed panzerotti into the heated oil and let them brown quickly on both sides. Transfer to a rack covered with paper towels.

When all the panzerotti are done, serve immediately.

CRISPY FRIED RICE BALLS WITH RAGÙ

Sicilian cities—Palermo, Catania, Messina—are famed for the quality and variety of their street-food offerings. Arancini, rice balls, shaped around a dollop of meaty ragù and deep-fried to a crisp dark golden color, are traditional and typical, sold at streetside friggitorie, or fry stalls, all over the island. But the best, everyone agrees, are the arancini sold at the bars on the jolly little traghetti that ferry people and cars back and forth all day between Messina and Villa San Giovanni on the mainland. As soon as the boat swings out into the straits, there's usually a rush to the bar to get an order in before the twenty-minute trip is over.

Arancini require a little patience to put together but are well worth the effort. If you happen to have leftover ragù from a pasta sauce, by all means use it in place of the ragù described here. Just make sure the meat is chopped quite small or shredded. (You will need a scant cup of leftover ragù.)

If you don't have any tomato sauce in the cupboard, it's easy to make with a can of plum tomatoes: Pour the contents of the can into a small saucepan and set over medium-low heat. Cook, breaking up the tomatoes, until the sauce is thick. For more flavor, sauté a crushed clove of garlic in olive oil before adding the tomatoes and season the tomatoes as they cook with salt, pepper, and fresh basil or dried oregano.

MAKES 8 LARGE OR 12 SMALL ARANCINI

FOR THE RAGÙ

- ½ pound very lean ground beef, veal, pork, or a combination
- 2 whole chicken livers, chopped
- 3 tablespoons extra-virgin olive oil
- ¼ cup finely minced yellow onion
- 1 garlic clove, minced
- ¼ cup finely minced carrot
- ¼ cup finely minced celery
- ½ cup frozen or blanched fresh green peas
- Pinch of ground or crumbled dried red chili, or to taste
- Sea salt and freshly ground black pepper to taste
- 1 cup tomato sauce

FOR THE RICE

- 1 quart Basic Chicken Stock (page 97)
- 2 tablespoons unsalted butter
- 1 tablespoon extra-virgin olive oil
- 2 cups arborio rice
- ¼ cup white wine
- Pinch of saffron threads
- Sea salt and freshly ground black pepper to taste
- ⅔ cup grated parmigiano reggiano
- 2 large eggs, lightly beaten
- 2 egg whites, beaten with 1 tablespoon water
- Fine dry bread crumbs
- Extra-virgin olive oil for deep-fat frying

You can make the ragù well in advance, even a day or two before you make the arancini. (Or use leftover ragù from another meal.) Combine the ground meat and chicken livers with a tablespoon of the olive oil in a small saucepan over medium-high heat. Cook, stirring and breaking up the meat, until it has browned lightly. As the meats cook, crush the chicken livers with a fork. Drain off and discard any fat and set the meat aside.

Combine the remaining olive oil and the minced onion, garlic, carrot, and celery in a sauté pan and cook over low heat until the vegetables are very soft. Stir the browned meat into the vegetables, then add the peas and seasonings. Add the tomato sauce and cook over medium-low heat for about 5 minutes, just to meld the flavors. If the ragù seems too dry, add a few tablespoons of hot water. If it seems too runny, cook it down to thicken. (The ragù should be quite dry so that it doesn't leak through the rice coating.) Taste and adjust the seasoning. Set the ragù aside, refrigerated if necessary, until ready to use, but bring it back to room temperature when you make the arancini.

When you're ready to make the arancini, bring the stock to a gentle boil and keep it just at the simmering point as you cook the rice.

In a saucepan, combine the butter and olive oil and set the pan over medium heat until the butter has melted. Stir in the rice and cook, stirring, until the rice has become opaque and starts to give off a nutty aroma. Add the white wine, raise the heat slightly, and cook, stirring, until the wine has been completely absorbed by the rice. Now add about ¾ cup of the broth and cook, stirring, until the broth has been absorbed. The rice should never dry, however, but should have a soupy consistency. Stir in the saffron, crumbling it in your fingers, and the salt and pepper.

Continue adding ladlesful of simmering stock, a little at a time—about ¾ of a cup, but you don't have to be too precise about this—and stirring each time until the stock has been absorbed by the rice before adding more. At the end of the cooking time the rice should be very soft—softer than for a regular risotto—and slightly sticky with its sauce. If you use up all the stock before the rice is done, add boiling water in the same manner.

When the rice is done, stir in the grated cheese and taste, adjusting the seasoning if necessary. Let the rice cool slightly, but while it is still quite warm, stir in the beaten eggs, mixing well.

Have the beaten egg whites ready in a soup plate. Spread the bread crumbs out on another soup plate or deep dish.

Take up a small handful of rice and shape it into a cup in the palm of your hand. Make a well in the center and add as much ragù as the rice ball will hold, then cover the ragù with additional rice, shaping it to make a small compact ball. Roll the ball briefly in the egg whites and then in the bread crumbs. Set aside until all the rice has been shaped into balls. (Leftover ragù may be frozen to use in the future or used as a sauce for pasta, with a little broth or more tomato sauce added.) Set the balls on a plate and transfer to the refrigerator for 30 minutes or so to let the balls firm up.

Add olive oil to a depth of 2½ inches in a deep fryer or saucepan and heat to a temperature of 360°F (a small cube of bread will brown in about a minute). Add the rice balls, a few at a time, and fry, turning them to brown them evenly all over. Cook for 3 to 4 minutes, or until the balls are crisp and golden brown. Remove and drain on paper towels set on a rack. When all the balls have been fried, serve immediately.

Frittata con Patate, Salsiccia, e Ricotta

POTATO, SAUSAGE, AND RICOTTA OMELET FROM BASILICATA

MAKES 4 TO 6 SERVINGS

1 medium potato (about 1 pound), peeled, halved, and thinly sliced	2 ounces hot cured sausage, such as capocollo, coarsely chopped	6 eggs
2 tablespoons extra-virgin olive oil	1 cup well-drained whole-milk ricotta, preferably made from sheep's milk	Sea salt and freshly ground black pepper Pinch of crumbled dried red chili (optional)

Combine the potato slices and olive oil in a skillet over medium heat. Cook, stirring frequently and breaking up the potato slices with the spatula rim, until the potatoes are very tender. Stir in the sausage and continue cooking.

In a bowl, combine the ricotta and eggs, adding salt, black pepper, and, if you wish, chili to taste.

Turn the heat down low under the skillet and pour the egg mixture over the potatoes in the pan, lifting the potatoes to let the egg batter run underneath. Cook, continually shaking the pan and running a palette knife or a narrow spatula around the edges of the frittata to keep the eggs from sticking. From time to time, lift some of the cooked egg off the bottom of the pan to let uncooked egg run beneath.

When the frittata is thoroughly cooked on the bottom, set a platter upside down over the skillet and turn the skillet over so that the frittata drops onto the plate. Now slide the frittata back into the skillet and continue cooking for 30 seconds to 1 minute, or until the frittata is firm on the bottom. Turn the frittata out onto a serving platter and serve immediately.

If turning the frittata and sliding it back into the skillet seems tricky, try simply running the skillet under a preheated broiler to brown the top very lightly.

Ciambutella

David Yeadon's loving description of ciambutella in his book *Seasons in Basilicata: A Year in a Southern Italian Hill Village* so engaged me that I set out to create a recipe for the dish. Yeadon's ciambutella was cooked by a villager (a man) outside over a wood fire, so if you have the opportunity at the beach or on a camping trip, by all means try it. But it is almost as good cooked at home on the kitchen range.

MAKES 6 SERVINGS, though if consumed outdoors, perhaps only 4

3 ounces pancetta, diced to make ⅓ cup	1 small hot fresh chili, trimmed and sliced	6 eggs, lightly beaten
¼ cup extra-virgin olive oil	1 medium yellow onion, coarsely chopped	3 or 4 fresh basil leaves, torn in strips
2 fresh Italian-style sweet sausages, preferably fennel-flavored	3 or 4 ripe tomatoes, chopped	Big pinch of dried oregano
	½ cup strong red wine	Handful of chopped flat-leaf parsley
1 large sweet red pepper, trimmed and sliced	Sea salt and freshly ground black pepper	

Combine the pancetta with a tablespoon of the olive oil in a heavy skillet over medium heat. Cook, stirring occasionally, until the fat in the pancetta starts to run and the dice begins to brown. Meanwhile, remove the skins from the sausages and break the meat up. Stir the sausage meat into the pancetta and brown thoroughly.

When the sausage is brown, add the sweet and hot peppers and onion, with a little more olive oil if the pan seems dry. Cook, stirring, until the pepper strips and chopped onion are soft. Now stir in the tomatoes and the red wine and raise the heat. Cook quickly to reduce the liquid in the pan and make a thick sauce; how long depends on the amount of liquid the tomatoes give off, but the result should be thick with very little visible liquid. Taste and add salt and pepper.

Combine the beaten eggs with the basil and oregano and pour over the contents of the pan. Cook as for a frittata (see page 90), shaking the pan and running a palette knife around the edge to loosen it, but do not try to mix it all up. Lift the vegetables and other ingredients gently to let a little of the egg run underneath. In the end you should have a layer of mostly vegetables on the bottom and a layer of mostly egg on the top.

If you are doing this outside over a wood fire, you probably don't want to risk flipping the cumbersome frittata over, so just keep cooking and lifting the ingredients until it is done to your taste. Just before removing from the fire, add the parsley.

If you are doing this at home on a kitchen range, preheat the broiler. Stir the parsley into the mix and slide the frittata under the broiler to set the top and brown it slightly.

Serve immediately with plenty of bread and red wine.

I PRIMI

First Courses

Thick, hearty, substantial soups, rustic potages dense with vegetables, legumes, potatoes, sometimes chestnuts, even pasta and bread, are often the main course, indeed the only course, for the evening meal throughout the southern Italian countryside. Yet these soups, humble as they are, rarely show up in recipe collections and almost never in even the most modest restaurants. On the other hand, chefs who are making a conscientious effort to preserve local traditions, like Federico Valicenti at La Luna Rossa in the Pollino Mountains of Basilicata and Berardino Lombardo at La Caveja in Campania, will often make a feature of such old-fashioned and appetizing fare. And these dishes are worth knowing about because, even when they require a long cooking time, they are easy-to-prepare, ample one-dish meals that can be stretched to serve a crowd; more often than not, they're also quite delicious. Even if these sometimes look like heavy fare, the fact that they're served on their own, with nothing but bread and a glass of wine, makes them lighter on the stomach. (I like these kinds of soups after a long afternoon walk on a chilly winter Sunday, when they seem especially restorative.)

Traditionally soups like these are made in a terra-cotta pignatta, and good southern cooks insist that only terra-cotta will give the soup the right flavor. I once bought a pignatta, along with a half dozen little serving bowls, in a ferramenteria, a combination hardware-housewares shop, in the little Casertano town of Pietravairano. The woman who sold it to me cautioned that the tall pignatta with its round belly should be rubbed inside and out with garlic before using it the first time. "It takes away the clay taste," she said. Then she turned it on its side and stretched her hand inside the pot. "Put the beans in up to here," she indicated, "with water and salt but no oil. The oil goes on after they've finished cooking."

It's fun to experiment with clay pots, but if you've broken as many in your lifetime as I have, you may be happier with a heavy-duty enameled cooking pot like the wonderful Le Creuset pots from France, which have just as good heat retention as the clay pots but are a lot less fragile.

The clear broths and simple purees of a single seasonal vegetable often found in France are not common in Italy, as Prince Fabrizio knew from experience and spared his rustic guests the embarrassment. When you come across a soup like that in the South, soup that's served as the opener to a meal rather than the meal in itself, it is evidence of French influence—and one must never forget that the French occupied the Kingdom of the Two Sicilies, off and on, for many years. That influence continues to this day, although there are few households that can still afford a *monzù*, a private chef trained in Franco-Italian cooking styles. It is in these monzù-influenced kitchens that you get the tradition, illustrated here, of rich, double meat or chicken broths to which something is added simply to delight the palate—a few vegetables (but very few), or some tiny meatballs, or even, at times, a pure white dollop of fresh sheep's milk ricotta floating on the amber-colored liquid.

Naples is home to this aristocratic cuisine, but Naples isn't just about refined food; there's one Parthenopean soup of legendary gusto for which I do not give the recipe simply because it would be impossible to prepare anywhere outside of Naples, and perhaps impossible to love except by the most dedicated napoletano. That's soffritto, much cherished in Naples as a kind of benchmark for how far toward the outrageous cooks are willing to go. It is made from the lungs, trachea, heart, and spleen of a recently slaughtered pig. The meats are chopped into bits and then cooked in melted lard and strong red wine, with lavish doses of conserva di pomodoro as well as conserva di peperoni rossi, both the sweet kind and the hot kind; if you're a Neapolitan cook, you buy this in thick, jellied slices from your local butcher, then thin it with water and pour the whole thing over slices of toasted bread. To say that soffritto is robust is to put it mildly. To say that it is an acquired taste is perhaps to say it all, but I should add that Neapolitans often croon about the heat, the fire, and the delightfully contrasting textures of soft bits of spleen, chewy bits of heart, and cartilaginous pieces of trachea. I leave it to adventurous readers to try soffritto on the spot in some waterfront tavern of Old Napoli.

Nevertheless, despite everything I've said about hearty soups, I want to begin with a few clear soups for serving at the start of the meal—soups that derive their goodness from a doubly rich stock and the addition of a few other ingredients to enhance but not detract from the basic flavor.

Brodo di Gallina e Brodo Ricco

BASIC CHICKEN STOCK AND RICH OR DOUBLE CHICKEN STOCK

The best chicken to use for stock is what used to be called a boiling fowl, but it's almost impossible to find one of these in North American supermarkets. However, if you know a chicken or egg farmer, possibly through a local farmers' market, one who raises free-range birds, ask if she ever has available such a big, tough old hen, maybe a layer past her prime. It does make a difference in flavor.

A Basic Chicken Stock to begin with is enriched by repeating the whole process, using the first basic stock to make the Double or Rich Stock. Either of these stocks or broths can be made ahead in quantities and frozen for long keeping. It's the sort of thing good cooks like to have on hand in the freezer for when it's time to make a risotto or add substance to a sauce.

MAKES 10 TO 12 CUPS

FOR BASIC CHICKEN STOCK		FOR RICH OR DOUBLE CHICKEN STOCK
4 to 5 pounds chicken parts, including wings and backs, preferably from a free-range bird	½ cup coarsely chopped flat-leaf parsley	4 to 5 pounds chicken parts, including wings and backs, preferably from a free-range bird
2 tablespoons extra-virgin olive oil	2 bay leaves	2 tablespoons extra-virgin olive oil
2 medium yellow onions, unpleeled but quartered	Big pinch of saffron threads, soaked in warm water (optional)	½ cup coarsely chopped flat-leaf parsley
2 garlic cloves, crushed with the flat blade of a knife	One 3-inch cinnamon stick (optional)	2 bay leaves
1 medium carrot, cut into chunks	1 dried red chili (optional)	1 tablespoon whole black peppercorns
1 green celery stalk, cut into chunks	1 tablespoon whole black peppercorns	Sea salt
	Sea salt	10 cups Basic Chicken Stock

Rinse the chicken pieces and dry with paper towels. If you wish to make a richly colored golden-brown stock, be sure the chicken pieces are very dry. Put them in a stockpot with the olive oil and the onions and set over medium heat. Brown slowly but thoroughly, turning frequently, until all the chicken pieces and the onions are golden, 20 to 30 minutes.

If, on the other hand, you want a clear, light chicken stock, omit this first step and simply put the chicken pieces and the onion in the stockpot.

Add the garlic, carrot, celery, parsley, and bay leaves. If you're making a golden stock, add the saffron with its soaking water. Add the cinnamon and chili, along with the peppercorns and a big pinch (a couple of tablespoonsful) of salt. Add about 3 quarts of cool water and set the pot over medium-low heat. Slowly bring to a simmer, carefully skimming the foam as it rises to the top. When the foam has ceased rising, cover the pot and simmer very slowly for at least 1½ hours, or longer if necessary—the chicken should be so thoroughly cooked that it is falling apart.

At the end of the cooking time, strain the stock through a double layer of cheesecloth or a fine-mesh sieve. Discard the solids, which will have given up all their savor. Taste the stock and add more salt if you wish, but keep in mind that if the stock is to be reduced later the salt will be concentrated.

Transfer the stock to the refrigerator to let the fat rise and solidify, after which it can be removed easily with a slotted spoon. (Once the fat has been removed, the stock can be frozen for longer keeping. I like to freeze it in 1 cup refrigerator containers for maximum efficiency.)

To make a Rich or Double Chicken Stock, simply repeat the whole procedure, using more chicken, oil, parsley, bay leaves, peppercorns, and salt. Add the already prepared Basic Chicken Stock, plus 2 cups water, and simmer the broth as for the basic stock, straining and degreasing it at the end as described above.

A soup that relies for its goodness simply on rich stock with the unassuming addition of a humble omelet, or frittata, this one is from Calabria. La mariola is the kind of thing a country farmwife will throw together at suppertime, especially on a feast day, when a lot of food may have been consumed at lunch and sated palates crave only lightness in the evening.

MAKES 4 TO 6 SERVINGS

6 cups Rich Chicken Stock (page 97)	2 tablespoons finely minced flat-leaf parsley	Pinch of crumbled dried red chili
4 eggs	2 tablespoons finely minced fresh herbs: marjoram, basil, sage, or another fresh green herb	Sea salt and freshly ground black pepper
¼ cup fine dry bread crumbs		
¼ cup grated aged pecorino or caciocavallo, plus more for serving		1 tablespoon extra-virgin olive oil

Bring the stock to a simmer and keep it very hot while you prepare the frittata or omelet. Mix together the eggs, bread crumbs, cheese, parsley, and any other herb you choose (if you don't have another fresh herb, it's perfectly fine just to use more parsley), beating the mixture with a fork. Stir in crumbled red chili, salt, and pepper to taste.

In a small skillet, heat the oil, using just enough to coat the bottom of the pan. Tilt the pan so the oil climbs the sides a little, then tip in the egg mixture, again tilting the pan to cover the bottom, and cook over medium heat until the eggs are thoroughly set. As the eggs cook, run a spatula knife around the edges of the pan to keep the eggs from sticking. At the same time, pull and lift the eggs with the knife to let the uncooked portion run underneath, but don't scramble them. They should cook to a flat pancake, without turning. When the omelet is done, and firm throughout, remove the pan from the heat and let the omelet set for a bit before slicing it—this will make it easier to slice into long, thin strips.

When you're ready to serve the soup, bring it back to a simmer, then transfer it to a tureen or individual soup bowls and add the strips of omelet. Pass more grated cheese separately.

Polpettine in Brodo

TINY MEATBALLS IN CHICKEN STOCK

Another example of how a simple but aromatic stock can be given extra interest by an addition, in this case small meatballs. The final garnish of parsley and chopped, toasted almonds gives elegance to what is a rather plain but full-flavored dish. You could make this with Basic Chicken Stock, but for a fuller flavor I recommend using Rich Chicken Stock.

MAKES 6 SERVINGS

½ cup roughly chopped yellow onion	1 egg	¼ cup minced flat-leaf parsley (optional)
2 garlic cloves, roughly chopped	¼ pound ground beef	¼ cup chopped toasted almonds
¼ cup chopped flat-leaf parsley	¼ pound ground pork	Grated aged caciocavallo or pecorino
⅓ cup chopped fresh basil, plus a few basil leaves for garnish	¾ cup fine dry bread crumbs	
½ cup grated aged caciocavallo or parmigiano reggiano	Sea salt and freshly ground black pepper	
	8 cups Rich Chicken Stock (page 97)	
	¼ cup extra-virgin olive oil (optional)	

Combine the onion, garlic, parsley, and basil in a food processor and process until finely minced. (Or chop to a fine mince on a board.) Mix in the grated cheese, egg, and ground meats. Add enough bread crumbs to make a mixture that is moist but holds together well—you may not need all the bread crumbs. Taste and add salt and pepper. Form into small meatballs about the size of a cherry and set aside—you should have 35 to 40 meatballs.

Bring the stock to a simmer. Tip the meatballs into the stock and simmer gently until they are cooked through—5 to 10 minutes, depending on the size of the meatballs. (Some cooks like to brown the meatballs in the optional olive oil before adding to the simmering stock. In this case, the meatballs don't need to cook in the stock for more than a minute or two before serving.)

To serve, sprinkle the surface of the soup, whether in a tureen or in individual soup bowls, with the optional minced parsley and toasted almonds. If you don't use parsley, garnish the soup with the reserved fresh basil leaves. Grated cheese may be passed at the table.

Zuppa di Riso al Pomodoro

RICE SOUP IN A TOMATO BROTH

This is a Neapolitan soup from the remarkable cookbook of Ippolito Cavalcanti, Duke of Buonvicino. *Cucina teorico-pratica* was first published in Naples in 1837, and the book represents for the south of Italy what the better-known *La scienza in cucina e l'arte di mangiar bene* by Pellegrino Artusi would come to mean for Tuscany and the North. Cavalcanti was a Neapolitan nobleman, but he wrote with gusto about the robust cuisine of his city, including a section of the book that was written in Neapolitan dialect. The book went through ten editions, the last one published in 1910, and is consulted by good cooks to this day. The recipe here is an adaptation of the version given by Jeanne Caròla Francesconi in her own superb compilation, *La cucina napoletana*.

This is a light soup, quite perfect for hot summer days, when it is served at room temperature or even slightly chilled. In that case, instead of the grated cheese, add about ½ cup of small dice of mozzarella, preferably imported *mozzarella di bufala* (buffalo-milk mozzarella).

MAKES 6 SERVINGS AS A FIRST COURSE

½ pound potatoes, peeled and diced	¼ cup extra-virgin olive oil	Sea salt and freshly ground black pepper to taste
1 medium yellow onion, coarsely chopped	2 tablespoons tomato concentrate or extract	¼ cup long grain rice
2 celery stalks, including green tops, coarsely chopped	4 or 5 cloves	¼ cup grated aged cheese: pecorino, caciocavallo,
2 carrots, chopped	1 small cinnamon stick	grana padano, or parmigiano reggiano, or
4 pounds ripe tomatoes, chopped	1 small dried red chili	½ cup diced mozzarella

In a soup pot, combine all the ingredients except the rice and cheese. Bring to a boil and turn the heat down to a mere simmer. Cover the pan and simmer for about 40 minutes, or until the vegetables are completely falling apart. Strain the soup through a fine sieve, letting all the juices drip through, then return the broth to a clean pan. Bring to a simmer again and add the rice. Simmer, covered, until the rice is done, then stir in the grated cheese and serve immediately. Or let cool to room temperature and serve garnished with diced mozzarella.

Minestra di Legumi Freschi

SOUP OF FRESH FAVAS AND PEAS

A fresh combination of fava beans and peas, this has all the flavors of a southern springtime blended together. Buy peas and, especially, fave that are really young and tender. Fava beans should be no thicker than your index finger. When they're that young, there's no need for that tedious business of peeling the individual beans. In Italy, we believe that if the individual beans need peeling (as opposed to simply shelling them from their pods), they're too old to eat anyway and should be kept for drying. The very best place to get good fava beans is at a farmers' market; otherwise, they do tend to be humongous, and old and tough as well.

MAKES 6 SERVINGS

8 scallions or spring onions (½ pound)	2 pounds fresh fava beans, shelled	5 or 6 small new potatoes, halved or quartered
¼ pound prosciutto or pancetta in 1 thick slice, diced	1¼ pounds fresh peas, shelled Sea salt and freshly ground black pepper	2 to 3 tablespoons minced fresh flat-leaf parsley, basil, or a combination
¼ cup extra-virgin olive oil		

Chop the scallions, including the green tops, into coarse uneven dice. Combine with the diced prosciutto and olive oil in a 3-quart saucepan. Set over medium-low heat and cook, stirring occasionally, until the scallions have started to soften but not brown and the fat in the prosciutto starts to run.

Add the shelled fava beans and peas, along with a tablespoon of salt and plenty of pepper. Stir well and let cook just until the legumes start to soften, about 7 or 8 minutes, then add the potatoes. Cover with boiling water by 2 inches and leave the soup to simmer for at least 20 minutes, or until the potatoes are soft and the legumes have cooked through. Just before serving, add the parsley and cook for 1 minute more, then serve immediately.

If you wish, although it would be anathema in southern Italy, a small dollop of unsalted butter is delicious on the top of each bowl of soup.

Cecamariti

PEA SOUP WITH CROUTONS

A pure dish of the Salento, the southeasternmost tip of Puglia, cecamariti (the name refers to something that will placate a hungry husband) is proof positive of the goodness of simple ingredients when they're combined as intelligently as they are here. This is real peasant fare, the kind that can easily be transported out to the fields or that will fill the farmer up in the morning before he leaves home, so he can pass the rest of the day with just a little piece of bread and cheese to keep him going.

Whole dried green peas are what's used in the Salento, but they're not always easy to find. I've made the soup very successfully with split peas instead, but the cooking time for the peas may be reduced by half.

Leftover cooked greens, such as dandelion greens or broccoli rabe, are often stirred in at the last minute before serving, along with the fried bread.

MAKES 6 TO 8 SERVINGS

1 pound whole dried peas, soaked for 6 to 8 hours or overnight (see headnote)	1 celery stalk, diced	4 or 5 slices coarse, country-style bread
1 medium yellow onion, diced	1 bunch of flat-leaf parsley, chopped (½ to ¾ cup)	½ cup plus 2 tablespoons extra-virgin olive oil
4 or 5 very ripe small tomatoes, peeled and diced, or 1 cup drained canned tomatoes, chopped	1 small dried red chili, crumbled	
	Sea salt and freshly ground black pepper	

Drain the peas and transfer to a terra-cotta pignatta or heavy soup kettle. Add fresh water to cover by 1 inch—about 1 quart of water. Set the pan over medium-low heat, and when the liquid begins to simmer, lower the heat and cover the pan. Simmer for about 1 hour, then stir in the onion, tomatoes, celery, parsley, and chili. Add salt and pepper to taste, then cover the pan and simmer for another hour or longer, until the peas are very tender and have started to dissolve into a mush—time depends on the age and size of the peas. Check the pan from time to time and add a little boiling water if the peas become too thick.

When the peas are thoroughly cooked, puree the contents of the pan, using a food mill or a stick blender. You should have a thick puree that is fairly smooth but with some discernible bits of peas and vegetables in it. Return the puree to the rinsed-out pan and keep hot while you pre-pare the bread.

Cut the bread slices into large croutons about 1 inch square, discarding the crusts. In a fry-ing pan over medium heat, heat ½ cup of the olive oil until it is just below smoking. Add the bread pieces and fry until crisp and golden brown on all sides. Remove and drain on a rack cov-ered with paper towels.

Transfer the pea puree to a heated serving dish, stir in the bread cubes, and serve immedi-ately, dribbling the remaining olive oil over the top.

Like most soups made with legumes, this one too is often served over slices of country-style bread, preferably toasted over an open fire, rubbed with a cut clove of garlic, and dressed liberally with fine extra-virgin olive oil. The parsley and garlic battuto or pesto that garnishes it, however, is a tradition in the Cilento, the breathtaking stretch of Campania's coastline that, backed by steep mountains, runs from Paestum south to the border of Basilicata. Cilentano cooks use this battuto for a soup made from a number of different dried legumes and grains, including corn, barley, and cicerchie, soaked overnight and cooked together. But it adds color and sparkle to any legume soup, such as this Zuppa di Ceci.

MAKES 6 SERVINGS

½ pound (1 cup) dried chickpeas, soaked for 6 to 8 hours or overnight	1 green celery stalk, including leaves, coarsely chopped	**FOR THE BATTUTO (PESTO)**
	1 bay leaf	½ teaspoon sea salt
1 garlic clove, coarsely chopped	1 small dried red chili	1 garlic clove, crushed
	Freshly ground black pepper	½ to ¾ cup coarsely chopped flat-leaf parsley
½ medium yellow onion, coarsely chopped		2 tablespoons extra-virgin olive oil

Drain the chickpeas and place in a soup kettle with fresh cold water to cover by about 1 inch. Set the kettle over medium-low heat and, when the water starts to boil, lower the heat, cover the pot, and simmer until the chickpeas are half cooked—30 to 45 minutes, depending on the age of the legumes. Add simmering water from time to time if needed.

Stir in the garlic, onion, celery, bay leaf, chili, and black pepper. Continue cooking, adding boiling water as necessary, until the chickpeas are tender. Remove the bay leaf and chili. Use a stick blender to make a creamy soup that still has considerable texture. (Or remove half the legumes and vegetables, transfer to a blender or food processor, and process until smooth, then return to the soup kettle and mix with the unblended portion.)

In a large heavy mortar, preferably one made of stone or of rough unglazed terra-cotta, crush the salt and the garlic together to make a paste. Add the chopped parsley and crush, turning the pestle against the walls of the mortar. When the parsley has been fully incorporated, gradually work in the olive oil to make a smooth emulsion. (This may also be done in a food processor or blender, but the result is more satisfying with an old-fashioned mortar and pestle.)

Serve the soup immediately, garnished with the parsley-garlic battuto. For an impressive presentation, transfer the hot soup to individual soup bowls or plates and swirl in the battuto so that each serving of pale soup is flecked with the dark green garnish.

VARIATIONS

🌿 A rustic garnish, occasionally served with this soup: about 2 ounces diced pancetta, toasted in 1 teaspoon olive oil until crisp, then scattered over the soup before serving.

🌿 In Basilicata, cooks often don't puree Zuppa di Ceci at all; instead, they stir into it for the final 15 or 20 minutes of cooking a handful of finely slivered cabbage and a couple of potatoes cut into small dice, both lightly toasted in olive oil in a skillet before being added to the soup to finish cooking.

Zuppa di Fagioli con Scarola

BEAN SOUP WITH ESCAROLE

Once upon a time Neapolitans were called *mangiafoglie*, leaf-eaters, because they ate so many greens. Times have changed, however, and today's Neapolitans are known as *mangiapasta* for the quantities of pasta they eat; still, I swear, Neapolitans eat more greens than anybody else in Italy, a country that is already total paradise for leaf-eaters. Escarole or *scarola* is one of many favorites, one that is not always easy to find in North America but worth snapping up when you do come across it.

Use white beans—cannellini, soldier, or navy beans—for this soup. Darker beans are fine in flavor, but they tend to make a muddy looking mixture.

MAKES 6 TO 8 SERVINGS

1 cup dried white beans, soaked for 6 hours or overnight	1 crisp green celery stalk, coarsely chopped	12 cherry or grape tomatoes, halved
1 large bunch of escarole (about 1 pound)	5 or 6 flat-leaf parsley sprigs, coarsely chopped	1 dried red chili (optional)
1 or 2 garlic cloves, coarsely chopped	2 tablespoons extra-virgin olive oil, plus oil for serving	Sea salt and freshly ground black pepper
		Toasted slices of bread, for serving

Drain the beans, put them in a saucepan, and add fresh water to cover by about 1 inch. Bring to a simmer over low heat, cover, and cook for 40 to 60 minutes, or until the beans are tender. Drain the beans, reserving the bean liquid.

Measure the bean liquid and add enough water to make 2½ cups.

Rinse and core the escarole. Chop the leaves into pieces about 1 inch long. Add them to the saucepan in which you cooked the beans, cover the pan and cook the escarole over gentle heat in the water clinging to its leaves until it is tender. Be careful not to let it scorch, adding a little boiling water to the pan if it starts to burn. When it is tender, set it aside with any liquid remaining in the pan.

Chop together the garlic, celery, and parsley to make about ½ cup finely minced aromatics. In a small skillet, cook the aromatics gently in the olive oil for about 10 minutes or until they give off fragrance but are not brown. Stir in the halved tomatoes and continue cooking until the tomatoes have shriveled somewhat and given off lots of juice.

Add the vegetable mixture to the escarole in the saucepan and set over medium-low heat. Break up the chili and add it, then stir in the beans plus the bean juice and water. Bring to a simmer, and season with sea salt and pepper. Let all the ingredients simmer together very gently while you toast the bread.

To serve, place a toasted bread slice in the bottom of each soup plate, then spoon the hot soup over. Pass a bottle of good olive oil at the table so diners can dribble on their own.

A small bowl of grated pecorino or caciocavallo cheese, passed at the table, would be welcome with this.

Pasta with Legumes (Pasta Fazool/Pasta e Fagioli)

The combination of pasta and beans, a tradition of humble tables from all over Italy, was immortalized by Dean Martin in a great song from half a century ago: "When the stars make you drool just like pasta fazool, that's amore!" Maybe it's not love, but it is certainly good eating—belly filling, nutritionally satisfying, and delicious to boot. Several of such combinations are typical of the South, and I include them here as soups although, with a little less liquid and a little more pasta, they could serve equally well as pasta courses.

Most beans used in Pasta e Fagioli are from the great New World family of *Phaseolus* beans—red-and-white streaked borlotti and creamy white canellini are probably the best known. But there's one unusual Old World bean that cooks should know about because it's so uncommon. That's the cicerchia (*Lathyrus sativus*), which looks like a cross between a chickpea and a small dried fava. This is a very old bean indeed, one that has been almost forgotten except in a few remote places, although, with the current fad for recovering lost and heirloom species, there's a push by groups such as Slow Food to reclaim cicerchie. You may well find them on the shelves of specialty food stores in the near future. To cook cicerchie, follow any of the recipes for bean soups, substituting cicerchie for the recommended beans. Cicerchie should be soaked overnight, then the water discarded and the beans rinsed thoroughly before continuing the cooking process.

Pasta Fasolu/Pasta e Fagioli

PASTA WITH BEANS

Pasta e fagioli is not beneath the attention of fine chefs like Alfonso Iaccarino, whose Michelin-starred restaurant Alfonso 2000 is in Sant'Agata sui Due Golfi, high on the Sorrento Peninsula overlooking the Bay of Naples. In an environment of hushed elegance, some variant of pasta and beans is often on the menu, along with far more refined selections. "Never use metal spoons to stir the beans," Alfonso advises, "only wooden ones." Metal spoons and metal ladles give beans a metallic flavor.

MAKES 8 SERVINGS

1½ cups dried borlotti or cannellini beans, soaked for 6 hours or overnight

2 whole garlic cloves, unpeeled

1 celery stalk, including green tops, coarsely chopped

2 tomatoes, peeled and sliced or chopped

1 fresh rosemary branch

1 medium yellow potato, peeled and diced

1 medium yellow onion, coarsely chopped

¼ cup diced pancetta

½ pound spaghetti, broken into 1-inch lengths

Sea salt

1 small dried red chili, crushed or crumbled

¼ cup extra-virgin olive oil

Handful of chopped flat-leaf parsley

Drain the beans, place in a pot, and cover with fresh cold water. Bring to a simmer and cook very gently, covered, until the beans are half done—about 30 minutes. Add the garlic cloves, celery, tomatoes, and rosemary and cook for another 15 minutes, then stir in the potato and onion. Continue cooking, adding boiling water as necessary to keep the beans always covered by about 1 inch, until the beans are very tender, about 1 hour.

Meanwhile, in a separate small skillet, brown the pancetta and drain on paper towels.

Bring 3 quarts of lightly salted water to a rolling boil, add the pasta, and cook until the pasta is just al dente, 5 to 7 minutes, then drain. (Time the pasta to be ready when the beans are done.)

When the soup is done, remove the garlic cloves and squeeze the soft garlic pulp into the soup. Add the chili, along with 2 tablespoons of the olive oil. Taste and add salt if necessary. Stir in the cooked pasta, transfer to a serving bowl, and garnish with the pancetta and chopped parsley. Dribble the remaining olive oil over the top and serve.

Cavatielli e Fagioli del Cilento

BEAN SOUP WITH CAVATIELLI PASTA FROM THE CILENTO

The Cilento, the region of the Campania coastline south of Salerno, is rugged, mountainous, poor, and wildly beautiful, with steep hillsides that often seem to plunge into the sea. This is the classic Mediterranean *macchia* landscape—wild, dry, resinous plants like broom (*ginestra*) and scrub oak. No one grows rich in the Cilento, except in the intangibles of clean air, good food, and staggering vistas wherever the eye comes to rest. As in many poor regions, local cooks have developed ways to add bright flavors to what are humble combinations of basic ingredients. The Cilentano technique is interesting and useful: Cook the beans and the cavatielli (with a little meat if you can afford it, without it if you can't), then sauté the aromatics to produce an extra bouquet of flavor and stir them into the soup at the end.

Commercially made cavatielli are not difficult to find, although in the Cilento they are often made by hand using semolina dough with no eggs. The pasta dough is rolled into a thin snake, then bits are cut off and rolled on a board, using one finger, two fingers, or three fingers, depending on the size of pasta required. (For bean soup, it's the robust three-finger version you want, according to my cavatielli coach, chef Pepe Zullo, who makes them almost every day.) If you can't find cavatielli, use another small complex pasta shape such as farfalle, fusilli, or small conchiglie (shells).

Butchers in Italian neighborhoods often have cotenne or cotiche, the salted rind of pork, which, diced and cooked along with beans, adds richness to any dish of legumes. It isn't always easy to find, however, so I substitute a couple of tablespoons of olive oil instead.

MAKES 8 SERVINGS

1 cup dried borlotti or similar dried beans, soaked for 6 hours or overnight	1 or 2 small dried red chilies, broken into pieces	¼ cup chopped flat-leaf parsley
1 piece cotenne (pork rind) or 2 tablespoons extra-virgin olive oil	3 garlic cloves, finely chopped	¼ cup chopped fresh basil
	3 celery stalks, finely chopped	1 pound cavatielli or other small pasta shapes
½ pound boneless pork shoulder, diced small	1 medium yellow onion, finely chopped	Sea salt and freshly ground black pepper
3 tablespoons extra-virgin olive oil, plus oil for serving	3 tablespoons tomato concentrate or extract diluted in ⅓ cup hot water	

Drain the beans and transfer to a saucepan with water to cover by 1 inch. If you have been able to find a piece of cotenne or cotiche (pork rind is known by both names), cut it into small dice or slivers and add to the saucepan; otherwise, stir in the olive oil. Set the pan over medium heat and bring to a simmer. Cover and turn down the heat to low, then simmer for 15 to 20 minutes while you prepare the pork.

In a small skillet, brown the pieces of pork in 1 tablespoon of the olive oil over medium-high heat. Stir in the broken bits of red chili, then scrape the contents of the skillet into the beans and continue simmering the beans, covered, over low heat until tender, 40 to 90 minutes, depending on the age of the beans.

In the same skillet, combine the remaining 2 tablespoons olive oil with the garlic, celery, and onion and cook over medium heat until the aromatics start to soften and give off a nice fragrance. Stir in the diluted tomato concentrate, along with the parsley and basil. Raise the heat and cook for just a few minutes more to concentrate the flavors. Set aside but keep warm.

When the beans are tender, bring water to a boil and add enough to the beans to be able to cook the pasta. Raise the heat to medium stir in the pasta and cook until the pasta is al dente. Scrape the vegetables in the skillet into the beans and pasta and stir to mix well. Taste and add salt and pepper to taste, then cook for another 5 minutes or so, just to meld all the flavors.

Serve immediately, passing more olive oil to dribble over the top.

Minestra di Pasta, Fagioli, e Verdure

SICILIAN PASTA, BEANS, AND GREENS

A beany-greeny soup, the Sicilian take on Pasta e Fagioli is sometimes made with a mixture of dried beans and dried favas, but it's perfectly legitimate to make it with dried beans alone, and I prefer it that way. White cannellini beans or red-streaked borlotti beans are good choices, but almost any bean will make a delicious and hearty soup. If you do use favas, be advised that it will be a much thicker soup, since they will disintegrate into a puree as they cook.

Like most uses of fennel in southern Italian cooking, this should really be flavored with the green tops of wild fennel, but if you lack a good reliable source of wild fennel (and most of us in North America do), use the green tops of cultivated fennel (bulb or Florentine fennel, sometimes sold as "anise") available in the produce departments of well-stocked supermarkets. I add a half teaspoon of dried wild fennel pollen (see Where to Find It, page 415) to boost the fennel flavor.

MAKES 6 TO 8 SERVINGS

1 cup dried beans, soaked for 6 hours or overnight	Sea salt	**GARNISHES (OPTIONAL)**
1 medium carrot, cut into chunks	1 cup coarsely chopped wild fennel fronds or cultivated fennel greens plus ½ teaspoon dried wild fennel pollen	Toasted slices of country-style bread
1 leek, white part only, thinly sliced		Extra-virgin olive oil
1 medium yellow onion, cut into chunks	1 cup slivered green chard or spinach	Freshly grated pecorino or parmigiano reggiano
1 celery stalk, cut into chunks	1 cup slivered green cabbage or kale	Minced flat-leaf parsley
2 bay leaves	1 cup pasta in small shapes— such as ditalini or tubetti— or spaghetti or maccheroni, broken into 1-inch lengths	Fresh whole-milk ricotta, preferably sheep's milk
1 piece parmigiano reggiano rind, if available		
1 small dried red chili, crumbled	Freshly ground black pepper	

Drain the beans and turn them into a soup pot—preferably one made from terra-cotta, but an enameled cast-iron pot will do. Cover with about 1 quart cool water and set over medium-low heat. Slowly bring to a simmer, then add the carrot, leek, onion, celery, and bay leaves. Add the parmigiano rind and red chili, cover the pot, and let the soup cook over very low heat, just barely simmering, for about 1 hour, or until the beans are tender.

Remove and discard the bay leaves, then puree about half the soup—you can do this right in the pot, using a stick blender, or remove about half the soup and puree it in a food processor, blender, or food mill. Add the puree back to the rest of the soup.

In a separate pot, bring 1½ to 2 cups water to a rolling boil. Add a pinch of salt and then the fennel, chard, cabbage, and the pasta. Season with salt and pepper to taste and cook until the pasta is tender. Using a slotted spoon, remove the greens and pasta and transfer them to the bean soup, setting aside their cooking liquid. Stir to mix, and if necessary, add some of the cooking liquid from the greens and pasta. If you have extra cooking liquid, keep it aside and add it, if necessary, when you reheat the soup before serving. (Bean soups thicken as they cool—the liquid from the greens and pasta is good for thinning it out again.)

When ready to serve the soup, toast the bread slices and dribble with oil. Set a bread slice in the bottom of each serving bowl and pour the soup over it. Garnish the soup with grated cheese and parsley or add a dollop of ricotta to each bowl.

Pancotto

Pancotto means "cooked bread," and that, more or less, defines this hearty soup, which was a constant on the tables of poor countryfolk before pasta came into widespread use. A combination of vegetables and aromatic herbs—whatever is in season—is simmered in plain water or broth, sometimes beans or legumes are added, and then at the end torn pieces of stale bread are stirred into the soup to thicken it. The soup may be enriched with a poached egg served on top of each bowl, along with grated cheese and a dollop of olive oil. It's a thrifty way of using up bread that's a little too old to eat fresh—and too fresh to toss out. A fundamental dish in the peasant diet, as it has been down through the ages, pancotto is still a welcome sight—and smell—on chilly winter nights.

To call this a soup is to be reminded of the incidental fact that the words *soup* and *sop* are as closely related as *bread* and *broth*. Bread is used thriftily to "sop" up the "broth:" the concept comes straight down from the medieval dining hall, where a thick slice of bread laid right on the tabletop was the plate on which the meal was served. In aristocratic households, once the meal was finished, the soppy bread was sent out to the poor at the gates of the castle, but in thrifty farmhouses it was, of course, consumed with grace—and thanks to the provider.

Pancotto should not be a thin, soupy sort of soup, but thick and ample. They are usually not made with broth at all—that is, stock made from meat, fish, or chicken—but simply with the water in which the vegetables have cooked, flavored with salt, pepper, the herbs that are at hand, and sometimes (often in Calabria and Basilicata) a dried red chili plucked from a braid of chilis hanging from a kitchen beam.

More important than any other ingredient is the quality of the bread used. For that, you will want a hefty loaf with a lot of texture. In the South, they use bread made with durum wheat (semolina), and if you can find that (or feel like making it—see recipe, page 26), it's ideal. Otherwise, use a good bakery loaf, whole wheat if you prefer, that's a couple of days old and firm without being dried out.

For a variation, simply substitute another vegetable (wild greens like dandelions or other chicories, turnip greens, potatoes, wild mushrooms, various cabbages, broccoli rabe, even salt cod is sometimes used) for the artichokes. If you wish, poach an egg for each serving and drop it on the top of the soup in the bowl, adding a dribble of olive oil and a few scraps of grated cheese.

MAKES 6 SERVINGS AS A MAIN COURSE, 8 servings as a first course

2 lemons	1 medium carrot, chopped	½ cup finely minced flat-leaf parsley and/or fresh mint leaves
4 to 6 large globe artichokes (about 3 pounds)	1 large or 2 medium potatoes, peeled and diced	
2 tablespoons extra-virgin olive oil, plus oil for garnish	Sea salt and freshly ground black pepper	3 to 4 slices stale country-style bread (crusts removed), torn into rough cubes
2 ounces pancetta or salt pork, diced	1 small dried red chili, crumbled (optional)	Grated aged cheese—pecorino, caciocavallo, parmigiano reggiano, or grana padano— for garnish (optional)
2 garlic cloves, chopped	1 tablespoon tomato concentrate or extract	
½ medium onion, chopped		

Use the lemons to prepare the artichokes as described on page 305, cutting each artichoke into 8 or 10 smaller pieces. Add 2 tablespoons olive oil to a 3-quart saucepan and set over medium-low heat. Stir in the pancetta and continue stirring until the fat starts to run. Add the garlic, onion, and carrot and cook, stirring occasionally, until the vegetables start to soften. Drain the artichokes and add to the vegetables in the pan along with the diced potato. Add salt and pepper to taste and, if you wish, the crumbled chili.

Bring water to a boil. Dissolve the tomato extract in a cup of boiling water and add to the pan with another 3 cups boiling water. Bring to a simmer, cover, and cook for about 20 minutes, or until the artichokes and potato cubes are tender. Taste and adjust the seasoning.

Set aside a couple of spoonfuls of minced herbs and add the rest to the soup. Stir in the bread cubes and continue cooking gently until the bread dissolves in the broth, 5 to 7 minutes.

Transfer to a soup tureen or individual soup bowls, sprinkle with the reserved herbs, and serve immediately, passing more oil and grated cheese, if you wish, to go on top.

Pancotto di Pomodoro

TOMATO PANCOTTO

A simple summertime pancotto, this reminds me of Tuscan pappa al pomodoro, which it strongly resembles. The addition of red chili, however, marks it indisputably as Calabrian. On really hot days, let the soup cool to room temperature before serving. Skip the cheese at that point and garnish it with a dollop of good oil and slivered fresh basil.

MAKES 4 SERVINGS

2 tablespoons extra-virgin olive oil	2 bay leaves	4 thick slices stale country-style bread, torn into smaller pieces
Finely chopped mixture of 1 small yellow onion, 2 garlic cloves, 1 celery stalk, and ½ cup coarsely chopped flat-leaf parsley	1 dried red chili, crumbled, or ground red chili to taste (optional)	Grated aged cheese—pecorino, caciocavallo, or parmigiano reggiano—for garnish
1½ pounds ripe tomatoes, peeled and coarsely chopped	1 teaspoon tomato concentrate, diluted in ¼ cup hot water	
	Sea salt and freshly ground black pepper	

Combine the olive oil and finely chopped vegetables in a heavy 3-quart pot over medium-low heat, and cook gently until the vegetables are soft but not brown. Add the chopped tomatoes, bay leaves, and red chili. Cook very gently, covered, for about 10 minutes.

Have ready 1 quart boiling water. When the tomatoes have released their juices, add the water to the pot, along with the diluted tomato concentrate and a good pinch of salt and plenty of black pepper. Cover and cook for another 15 or 20 minutes, until the tomatoes have completely fallen apart. Remove the bay leaves and, if you wish to have a less chunky soup, use a stick blender to partially puree the vegetables, then stir in the broken-up slices of bread and cook, covered, for 10 minutes longer, or until the bread has dissolved in the tomato broth.

Taste and adjust the seasoning. Serve hot with grated cheese sprinkled on top or see the note above for an alternative suggestion.

Minestrone di Montagna

SOUTHERN ITALIAN MOUNTAIN MINESTRONE

This is really a meat stew, based on the omnipresent lamb of southern mountain pastures, along with plenty of potatoes and cabbage. Far from the idealized Mezzogiorno of eternal sunshine, sparkling waters, and Greek ruins against brilliant blue skies, the home of this hearty, one-dish meal is up on the steep, rocky slopes where, in winter, winds howl and snow bears down on obstinate mountain villages clinging to cliffsides.

A village cook would use pure lard for the fat in this dish, but since lard without added preservatives is hard to come by in North America, I use extra-virgin olive oil instead.

MAKES 6 SERVINGS

2 tablespoons extra-virgin olive oil	¼ cup coarsely chopped flat-leaf parsley	2 large potatoes, peeled and diced
½ to ¾ pound lean boneless lamb, cut into bite-sized chunks	2 bay leaves	½ pound green cabbage, slivered
	1 teaspoon dried oregano (optional)	½ pound linguine or other long, thin pasta, broken into 1-inch pieces
¼ pound lean pancetta, diced	1 dried red chili (optional)	
1 medium onion, halved and sliced	1 tablespoon tomato extract, concentrate, or paste, diluted in 1 cup hot water	Freshly grated aged pecorino for garnish
1 green celery stalk, cut into chunks	Sea salt and freshly ground black pepper	
2 garlic cloves, crushed with the flat blade of a knife		

In a terra-cotta pignatta or heavy stew pot, combine the olive oil, lamb, and pancetta and set over medium heat. Cook, stirring, until the meats are brown. Lower the heat and add the onion, celery, garlic, parsley, and bay leaves, stirring to mix well. Stir in the oregano and chili. Add the diluted tomato extract to the pot along with another 2 cups water. Add salt and pepper to taste and bring to a simmer. Cover the pot and cook at a very slow simmer until the meats are thoroughly cooked and starting to fall apart, 1 to 1½ hours.

Once the meats are cooked, add the diced potatoes along with another 2 cups boiling water to the pot and cook until they are just tender, then stir in the cabbage and pasta, adding a little more boiling water if necessary, and continue cooking until the pasta is done. Serve immediately, garnishing each serving with a little grated cheese.

HEARTY VEGETABLE MINESTRONE

The recipe comes from Cosenza in Calabria—you can tell because like almost everything from down in the toe of the Italian boot, it includes crumbled dried red chilies—*peperoncini rossi*. You should feel the heat as a pleasant piquancy in the soup but not something that sends you rushing for the water pitcher.

As with most minestrone, wherever in Italy they come from, the ingredients can be, and should be, varied according to what's in season, what's in the market, and what's in the larder. You could add some celery, for instance, or a small amount of slivered cabbage; when I have leftover beans or chickpeas, I often stir half a cup or so into the soup to add heft. Use your imagination, but remember that it's the flavor of the onions that should predominate.

Apart from the red chili, the most important ingredient, the one that defines this soup as Calabrian, is the red onion. In Calabria, these are the sweet firm red onions from Tropea; in America we use sweet Walla Walla reds or the like.

MAKES 8 SERVINGS

1 pound sweet red onions (2 to 3 medium)	1 quart vegetable or chicken stock	2 dried red chilies, crumbled, or crushed dried red chili to taste
1 garlic clove, chopped	Sea salt	8 thick slices country-style bread, toasted
¼ cup extra-virgin olive oil, plus more for garnish	8 to 10 Swiss chard leaves and/or other greens	Freshly ground black pepper
1 tablespoon red wine vinegar	1 cup shelled fava beans or other vegetables	Grated aged cheese such as caciocavallo or pecorino for serving
2 medium white potatoes, peeled		
3 medium carrots		

Cut the onions in half and thinly slice. Combine with the garlic and 2 tablespoons of the olive oil in a large saucepan. Add the vinegar, which should help to keep the onions from losing all their bright color. Set over medium-low heat and cook very gently, uncovered, stirring frequently, until the onions are very soft but not brown, 20 to 30 minutes.

Meanwhile, cut the potatoes and carrots into large dice and combine in another pan with the stock, adding salt if necessary. Cover and set over medium-low heat. Simmer gently for about 45 minutes, or until the vegetables are very soft.

Trim the chard of its thick stems if necessary, then slice the chard into strips. When the potatoes and carrots are done, add the chard, fava beans, and chilies. Cook for another 10 minutes.

Meanwhile, cut the toasted bread slices into large croutons. Heat the remaining 2 tablespoons olive oil in a skillet over medium heat and fry the croutons until crisp on all sides. Remove and set aside.

Taste the minestrone and adjust the seasoning, adding more salt if necessary and plenty of black pepper. Serve the soup with the croutons, dribbling a little extra olive oil over the top of each serving. Pass the grated cheese.

Southern Italy is a land of wheat, specifically hard, golden durum, called *grano duro,* "hard wheat" in Italian. *Triticum turgidum,* var. *durum* is the species name, to distinguish it from *T. aestivum, grano tenero*, or soft wheat (often called *bread wheat* in English), from which is derived our all-purpose flour. Among the oldest species of cultivated wheat, durum moved into the Mediterranean Basin very early in human prehistory, brought by early farmers and traders from somewhere east of Syria. In the distinctive Mediterranean environment of hot, dry summers and cool, rainy winters, grano duro flourished. Puglia's great food historian Luigi Sada said that the Pugliese "arrived at the dawn of their history" already aware of wheat and its uses—witness, he pointed out, the spikes of wheat that appear on silver coins called *stateri* from ancient Metapontum, settled by Greeks in the late eighth century B.C.E. (In fact, although there are indeed spikes of wheat on some Metapontum coins, barley ears are far more numerous, not surprising given the importance of barley in the ancient Greek diet.)

The rolling plains of Puglia, from Foggia down across the grassy Murge west of Bari, as well as the uplands of central Sicily were vital contributors to the granary of Imperial Rome, so the history books tell us, and they still represent a major source of Italy's hard wheat production. In today's world, however, durum represents a very small proportion of the annual world wheat harvest—small but nonetheless significant because it is from the vitreous grains of durum, ground to a gritty, mealy flour called *semola* in Italian and *semolina* in English, that the finest pasta is made. Indeed, in Italy all commercial pasta must be made from grano duro—that's the law of the land, consumer protection legislation written to ensure that the Italian dietary staple is made from the best high-quality, high-protein wheat.

After the grain harvest in June, the southern Italian landscape seems burnt by the sun, dusty and yellow as an old lion's pelt, and it lies that way for months as if exhausted. In the Mediterranean wheat is a winter crop: the broad fields are turned in autumn, revealing the rich red-to-black colors of the soil, then plowed and sown. Throughout the winter months, the wheat grass grows, ever so slowly, then quickening with the sun's increasing strength and warmth. Travel through the same landscape the following April or May, and the multiplying greenness of the rippling grass will take your breath away.

With such a long history of wheat growing, it is not surprising that pasta reached a kind of apotheosis here in the old lands of Magna Graecia. I would not venture to say that pasta was invented here. Pasta, made simply from durum-wheat semola and water, unlike the egg-and-soft-flour pasta of the North, may in fact have been invented in many places around the Mediterranean and at more or less the same time. What is undeniable, however, is that pasta evolved here into one of the most astonishing food products on the world's table—quick, easy, filling, cheap, and infinitely adaptable.

Each province, each town and village, maybe even each family, it seems, has its own pasta traditions, whether the shape of the pasta itself or the sauce that is considered obligatory to serve with it. The round mushroom caps of orecchiette from Altamura and surrounding towns in Puglia's Murge, the twisted busiate fabricated by Trapanesi cooks in western Sicily, the strascinate made by dragging disks of pasta across a rough board in Basilicata and Puglia alike, and the cavatielli from Campania that are shaped with one finger, two fingers, or three fingers depending on the sauce that will accompany them—these are but the most obvious examples of what could easily become an encyclopedia if a person ever set out to document every single style of pasta made in southern Italy.

And then there are the sauces, the flavor combinations that give the pasta a reason to be eaten: Basilicata, for instance, far from trans-Alpine German influences, is probably the only place south of the Alps where it's traditional to serve spaghetti with an absolutely normal tomato sauce over which the cook grates fresh horseradish. (It's a remarkable combination—try it sometime when you come across a horseradish root, often available at natural-food stores.) Basilicata is also a place, like Calabria, where it's customary to cook pasta in milk for the Feast of the Ascension, forty days after Easter—the pasta dressed with a sauce of the milk in which it has cooked, reduced and thickened with grated pecorino or sweetened with sugar and cinnamon. Another astonishing combination (astonishing both because it seems so unusual to North American palates and then, of course, because it is astonishingly good) is Sicily's great dish of pasta colle sarde, pasta cooked with wild fennel, sweet raisins, pine nuts, and humble sardines; or the Barese dish of spicy tomato and lamb ragù atop ravioli stuffed with sweetened ricotta.

These are all amazing dishes, but there is plenty of pasta that is equally delicious but a good deal simpler and easier to prepare—less spectacular for dinner guests and more adaptable to family meals. These pasta dishes come from all over the South, pasta with a seasonal vegetable, whether artichokes or tomatoes or sliced zucchini; pasta with a sauce mixed with whatever fish was available in the market that day; pasta with nothing but good olive oil, grated cheese, and a hefty sprinkling of freshly ground black pepper. Some of these pasta dishes are tied to a particular place for historical or other reasons, like Orecchiette alla Barese, made with broccoli rabe and traditional in the Terra di Bari in Puglia, or eggplant-garnished Pasta alla Norma, invented in lively Catania in Sicily, birthplace of the composer Bellini and named for one of his best-loved operas. Others are more generically southern and can be found, with slight variations, in much of the South but seldom, I think, in central or northern Italy, unless at the hands of a transplanted southern cook.

Like southern bread, the pastas of southern Italy are made from semola, the gritty flour of hard-grain durum wheat, often locally grown. This holds whether the pasta is handmade at home or machine-produced in small family factories like that of Benedetto Cavalieri in Puglia or Pastificcio Fratelli Setaro in Torre Annunziata, one of the towns south of Naples that is famous for the quality of its pasta. While it's true that all commercial, boxed pasta in Italy must be made from durum wheat, pasta made at home or by hand in central and northern Italy, is made with flour from bread wheat, which almost always has eggs added to the dough to hold it together. But in the South it is almost always made with semola di grano duro, and woe betide the cook who thinks of adding eggs to the dough "just to hold it together"—a sin I confess to having committed on many occasions.

One question often asked about southern Italian pasta traditions: What cheese should I grate on top, and when should I do so? To be absolutely authentic, you would want to use a hard aged caciocavallo, made from cow's milk, or an aged ewe's milk pecorino, such as those made in various regions of the South. (I caution against the cheese called "romano" that is widely sold in American supermarkets. It has a nasty taste that is not at all like true pecorino romano.) In fact, however, authentic or not, these days many southern cooks use northern cheeses, parmigiano reggiano or its cheaper cousin grana padano, that have acquired national distribution.

And when should you garnish with grated cheese? Whenever you wish, and don't let anyone tell you different! "But I thought Italians never eat cheese with fish?" you say. Never say *never*: Italians do many, many things in the kitchen that you will have heard they "never" do. The great gift of la cucina italiana, especially of la cucina del mezzogiorno italiano, is that there are no hard-and-fast rules. So cheese with fish? By all means, if it pleases your palate, go right ahead. Enjoy!

Sauces

When it comes to saucing pasta, the cooks of southern Italy display infinite imagination, combining fresh vegetables, tomatoes, of course, preserved pork and sausages, a wealth of fish and seafood, grated and sliced cheeses, humble beans, and even bread crumbs, along with capers, black and green olives, anchovies and bottarga, pine nuts, grated citrus zest, fresh and dried herbs, and onions, garlic, carrots, and all the usual aromatics from the garden or the larder. And, of course, not to be forgotten, the good dense olive oil, a richly flavored ingredient in its own right, that is made throughout the region.

With all this wealth of ingredients, however, pasta remains in essence a modest, unassuming, everyday sort of dish, one that graces the tables, sometimes twice a day, of rich and poor alike, though more often it may be the *only* dish on a poor table and hence served in comparative abundance. With a belly full of pasta, even pasta that has been dressed meagerly with bread crumbs and anchovies, there's less need for the luxuries of meat.

With all this variety, too, pasta is sauced with a natural restraint from which we North Americans might take a lesson. Pasta, after all, is the point of the dish, in rich households and in poor; the sauce is there to add interest to the pasta and not vice versa. It should not dominate the dish. There should be enough sauce to cling to the strands or rounds or mounds of pasta, but not so much that it leaves a deep puddle in the bottom of the plate.

The following sauces are for the most part basic, simple, tomato-based sauces that can be used with almost any kind of pasta, from vermicelli to lasagna, although I have given some suggestions for appropriate shapes and sizes. The ragù recipes are more complex, but they too can be used with just about any pasta. Short stubby ziti and rigatoni are the usual pasta shapes for a ragù, but there's no rule that says you can't serve it with long, skinny spaghetti or vermicelli, and of course ragù is the basic sauce for many lasagne and paste al forno.

Sugo di Pomodoro

BASIC TOMATO SAUCE

A basic, all-purpose tomato sauce, this can be varied in many ways, adding more garlic (or, alternatively, leaving the garlic out entirely) or finely chopped onions, minced fresh or dried herbs such as fresh basil or parsley or dried oregano, or a crumbled dried red chili. In essence, this sauce is the foundation of much Italian cooking, from pasta to pizza to soups to stews, and not just in the South either, although tomatoes grown in southern Italy reach an apogee of flavor and texture like no other tomatoes in the world.

Tomatoes are one of the few vegetables that take well to canning, and I have no qualms about using canned tomatoes to make a sauce when good-quality fresh ones are not available. Try out several different brands and find one that pleases you.

The recipe makes about 2 cups, which is all you will need for most recipes. If you double the quantities, you can keep half the sauce in the refrigerator for several days, or in the freezer for weeks, to have on hand. A half cup or more of the sauce, added during cooking, will also enliven a *zuppa di fagioli*, bean soup, or minestrone considerably.

If you should come across an abundance of good, fresh, garden-ripened tomatoes from a local farmer, you can also make the sauce in still larger quantities and freeze it or preserve it; see page 129 for directions.

MAKES ABOUT 2 CUPS, enough for 4 to 6 servings of pasta if used on its own as a pasta sauce

1 to 3 garlic cloves, sliced 2 tablespoons extra-virgin olive oil	3½ pounds ripe fresh tomatoes, preferably plum, peeled, seeded, and coarsely chopped, or one 28-ounce can whole tomatoes, with juice, chopped	1 teaspoon sea salt (for fresh tomatoes only) ½ teaspoon sugar (optional)

In a heavy nonreactive saucepan over medium-low heat, sweat the garlic gently in the olive oil until it begins to soften, about 5 to 7 minutes. If by mistake you let the garlic brown, throw it out and start over—overly browned garlic will give an acrid flavor to the sauce. Add the tomatoes and, if you wish, salt and sugar, raise the heat slightly, and cook rapidly, stirring frequently, while the tomatoes give off their juice and cook down to a thick mass—15 to 20 minutes. Watch the mixture carefully toward the end to make sure it doesn't scorch. (If you use canned tomatoes, they will take less time to cook down since they are already processed.)

Turn the tomatoes and their juices into a colander over a bowl and let them drain. Set aside the drained liquid and put the tomatoes through a food mill to get rid of skins and seeds. Whether you use the fine, medium, or large disk is up to you. I use the disk with the largest holes because, for me, chunkiness is part of the sauce's appeal, but you might find that for some purposes a finer-textured, smoother sauce is more to your taste. (For a very fine texture, transfer the pureed sauce to a food processor and process briefly in spurts.)

Return the pureed sauce to the saucepan and set over medium-low heat. If the sauce is thicker than you wish, add some of the reserved liquid from the bowl. If, on the other hand, it seems too thin, continue cooking, stirring constantly and watching very carefully, until it reaches the desired consistency.

VARIATION

For Salsa alla Pizzaiola, Sauce of the Pizza Maker (or of the Pizza Maker's wife) add the following to the pureed Sugo di Pomodoro when you return it to the saucepan:

½ teaspoon crumbled dried red chili, or more to taste	1 teaspoon dried oregano, or more to taste	2 tablespoons minced flat-leaf parsley

Don't think, because of its name, that this sauce has to be restricted to pizza. It's also a quick and easy sauce to serve over almost any kind of pasta, from spaghetti to short stubby cuts like farfalle and rigatoni. Bistecca alla pizzaiola is another use for this sauce—a simple dish of thin boneless beef steaks (minute steaks are appropriate), quickly seared on both sides and then finished in the pizzaiola sauce.

San Marzano Tomatoes—L'Oro di Napoli

Whether creating a rich meat ragù for Sunday lunch or a simple pummarola to top a pizza, Neapolitan cooks swear by the thin-skinned, fragrant San Marzano plum tomatoes that are a traditional crop on the fertile plains south of Vesuvius. Fleshy and juicy at the same time, these tomatoes profit from a combination of mineral-dense volcanic soils and salty breezes off the Bay of Naples, a balance that adds intense flavors to all the fruits and vegetables grown in the region—to apples and apricots, to artichokes, peas, and lemons, but especially to tomatoes. These prized tomatoes are grown mostly for processing, for which they seem uniquely suited, although local cooks may slice up a few San Marzanos for a salad or a fresh pasta sauce. Italians conventionally refer to canned tomatoes as *pelati,* meaning "peeled," but true, authentic San Marzanos need no peeling, unlike canned tomatoes from other parts of Italy (and of the world). The San Marzano's tender skin, which helps conserve its flavor, easily melts into a sauce when cooked.

But it also makes for very fragile fruits, ones that cannot be harvested easily or transported far from their growing region. The ripe tomatoes must be selected by hand, each plant visited six, eight, or even more times throughout the season as the fruits mature, explained Sabato Abagnale, a young, enthusiastic tomato grower and processor in Sant'Antonio Abate, the tomato capital of the volcanic plain. The harvest begins in July and extends till September, the hottest time of the year, said Sabatino (as his friends call him), made bearable only by the fact that the tomatoes are picked in the evening, when the sun has left the fields. "For thirty-five days," Sabatino said, "we don't stop working, literally, only to sleep. But it's worth it." Within twenty-four hours of harvest, the tomatoes are washed and packed in cans or jars, processed for sixty minutes—"*e basta*, that's it! No, no preservatives, no additives, nothing like that."

Abagnale is head of a Slow Food presidium, organized to create a market for these special fruits. The presidium, which came to birth under the direct influence of Slow Food founder Carlo Petrini, brought together a handful of farmers who were passionate about their heritage, then helped to educate the tomato-consuming public about what was at stake, all with the goal of preserving and protecting true San Marzano tomatoes, a small but significant niche of Italian culture and cuisine.

Preservation? Protection? Why do San Marzanos need special protection? Isn't that what I buy just about every time I buy a can of imported Italian plum tomatoes?

Well, it turns out there are San Marzanos and then there are *real,* authentic San Marzanos, which is what Sabatino and a very few other growers are known for. In recent decades the authentic San Marzano, the one with the thin skins and the fragile fruits and the incomparable flavor—itself a product of early-twentieth-century breeding efforts—had simply disappeared. True San Marzanos, wiped out by disease, were replaced by new cross-breeds that produced tough, virus-resistant fruits that could be harvested mechanically, tossed into a bin, and hauled off to processors without damage. Furthermore, they could be grown anywhere and still called San Marzanos, even in the Po Valley far away to the north, leagues from the sun, the sea, and the incomparable Vesuvian soil. It's a familiar story, especially to Americans cognizant of the loss of flavor in our own food products developed for long-distance shipping and rough handling. And, it was said, that was the fate of the true San Marzano.

Until a couple of years ago, when someone—it's not clear who—uncovered a cache of original seeds kept in cold storage by Cirio, the first and still one of the largest industrial processors of tomatoes in the world. A mere handful of these seeds were grown out and grown out again, and today there are four growers in the Agro Nocerino-Sarnese, the farmland south of Vesuvius that was the San Marzano's original home. The task has not been easy, at least in part because of the intense development of greenhouse floriculture in the region. Methyl bromide, used to sterilize greenhouse soil (and supposed to have been phased out by 2005) fouls much of the soil, and overbuilding of cheap, nasty housing and small factories has crowded farmers completely off their fields.

And it's the soil in the fields that is ultimately responsible for the quality of these exceptional tomatoes. Sabatino calls it *arapilla,* a word that has no English or even Italian equivalent. It refers to the ashes washed down from the volcano over the millennia and compacted into this soil, which extends one to three meters down (three to nine feet). It provides rich fertilizer and fine drainage for anything that grows here.

"You can take the seeds anywhere you want," Sabatino explained to me one early summer morning when I visited him in a small tidy field where the baby tomato plants were just inches high, "but without this soil, you won't get the flavor." He picked up a handful of rust-colored soil from the tomato patch and held it out for my inspection. "This," he said, "this is our secret ingredient." It looked like fairly ordinary earth to me, friable, slightly reddish in color, bits clumping together from the moisture it holds. But I'm willing to credit him with knowing what he's talking about, especially when I taste his tomatoes. The proof is there, in the tasting.

Sabatino Abagnale's tomatoes are available in North America through the website gustiamo.com. They are expensive, but worth it.

La Pomarola

PRESERVED TOMATO SAUCE

Anytime in the late summer or early fall when you come across an abundance of good, fresh, garden-ripened tomatoes from a local farmer, make Sugo di Pomodoro (Basic Tomato Sauce, page 125) in large quantities and either freeze it or do as families do all over Italy and preserve it in pint or half-pint canning jars. This farmhouse-bottled sauce is often called *pomarola,* and it's so easy and simple that Americans who care about the quality of their food should be doing it too. It's a great way to spend a late-summer or early-autumn Saturday, after a trip to the farmers' market. Here's how to do it:

First, make sure you have enough Mason jars, screw-tops, and lids for the tomatoes—it's difficult to judge, since a lot depends on the amount of liquid in the tomatoes. Most of that will evaporate, leaving the thick sauce behind, so err on the side of caution. The jars must be scrupulously clean, rinsed in hot soapy water, then again in clear hot water, then set aside to drain. Set the jars on a wooden countertop or on several layers of newspaper so they don't crack when the boiling liquid or sauce is poured in. Have the tomato sauce ready and simmering. To be extra careful, just before you plan to transfer the sauce to the jars, fill each jar with boiling water. Then carefully pour the hot water out of a jar, immediately fill it with hot tomato sauce to within ½ inch of its top, screw down the lid, and go on to the next jar. When all the jars are filled, immerse them in water to cover by at least 1 inch in a stockpot or canning pot (put a layer of newspapers on the bottom of the pot to keep the jars from banging about). Set the pot over medium-high heat and bring the water to a boil; process (boil) for 20 to 30 minutes. Turn off the heat and, using tongs, remove the jars from the water and set them aside on a cloth towel or a wooden board until the lids ping, indicating that they are fully sealed. Tighten the lids once more and secure. Store in a cool, dark place—a collar or a cool pantry cupboard.

Incidentally, if any of the lids refuse to ping and seal, you can still use the sauce, but it would be better to store it in the refrigerator and use it within a week or so.

Salsa alla Sangiovanella

TOMATO SAUCE FOR THE FEAST OF ST. JOHN THE BAPTIST

June 24, the feast of St. John the Baptist (San Giovanni Battista), is traditionally celebrated as Midsummer's Eve. This is true not just in Italy or the Mediterranean but throughout Europe, even far north in Scandinavia and Scotland. The longest day (and the shortest night) of the year is a magical time-out-of-time, and that's been so since long before Shakespeare's dazzling mind-twister about faerie land and the fools we mortals can become under Puck's enchantment. Even if June 21st is the true solstice, the 24th is celebrated with traditional rituals, bonfires, and, of course, dishes. In Bari, Puglia's ancient port city fronting on the southern Adriatic, that dish is Vermicelli alla Sangiovannella, with this delicious and imaginative sauce. Why? "Because we've always done it this way."

Salsa alla Sangiovannella is good on any kind of pasta, not just vermicelli, and it also makes a splendid topping for pizza or crostini.

MAKES ABOUT 3 CUPS, enough for 6 servings, about 1 pound of pasta

6 anchovy fillets	½ small dried red chili or ¼ teaspoon crushed dried red chili, or to taste	¼ cup chopped pitted black or green olives
1 garlic clove, chopped		½ cup finely chopped flat-leaf parsley
⅓ cup extra-virgin olive oil	1 or 2 tablespoons capers, preferably salt-packed, rinsed and drained	Sea salt and freshly ground black pepper
2 cups Basic Tomato Sauce (page 125)		

If you are using salted anchovies, rinse them thoroughly under running water to get rid of excess salt, then strip away their bones and chop them coarsely. (If you're using oil-packed anchovy fillets, simply chop them.)

In a saucepan over medium-low heat, gently sweat the garlic in the oil. When it is soft, add the anchovies and cook, stirring with a fork and pressing down on the anchovies to melt them into the oil. Add the tomato sauce and cook just long enough to meld the flavors, then stir in the chili, capers, olives, and parsley. Taste and add salt if necessary and lots of black pepper.

VARIATION

This is very similar to the Neapolitan sauce called *alla puttanesca*. To make puttanesca, simply add 1 medium onion, finely chopped, to the garlic and season the sauce with dried oregano.

Pumadoru a Picchiu Pacchiu

RAW TOMATO SAUCE FOR PASTA

What does *picchiu pacchiu* mean? A long bout of research led me to an answer—"bottom smacker." But what that has to do with this quick and easy Sicilian pasta sauce, I haven't a clue. Meaning aside, however, it's a good quick dish because, even if the sauce requires some preparation (but not very much!), once it's done it simply sits in its bowl, which it can do for hours, until the pasta is ready to serve. Use spaghetti or a similar long, thin pasta.

MAKES ENOUGH FOR 1 POUND OF PASTA; 4 to 6 servings

2 pounds very ripe tomatoes, peeled, seeded, and chopped	Sea salt	⅓ cup chopped fresh basil, plus 2 tablespoons for garnish
4 garlic cloves, chopped or very thinly sliced	½ teaspoon crumbled dried red chili	½ cup extra-virgin olive oil

To make the sauce, simply combine the tomatoes, garlic, a teaspoon or so of salt, the chili, ⅓ cup basil, and oil in a large bowl. Cover and set aside at room temperature to marinate for several hours. If you must refrigerate the sauce at any point, be sure to give it plenty of time to come back to room temperature before serving it.

When ready to serve, simply cook the pasta as usual, drain, turn into a heated serving bowl, and immediately toss with the sauce. Garnish with the extra basil and serve immediately.

VARIATION

Giuseppe Coria, in his authoritative book about Sicilian cuisine, *Profumi di Sicilia,* makes "picchi pacchi" quite differently, sautéing sliced onion gently in oil until golden, then adding peeled, seeded tomatoes, salt, pepper, and a quantity of basil. This sauce is then used as the medium for cooking other things—snails, for instance, meatballs, or chunks of swordfish—or for reheating slices of roasted meat.

On the Importance of a Tasty Ragù

One Sunday morning years ago, I chanced to meet an old man on the street in Carroll Gardens, back in the days when that Brooklyn neighborhood was still solidly Italian-American. I asked him about places to eat. "Eat? Ohhh," he groaned, "you shoulda been here back in the old days. You could walk around on a Sunday morning and the smell of red gravy coming outa every house on the block—it was wonderful!"

When Italian-Americans wax nostalgic about the red gravy of their childhoods, it is this ragù napoletano of which they dream, bubbling away on the back of nonna's kitchen stove as the family gathers after Mass on Sunday. If pizza is the most famous of all Neapolitan preparations, one that has been cheerfully exported all over the world, there is no question that what a true Neapolitan craves first of all when returning home is spaghetti al ragù, a simple plate of pasta dressed with the rich, meaty, tomatoey, spicy, fragrant sauce that is traditional for Sunday lunch in Naples and the surrounding countryside, in fishing ports, and tourist resorts along the Amalfi Drive and in mountain villages and farmhouses deep in the interior. *Pippiare* is the word in Neapolitan that describes the gentle, genteel bubbling of the sauce, not even a simmer but just a little pip-pip-pip as it slowly cooks and reduces over a long period of time—the very essence of slow food.

Certain ingredients, it goes without saying, are required for a proper ragù—meats, of course, in a variety to lend complexity and richness to the sauce; onions, masses of them, very thinly sliced and stewed until they melt in a tasty combination of olive oil and *strutto*, lard; and, most important of all, tomatoes made into a simple sauce that is added to the simmering meats a little at a time, each addition cooked down to a dark mahogany-red sauce before the next bit is added.

To make a good, savory ragù, with the correct balance of sweet and tart flavors, you must use either summer tomatoes, preferably meaty plum tomatoes, fresh from the garden, ripe and plump and tasty, or the same tomatoes, preserved whole for the winter. Where I live in North America, it is almost impossible to find tomatoes good enough for a ragù, even at the height of summer, even the San Marzanos that local farmers raise from seed in a vain attempt to produce a Neapolitan flavor, so I almost always make ragù with canned tomatoes. Not all canned tomatoes are alike by any means; furthermore, just because tomatoes come from Italy doesn't make them better than American industrially produced ones. If you can't put up your own home-grown tomatoes, buy and taste several brands before settling on one that's right for you.

In any case, it is always better to make your own sauce from canned whole tomatoes than to use a canned tomato sauce. Canned sauces too often have artificial flavors and other undesirable ingredients that interfere with the pure taste of the tomatoes. You're going to spend some time and effort on this recipe, and for that reason alone you should be using the best ingredients you can find.

In addition to the tomatoes, you will need a single piece of meat, one with a good quantity of cartilage to give body to the sauce. You may use either beef (ask the butcher for a piece of chuck, the same cut you'd use for a pot roast—a boneless top blade roast or the so-called seven-bone roast, so called from the shape of the blade bone) or pork (shoulder is a good cut for this). Neapolitan recipes often call for veal, but the pale, anemic manufactured veal we get in North America is not appropriate (for this or anything else, in my opinion). If the meat doesn't naturally hold together in one piece, have the butcher tie it for you. You'll also need five or six pork ribs in one piece—but don't get so-called country-style ribs, which are more meat than bone. It's the bone and connective tissue that's important to enrich the ragù. If your butcher is the old-fashioned kind who sometimes has a piece of oxtail, add that to the meat selection as well; or consider a nice osso buco, a thick slice of shank, more bone than meat, if it is available. If you have an Italian pork butcher, ask for a piece of guanciale (gwan-CHA-lay)—cured pork cheek, which is very flavorful. Otherwise, substitute pancetta.

One other traditional meat addition is well worth considering if you can find it. That is a piece of pork rind, called in Italian *cotenne* or *cotiche,* which you may find in butcher shops in Italian neighborhoods. Often the rind will be rolled up and tied, making it easy to pull out of the sauce after you've extracted all its rich flavor and gelatinous qualities.

Because it takes a long time to prepare—the longer the better for this slow-cooked sauce—ragù is often made a day ahead and reheated and in fact seems to benefit from this treatment.

Jeanne Caròli Francesconi cautions readers of her magisterial *Cucina Napoletana* that ragù napoletano is not a simple sauce; rather "It is a ritual celebrated weekly in every Neapolitan family worthy of the name."

Ragù Napoletano

NEAPOLITAN MEAT SAUCE FOR PASTA

Traditionally, ragù is used to sauce spaghetti or rigatoni for a first course, while the beef or pork is thinly sliced and served as a second course with a little of the ragù to dress it. As an alternative, you may shred all or part of the meat, discarding the excess fat and the bones. Stir the shredded meat into the ragù to make a super-rich sauce for pasta.

MAKES ENOUGH FOR 3 POUNDS OF PASTA; 10 to 12 servings

3 tablespoons extra-virgin olive oil, or more if necessary	2 plump garlic cloves, chopped	1 teaspoon freshly ground black pepper
2 tablespoons pure pork lard or olive oil	½ cup chopped flat-leaf parsley	½ teaspoon freshly grated nutmeg
2 pounds boneless beef, pork, or veal in one piece	¼ pound pancetta or guanciale, diced	Two 2-inch cinnamon sticks
5 or 6 bony pork ribs	2 medium yellow onions (about 1 pound), halved and thinly sliced	Sea salt
1 piece oxtail or a bony veal shank (osso buco) if available	2 cups dry red wine	
1 large carrot, chopped	6 to 8 cups Basic Tomato Sauce (page 125)	
1 large green celery stalk, including leaves, chopped	1 tablespoon tomato extract, concentrate, or paste (optional)	

Combine 3 tablespoons of the olive oil and the lard in a large stockpot or soup kettle over medium heat. While the lard is melting, dry the meats thoroughly with paper towels, then add them to the fat in the pan and brown them on all sides, turning frequently. When the meats have developed a nice brown crust on all sides, remove and set aside.

Meanwhile, chop together the carrot, celery, garlic, and parsley to make a fine mince.

Add more oil to the pot if necessary to make about ¼ cup of fat. Stir in the diced pancetta and cook until the fat begins to run and the dice start to brown a little along the edges. Stir in the sliced onions, reduce the heat to as low as you can go and cook very gently, stirring frequently, and watching carefully to make sure the onions do not brown, until the onions have softened considerably, as long as 30 minutes. If the onions start to color, add a few tablespoonsful of water to the pot. When the onions are done, stir in the minced vegetables and continue cooking over low heat until the vegetables are all quite soft, another 15 minutes.

Return the meats to the pot, pushing them down into the softened vegetables. Add about ½ cup of the wine and cook uncovered, very gently, until the wine has almost evaporated. Keep adding half-cups of wine, letting each addition evaporate almost entirely before the next ½ cup is added. Turn the meats from time to time. This should be a very slow process, taking as much as 1½ to 2 hours.

While the wine is cooking down, prepare the tomato sauce if you do not have it already. Make the sauce from fresh tomatoes if you have available very ripe and flavorful local tomatoes, peeling and seeding them before cooking; otherwise, use canned tomatoes, or a combination of fresh and canned. If you wish, stir a spoonful of tomato extract into the tomato sauce to boost the flavor. Add black pepper, nutmeg, and cinnamon to the tomato sauce and bring to a simmer before adding to the ragù.

When all the wine has been added and left to evaporate, start stirring in the tomato sauce, again in increments of ½ to 1 cup. Cover the pan between additions and let each addition cook down, thicken, and darken to a dark, rusty mahogany before adding more. Again, this should proceed very slowly and take up to 1½ to 2 hours. When all the tomato sauce has been added, cover the pan with aluminum foil and then with the lid. Let the ragù continue to cook very, very slowly and gently for 1½ hours—use a heat diffuser if necessary to keep the heat as gentle as possible. You may add a little water from time to time if the sauce appears to be thickening too much.

When the ragù has finished cooking, the sauce will be dense and dark mahogany red in color and the meats will be fork-tender. Remove the meats from the sauce and set aside. If you wish, puree the sauce by whirling it in a blender or food processor or using a stick blender right in the pan. The stick blender is my preferred method since it gives the sauce a slightly pureed texture but still keeps some of the interesting chunkiness. Of course, you may also choose not to puree it and leave it as a chunky sauce—there are no rules or regulations about this. Taste and add salt if necessary.

Quick and Simple Ragù

Cooks in a hurry but looking for a richer, meatier sauce than the usual Sugo di Pomodoro often short-cut a ragù by browning ground meats and mixing them with the basic tomato sauce, making a quick ragù to serve with pasta for a family supper.

MAKES 3 CUPS SAUCE, enough for 6 servings of pasta

1 medium onion, finely chopped	¼ pound lean ground beef or veal	Sea salt and freshly ground black pepper
2 tablespoons extra-virgin olive oil	1 or 2 fresh chicken livers, chopped (optional)	¼ cup minced flat-leaf parsley or mixed fresh basil and parsley
1 medium carrot, finely chopped or coarsely grated	2 cups Basic Tomato Sauce (page 125)	
2 fresh Italian-style sausages		

Combine the onion, olive oil, and carrot in a heavy skillet over medium-low heat. Cook, stirring occasionally, until the vegetables are softened. Meanwhile, remove the casings from the sausages.

As soon as the vegetables in the pan are soft, raise the heat to medium and add the meats. Cook briskly, stirring constantly with a fork and breaking up the meats. If you are using chicken livers, crush them into the other meats with the fork. When the meats are brown and fragrant, stir in the tomato sauce. Taste for seasoning, adding salt and pepper. Cook slowly, covered, for about 30 minutes, or until the sauce has come together. Just before serving, stir in the minced herbs.

Ragù del Pastore

SHEPHERD'S RAGÙ

A Pugliese ragù is often made from a variety of meats—a little pork, a little lamb, a little veal. But when it's made with lamb alone, it's always called shepherd's ragù, for obvious reasons.

This is the sauce to be used for Calzoni di Ricotta con Ragù del Pastore (page 172), but it's also a great sauce for any of the homemade semolina pastas for which Pugliese cooks are said to have *una manina,* a gifted little hand. Favorite shapes include round, disklike *orecchiette;* long, oval *strascinate;* and *troccoli,* which are long, thin strings of pasta like spaghetti but square in section. The wooden rolling pins with regular sharp ridges that you sometimes come across in shops in Italian neighborhoods are specially made for cutting troccoli. You may also, of course, use this with a good grade of commercial pasta, such as Benedetto Cavalieri pasta from Puglia or Setaro pasta from Torre Annunziata on the Bay of Naples, both brands available in North American markets and by mail order (see Where to Find It, page 415).

In the Italian South, lamb ragù is made with a whole shoulder of very young lamb, weighing about 1½ pounds, including the bones, the collagen from which gives richness and body to the sauce. Such young lamb is almost impossible to find in North America unless you have access to a butcher in a Greek or Italian neighborhood, where baby or spring lamb is highly appreciated. If you can get a piece of lamb shoulder with the bones attached, even if it comes from an older animal, so much the better. You will need 1½ to 2 pounds; otherwise, make do with regular boneless stewing lamb from a good butcher or supermarket, in which case a pound will be sufficient. Trim away any excess fat and cut the boneless lamb into small pieces.

MAKES ENOUGH FOR 1½ TO 2 POUNDS OF PASTA; 8 servings

1 large or 2 medium yellow onions (about ¾ pound), halved and thinly sliced	1 cup dry red wine	1 tablespoon tomato extract, concentrate, or paste, diluted in ¼ cup hot water
¼ cup extra-virgin olive oil	One 28-ounce can plum tomatoes	Sea salt
1 pound lean boneless lamb or 1½ to 2 pounds on the bone, preferably shoulder	1 small dried red chili, crumbled, or to taste	2 bay leaves
	5 or 6 cloves	Freshly ground black pepper

In a saucepan large enough to hold all the ingredients, gently sweat the onion slices in the olive oil over low heat, stirring frequently, until the onion is very soft and just beginning to turn golden.

Push the softened onion to the sides of the pan and add the meat to the middle. Raise the heat slightly and cook, turning frequently, until the meat is brown on all sides and any liquid it gives off has evaporated. Add the wine, stirring to scrape up any brown bits from the bottom of the pan, and cook slowly until it has reduced to just a few tablespoons.

Drain the tomatoes, reserving the juice. Chop the tomatoes and add them to the meat, along with the chili, cloves, diluted tomato extract, and a pinch of salt. Stir to mix well. Lower the heat so that the sauce just bubbles very gently, stir in the bay leaves and several grinds of black pepper, and cover the pot. Leave over gentle heat for 2 to 2½ hours, adding the juice from the tomato can or boiling water from time to time to keep the sauce from becoming too thick. (You may add as much as 1½ cups of liquid before the sauce is done.) At the end of the cooking time, taste the sauce and adjust the seasoning. If the sauce seems thin, boil it down rapidly. If it is too thick, add a little boiling water and cook just long enough to meld everything together, about 5 minutes or so.

Remove and discard the bay leaves and cloves before serving.

Making Bread Crumbs

Sooner or later, any cook who plans on building a repertoire of southern Italian dishes discovers the virtue of a ready supply of bread crumbs. You can, of course, buy commercially packaged crumbs, and they are fine for many purposes—but don't bother with bread crumbs flavored with dried herbs or "Italian seasoning," whatever that is.

Fortunately, making bread crumbs is easy, especially with a food processor. Use stale country-style white bread, the kind that has good bready flavor and a lot of texture in the internal crumb. (Keep a bag of leftover bits of bread in the freezer, adding to it whenever you have an extra piece.) Italians call this *pane raffermo,* or "firmed-up bread," meaning bread that has lost a lot of its moisture but isn't too hard to slice. If the crusts of the bread are thick, cut them off, then slice the white crumb into big cubes. Add to the bowl of a food processor and process in quick pulses until the crumbs are the desired consistency.

This will give you "fresh" bread crumbs, ideal for soaking in water or milk and adding to meatballs or meat loaf recipes. Fresh bread crumbs can be frozen, sealed in a plastic bag or freezer container, until ready to use, but if they're not frozen, they should be dried before being stored—otherwise they will turn moldy. To dry bread crumbs further, spread them on a cookie sheet and toast them gently in a 350°F oven until golden; or brown them on top of the stove in a very small amount of olive oil, stirring constantly over medium heat until the crumbs are crisp and golden. Toasted or browned bread crumbs should keep well in a sealed jar or container without being refrigerated.

Spaghetti alle Olive Verde

SPAGHETTI WITH GREEN OLIVES AND LEMON ZEST

This Pugliese pasta is quick and easy, relying on the kinds of ingredients good cooks have on hand.

MAKES 4 TO 6 SERVINGS

3 to 4 tablespoons extra-virgin olive oil

2 garlic cloves, sliced

¾ cup fresh bread crumbs, preferably homemade (page 139)

¼ to ⅓ cup well-drained canned tuna, preferably oil-packed

2 tablespoons capers, preferably salt-packed, rinsed and drained

½ cup mixed flat-leaf parsley and fresh basil leaves

⅔ cup coarsely chopped pitted green olives (about 1 pound with pits)

Sea salt

Crumbled dried red chili

1 pound spaghetti

Grated zest of 1 lemon, preferably organic

Combine 2 tablespoons of the olive oil with the garlic in a small skillet and cook over medium-low heat for a few minutes, stirring frequently, until the garlic starts to turn golden. Remove the garlic slices from the oil and discard. Add the bread crumbs to the oil in the pan and toast, stirring frequently, until the crumbs are golden and crisp. Remove from the heat and set aside.

In a food processor, combine the tuna, capers, parsley, and basil with the chopped olives. Process briefly to make a coarse paste, then add 1 or 2 tablespoons of olive oil and process again. Taste and add salt if necessary (the olives may provide enough salt) and chili to taste.

Bring 6 quarts of water to a rolling boil, add sea salt and the spaghetti, and boil rapidly until the pasta is done. Drain, turn into a bowl, and dress immediately with the olive paste. Toss it to mix the paste throughout, then add the grated lemon zest and toss again. Finally, top the spaghetti with the toasted bread crumbs and serve immediately.

Lasagnette di San Giuseppe

ST. JOSEPH'S DAY PASTA

An old tradition links the feast of San Giuseppe (St. Joseph) on March 19 with mid-Lent festivals, a brief but joyful holiday reminding us that we're halfway to Easter—but still within the constraints of the Lenten fast. Pino Marchese, who grew up in the *centro storico,* the old town center, of Bari, the capital of the Region of Puglia, remembers the huge bonfires (*falò*) that were lit for San Giuseppe in the main piazzas of the old town, bonfires fed with all the wooden objects that had been discarded during the previous year—broken furniture, cracked wooden kitchen bowls, even the heavy wooden gates that swung open into family courtyards. Anything broken beyond repair became fuel for the San Giuseppe bonfire. The fires have become a thing of the past in Bari, but the feast continues to be celebrated with this dish—another illustration of the use of bread crumbs over pasta, this time, however, enriched with chopped toasted almonds. Lasagnette are not what we call lasagna pasta. Rather they are inch-wide strips of curly-edged ribbon pasta, but similar shapes will also do. If you can't find anything else suitable, use the widest tagliatelle or fettuccine available.

MAKES 4 TO 6 SERVINGS

¾ cup blanched almonds	Freshly ground black pepper	6 to 8 fresh basil leaves, shredded
½ cup extra-virgin olive oil	1 garlic clove, finely chopped	
1 cup fresh bread crumbs	1 small onion, finely chopped	Sea salt
8 to 10 anchovy fillets, coarsely chopped	1½ cups Basic Tomato Sauce (page 125)	1 pound lasagnette or similar pasta

Preheat the oven to 350°F.

Mix the blanched almonds with a teaspoon of the olive oil, tossing to coat the almonds with the oil, then spread the almonds on a baking sheet and transfer to the preheated oven. Toast until the almonds are golden, stirring occasionally—this should take 10 to 15 minutes and can be done ahead of time, even several days ahead if necessary. Transfer the almonds to a cutting board and chop them as fine as you can. (Don't be tempted by the food processor—it will grind some of the almonds to a paste while leaving others way too big for the dish.)

Add another teaspoon or so of oil to the baking sheet and toast the bread crumbs in the oven until they are golden brown and very crisp, about 10 minutes. Combine the crumbs with the almonds in a small bowl.

Place 2 tablespoons of the oil in a skillet over medium-low heat. Stir in the anchovies and cook, crushing the anchovies into the oil with a fork. Mix the anchovies and oil into the bread crumbs and almonds, add lots of black pepper, and set aside.

Add the remaining oil to the skillet and gently sweat the garlic and onion over low heat until they are soft and melting but not browned. Add the tomato sauce and cook for just 3 or 4 minutes to combine the flavors. Stir in the basil and set aside.

Bring a pot of lightly salted water to a rolling boil, drop in the pasta, and cook until al dente, 10 to 12 minutes. Drain and dress with the tomato sauce and half the bread crumb–almond mixture. Sprinkle the remaining crumb-almond mixture over the top and serve immediately.

Quick Pasta Ideas from la Dispensa

The *dispensa* is the pantry or dispensary, the place from which food is dispensed to the kitchen. In a southern Italian family, even in a Bari or Palermo apartment where the dispensa is a closet, there will surely be boxes of commercial pasta in various shapes and sizes, a jug or two of local olive oil, jars and cans of preserved tomatoes and anchovies in oil, braids of garlic and onions, dried oregano, a wedge of pecorino for grating, and perhaps half a prosciutto or a fat salami from the last visit to a cousin's farm—all the necessary ingredients for the quick assembly of a last-minute meal.

Often such a last-minute meal will consist of nothing but a big bowl of pasta (*pasta e basta*, they often say), truly the Italian fast-food invention of the last millennium. For getting a quick, easy, and satisfying meal into a lot of hungry mouths, nothing beats pasta.

You'll need a pound of dried pasta to make four to six servings—four if the pasta is the focus of the meal, six if it is served as a *primo,* or first course. Whatever shape you decide on, cook it in at least six quarts of rapidly boiling salted water. Cooking time depends on the pasta shape—obviously, very skinny vermicelli will cook more quickly than complex shapes like conchiglie (snails), farfalle (butterflies), or similar shapes. You're the best judge of when pasta is done to your liking. Drain the pasta, turn it into a heated bowl, dress rapidly, and send to the table.

PASTA AL CACIOPEPE: While the pasta is cooking, coarsely grate ½ to ¾ cup of pecorino toscano or pecorino sardo. (The pecorino romano available in U.S. supermarkets is usually of very poor quality and not recommended.) As soon as the pasta is drained, turn it into the heated bowl and toss with 2 tablespoons or more extra-virgin olive oil and the grated cheese. Top with lots and lots of freshly ground black pepper and serve.

PASTA AL LIMONE: While the pasta is cooking, prepare a good ½ cup of finely chopped fresh herbs—flat-leaf parsley and basil are indispensable, but with them you could also use a small amount of rosemary, some fresh thyme, and/or borage; other herbs, not common in the southern Italian kitchen but delicious in the dish, include tarragon leaves, or, even more unusual, lovage or lemon verbena. Along with the herbs, chop the zest only of a well-washed, preferably organic, lemon. Mix the juice of the lemon (about 3 tablespoons) with an equal quantity of extra-virgin olive oil and toss with the drained pasta and the herb mixture. Add salt and pepper, a very small amount of grated cheese if you wish, and send to the table.

PASTA ALLA BOTTARGA DI TONNO: Maria Titone, whose family makes the gorgeous Titone organic olive oil on its estate north of Marsala in Sicily, made this dish for me one day when I dropped in for lunch during the olive harvest. Bottarga di tonno is preserved tuna roe. (There's also bottarga di muggine, mullet roe bottarga, from Sardinia.) You may not keep bottarga in your dispensa, but it's worth considering. It's easy enough to find in fine food shops or by mail order (see page 415), and it keeps well—that's what it's meant to do.

To make the dish, grate enough bottarga to make about ¾ cup and cover it with 1 cup olive oil (extra-virgin, of course). While the water is boiling and the pasta is cooking, coarsely chop enough parsley leaves to make a loosely packed cup and dice 3 or 4 very ripe medium tomatoes—or use a dozen sweet little cherry tomatoes and simply quarter them. Mix all this together—bottarga, oil, parsley, and tomatoes—and toss with the drained pasta while it's still very hot. Add a lot of freshly ground black pepper and serve immediately.

Pasta col Pesto Trapanese

PASTA WITH TOMATO AND TOASTED ALMOND PESTO

For those who think pesto comes *only* from Liguria and *always* includes masses of basil and pine nuts, this delicious alternative, from Trapani, a fishing and salt port on Sicily's far western headland, will come as a surprise. Pounded nut sauces like pesto, Sicilian food authorities claim, are characteristic of the cuisine that evolved during the centuries of Arab control of Sicily. Trapanese cooks usually serve pesto with busiate, a short twisted pasta shape typical of the region; as far as I know, busiate are not available in North America, so I've suggested using fusilli instead.

Yes, you can make the sauce in a food processor, although the texture will be much better and more typical if you take the time to make it with a mortar and pestle.

MAKES 4 TO 6 SERVINGS

4 or 5 ripe tomatoes, peeled, seeded, and chopped	6 to 8 large fresh basil leaves, torn into small pieces	About 5 tablespoons extra-virgin olive oil
Sea salt	Freshly ground black pepper	1 pound curly pasta such as fusilli
½ to ¾ cup blanched almonds	Crumbled dried red chili (optional)	
2 garlic cloves, coarsely chopped		3 tablespoons dry bread crumbs

Sprinkle the chopped tomatoes with about a teaspoon of salt and set in a colander in the sink to drain excess liquid while you prepare the other ingredients. Preheat the oven to 350°F.

Spread the blanched almonds on a baking sheet and put in the preheated oven for about 10 minutes, checking frequently and stirring the almonds to make sure they toast evenly to a light golden brown. Be careful not to overtoast the almonds—dark brown almonds will make a bitter sauce. Remove and set aside to cool slightly, then chop with a chef's knife to a very fine texture.

In a large, heavy mortar, crush about ½ teaspoon salt and the garlic together to make a paste. Add the basil leaves and crush, turning the pestle against the walls of the mortar. When the basil has been fully incorporated, gradually add the chopped drained tomatoes, a few pieces at a time, crushing them into the sauce and adding black pepper to taste, red chili if you wish, and more salt if needed as you crush. The sauce should be thick and rather chunky. Stir in, without crushing them, the finely chopped almonds. Gradually, as if you were making a mayonnaise, mix in 3 or 4 tablespoons of olive oil in a thin thread, stirring constantly. By the time you finish, the sauce should be as thick as a homemade mayonnaise.

Bring at least 6 quarts of lightly salted water to a rolling boil. Drop in the pasta and let cook until done, 8 to 10 minutes.

Meanwhile, heat the remaining tablespoon of olive oil in a small skillet over medium heat and add the bread crumbs. Cook, stirring, until the crumbs turn brown and crisp. Remove and set aside.

When the pasta is done, drain thoroughly and turn into a preheated bowl. Mix in about half the pesto and top with the rest. Sprinkle the bread crumbs over the top and serve immediately.

Using a Mortar and Pestle

I sometimes have trouble convincing friends that the use of a mortar and pestle really makes a difference in the outcome of a sauce. I didn't believe it myself at first, and it was actually a Ligurian cook, Melly Solari of the Ristorante Ca'Peo in Leivi, who convinced me when she made a classic Ligurian pesto in her big stone mortar. Yes, it does take more time than whizzing sauces in the food processor, and for many things (mayonnaise, for instance) the food processor is actually an improvement over the old-fashioned mortar. But for pesto, whether the basil–and–pine nut variety from Liguria or the spicier tomato-and-almond kind from Trapani, you just can't beat the texture that you'll get from a stone or terra-cotta mortar, preferably one with rather roughened sides.

Don't just pound the pestle up and down over the contents of the mortar. Instead, stroke the pestle diagonally down the walls of the mortar. If you're right-handed, like me, you'll move in a countorclockwise direction; I imagine if you're left-handed, you'll find clockwise more comfortable. Keep stroking rhythmically and rotate the mortar as you do so; the crushed ingredients will blend naturally with the rest, and eventually you will have a most unctuous paste with a slight unevenness that seems to contribute mightily to the flavor of the sauce.

U Spaghett' Anatalina

NEAPOLITAN CHRISTMAS EVE SPAGHETTI WITH WALNUTS

Plump, fresh, and incomparably flavorful, walnuts from the Sorrento peninsula, just south of Naples, are renowned throughout Italy. The arrival of the annual harvest in Neapolitan markets and food shops is as much a harbinger of the Christmas season, when this walnut sauce is traditionally served, as is the opening of the sidewalk stalls along via San Gregorio Armeno in Spaccanapoli. There in the heart of the old city a market springs to life with hundreds and thousands of *figure*—molded and carved plastic, terra-cotta, wooden, or papier-mâché figures in a fantastic array of shepherds, magi, saints, iconic Holy Family images, modern-day politicians (Berlusconi is always popular), and film and pop stars (from Elvis to an eternally youthful Sophia Loren to the blind singer Andrea Bocelli). In the weeks preceding Christmas, these are eagerly bought and carried home to add to the personalities of the traditional Neapolitan Christmas *presepio* or crèche, which is more often a panorama of modern or nostalgic Naples than it is a depiction of Palestine in the Year One.

The Christmas Eve meal in Italy, as in other Mediterranean Catholic countries, is invariably meatless, a relic of what was once the Advent fast that stretched from December 1 to Christmas Eve. Fasting is no longer obligatory for the faithful, but many still observe the injunction to go meatless, especially on Christmas Eve.

MAKES 4 TO 6 SERVINGS

1 cup walnuts, the fresher the better	1 pound spaghetti	8 anchovy fillets, coarsely chopped
Sea salt	½ cup extra-virgin olive oil	½ cup minced flat-leaf parsley
	6 garlic cloves, finely chopped	

Preheat the oven to 400°F.

Spread the walnuts on a baking sheet and toast in the oven for several minutes, or until the nuts begin to release their fragrance. It's okay if the nuts turn a little golden, but don't let them turn deep brown. Remove from the oven and transfer to a kitchen towel spread out on a countertop. Rub the nuts together in the towel to remove and discard as much of the flaky skin as you can. Chop the nuts coarsely and set aside. (This can be done ahead, even several days ahead, and the chopped nuts stored in a tightly sealed canister or glass jar.)

When ready to cook, bring 6 quarts of lightly salted water to a rolling boil. Add the spaghetti and cook until almost al dente.

Meanwhile, finish the sauce: Set a saucepan large enough to hold the cooked pasta over low heat. Add the oil and garlic and cook gently, stirring occasionally, until the garlic starts to soften. Add the chopped anchovies and continue cooking, using a fork to mash the anchovies into the oil. Stir in the chopped walnuts and cook for about 1 minute.

When the pasta is almost al dente, remove about ½ cup of the pasta water and add it to the sauce. Let it simmer while you drain the pasta, then add the pasta to the walnut sauce, turnng to coat it well with the sauce as it finishes its last minute or so of cooking. Taste and add salt if necessary, although there may be sufficient salt from the anchovies.

Turn onto a warm platter, garnish with the minced parsley, and serve immediately.

Mostaccioli con Carciofi

MOSTACCIOLI WITH ARTICHOKES

Mostaccioli is a short, stubby pasta shape used in Calabria, and I have to confess I haven't found it much elsewhere. Use another shape instead—penne or farfalle, conchiglie (snails), or the little round wheels made by Benedetto Cavalieri, pasta makers in Puglia with a good distribution in North America.

MAKES 4 TO 6 SERVINGS

2 lemons	Sea salt and freshly ground black pepper	½ cup freshly grated pecorino or other hard aged cheese, plus more for serving
6 medium or 4 very large artichokes	1 teaspoon tomato extract, concentrate, or paste, diluted in ½ cup hot water	2 tablespoons minced flat-leaf parsley
2 tablespoons extra-virgin olive oil	1 pound short, stubby pasta	2 tablespoons minced fresh basil
1 ounce pancetta, diced	3 eggs	
1 medium yellow onion, finely chopped		

Use the lemons to prepare the artichokes as described on page 305, cutting each artichoke in half or, if very large, into quarters.

Put the olive oil in a skillet large enough to hold all the ingredients, including the pasta. Set over medium-low heat and add the pancetta. Cook until the pancetta releases its fat and starts to turn a little brown along the edges. Stir in the onion and cook gently until the onion is softened and golden but not brown. While the onion is cooking, cut the prepared artichokes vertically into thin slices. When the onion is soft, stir the sliced artichokes into the skillet. Add salt and pepper to taste and the diluted tomato extract and cook gently until the artichokes are tender, 5 to 10 minutes. (If necessary, occasionally add a ladleful of boiling water from the pasta pot to keep the artichokes from drying out. There should always be a small amount of liquid to coat the artichokes.)

Meanwhile, bring 6 quarts of water to a boil in a large pot. Add a generous pinch of salt and the pasta, and cook the pasta at a rolling boil until it is almost, but not quite, done. (It will finish cooking in the sauce.)

While the pasta is cooking, beat the eggs with the grated cheese. When the pasta is almost done, add a final ladleful of pasta water to the artichokes. Drain the pasta quickly and stir it into the artichoke sauce. Finish cooking the pasta in the sauce—it will take another 1½ to 2 minutes. When the pasta is tender, remove the skillet from the heat and immediately pour the beaten eggs over the pasta in its sauce, stirring vigorously to combine everything very well. The eggs will cook and thicken from the heat of the pasta and make a sauce. (If you've ever made pasta alla carbonara, you'll be familiar with the process.)

Stir in the minced fresh herbs and serve immediately, accompanied by extra cheese at the table.

Pasta alla Norma

PASTA WITH EGGPLANT AND TOMATOES

This, says cooking teacher Eleonora Consoli, is Catania's greatest dish, named for that town's most famous citizen, Vincenzo Bellini and his opera *Norma,* a bel canto tour de force first performed in 1831. The recipe doesn't date from Bellini's time but was offered as a tribute to him many decades later. It has since become a standard of orthodox East Sicilian cuisine. In the most traditional version, this is simply pasta dressed with a tasty tomato sauce and topped with cubes of fried eggplant and grated cheese. Eleonora's recipe is a little more elaborate, adding olives, pine nuts, capers, and basil. Ricotta salata is the cheese Sicilians use, and it should not be difficult to find. In its absence, however, use any hard aged grating cheese (caciocavallo, aged pecorino, parmigiano reggiano, or grana padano).

MAKES 4 TO 6 SERVINGS

1 pound eggplant (1 or 2 medium), cut into ½-inch cubes	2½ cups chopped peeled fresh tomatoes or well-drained canned plum tomatoes	2 tablespoons capers, preferably salt-packed, rinsed and drained
Sea salt	1 teaspoon sugar, more or less (optional)	½ cup fresh basil leaves, slivered
2 tablespoons extra-virgin olive oil, plus oil for frying	Freshly ground black pepper	1 pound spaghetti or other long, thin pasta
1 garlic clove, coarsely chopped	⅓ cup coarsely chopped pitted black olives (optional)	1 cup freshly grated ricotta salata or other hard aged cheese
	¼ cup pine nuts	

Toss the eggplant cubes in a colander with a liberal handful of sea salt. Set the colander in the sink and weight the eggplant with a plate and a can of tomatoes or other weight on top. Leave for 30 minutes to 1 hour, then rinse the eggplant thoroughly and dry with paper towels.

Meanwhile, heat about 2 tablespoons of olive oil in a saucepan and cook the chopped garlic over gentle heat until it is softened. Do not let it brown. Stir in the chopped tomatoes and raise the heat slightly so that the liquid in the tomatoes cooks quickly. Cook the tomatoes, stirring frequently, until they start to fall apart and make a chunky sauce. Taste the sauce and add sugar if it seems too acidic, along with a little salt and several grinds of black pepper. Stir in the olives, if you wish, along with the pine nuts and capers, and simmer for 5 minutes longer. Stir in the slivered basil. Once the sauce comes to a simmer again, turn off the heat and set the saucepan aside. (The sauce may be prepared well ahead of time and reheated when ready to serve.)

Add about an inch of olive oil to a deep frying pan or skillet and heat to about 360°F (a small cube of bread will brown in about a minute). Fry the eggplant cubes until golden on all sides, transferring to a rack covered with paper towels to drain. You may have to do this in several batches. (Do not add more oil while frying: If the temperature of the oil drops, the eggplant will absorb it like a sponge. Add more oil only when there are no eggplant pieces in the pan and let it reheat to 360°F before adding more eggplant.)

Meanwhile, bring 6 quarts of lightly salted water to a rolling boil. When all the eggplant has been fried, cook the pasta in the boiling water until it is al dente or done to your taste. Drain, turn into a warmed bowl, and immediately dress the pasta with the hot tomato sauce. Top with the eggplant, then sprinkle a small amount of grated cheese over it and serve immediately, accompanied by the rest of the cheese in a bowl.

VARIATION

Some Catanese cooks use a technique called *saltare in padella* to finish the pasta. Once the spaghetti is almost, but not quite, done, drain it and stir it into the pan with the tomato sauce. Cook briefly, just long enough to finish the pasta, then serve garnished with the fried eggplant and the grated cheese.

Maccheroni all' Ischitana

MACARONI FROM THE ISLAND OF ISCHIA

Tomatoes from the island of Ischia are born of a dry climate and raised in the salty air of the island—the ideal ambience for tomatoes with incomparable flavor. Try this recipe with local, garden-ripened tomatoes at the peak of the season, when their flavor impact will be greatest. Dip them in boiling water for 10 to 12 seconds, then lift the skin off with a sharp knife.

This dish is usually served at room temperature or a little warmer, not piping hot from the stove. Maccheroni, or macaroni, is a long, thin pasta that looks like spaghetti but has a hole in it. If you can't find maccheroni, by all means use spaghetti instead.

MAKES 4 TO 6 SERVINGS

3 tablespoons extra-virgin olive oil	¼ cup capers, preferably salt-packed, rinsed and coarsely chopped	Pinch of dried oregano
2 plump garlic cloves, minced		½ cup bread crumbs
6 anchovy fillets, coarsely chopped	⅓ cup coarsely chopped pitted black olives	1 pound maccheroni
2 pounds ripe tomatoes, peeled and coarsely chopped	Sea salt (optional)	¾ cup diced mozzarella, preferably buffalo-milk
	Pinch of crumbled dried red chili	½ cup torn basil leaves

Combine 2 tablespoons of the olive oil and the garlic in a skillet over medium-low heat. Gently sweat the garlic until it is very soft, but do not let it brown. Add the anchovies and mash them with a fork into the garlicky oil. Stir in the tomatoes, capers, and olives and cook about 10 minutes. Taste and add salt if you wish. Now stir in the chili and oregano and simmer for about 10 minutes. Add a little water from time to time if the sauce starts to stick.

Meanwhile, bring 6 quarts of lightly salted water to a rolling boil. In a separate small skillet, combine the bread crumbs with the remaining tablespoon of olive oil. Set over medium heat and toast the crumbs, stirring occasionally, until golden brown and crisp. Set aside.

Cook the pasta until done to taste, then drain. Or cook until slightly underdone, drain, and let it finish cooking in the simmering sauce. Mix the pasta and sauce together and stir in the cubes of mozzarella and some of the basil, along with a couple of tablespoons of crisp bread crumbs. Transfer to a serving dish and garnish the top with the rest of the bread crumbs and basil. Let rest for at least 15 minutes before serving.

Rotelle con Salsiccie e Porcini

WINTERTIME PASTA WITH SAUSAGES AND DRIED WILD MUSHROOMS

This recipe originated with Benedetto Cavalieri, whose grandfather established the pasta factory of the same name in Maglie, just south of Lecce in Puglia, in 1918. (After three generations, Pastificio Benedetto Cavalieri is now passing into the fourth, as Benedetto's son Andrea begins to help out with the family firm while continuing his university studies.) Cavalieri pasta is still made the old-fashioned way, with flour from hard durum wheat grown on the Tavoliere, the grain fields of northern Puglia, then shaped with bronze dyes that give a rougher surface to each pasta shape, allowing the pasta itself to "marry," as Italians say, with the sauce. Finally, it is dried slowly at relatively low temperatures so that the nutty flavor of the wheat remains intact. You can taste the difference—but you can see the difference too when you compare the pale rough surface of Cavalieri pasta with the shiny, glossy, toasted yellow exterior of more industrial products. (Benedetto Cavalieri pasta is available in North America at many gourmet stores. See page 415.)

In the Cavalieri kitchen, this dish is made with rotelle, wheel-shaped pasta. It's a complex shape, Benedetto says, meaning parts of it will be almost overcooked, other parts undercooked, and still others just right. "It's more interesting that way," he explained. Besides rotelle, other small, stubby shapes such as farfalle (butterflies) and lumache (snails) do well here.

Try to find fresh pork sausage that has no added flavors (such as garlic, cheese, or parsley).

MAKES 6 TO 8 SERVINGS

2 ounces dried porcini or other flavorful dried mushrooms	1/2 cup finely chopped flat-leaf parsley	2 bay leaves
1/4 cup extra-virgin olive oil	1/2 to 3/4 pound fresh Italian-style sweet (mild) sausage	Freshly ground black pepper
1 cup finely chopped onion		Sea salt (optional)
1/4 cup finely chopped celery	3/4 cup Basic Tomato Sauce (page 125)	1 to 1 1/2 pounds short, stubby pasta
1/2 cup finely chopped carrot		Freshly grated aged cheese for serving

Put the dried mushrooms in a bowl and cover them with very hot water. Set aside to soak for at least 30 minutes while you prepare the sauce.

Put the olive oil in a skillet large enough to hold all the sauce ingredients and set over medium heat. Stir in the onion, celery, and carrot. Set aside half the parsley to be used later as a garnish and stir the remaining parsley into the vegetables. Cook, stirring, until the vegetables are soft.

While the vegetables are cooking, remove the sausage from the casing. Break up the sausage meat with your fingers and distribute it all over the vegetables. Stir the sausage meat into the vegetables and continue cooking until the meat has lost its raw color.

Meanwhile, remove the mushrooms from their soaking liquid, *reserving the liquid.* Rinse the mushrooms quickly under running water to get rid of any residual earth clinging to them, then chop very coarsely and add to the skillet with the sausages, stirring to mix well.

Put a layer of paper towels in a sieve or colander and strain the mushroom liquid through the paper into a bowl. Add the filtered liquid to the skillet. Let it cook down briefly, then stir in the tomato sauce. Turn the heat down to a low but steady simmer. Add the bay leaves and lots of black pepper, cover the pan, and simmer for about 20 minutes. If the sauce seems too thick, add a small amount of boiling water. If it seems too thin, raise the heat slightly and boil away any excess liquid. When the sauce is ready, taste and add salt if necessary, though there may be sufficient salt in the sausages.

Bring about 6 quarts of water to a rolling boil and add a generous pinch of salt and the pasta. Stir the pasta with a long-handled spoon and boil it rapidly for 8 to 10 minutes.

Just before the pasta is done, add several ladles of boiling water to a large serving bowl to warm it. Turn the water out, then add a couple of ladles of the simmering sauce to the bowl. Drain the pasta in a colander and add to the bowl, mixing well. Spoon more of the sauce over the top and turn the pasta to mix. Serve the pasta with the remaining sauce spooned over the top. Garnish with the reserved parsley and serve immediately, passing the grated cheese at the table.

Oven-Baked Pasta Dishes (Pasta al Forno)

Pasta al forno is really another way of saying "pasta casserole," but it's been a couple of generations since casseroles were fashionable in North American kitchens. Pasta al forno, on the other hand, has never gone out of favor with southern Italian cooks. And with good reason. It's a dish that can be assembled ahead of time and baked at the last minute before service. Moreover, most oven-baked pasta dishes are capable of almost infinite expansion and contraction, from a little dish for one or two people to a big tray that will feed a crowd.

Pasta al Forno con Melanzane

OVEN-BAKED PENNE WITH EGGPLANT

Pugliese cooks always fry the eggplant before assembling the dish, but it's possible to cut down on the amount of oil used by baking the eggplant slices. See the note at the end of the recipe.

MAKES 6 TO 8 SERVINGS

2 pounds eggplant, sliced about ¼ inch thick	1½ cups Basic Tomato Sauce (page 125)	½ cup unseasoned dry bread crumbs
Sea salt	1½ pounds ripe fresh plum tomatoes, sliced about ¼ inch thick, or one 28-ounce can plum tomatoes, drained and coarsely chopped	Freshly ground black pepper
¾ cup extra-virgin olive oil (less if you are baking the eggplant)		⅓ cup grated pecorino or other hard aged cheese
1 pound penne or other short, stubby pasta		2 tablespoons coarsely chopped fresh basil

Layer the eggplant slices in a colander, sprinkling each layer liberally with salt. Weight the slices (a can of tomatoes on a small plate works well) and set in the sink to drain for 30 minutes to 1 hour, then rinse the slices under running water and pat dry with paper towels.

Heat the olive oil in a deep skillet over medium-high heat and fry the eggplant slices on both sides until they are golden brown, transferring them to a rack covered with paper towels to drain. Reserve the oil in the pan to use in the rest of the recipe.

Bring about 6 quarts of water to a rolling boil, add salt to taste and the pasta, and cook until the pasta is not quite done, rather firm in the center. Drain the pasta, transfer to a bowl, and immediately toss with 1 cup of the tomato sauce.

If you are going to bake this immediately, preheat the oven to 375°F.

Use about a tablespoon of the reserved oil to grease the bottom and sides of a baking dish—a 2½- to 3-quart soufflé dish will be fine. Layer half the tomatoes over the bottom and sprinkle with half the bread crumbs, plus salt and pepper to taste. Spread half the sauced pasta on top, then half the eggplant slices in a layer. Spoon about ¼ cup of the remaining tomato sauce over the eggplant and sprinkle with half the cheese and half the basil.

Add in layers the remaining pasta, eggplant, tomato sauce, cheese, and basil. (The dish can be made ahead to this point and set aside, covered with foil or plastic wrap, for up to 4 hours. Preheat the oven before baking.)

Top the dish with the remaining tomatoes and bread crumbs. Dribble ¼ cup of the reserved oil over the top and transfer the dish to the preheated oven. Bake for 1 hour.

Remove from the oven and set aside to rest for at least 30 minutes before serving.

NOTE: *To bake the eggplant instead of frying, preheat the oven to 450°F. Rinse and dry the salted eggplant slices, then set them on a lightly oiled baking sheet and, using a pastry brush, dab the top of each slice with a little oil. (You'll need only a couple tablespoons of oil for this, plus 5 tablespoons for the rest of the recipe, instead of ¾ cup.) Bake the eggplant slices until golden on both sides, about 15 minutes. (They should brown on both sides without being turned.) Proceed as directed.*

Ziti Alerti/Pasta al Forno con Ragù e Ricotta

BAKED PASTA WITH A RICH RAGÙ

"Almost no one makes this dish anymore," Michele Giugliano, co-owner and chef at the famous old Neapolitan restaurant Mimì alla Ferrovia, told me. Perhaps with good reason—it's one of those preparations ideally suited to grandmothers with plenty of time on their hands. Nonetheless, for special occasions it's well worth the effort, for it's one of the most amusing and delicious dishes I've ever tried.

In Napoli, where ziti is a favorite pasta shape, this is also known as *ziti alerti* or *ziti in piedi* ("alert" or "standing ziti") because the pasta shapes are set to stand on their ends in the baking dish. Now, ziti are rather long, round strands of pasta with hollow centers, similar to maccheroni but fatter. I can't imagine that even a Neapolitan grandmother would have the patience to stuff these things, so I make this with manicotti shells, first partially cooking the pasta to make it flexible and then cutting the tubes in half to make them shorter and easier to fill.

Of course, you could also make this as a conventional baked pasta dish, parboiling the pasta, mixing it with the ragù and ricotta, then topping it with more ragù and grated parmigiano reggiano and baking it until the top is nicely browned. But the following is the way, according to Dottore Giugliano, that old-fashioned nonne napoletane do it.

MAKES 8 TO 10 SERVINGS

¼ cup extra-virgin olive oil, plus a little oil for the dish	1 pound beef shank	6 tablespoons finely minced flat-leaf parsley
1 medium yellow onion, finely chopped	Sea salt and freshly ground black pepper	2 tablespoons finely minced fresh basil
2 garlic cloves, thinly sliced	1 cup dry red wine	1½ pounds manicotti
1 green celery stalk, finely chopped	One 28-ounce can crushed tomatoes	1¼ pounds ricotta cheese
1 medium carrot, finely chopped	1 tablespoon tomato extract, concentrate, or paste, diluted in ½ cup hot water	½ cup freshly grated aged pecorino or parmigiano reggiano
2 pounds very meaty ("country-style") pork ribs	Freshly grated nutmeg	
	Crumbled dried red chili	

Combine ¼ cup of the olive oil, the onion, garlic, celery, and carrot in a large, heavy saucepan over low heat. Cook gently, stirring often, until the vegetables are softened but not brown.

Push the vegetables out to the edge of the pan and add the pork and beef to the center. Add salt and pepper to taste, raise the heat to medium, and brown the meats on all sides, turning frequently. Add the red wine and combine with the vegetables. Let the wine cook until it is reduced by half, then stir in the crushed tomatoes and dissolved tomato paste. Add nutmeg and chili to taste (the sauce should have a little piquancy from the chili, but it should *not* be hot as an American chili sauce) and bring to a simmer. Cover and cook at a bare simmer for up to 3 hours, stirring from time to time and adding a tablespoon or so of boiling water if the sauce gets too thick and starts to stick. Remove the meats from the pan, scraping off the sauce. Shred the meats with a fork, discarding bones and fat, and return the meats to the sauce. Stir in 2 tablespoons of the parsley and the basil. Taste and adjust the seasoning if necessary. You should have about 8 cups of sauce. (The sauce may be prepared to this point and refrigerated for 3 or 4 days. Heat the sauce to simmering before continuing with the recipe.)

Preheat the oven to 375°F.

Bring a large pot of lightly salted boiling water to a rolling boil and add the manicotti. Partially cook the manicotti, for about 6 minutes, until the pasta is beginning to soften but is still firm in the middle, then drain and rinse under cool water to stop the cooking. Cut each manicotti in half crosswise to make 2 shorter tubes. You will need 40 half-tubes of pasta.

Lightly oil the bottom and sides of a 12-inch round baking dish. Spread about 1½ cups of the ragù over the bottom. Now stand the manicotti tubes upright in the ragù, wedging the tubes in closely together; some of the tubes may have split, but you should have about 40 standing tubes when you finish.

Mix 2 cups of the ragù with 2 cups of the ricotta. Taste and add salt if necessary. Carefully spoon the ragù-ricotta mixture into each manicotti tube, filling it about two-thirds of the way. Dollop a bit of the remaining plain ricotta on top of each tube. Spoon the remaining ragù (unmixed with ricotta) over the stuffed pasta and top with the grated cheese and remaining parsley. Cover the dish with aluminum foil, sealing the edges around the dish but tenting the foil slightly over the stuffed pasta. Set the dish in a larger roasting pan, then transfer to the preheated oven. Carefully pour about ½ inch of boiling water into the roasting pan. Bake for 15 minutes, then remove the foil, raise the oven temperature to 400°F, and continue baking for 5 to 10 minutes, or until the manicotti are lightly browned on top. Remove from the oven and let settle for about 10 minutes before serving.

Pasta di Grano Duro Fatta in Casa

HOMEMADE SEMOLINA PASTA

There used to be a myth that pasta was made with hard durum wheat semolina only in pasta factories, but the truth is that all over the south of Italy women make fresh pasta at home from semolina—perhaps not as often as they used to before so many Italian women had to go out to work, leaving them with precious little time to spend rolling out pasta dough, but still, for special occasions, nothing beats homemade pasta, even if everyday pasta most often comes from a box.

I am not going to tell you how to make *pasta all'uovo*, the rich, egg-based pasta made with regular all-purpose flour that is a glory of northern Italian cooking, because there are plenty of cookbooks that do exactly that, including my own, *The Essential Mediterranean*. But you can also make semolina pasta, either the purist version with no eggs or with a few eggs added to the dough, as many people do (see the variation). Pasta dough with eggs in it has more elasticity and can be rolled out to a thinner sheet than dough without eggs. I confess that I often add a couple of eggs when I'm feeling a little anxious about how things are going to turn out. But for normal days, full of self-confidence, here's how it's done.

MAKES ENOUGH PASTA FOR 6 TO 8 SERVINGS

2¼ cups semolina	Sea salt

Put 2 cups of the semolina in a mixing bowl and make a well in the center. Dissolve a big pinch of sea salt (1 to 2 teaspoons) in ⅔ cup of warm water. Slowly, using a little at a time, pour the salty water into the flour, gradually mixing until all the water has been added. (You may need a little more water or a little more semolina, depending on the weather and the ambient humidity.)

Knead the pasta in the bowl for a few minutes. You will feel the semolina granules start to soften and relax. Once the dough is well mixed, turn it out onto a wooden board. If it feels stiff, brush a little water onto the board with your fingers and knead it into the dough. On the other hand, if it feels too loose and sticky, scatter just a tablespoon or two of semolina on the board and knead it in. Continue kneading for about 10 minutes, or until the dough has reached a soft, silky texture. Cover the dough with plastic wrap or an inverted bowl and set aside to rest for 30 minutes. It's important to cover the dough well to keep it from drying out.

When you're ready to roll out the pasta, divide it in half and keep the half you're not working under wraps. Roll the pasta out into the thinnest possible sheet. You may use a pasta rolling machine, if you wish, and roll the pasta up (or down) to the #5 setting, but it's quite impossible to roll this kind of pasta into as thin a sheet as you can do with an egg-based dough. Cut the pasta into whatever shape you need and transfer it to spread-out kitchen towels, lightly strewn with semolina, to dry slightly before cooking.

VARIATION

To make an egg-based pasta, stir 2 eggs into the semolina before you start adding water. Because of the liquid in the eggs, you will need much less water. Dissolve the salt into just ⅓ cup of warm water; you can always add more water later if necessary.

Ciceri e Tria Salentino

PASTA WITH CHICKPEAS AND A GARNISH OF FRIED PASTA

From the Salento Peninsula, the tip of the heel of the Italian boot, this combination is exemplary. *Ciceri* is a dialect word for chickpeas, and *tria* comes from an ancient Greek word for pasta, *itrion*, perhaps the original of all the pastas made from durum wheat. The combination of boiled and fried pasta is unusual and intriguing—one vegetarian friend, to whom I served this dish, insisted that I had put fried bacon on top. Soak the chickpeas the day before to soften them up before cooking.

MAKES 6 TO 8 SERVINGS

1½ cups dried chickpeas, soaked for 6 hours or overnight	1 medium yellow onion, quartered	Homemade Semolina Pasta dough (page 159)
2 garlic cloves, crushed with the flat blade of a knife	2 bay leaves	Extra-virgin olive oil for deep-fat frying
	1 celery stalk, coarsely chopped, including leaves	1 small dried red chili

Drain the soaked chickpeas and transfer them to a saucepan with enough fresh water to cover them by about 1 inch. Add 1 crushed garlic clove, plus the onion, bay leaves, and celery, and bring to a simmer. Cover the pan and simmer gently over low heat until the chickpeas are very tender, about 40 minutes (but cooking time will vary depending on the age of the chickpeas). Add boiling water from time to time if necessary. The legumes should always be covered by about an inch of water.

Meanwhile, roll out the pasta. Divide the dough in half and keep the part you're not working with covered. Roll out the dough on the board into a circle, as thin as you can make it. Or put the dough through a pasta machine, gradually decreasing the space between the rollers. Once the dough is as thin as you can get it, slice it into long, straight noodles, about ½ inch wide. Drape the pasta over a rack or arrange it on clean kitchen towels and leave to dry briefly—15 to 30 minutes.

When the chickpeas are very tender, start to assemble the dish. First separate out about a third of the pasta to be fried. Put 1 inch of olive oil in a saucepan or a deep frying pan over medium heat and toss in the remaining garlic clove and the red chili, broken in half. As the oil warms up, the garlic will start to brown. Before it is completely brown, remove it from the oil, along with the chili, and discard. Add the pasta to the hot oil, a few strips at a time. Quickly fry the pasta until it is crisp and brown. Transfer to a rack covered with paper towels to drain.

Remove the bay leaves from the chickpeas and discard. Raise the heat under the chickpeas to medium-high, adding boiling water to keep them covered to a depth of 1 inch. Gently stir the remaining, unfried pasta into the chickpeas and cook until the pasta is done, 5 to 7 minutes. When the pasta is al dente, remove the pan from the heat and serve immediately, without draining and with all the thick soupy juices intact. Garnish each bowl with a generous handful of the fried pasta.

The Fastest Orecchiette in the World (L'Orecchietta più Veloce del Mondo)

Onofrio Pepe is a tireless, unpaid promoter of his hometown, Altamura, a beautiful walled city of Renaissance palaces and medieval churches that sits high in the midst of the rolling grass plains of the Alta Murge of central Puglia. Not that Altamura needs much promotion. The town, which dates back to 1230, when Emperor Frederick II established it on the ruins of an ancient acropolis, is widely acclaimed throughout Italy as the home of the best bread in the entire country.

Altamura bread, dense, chewy, richly colored from the golden semolina of which it is made, is well worthy of its reputation, but the cooks of this region, where durum wheat has been cultivated since antiquity, are also famed as pasta makers. This is not the egg-rich pasta of northern Italy; rather, like the bread, it's a dense, chewy pasta, made from the hard durum grown across the uplands of the Murge surrounding Altamura, as well as in other parts of southern Italy. This pasta takes many forms, but one of the best known is orecchiette, or little ears, disks of pasta stretched with a knife, then flipped gently over the thumb to make a little hat or ear in which to capture the sauce.

And that leads me back to Onofrio, who had the idea a few years ago of promoting local cuisine with a contest to determine the maker of *l'orecchietta più veloce del mondo,* the fastest orecchiette in the world. It was in December, a restful season when the major harvests are done, the fields have been sown with winter wheat, and the end-of-the-year festivities are on the near horizon. At Masseria San Giovanni, an imposing old farming estate transformed into a hotel and restaurant outside the walls of Altamura, a crowd gathered around the 16 contestants, all women of varying ages except for one man, a pensioner who had taken up cooking as a hobby. Each contestant was given a kilo (2.2 pounds) of semolina kneaded into a dough with the correct amounts of water and salt, nothing more. At a long table they faced the television cameras and throngs of supporters, each contestant holding a blunt-edged paring knife, the only tool necessary for the job—and presumably blunt-edged so they wouldn't risk stabbing one another in the fury of the contest.

Ready, steady, go—and off they went, fingers flying, as they quickly kneaded, rolled, chopped off disks of pasta dough, stretched them gently with the knife blade, then nimbly flipped them over their thumbs and dropped them in a pile in front of themselves. At first they were lighthearted, but their faces grew grim as time wore on and the chants of the two clock-watching referees intensified. Who could make the most? Who could make the best? Who could make the thinnest and most delicate? Clearly, these were questions whose answers might well cancel each other out.

As the gong struck, an audible sigh went up from the crowd. Now it was time to count—and time for the jury to begin its own contest, because of course the woman who made the most (891 orecchiette in one hour) didn't actually have a very fine hand: her orecchiette were lumpy and misshapen. And the first to finish? She was done with her dough in forty-five minutes but made only 715 orecchiette. And the woman who made 865 orecchiette—well, she didn't finish at all, and at five minutes past eight, she was still steadily churning them out! The jury members (I knew because I was one, albeit reluctantly) began shouting among themselves. In the end Onofrio announced a great number of honorable mentions—one to the male pensioner just for appearing, one to a gum-chewing teenager for the same, special mentions for fine quality to three other women, and finally first prize to Antonia Pugliese, who made 847 orecchiette in forty-seven minutes, very fast, very regular, but just possibly, the jury suggested, a little too thick.

Orecchiette alla Barese/Orecchiette con Cime di Rape

ORECCHIETTE WITH BROCCOLI RABE (RAPINI)

I have included directions for making the orecchiette by hand, but I suspect you will be more likely to buy ready-made orecchiette. If so, look for a Pugliese brand of pasta—Benedetto Cavalieri is one; another is Pastificio Benagiano, located in Puglia but using wheat grown in nearby Basilicata.

Cime di rape are what is called *broccoli rabe* or *rapini* in American produce markets. This remarkable vegetable is both delicious, with a pleasantly bitter bite, and nutritious, with all the healthful properties of the cabbage family, loaded with vitamins, antioxidants, and other good things. If necessary, substitute ordinary broccoli, but the dish will lack the complex flavors of bitter broccoli, sweet garlic and oil, salty anchovies, and pungent chilies.

MAKES 4 GENEROUS SERVINGS

Homemade Semolina Pasta dough (page 159) or 1 pound store-bought orecchiette	6 anchovy fillets, coarsely chopped	1 pound (2 bunches) broccoli rabe (rapini), rinsed and trimmed
½ cup extra-virgin olive oil	1 small dried red chili, coarsely chopped, or ½ teaspoon crumbled dried red chili, or to taste	Sea salt and freshly ground black pepper
2 garlic cloves, thinly sliced		

Divide the pasta dough into 8 more or less equal portions. Roll each portion out into a long snake not more than 1 inch thick, then cut the snake into thumbnail-sized pieces, similar to small gnocchi. Using the thick side of a table knife, drag each of these across a rough wooden surface to elongate it and give it a rough texture on one side.

These are what is called *strascinate* or *stacchjoddi*. To turn them into orecchiette, flip each one gently over your thumb to make a little hat or "ear." When done, you should have about 50 orecchiette, or enough for 4 generous servings. Set the finished pasta aside on a lightly floured cloth to dry for about 30 minutes.

While the pasta is drying, prepare the rest of the ingredients: Put the olive oil in a small skillet over medium heat and add the garlic. When it begins to soften and turn color (don't let it brown), add the anchovies. Cook over medium heat, crushing the anchovy fillets with the back of a fork to make a coarse paste in the skillet. When the anchovy fillets are well mashed into the oil, add the chili. Stir to mix well and set aside in a warm place until ready to use.

Coarsely chop the leaves and stems of the broccoli rabe, leaving the little flower clusters intact. Bring a large pot of lightly salted water to a rolling boil, drop in the broccoli rabe pieces (and the pasta if you're using store-bought), and boil, uncovered, for 12 to 15 minutes, or until the pasta is al dente.

If you're using homemade pasta, add it to the water after the broccoli has cooked for 3 minutes, and boil with the broccoli rabe until the pasta is just tender—7 to 9 minutes longer.

Drain the pasta and broccoli rabe in a colander, transfer to a heated bowl, and toss with the anchovy-garlic sauce. Taste and add salt if necessary (the anchovies may give it plenty of salt) and lots of black pepper. Serve immediately.

Gran'Arso

There is one type of orecchiette that you will not, I think, find in North America, because it's hard enough to find even in Puglia. If you go to Puglia, however, especially in the North, in the great wheat-growing Tavoliere around the city of Foggia, you may find on a restaurant menu a reference to *orecchiette al gran'arso* or *al grano brusciato*. This is a peculiar local usage that dates from times when, after the annual harvest of durum wheat and the burning of fields to rid them of chaff, poor people gleaned whatever bits of wheat remained behind and used them to make into flour. Years later, long after poor people had ceased to glean and fields to be burned, the burnt, smoky flavor of the flour became desirable; nowadays, the grains of wheat are burned deliberately, and, as with so many items in the meager larder of poor countryfolk, *gran'arso* has arrived on the tables of even rather fancy restaurants. It's a curious-looking dish, because the pasta made from the burnt flour has a grayish tinge, but the smoky flavor goes well with tomato sauces made with pancetta or prosciutto.

Easter in southern Italy is a magical holiday, one that leads observers and believers alike back to the origins of Christian faith and the old religion from which Christianity evolved. Death and resurrection are age-old themes in the Mediterranean, so it is not surprising to find rituals that have little to do with Catholic orthodoxy—like the Palm Sunday blessing of olive branches that may later be used to encourage the wheat to grow strong and straight. What is celebrated at this moment is the miracle of spring and the new planting season. Many foods, many dishes associated with the great feast, give testimony to these ancient associations. One such is this Easter dish from Basilicata. Sagne Chine (the name means *lasagna ripiena,* "stuffed or filled lasagna") is full of the good things of springtime, from peas to artichokes to fresh eggs and cheese. The mozzarella can be either cow's milk (*fior di latte*) or buffalo-milk (*mozzarella di bufala*). (For some other Easter dishes, see Torta Rustica, page 63, and Pastiera di Grano, page 401.)

MAKES 8 TO 10 SERVINGS

Homemade Semolina Pasta dough made with eggs (page 159)

3 large artichokes

1½ lemons for preparing the artichokes

1½ pounds fresh peas, shelled

Sea salt

½ pound fresh wild mushrooms, sliced, or 1 to 2 ounces dried porcini

4 eggs

½ pound fresh Italian-style sausage, hot, sweet, or both

1½ cups grated hard aged cheese: pecorino, caciocavallo, or parmigiano reggiano

Freshly ground black pepper

Dry bread crumbs, if necessary

Unbleached all-purpose flour

About ¾ cup extra-virgin olive oil

½ pound lean pork tenderloin, diced small

2 cups Basic Tomato Sauce (page 125)

¼ cup finely minced fresh basil

1 teaspoon ground chili pepper or crumbled dried red chili to taste

2 celery stalks, including leaves, minced

1 medium yellow onion, minced

¼ cup finely minced flat-leaf parsley

2 bay leaves

½ pound fresh mozzarella, sliced

Make the pasta dough as described, mixing the flour with the eggs and salt water to make a firm dough. Knead until the dough is smooth, then set aside to rest, covered, while you prepare the rest of the ingredients.

Prepare the artichokes as described on page 305, using 1 of the lemons. Cut each artichoke in half before adding it to a bowl of acidulated water.

Bring a small pan of water to a rolling boil, add a good pinch of salt, and toss in the peas. Cook, uncovered, for 5 to 7 minutes, or until the peas are soft but not mushy. Drain and set aside.

If you are using dried mushrooms, put them in a bowl of very warm water to soak. If using fresh mushrooms, rub them clean, trim them, and slice.

Set aside one of the eggs. Add the remaining eggs to a small pan of cool water and bring to a boil. Cook until they are hard—8 to 10 minutes—then run under cold water and peel. Slice lengthwise into wedges.

Remove and discard the sausage casing and combine the meat in a bowl with about ½ cup of grated cheese. Add the remaining egg, along with plenty of pepper. Mix very well, using your hands, then, wetting your hands in cool water, shape the mixture into 20 to 24 meatballs. If the mixture is too liquid to shape easily, add ¼ to ½ cup bread crumbs. When all the meatballs have been formed, sprinkle flour on a plate and roll the meatballs in the flour to coat them lightly. Add about ½ cup olive oil to a small saucepan and set over medium heat. When the oil is hot, add the meatballs and brown them on all sides, turning frequently. (You may have to do this in 2 or more batches.) As the meatballs brown, transfer them to a rack covered with paper towels to drain.

Discard all but about 2 tablespoons of the oil from the pan and return to medium heat, adding the diced pork. Cook, again turning frequently, until the pork bits are brown on all sides. Remove and set aside.

Heat the tomato sauce in a small saucepan and, when it is simmering, stir in the basil and chili to taste. Set aside but keep warm.

In a clean skillet, combine the celery and onion with 2 tablespoons fresh olive oil and set over medium-low heat. Cook, stirring occasionally, until the vegetables are very soft, then stir in the parsley.

While the vegetables are cooking, drain the reconstituted dried mushrooms, reserving their soaking water. Rinse the mushrooms and slice. Filter their soaking water through a sieve lined with a paper towel to remove any earth. When the vegetables in the pan are soft, add the mushrooms, whether dried or fresh. As the mushrooms start to cook down, cut each half artichoke into 4 to 6 smaller pieces and add to the mushrooms. Stir to mix well and add about ¼ cup of the strained mushroom-soaking liquid or fresh water to the pan, along with the bay leaves. Bring to a simmer, cover, and cook very gently for about 15 minutes, or until the artichoke pieces are soft. Remove from the heat and stir in the peas. Add the juice of the remaining ½ lemon and set aside. (The recipe may be prepared to this point up to a day ahead, but the ingredients should all be at room temperature and the tomato sauce should be just below simmering before you continue with the recipe.)

Divide the pasta dough in half, keeping the half you're not working with well covered. Roll the dough out on a lightly floured board and cut it into wide strips (sagne or lasagne), about the width of your knuckles and twice as long. Set the pasta strips aside on kitchen towels to dry slightly.

Bring about 6 quarts of water to a rolling boil, and when it is boiling, add a good pinch of salt. Now parboil the lasagne strips: Add about 6 strips at a time to the boiling water and let them boil for about 1½ minutes, just enough to soften them. Spread kitchen towels on a countertop and, as you remove each strip with a slotted spoon or ladle, lay it on the towels to drain.

Preheat the oven to 350°F.

Use a little olive oil to grease the bottom and sides of a 9 × 12 baking dish, then line the bottom of the dish with about a third of the lasagna strips. Spread a third of the tomato sauce over the lasagna layer and distribute over it half the meatballs, half the pork dice, half the sautéed vegetables, and half the hard-cooked egg. Distribute a third of the mozzarella slices on top and a third of the remaining grated cheese.

Set another layer of lasagna strips on top and continue with a third of the tomato sauce and the remaining meatballs, pork, vegetables, and eggs, then add another third of the mozzarella and grated cheese. Finally, cover the top with the remaining lasagna strips. Spread the remaining tomato sauce on top, carrying it out to the edges of the dish and covering the lasagna strips completely. Distribute the remaining mozzarella over the top and sprinkle with the remaining cheese.

Finally, dribble olive oil over the top of the cheese and transfer the dish to the preheated oven. Bake for about 30 minutes, or until the top of the dish is golden brown. Remove and let sit for about 10 minutes to consolidate the flavors, then serve.

According to the Florentine food historian Kyle Phillips (you can find him talking about Italian food on italianfood.about.com), cannelloni are a modern invention. Phillips points out that they don't exist in Pellegrino Artusi's *La scienza in cucina* (first published in 1891), but they do in Ada Boni's *Talismano della felicità* (first published in 1929), two cookbooks that are, or were, as widely used in Italy as *The Joy of Cooking* has been in North America. So somewhere in between those two dates cannelloni came into existence—possibly according to somewhat suspect folklore, invented in 1924 precisely, in the kitchen of the Hotel Cappuccini in Amalfi.

By now, however, cannelloni are standard banquet fare, served at just about every wedding reception in southern Italy and many in the Center and North, as well they ought to be, for cannelloni are delicate and delicious, perfect for wedding feasts. In southern Italy they are, naturally enough, more often made with semolina rather than with all-purpose flour.

I give two different recipes for filling, one with meat and one without.

MAKES 12 CANNELLONI; 6 servings as a primo piatto or first course

For the pasta, follow the recipe for egg-based pasta on page 160, using 1 cup of semolina and 1 egg. Prepare the pasta dough and set it aside, covered, to rest for at least 30 minutes.

Select one of the following two fillings, either the meat for Cannelloni al Ragù, or the ricotta that follows it for Cannelloni alla Ricotta. Have the filling prepared before you roll out the pasta.

For filling and baking, follow the directions for each separate filling.

Filling for Cannelloni al Ragù

Note that the ragù must cook for several hours. It may be prepared a day or more in advance and reheated when you're ready to make the cannelloni. Or, if you have leftover ragù, use that instead.

About 1¾ cups ragù sauce (page 134)

About 1 cup shredded meats from preparing ragù

1 small fresh spring onion, chopped

1 teaspoon extra-virgin olive oil, plus oil for the baking dish

About ¾ pound fresh peas, shelled (½ to 1 cup shelled peas)

3 to 4 ounces fresh (young) pecorino or provolone, diced (½ cup)

¾ cup freshly grated hard aged cheese: pecorino, caciocavallo, parmigiano reggiano, or grana padano

Ground or crumbled dried red chili (optional)

½ pound cow's milk mozzarella, very thinly sliced

Have the Neapolitan ragù ready, with the pureed ragù sauce separate from the shredded meats. Chop the shredded meats on a board to a fine texture, then transfer to a bowl.

Combine the chopped spring onion with the teaspoon of olive oil in a small saucepan. Set over low heat and cook gently until the onion softens, then stir in the peas. When the peas start to sizzle gently, add boiling water to cover and cook over medium heat until the peas are tender. Drain and add the peas and onion to the shredded and chopped meat. Add the diced pecorino and ¼ cup of the grated cheese. Stir in about ¾ cup of the ragù sauce. This should be sufficient to make a mixture that will hold together well. Taste the mixture and adjust the seasoning if necessary, adding a good pinch of chili.

When ready to prepare the cannelloni, roll the pasta out into a broad circle, as thin as you can possibly make it. Cut the pasta into 12 rectangles approximately 5 × 2½ inches. Bring a large pot of water to a rolling boil, add a good pinch of salt, then add the cannelloni rectangles—for greater convenience, you may do this in 2 or more batches. Cook the pasta rectangles until barely al dente, pliable but not yet soft enough to eat—1½ to 2 minutes in all. Retrieve them from the boiling water with a slotted spoon and drain on kitchen towels spread on a countertop. Let them dry, but do not leave them for more than half an hour or so before stuffing them or they will get stiff again.

Preheat the oven to 450°F.

Use olive oil to grease generously the bottom and sides of a baking dish about 8 × 11 inches. Use ¼ cup of the remaining ragù sauce to distribute over the bottom of the dish.

Now lay out a prepared pasta rectangle on a board or other work surface. Spoon 2½ to 3 tablespoons of the meat-pea mixture down the long side of the rectangle and roll it up like a loose, hand-rolled cigarette—or more like a cigar. As each pasta roll is done, set it in the dish—they can be set very close, with the long sides wedged together. When all the cannelloni are done, layer thin slices of mozzarella over the top, then spoon on the remaining ragù sauce and sprinkle with the remaining grated cheese.

Dribble the top generously with olive oil and transfer to the preheated oven. Bake for 20 minutes, or until the top is bubbling and blistering brown. Remove and let rest for about 20 minutes before serving.

Filling for Cannelloni alla Ricotta

Note that if you omit the prosciutto, you'll have a very acceptable vegetarian (not vegan) first course or a main dish if you wish.

½ pound cow's milk mozzarella, diced	1 cup grated mild pecorino or parmigiano reggiano	2 cups Basic Tomato Sauce (page 125)
1 pound whole-milk ricotta, preferably sheep's milk, well drained	¼ cup minced flat-leaf parsley Sea salt and freshly ground black pepper	¼ cup slivered fresh basil ½ teaspoon crumbled dried red chili
¼ pound prosciutto, diced (optional)	Extra-virgin olive oil for greasing the baking dish	
2 eggs, lightly beaten	and dribbling on top	

Combine the mozzarella, ricotta, prosciutto, and eggs in a bowl. Stir to mix well, then add ½ cup of the grated cheese and the parsley. Taste for salt (sometimes the cheese will be sufficiently salty), then add it, if you wish, along with plenty of pepper.

Have the precooked pasta rectangles ready, as described on page 170.

Preheat the oven to 450°F. Use olive oil to grease generously the bottom and sides of an 8 × 11-inch baking dish. (Note that no sauce goes in the bottom of the dish, unlike in the Cannelloni al Ragù.)

Bring the tomato sauce to a simmer and stir in the slivered basil and chili.

One by one, lay the precooked pasta rectangles out on a board or work counter. Spoon 2½ to 3 tablespoons of the prepared filling down the long side and roll the rectangle up, like a loose, hand-rolled cigarette—or like a cigar. As each roll is finished, set it in the dish—they can be set very close, with the sides wedged together. When all the cannelloni are done, if you have leftover filling, dab or spread it over the top of the cannelloni, then spoon the tomato sauce all over the cannelloni—you may not need all the sauce. Sprinkle with the remaining grated cheese and dribble generously with olive oil. Transfer the dish to the preheated oven. Bake for 20 minutes, or until the top is bubbling and browning slightly. Remove from the oven and set aside for 10 to 20 minutes before serving.

Calzoni di Ricotta con Ragù del Pastore

CALZONI OF SWEETLY SPICED RICOTTA WITH A PEPPERY LAMB RAGÙ

Domenico Maggi, a fine Pugliese chef and cooking instructor who heads up Italy's team for the annual culinary Olympics, often does guest stints at the Culinary Institute of America. I've adapted the following recipe from one he made while teaching Pugliese dishes at the CIA's Greystone campus in California. As this dish shows, "Mino" Maggi is something more than a first-rate chef—he is also thoroughly grounded in the treasured culinary traditions of his native region. I added eggs to the pasta dough to be able to roll it out as thin as possible; if you prefer to make an eggless dough like Chef Maggi (and like most Pugliese cooks), you will need to use more water to make up for the missing eggs, as directed on page 159.

If you can get sheep's milk ricotta, it will give the calzoni a more authentic flavor. For another flavor booster, grind a piece of cinnamon stick and a dozen or so cloves in a spice grinder or coffee mill until fine and use in place of preground packaged spices.

Note that the lamb ragù must be prepared in advance since it should cook for at least 2½ hours. It may also be made several days ahead and refrigerated until ready to heat and serve. The ricotta will also benefit from being drained overnight in a fine-mesh sieve to get rid of excess whey.

MAKES 45 TO 50 CALZONI; 8 servings

1¼ pounds whole-milk ricotta, well drained	1 egg beaten with 1 teaspoon water to seal the calzoni	Sea salt
1 egg plus 1 egg yolk	Semolina for the pasta tray	Grated hard aged cheese— pecorino, caciocavallo, or parmigiano reggiano—for serving
1 teaspoon mixed ground cinnamon and cloves	Homemade Semolina Pasta, made with 1 egg (page 159)	
1 tablespoon sugar	Unbleached all-purpose flour for the work surface	
Grated zest of 1 lemon, preferably organic	Ragù del Pastore (page 137)	

Using a wire whisk, beat together the ricotta, whole egg, and egg yolk until the mixture is smooth and creamy. Add the spices, sugar, and lemon zest and beat to mix thoroughly. Set aside.

When you're ready to make the calzoni, have the egg wash ready and strew semolina over a platter or tray on which to set the finished pieces. Divide the pasta dough in half, keeping the half you're not working with under a bowl to prevent it from drying. Lightly flour a wooden board or other work surface and roll out the pasta dough until it is very thin—less than ⅛ inch.

Using a cookie cutter or a wineglass, cut out circles 4 to 5 inches in diameter from the rolled-out dough. (You should be able to get 20 to 25 circles from each half of dough.)

Drop about a teaspoonful of the ricotta filling in the middle of each circle, but slightly off center. Lightly paint the edge of the circle with the egg wash, fold it over to make a crescent, and press the edges together, using a fork or your fingers to make a tight seal. As you finish each crescent, transfer it to the platter or tray to rest. (The crescents may be made an hour or so ahead of time without any damage if they are covered with a lightly dampened cloth.)

When ready to cook, bring the lamb ragù to a simmer. Bring about 6 quarts of salted walter to a rolling boil and add half the calzoni. Let them cook until tender all the way through—about 5 to 7 minutes.

Meanwhile, layer some of the lamb ragù over the bottom of a heated serving bowl. When the calzoni have finished cooking, lift them out of the pot using a slotted spoon. Transfer the cooked calzoni to the serving bowl and spread more ragù over the top. Cook the remaining calzoni and add them to the bowl. Turn all the remaining ragù over the calzoni and stir very gently to mix. Serve immediately, passing the grated cheese separately.

Pasta colle Sarde

PASTA WITH SARDINES AND WILD FENNEL

Another of the many recipes associated with the feast of San Giuseppe, this Sicilian dish is truly an extraordinary complex of flavors—humble peasant flavors like wild fennel and cheap sardines, together with glamorous saffron, pine nuts, and raisins. It's no longer restricted to the March 19 feast but is served throughout the spring and has become an emblem of Sicilian cuisine.

I must confess that I publish this recipe with the expectation that most readers will not be able to reproduce it. You can't really make pasta colle sarde in North America unless you happen to have fresh sardines and fresh wild fennel, and both at the same time. Cultivated Florentine bulb fennel and canned sardines just won't do, no matter how you tweak the recipe. I include the recipe here as a matter of record, because it's an important dish, as well as for those lucky souls who live in parts of the country—California, for instance—where wild fennel brightens hillsides with its mustard-yellow blossoms. If you can get fresh sardines at the same time, you are lucky indeed, and this recipe is for you.

In Sicily, this is made in early spring, when the wild fennel shoots are tender and green. If more mature fennel is used, the tough stems must be discarded, leaving only the tender green tops, which can be snipped easily with a paring knife, and the fronds. (Do not harvest wild fennel from the roadside, where it often grows; it may well be contaminated by automobile pollution.)

At the great wine estate of Regaleali in the center of Sicily, Monzù Mario, the family chef of the Tasca d'Almerita family, served pasta colle sarde as a simple pasta with a sauce, using long pasta such as bucatini. Other Sicilian cooks often make it as a pasta al forno, an oven-baked pasta, cooking short, stubby pasta—rigatoni or ziti, for instance—until not quite done, then dressing it with the sauce and baking it in the oven to finish.

To toast bread crumbs, simply stir them in a skillet over medium heat until golden brown and crisp. Remove from the heat and set aside.

3 or 4 big bunches of wild fennel, including the feathery green tops, or enough to make 4 packed cups sliced fennel	1 large onion, coarsely chopped	Salt and freshly ground black pepper
1 pound fresh sardines	4 anchovy fillets, chopped	½ cup unbleached all-purpose flour
Pinch of saffron threads	2 tablespoons tomato puree	1 pound pasta, either bucatini or short, stubby pasta like rigatoni
About ¾ cup extra-virgin olive oil	¼ cup dry white wine	About ½ cup toasted coarse bread crumbs
	2 tablespoons golden raisins	
	2 tablespoons pine nuts	

Snip the tender stalks and fronds of the wild fennel into pieces about an inch long. Use only the tender part that can be cut easily with a paring knife. If you have to saw the stalk to cut it with the knife, it's too tough. Rinse the fennel well under running water. You should have about 4 well-packed cups of greens.

Bring a large pot of water to a rolling boil and drop in the fennel. Boil for 15 to 20 minutes, or until the thickest pieces are easily pierced with the tip of a knife. While the fennel is cooking, prepare the sardines. Cut off the head and tail of each sardine, pulling out the entrails as you do so. Slit along the belly and open the sardine. Gently pull out the backbone and cut away any prickly fins, but don't worry about getting every last little bone. Sardine bones are soft and fine and won't be any problem in the sauce. Cut each sardine into 2 fillets. When all the fish are prepared, rinse the fillets very quickly in cool water. Set aside a fourth to a third of the fillets to be fried and chop the rest into bite-sized pieces. Pat the sardines dry with paper towels.

Drain the fennel but *do not discard the cooking water*—this should yield about 2 cups of drained greens.

Remove about ½ cup of the cooking water and add the saffron to it. Set aside to steep.

As soon as it's cool enough to handle, chop the fennel coarsely. In a medium skillet, heat 2 to 3 tablespoons of olive oil and sauté the chopped fennel over medium heat until it absorbs the oil and starts to give off a pleasant aroma. Remove the fennel from the skillet and set aside.

Add 2 to 3 more tablespoons of olive oil to the skillet and set over medium-low heat. Add the onion and cook gently, stirring frequently, until the onion is soft and golden but not brown. Stir in the anchovy bits and press them with a fork to mash them into the sauce. Stir in the tomato puree and wine and simmer for 2 to 3 minutes. Add the chopped sardines to the sauce and cook, stirring, until they have turned opaque, then stir in the chopped fennel, mixing well. Add the raisins, pine nuts, and saffron water to the sauce along with salt and pepper to taste. Simmer very gently while you fry the reserved sardine fillets and cook the pasta.

Dry the remaining fillets once more with paper towels, then lightly coat them in flour. Heat about ¼ cup of olive oil in a small skillet over medium heat, and when it is hot, brown the fillets on both sides. Transfer to a rack covered with paper towels to drain. Make sure you have a fillet to top each serving.

Add enough water to the remaining fennel water to make 6 quarts. Bring to a boil and add salt.

If you are going to serve this as a simple pasta with sauce, add the pasta to the boiling water, cook until done to taste, drain well, and dress immediately with the hot fennel and sardine sauce. Garnish with the fried fillets and serve immediately, sprinkling with toasted bread crumbs.

If you wish to make pasta al forno, preheat the oven to 325°F. Use a little more oil to grease the bottom and sides of a 2½- to 3-quart baking dish. Sprinkle three fourths of the bread crumbs generously all over the inside of the greased dish.

Boil the pasta vigorously until it is almost, but not quite, done. Drain thoroughly and immediately mix all of the pasta with half of the sardine-fennel sauce. Transfer half of the mixed pasta to the prepared baking dish and top with half of the remaining sauce. Add the remaining mixed pasta and arrange the fried sardine fillets over the top, then top this off with the remaining sardine-fennel sauce. Sprinkle with 2 tablespoons of bread crumbs and dribble a little more olive oil over the whole. Place in the preheated oven and bake for about 30 minutes, or until the top is bubbly and starting to brown.

Remove and set aside for 5 or 10 minutes to let the flavors develop and the dish cool down slightly, then serve.

Penne al Pesce Spada

PENNE WITH A SWORDFISH RAGÙ

The best recipes for swordfish always seem to come either from Messina in Sicily or from Reggio Calabria on the mainland, which stands to reason since the best swordfishing in the Mediterranean is in the straits of Messina that divide these two provinces. Although this recipe is said to come from Sicily, I'd be willing to bet you can find the like in any of the little seafood restaurants that dot the coast from Reggio north up to Pizzo and beyond, all good swordfishing waters once upon a time, before the big fish began to get smaller and fewer.

MAKES 4 TO 6 SERVINGS

½ cup extra-virgin olive oil	½ cup dry white wine	1 small eggplant, diced
1 medium red onion, minced	2 pounds ripe tomatoes, preferably plum tomatoes, peeled, seeded, and chopped	1 pound penne or similar short, ridged pasta
1 garlic clove, minced		Leaves from 1 small bunch of fresh mint, slivered
½ cup minced flat-leaf parsley		
1 pound fresh swordfish, diced into ½- to 1-inch cubes	Sea salt and freshly ground black pepper	

Add ¼ cup olive oil to a skillet and set over medium-low heat. Add the minced vegetables and as soon as they start to sizzle slightly, add the swordfish dice. Cook, turning and stirring, until the fish dice start to change color. Add the wine, raise the heat, and cook rapidly until the wine has reduced to a couple of tablespoons. Stir in the tomatoes, add salt and pepper to taste, and cook for about 30 minutes, stirring occasionally. If the tomatoes start to stick to the bottom of the pan, stir in a few more tablespoons of wine or hot water.

Meanwhile, pat the eggplant dice dry with paper towels. Heat the rest of the olive oil in another skillet and saute the eggplant dice until brown on all sides. Remove from the oil and drain on paper towels.

Bring 6 quarts of water to a rolling boil, then add salt and the penne. Cook for about 7 minutes, until the penne are not quite done. Drain and add to the pan with the swordfish. Let the penne finish cooking in the sauce, then transfer to a heated serving bowl and garnish with the fried eggplant dice and slivered mint. Serve immediately.

Pasta del Principe

SPAGHETTI WITH GREEN HERBS AND CRUMBLED TUNA

I found this quick and easy pasta dish in the Monte Iblei, the mountainous region inland from Siracusa in southeastern Sicily, although no one could tell me why such a humble dish would be called "the prince's pasta." It leads to romantic daydreams of some rustic Cinderella preparing this for a hungry prince and thereby winning his heart, but that is not a very likely Sicilian story.

MAKES 4 TO 6 SERVINGS

¼ cup chopped mint leaves	⅓ cup dry bread crumbs, preferably homemade	Grated zest of ½ lemon, preferably organic
¼ cup chopped flat-leaf parsley	¼ cup extra-virgin olive oil, preferably from the Monte Iblei	1 pound spaghetti
2 garlic cloves, chopped		Freshly ground black pepper
Sea salt	⅓ cup drained canned tuna, preferably oil-packed	¼ cup finely chopped toasted almonds
2 or 3 anchovy fillets, chopped		

Combine in a mortar the mint, parsley, and garlic with a small pinch of salt. Work together to make a creamy paste, as you would a pesto (see page 145). Add the anchovies and continue working until the anchovy bits are incorporated. In a small saucepan, toast the bread crumbs with 1 tablespoon of the olive oil, stirring, until the crumbs are crisp and golden brown. Remove from the heat and set aside.

In a serving bowl large enough to hold the pasta, break up the tuna with a fork to make a coarse paste, as if you were making tuna salad. Blend in the herb-anchovy mixture, along with the remaining olive oil, using only as much oil as you need to make a thick sauce. Stir in the lemon zest. If you are going to be using the sauce right away, add the bread crumbs now. If not, wait until the pasta is done before adding the bread crumbs; otherwise they may get soggy. Taste and add more salt if necessary and several grinds of black pepper.

Bring 6 quarts of water to a rolling boil, add a tablespoon or so of salt, and turn in the spaghetti. Cook until the pasta is done. Just before draining the pasta, remove a ladleful of hot pasta water and stir it into the sauce in the bowl. Drain the pasta and quickly turn into the sauce, stirring and tossing. When the pasta and sauce are well mixed, sprinkle with the almonds and serve immediately.

Spaghetti al Pescatore Calabrese/Spaghetti du Piscaturi Calabrisi

CALABRIAN FISHERMAN'S SPAGHETTI WITH A FRESH SEAFOOD SAUCE

Similar fresh seafood pastas are made all up, down, and around Italy's long, long coastline, the ingredients varying with the daily catch. What marks this one as particularly Calabrian is the addition of green olives, capers, and red chili along with the merest brush of tomato. If you want to emphasize the Calabrian nature of the dish, add plenty of chili.

In Italy, this would be served with the mussels and clams in their shells. Americans may find that a little awkward, so I've suggested discarding the shells and simply adding the meaty insides to the stew to finish cooking.

Please don't feel that this can be made only with the ingredients listed here. If you can't find Manila clams, for instance, simply increase the amount of mussels or shrimp. If you can't find fresh squid, add about ½ pound of sea scallops, cut into smaller pieces. You could even make this with all mussels or all clams if you wish.

MAKES 6 SERVINGS

1 pound mussels in their shells

1 pound small Manila clams in their shells

1 medium yellow onion, finely chopped

2 garlic cloves, finely chopped

3 tablespoons extra-virgin olive oil

1 medium squid, cleaned

½ pound shrimp, peeled and cut into bite-sized pieces

About ¼ cup pitted green olives, coarsely chopped

2 heaping tablespoons capers, preferably salt-packed, thoroughly rinsed and drained

Sea salt

Crumbled dried red chili

1 tablespoon instant flour

½ to 1 cup dry white wine

1 tablespoon tomato extract, concentrate, or paste, diluted in ¼ cup hot water

1 pound spaghetti

½ cup coarsely torn fresh basil leaves

¼ cup minced flat-leaf parsley

Clean the mussels and clams very well, brushing them under running water to get rid of any earth or sand that clings to them. The shells should be tightly closed—discard any that gape open or that feel suspiciously heavy for their size, an indication the mollusk is probably full of mud.

Transfer the mussels and clams to a saucepan that will hold them all in no more than 2 or 3 layers. Set over medium heat, add about ¼ cup of water, and cover the pan. Cook the bivalves, shaking the pan from time to time, until they are all open. Any that fail to open after 10 or 15 minutes should be discarded.

Remove the pan from the heat and, using tongs, remove the mussels and clams and set aside. When cool enough to handle, remove the meats and discard the shells. Filter the liquid left in the bottom of the pan very carefully through several layers of cheesecloth to rid it of any sand, then set aside.

Combine the onion and garlic with the olive oil in a heavy saucepan large enough to hold all the ingredients, including the pasta. Set over medium heat and gently cook the vegetables until they start to change color, but don't let them get really brown.

Bring a large pot of water to a rolling boil for the pasta.

Rinse the squid and slice the hood into rings. Cut the tentacles lengthwise into 6 pieces. Add the squid to the vegetables in the pan, along with the shrimp pieces, olives, and capers. Sprinkle with salt and chili to taste. Stir in the instant flour and add ½ cup of wine. Raise the heat slightly and let the wine almost evaporate—there should just be a few tablespoons of liquid left in the bottom of the pan. Stir in the diluted tomato concentrate. If the sauce is still very thick, add more wine. Remove the sauce from the heat, but keep it warm while you cook the pasta.

When the pasta water comes to a rolling boil, add a good big pinch of salt. Add the spaghetti and cook for about 6 minutes.

Meanwhile, add the clams and mussels to the sauce, with about ½ cup of their cooking liquid. Stir in the basil and parsley, return the sauce to low heat, and simmer for 3 minutes, no more.

Drain the spaghetti and immediately add to the pan in which the seafood is cooking. Let the pasta finish cooking in the pan, about 3 minutes, stirring, tossing, and swirling the pan to mix all the flavors together well. Remove from the heat and serve immediately.

Spaghetti al Nero di Seppia

BLACK SPAGHETTI WITH A SQUID INK SAUCE

It's not always easy to find squid (calamari, seppie, etc.) that still have their silvery ink sacs intact, but when you do come across them, it's worth buying in quantity. Use what you need to make this recipe, but clean the rest and freeze them. You can remove the ink sacs and freeze them all together, if you wish, in a plastic freezer bag.

Occasionally you might come across frozen squid ink at fancy fishmongers, but I find the usually astronomical price such an absurdity that I cannot be persuaded to buy it. On the other hand, you might look for dried squid ink, such as that produced in Sicily at the Campisi plant in Marzamemi (www.specialitadelmediterraneo.it). It lacks the well-developed flavor of fresh squid ink, but it makes an acceptable substitute for this dish or for an equally delicious risotto al nero di seppia.

MAKES 6 SERVINGS

½ pound whole squid with ink sacs attached	1 pound ripe fresh tomatoes, peeled, seeded, and chopped, or 1 cup canned plum tomatoes, drained and chopped	1 pound spaghetti
¼ cup extra-virgin olive oil		Ground or crumbled dried red chili
3 garlic cloves, coarsely chopped		¼ cup finely minced flat-leaf parsley, plus a little parsley for garnish (optional)
½ cup dry white wine	Sea salt	

Carefully clean the squid by pulling out the interiors. Amid the innards you will see a small silvery sac that contains the squid ink. Remove this, without cutting into it, and set it aside. Discard the innards. Rinse the squid hoods (mantles) and tentacles and slice into pieces ¼ to ½ inch thick.

Hold the reserved ink sacs over a small saucer. Using scissors, cut a slit at one end and gently squeeze the few drops of ink into the saucer. Set aside. (The squid may be cleaned well ahead of time, but if you are not going to prepare the recipe right away, cover the ink thoroughly with plastic wrap to keep it from drying out.) It may look like very little, but, believe me, a little goes a long way.

In a saucepan large enough to hold the cooked pasta with its sauce, heat the olive oil and gently sweat the garlic until it is soft but not brown. Remove the garlic with a slotted spoon and set aside. Raise the heat under the pan, and when it is medium-hot to hot, add the squid pieces.

Cook quickly, stirring, until the squid pieces are golden. Add the white wine and continue cooking over medium-high to high heat while the wine evaporates to a few spoons of liquid, then stir in the tomatoes, reserved garlic, and salt. Lower the heat to simmer and cook gently for about 20 minutes to soften the tomatoes and tenderize the squid.

Meanwhile, bring a large pot of lightly salted water to a rolling boil. Cook the spaghetti, timing it to have almost finished cooking by the time the squid sauce is ready. At that moment, stir the red chili, parsley, and reserved squid ink into the sauce. Drain the pasta and turn it into the squid sauce. Let the pasta finish cooking for a minute or two in the sauce, then serve it, garnished, if you wish, with a few sprinkles of minced parsley.

Cùscusu Trapanese

COUSCOUS FROM TRAPANI

Odd as it may seem, couscous actually has a long history on the island of Sicily, especially along the western coast, where a strong connection with North Africa goes back at least to the Carthaginians. And why not, since couscous is really just another form of pasta, prepared in a slightly different manner, given a slightly different shape, and steamed rather than boiled?

If couscous was a technique developed in North Africa (although not by Carthaginians), as many food authorities claim, it must have been transmitted thence to Sicily. As with most questions about the history of pasta, however, nothing is certain. French historian Marcel Aymard traced couscous in Sicily back at least to the sixteenth century, when, he said, it appeared regularly in Palermo accounts. The nuns of the Convent of San Salvatore enjoyed couscous for their Christmas feast, Aymard found, in the late seventeenth century, at a time when pasta and couscous were both considered holiday dishes, not everyday meals. Since Christmas is a major feast, the nuns most likely were not eating their couscous with seafood; possibly they had a sweetened version with toasted almonds and pistachio nuts, such as the one Sicilian food authority Giuseppe Coria describes as prepared to this day at the Cistercian convent of the Santo Spirito near Agrigento.

Cooks familiar with North African couscous will find the Sicilian version different both in the way it is made and in the way it is cooked. One Italian cookery writer refers to the preparation of couscous as *"un'impresa disperata."* I would not go so far as to call it a desperate undertaking, but it is not a dish for cooks in a hurry, requiring, as it does, time and patience in notable quantities. For those like me, however, who really enjoy taking a day off from the run of the mill and passing time in the kitchen making something unusual and truly delicious well, this is for you.

But if you don't have the time and still want to try the recipe, you may simplify the process considerably by using commercially available couscous. Despite what it says on the couscous box, however, it will need at least an hour of cooking and another thirty minutes of resting in its sauce.

Making couscous by hand is by no means as laborious as it is often said to be, but you will need to use durum wheat semolina, in the coarsest grind you can find. (In Trapani, shops sell a very coarse grind called *semolato*.) A flat-bottomed bowl with sloping sides, like something in which you might serve fruit, is a useful piece of equipment. The Sicilian equivalent, a *mafaradda*, made either from wood or from terra-cotta, is intended specifically for the *incocciata*, or shaping, of the little grains of couscous.

For cooking the grains, it is helpful but not mandatory to have a couscoussière (*cuscusera* in Sicilian). Franco–North African couscoussières, usually made of aluminium, are available from Sur la Table, Williams-Sonoma, and other mail-order purveyors (see Where to Find It, page 415), but I should point out that a traditional Sicilian cuscusera is made of terra-cotta, both the bottom pignatta, which holds the liquid, and the top part, with the holes in it, which holds the actual couscous. Apart from that detail, it works in exactly the same way as a North African couscoussière—the steam from the boiling liquid rises through the holes and steams the couscous that sits on top.

You can also improvise a cuscusera, as many cooks do, with a colander that sits snugly into the pot in which the liquid boils. It is most important, however, that the couscous itself come in contact *only* with the steam, *never* with the boiling liquid. Whether you use a proper cuscusera or an improvised one, when it comes time to cook, you must seal the edge where the top pot or colander joins the lower pot that holds the liquid. This is easily done: Make a simple paste of flour and water and roll into a long snake, then use this as caulking between the two pots to keep the steam from escaping. The steam will then be forced through the holes of the top pot or colander and up through the couscous.

Although I've heard of different versions of Sicilian couscous (with a puree of dried favas, with a duck and lentil broth, with pork and cauliflower, for example), as well as the sweet couscous from Agrigento, in my own experience, couscous in Trapani, on the island of Favignana, and in other parts of western Sicily is invariably served with seafood—fish or shellfish or sometimes both together. Unlike North African couscous, which is usually steamed over a stew that will be served with the grains, in Sicily the couscous and its sauce are cooked separately—just like pasta—and then brought together when it's time to serve them. The couscous itself steams over an aromatic bath of bay leaves and lemons, sometimes saffron too, but the bath is discarded when the couscous is done.

Cooks like Rosa Ponzio at El Pescador, on the island of Favignana, and Pino Maggiore, chef-owner of Cantina Siciliana in downtown Trapani, make a savory seafood broth that is used to dress the couscous once it is cooked. Rosa uses more of the same broth to make a seafood stew, which she serves as a second course following the couscous. Pino, on the other hand, likes to serve fish, shrimp, or calamari rings, crisply fried in olive oil, on top of the brothy couscous. In any case, more broth is passed in a pitcher for diners to add at the table.

The recipe describes how to prepare and steam Sicilian-style couscous, whether handmade or commercially available. The couscous may be served with its garnishing Brodo di Pesce (Seafood Broth, page 250) and an almond pesto (recipe follows) as a first course, perhaps followed by a plain roasted or grilled fish. Be sure to have enough Brodo di Pesce ready—you will need 5 cups for the couscous.

For a richer presentation, serve the couscous with a Ghiotta di Pisci Siciliana, an abundant seafood stew (page 251), garnished with the almond pesto.

TO MAKE THE COUSCOUS FROM SCRATCH	About ¼ cup extra-virgin olive oil	FOR THE ALMOND PESTO
4 cups semolina, the coarser the better	Freshly ground black pepper (optional)	1 egg
		Sea salt
2 teaspoons sea salt, dissolved in ¾ cup warm water	6 to 8 bay leaves, or more if necessary	½ cup coarsely chopped toasted almonds
About 2 tablespoons extra-virgin olive oil	2 lemons, each cut into 8 pieces	4 or 5 garlic cloves, crushed
		½ to ¾ cup extra-virgin olive oil
Otherwise, use 4 cups commercial couscous	Pinch of saffron threads (optional)	Juice of ½ lemon
1 medium yellow onion, very finely minced (1 cup)	About ½ cup all-purpose flour to make a paste to seal the pot	½ cup slivered fresh basil leaves
½ cup very finely minced flat-leaf parsley	5 cups Brodo di Pesce (page 250)	½ cup coarsely chopped toasted almonds

To make couscous from scratch, spread the semolina out in a wide, flat-bottomed bowl. Have a smaller bowl with salty water in it at one side. Assuming you are right-handed, dip your left hand in the water and dribble it all over the semolina. Spread your right palm out, fingers stretched, and gather your fingers together again, rubbing the semolina gently as you do so. Keep dipping one hand and rubbing and gathering with the other, always moving in the same direction and gathering in the dryer grain from the sides; gradually the semolina will form up into very small balls—the couscous. Don't use too much water at one time as the balls will turn into big lumps, which you don't want at all. It will take 10 to 20 minutes to work in all the salty water; if you run out of water before you feel the process is complete, simply add a little more. Finally, take a tablespoon or two of olive oil in the palm of your hand and, using both hands, rub it lightly into the couscous in the same manner. When the oil has been worked in, continue to rub the couscous lightly between your palms to reduce any lumps to little balls—the gesture used is as if you were lightly scrubbing laundry. In the end, the couscous grains should be as consistent in size as possible, but keep in mind that part of the charm of homemade couscous is in its very irregularity.

Spread the couscous in a thin layer over a large tray or a baking sheet to dry slightly for at least 30 minutes, tossing and rubbing it every few minutes to keep it from clumping together.

Sicilians usually cook the couscous right away after this initial drying. If you are using commercially made couscous, you should dampen it lightly with up to ½ cup warm water sprinkled over it and raked through with your fingers, then spread it on a tray to swell for about 20 minutes as it absorbs the water.

Transfer the dampened couscous to a bowl and combine with the onion and parsley. Dribble about ¼ cup of olive oil over the grains and sprinkle them, if you wish, with plenty of black pepper. Take up a handful of couscous and rub it lightly between your palms. Continue doing this, a handful at a time, until the oil, onion, and parsley are all well incorporated into the couscous.

Add enough water to the lower pot of the cuscusera to come within 2 inches or more of the top pot so that when the water comes to a boil only steam, but not the boiling water, will come into contact with the top. Add the bay leaves and the lemon wedge to the water, squeezing the lemons slightly. Add the saffron if you wish. Set over medium-high heat and bring to a boil.

Couscous that has been treated with water and oil usually holds together pretty well, but if you're afraid the couscous might drop through the holes in the top part of the cuscusera, cover the holes with more bay leaves. Transfer the treated couscous to the top part of the cuscusera and set it over the boiling water to steam. Mix a little water into the flour to make a paste and roll it into a thin snake. Use it to caulk the join between the bottom and top parts of the cuscusera.

When the couscous has steamed for 30 minutes, use a fork to fluff the grains gently, tossing them so that what was on the top goes to the bottom and vice versa. Leave the couscous to steam for another 30 minutes and then repeat. Test the couscous: It should be close to done but might need another 15 to 30 minutes to arrive at the right soft, tender consistency.

While the couscous is steaming, bring 5 cups of prepared Brodo di Pesce to a simmer; keep the broth warm for dressing the couscous.

Make the almond pesto: Add the egg to the bowl of a food processor with a pinch of salt. Process to combine the yolk and white, then, with the motor running, add the almonds and garlic. As soon as the mixture is homogenous, start adding the oil, as you would with a mayonnaise, a few drops at a time with the motor running. As the sauce starts to incorporate the oil, you may add it more liberally, but never more than a thin stream. At the end it should be as thick as mayonnaise. Whizz in the lemon juice and taste, adding a little more salt, olive oil, or lemon juice if necessary. Transfer to a bowl to serve with the couscous.

When the couscous is done, tip it out onto a serving tray and gently dribble the warm Brodo di Pesce over it, tossing with a fork to make sure the grains absorb as much as possible. (You may not need to use the entire amount of seafood broth, but use as much as the couscous will absorb and keep the rest warm to pass when you serve the couscous.) Cover the tray with kitchen towels and keep in a warm place for 20 to 30 minutes. When ready to serve, garnish the couscous with slivered basil and chopped toasted almonds and pass the bowl of almond pesto to spoon on top. Or reserve the basil, almonds, and almond pesto and serve the couscous with Ghiotta di Pisci Siciliana (page 251).

Beans, Rice, and Other Grains

The distinction between rice and beans in the Mezzogiorno, it always seems to me, is this: Rice is urban, while beans are more characteristic of the countryside. But in cities like Palermo, Napoli, and Bari, beans are also on the humble tables of the poor. As they have always been, for legumes are the cheapest source of good protein and poor cooks all over the Mediterranean—indeed, all over the world—have always relied on beans to fill hungry bellies.

The most popular beans in southern kitchens are some of the oldest foods known to humankind. I'm thinking of the lentil pottage for which Esau sold his birthright, of the lentils and favas that fed the builders of the pyramids, and of chickpeas, evidence for which archeologists turn up in even more ancient contexts. Fave, lenticchie, ceci, and that little known bean the cicerchia (*Lathyrus sativus*) have been fundamental in the Mediterranean diet for thousands of years. The combination of beans like these with wheat products—originally bread, nowadays more often pasta—has, as vegetarians know, important nutritional synergy, the two together being greater than the sum of their parts. Does this account for the generally good health of southern Italian bean-eaters? Put in the context of the overall diet, including olive oil, plenty of fresh vegetables, and seafood and meat in small quantities, apparently it does.

Rice is different. There has never been a lot of rice cultivation in southern Italy and, even though some food historians say that Arabs brought rice to the South, there is no hard evidence of that. More likely rice came into the diet during the long centuries of Spanish occupation (that the Spanish themselves got rice from the Arabs, on the other hand, is indisputable).

In the South, rice is of greatest importance in Puglia, where it is often part of the multilayered casserole called a *teglia* or *tiella* or *taieddha,* depending on where in Puglia the kitchen is located. The tiella takes many forms but basically is made of layers of potatoes, vegetables, often mussels on the half-shell, bits of salt cod, or other kinds of seafood, and frequently, if not always, of rice. Another great layered rice dish, suggesting the urban and aristocratic (or at least foreign) connotations of this ingredient, is the Neapolitan sartù or timballo di riso with its rich and complex assemblage of veal meatballs, chicken livers cooked in Marsala, saffron, nutmeg, and ragù, reminiscent of the timballo di macaroni that the Leopard Prince Fabrizio offered to his guests at Donnafugata, a Sicilian version of the extravagant dish. But rice is also central to that exuberant street snack of Palermo, *arancini,* balls of saffron rice wrapped around a dollop of ragù (see page 87), then deep-fried.

Other grains play minor roles in southern Italian cooking, but they deserve mention. Maize corn, *granoturco,* is not as well known and appreciated as it is in northern Italy, but typically even as bland a dish as cornmeal polenta is made lively and more interesting in country districts of Campania by adding to it chunks of cheese and sausage; in Calabria, the addition typically is of plenty of red chilies. Barley, a holdover from ancient Greece where it was a staple, is occasionally used in breads but not, as far as I know, ever eaten on its own.

The one grain that holds center court throughout the South is of course wheat, and while wheat is most often turned into flour or semolina, the whole grains or berries are also consumed, especially in Puglia and Basilicata, in the form of *grano pestato,* or pounded wheat. Many of the older durum varieties (including farro, incidentally) have an inherent difficulty in that, even after threshing, individual grains retain an indigestible hull or pellicle. Over the centuries, indeed over the millennia, techniques were developed for dealing with this. In Puglia, the most important one was pounding the soaked grains in a mortar to release that outside husk. This is an ancient technology. Pugliese food historian Luigi Sada found evidence for grano pestato in Cato's instructions for *"Graneam triticeam sic facito"*: "Put a half-pound of selected wheat in a clean mortar," Cato instructed, "wash it well, flay it well, rinse it well. Then turn it into a cooking pot, add pure water, and cook." Many of the rice dishes from the Italian South—the teglias from Puglia, for instance, multilayered dishes of rice, seafood, potatoes, and vegetables—were originally made with peeled wheat or with barley; the switch to rice, I think, came about with the Spanish, who ruled southern Italy for many centuries.

Note that you will also find delicious bean soup recipes on pages 102 to 112.

Lenticchie con Salsiccie

GRATIN OF LENTILS WITH SAUSAGE

For the sausages, use either sweet or hot—or one of each. You can do variations on this as well: You could chop a bunch of escarole and steam it till tender, then stir it into the lentils before putting them in the oven; you could also sauté a handful of fresh wild mushrooms and add them to the lentils with the sausages and aromatics; when tomatoes are fresh and ripe, you could arrange thin slices over the top of the lentils, dribble a little olive oil over the tomato slices, and put the dish into the oven to finish cooking.

MAKES 2 TO 4 SERVINGS

1 cup small lentils	Sea salt and freshly ground black pepper	2 fat, fresh sweet (mild) or hot Italian-style sausages (about 1 pound), sliced ¼ to ½ inch thick
3 garlic cloves	1 thick green celery stalk, chopped	
2 small yellow onions		½ cup dry white wine
1 bay leaf	2 tablespoons extra-virgin olive oil	
1 or 2 small dried red chilies		

Rinse the lentils thoroughly and place in a small stockpot along with 2½ cups water. Set over low heat and bring to a simmer while you peel one of the garlic cloves and one of the onions. Add them, whole, to the lentils along with the bay leaf, one of the chilies, and lots of black pepper. When the liquid is simmering, cover the pan and cook slowly for 30 minutes, or until the lentils are tender. Taste and add salt if necessary.

Meanwhile, coarsely chop the remaining garlic and onion and place in a skillet along with the celery and olive oil. Set over medium-low heat and cook gently until the vegetables are softened but not brown.

Preheat the oven to 400°F.

When the lentils are done, remove from the heat and discard the onion, garlic clove, and bay leaf, or as much of it as you can extract from the pot—don't be too finicky about this. Stir in the sautéed vegetables. Taste and add more chili if you wish. Transfer the lentil mixture to an oval gratin dish.

Add the sausage slices to the skillet in which you cooked the vegetables and set over medium heat. Cook, turning frequently, to brown the sausage slices, then transfer them to the lentils. Add the wine to the pan in which the sausages were cooked and set the pan over high heat, boiling down the wine and scraping up the brown bits left in the pan. When the liquid is reduced to about 2 or 3 tablespoons, pour it over the lentils. Set the gratin dish in the preheated oven and bake for 30 to 40 minutes, or until the liquid in the pan has been almost fully absorbed. Remove from the oven and let sit for 10 minutes or so before serving.

'Ncapriata/Fave e Cicoria

PUREED FAVA BEANS WITH BITTER GREENS

This sweetly satisfying combination, pureed beans with bitter greens dressed in rich Pugliese olive oil, is irresistible. Small wonder that it is one of the hallmarks of Puglia's food traditions. Dried fava beans can usually be found in food shops in Italian and Greek neighborhoods. If you can get them, peeled dried fave are best for this preparation since they dissolve into a puree without any further treatment. Otherwise, you will have to use dried fave with the peel or skin attached. To clean them, simply soak them overnight in lots of water. Then the skin should slip right off, perhaps with the help of a paring knife to make a little slit at one end.

The *cicorie,* or wild bitter greens, are another problem, unless you're willing to go out in early springtime with a kitchen knife and a basket to harvest dandelion greens—a good substitute for the wild Pugliese chicories, as long as you're careful to forage in an area that has not been treated with weed-killers or pesticides. Otherwise, try a good produce vendor for farmed bitter greens like dandelions or various chicories. They won't have that nervous, edgy quality of wild ones, but they will do.

You could also serve the fava puree with cultivated bitter greens such as turnip tops or broccoli rabe (rapini). Chinese broccoli, prepared as in this recipe, is a wonderfully pungent foil for the sweet bean puree.

Some Pugliese cooks add a peeled potato, cut into chunks, to cook with the beans and thicken the puree.

A similar fava bean puree is called *macco* in some parts of southern Italy. It is served in Palermo with yellow squash, and with wild fennel in Catania; in Basilicata, fave are cooked to a puree with thinly sliced onion and peeled, seeded, chopped tomatoes. Then broken spaghetti, still quite al dente, is dressed with oil and added to the fave, along with lots of pepper and grated cheese.

MAKES 8 SERVINGS AS A FIRST COURSE

½ pound dried peeled fava beans (*fave sgusciate*), or ¾ pound whole (unpeeled) dried fave	Sea salt ½ cup extra-virgin olive oil	1 pound bitter greens: wild dandelion greens, broccoli rabe, turnip greens, or other

Soak the fave overnight, then drain and, if using unpeeled fave, pull the outer skins away and discard them. Place the peeled fave in, preferably, a terra-cotta cooking vessel that is taller than it is broad—a pignatta is just right, although an old-fashioned bean pot will do the trick too. Add fresh water to cover the beans, cover the pot, and place over low heat to come to a boil. You can gradually increase the heat as the pot warms, but of course, a terra-cotta pot should never be set on an electric burner; if you have an electric stove, put the beans in a heavy soup or stock kettle instead.

As the beans start to boil, they will give up foam, which, Pugliese housewives say, should be skimmed off with a spoon. Once the foam ceases to rise, add a good pinch of salt and, as the beans cook down, stir them thoroughly with a long-handled wooden spoon. The beans will gradually dissolve into the cooking liquid; keep a kettle of water simmering on the back of the stove and, if necessary, add boiling water from time to time to keep the beans from scorching. The beans should take about an hour to cook—you will need to stir them fairly constantly during the last 10 or 15 minutes. When they are completely dissolved, without any lumps, they should have the consistency of clotted cream. Using the wooden spoon, beat in ¼ cup of the olive oil and taste, adding salt if necessary.

While the beans are cooking, clean the greens thoroughly in several changes of water. Place them in a large kettle and boil them in the water clinging to their leaves until they are thoroughly cooked and tender. (You may have to add a very little boiling water from time to time.) Drain in a colander, turning into a bowl, and dress the hot greens with the remaining ¼ cup of olive oil and salt to taste. Toss to mix well.

Pile the fava puree on one side of the serving platter, the greens on the other, and serve with lots of thick slices of country-style bread, fried in olive oil if you wish, or toasted and dribbled with olive oil. Eat the greens and puree together, accompanied by the crisp bread.

NOTE: *Paola Pettini, who ran a highly regarded cooking school in Bari (Italian only), served me fave e cicoria beautifully mounded on a heavy antique platter and surrounded by the following garnishes: red onions, slivered rather thickly and steeped in vinegar; whole small green peppers, spicy but not burning hot, deep-fried in olive oil; black olives sautéed in olive oil and mixed with a little tomato sauce. The whole platter was topped with a scattering of thick bread crumbs, sautéed in olive oil until they were crisp.*

Risotto con Verdure

RISOTTO WITH GARDEN VEGETABLES

Costanza Tasca, of the Tasca d'Almerita wine family at Regaleali in central Sicily, is not so well known in North America as her cookbook-writing sister Anna, but she is just as good a cook, as even Anna admits, and often helps out with the classes that Anna conducts at her farmhouse on the estate (for information, see page 432). This is a risotto Costanza prepared for lunch one spring day when I was visiting. The peas and the artichokes both came from the vegetable garden right outside the kitchen courtyard, the lemon from a tree just around the corner, and the tomato concentrate had been put up by Anna the previous summer. Be sure to have the artichokes ready and trimmed and the peas shelled before you begin cooking.

MAKES 4 TO 6 SERVINGS

1 lemon	1¼ pounds fresh peas, shelled (about 1¼ cups)	4 to 6 cups vegetable or light chicken stock
2 large artichokes	Sea salt and freshly ground black pepper	2 cups round-grain risotto rice (see Note)
1 medium yellow onion, finely chopped	1 tablespoon tomato concentrate, extract, or paste	Grated aged cheese, such as parmigiano reggiano, for garnish
2 tablespoons unsalted butter		
2 tablespoons extra-virgin olive oil		

First prepare the artichokes as described on page 305, using the lemon to keep them from blackening. Slice the artichokes lengthwise about ¼ inch thick and add to the acidulated water.

Combine the onion, 1 tablespoon of the butter, and 1 tablespoon of the olive oil in a heavy saucepan over medium-low heat. Cook until the butter melts and the onion starts to soften and give off its aroma but is not brown.

Drain the artichokes and add them to the pan, stirring to mix with the onion. Cook for 3 or 4 minutes, then stir in the peas, along with salt and pepper to taste, and cook for a few minutes.

In a small bowl, combine the tomato concentrate with about ½ cup boiling water. Stir to dissolve the concentrate and, when it is fully dissolved, add it to the pan with the vegetables. Cook the vegetables until they are just barely tender, about 10 minutes.

Have the stock simmering gently on the stove.

Add the second tablespoon of olive oil to the vegetables, then stir in the rice to mix it well. Cook until the rice loses its raw look, stirring occasionally to keep the rice from catching. Now add about a cup of the simmering stock and cook, stirring occasionally, until much of the stock has been absorbed. Continue to add cups of stock one at a time, waiting for each one to be absorbed before adding the next. The rice should never become dry, but there should be a shimmer of liquid around the grains. You may not need to use all the stock. The rice is done when it is al dente, with a little resistance at the center to the bite, usually in about 20 minutes since you started adding stock. At that point, remove it from the heat and immediately stir in the remaining tablespoon of butter. Cover the pan and let rest for 10 minutes, during which time the rice will continue to soften and absorb the flavors of the vegetables.

Serve the rice, passing a bowl of grated cheese to sprinkle on top.

NOTE: *Most Italian chefs agree that the best rice for risotto is either carnaroli or vialone nano, both of which are usually easy to find in specialty food shops and mail-order outlets. Note that these are not brand names but rather varieties of rice. A more common variety, often available in supermarkets, is arborio. Do not try to make risotto with long-grain rice, such as carolina or basmati. The starch structure is different, and such varieties simply won't work for risotto.*

This may seem like—and it is—a long, complex preparation, but it is worth every minute. Obviously it's not a dish for every day but rather for those special occasions, birthdays and anniversaries, when you want to take the time to make an impression. In fact, the recipe can be prepared a day or more ahead up to the point where you must cook the rice. Refrigerate the prepared ingredients, and then, early in the day on which you will serve the sartù, prepare the rice and the besciamella sauce and assemble the whole thing an hour before serving.

Note the quantities of butter used in the recipe—most unusual in southern Italy and indicative of the dish's origins in the aristocratic kitchens of the monzù, native chefs trained in French haute cuisine, or in what passed for haute cuisine in Napoli, and employed almost exclusively in the palaces of the nobility.

MAKES 10 SERVINGS AS A FIRST COURSE, 8 servings as a main course

10 ounces ground veal	2 ounces dried porcini	One 35-ounce can plum tomatoes
1⅔ cups freshly grated parmigiano reggiano	½ pound chicken livers	4 to 5 cups chicken stock (page 97)
3 eggs plus 1 egg yolk	¼ cup Marsala	1 pound rice for risotto
Salt and freshly ground black pepper	¾ cup shelled fresh or frozen peas (from about ¾ pound in the pods)	½ teaspoon powdered saffron
A few tablespoons unbleached all-purpose flour	¼ pound prosciutto in one thick slice, diced	1 cup milk
About 1½ sticks (6 ounces) unsalted butter	1 medium carrot, diced	Nutmeg for grating
¼ cup extra-virgin olive oil	1 celery stalk, diced	½ cup fine dry bread crumbs
	1 small onion, diced	¼ pound fresh buffalo-milk mozzarella, finely diced

Combine the ground veal with ½ cup of the grated cheese and 1 whole egg and mix well. Add salt and pepper to taste, then form the mixture into very small meatballs—a little over a teaspoonful each. Sprinkle some flour on a plate and roll the meatballs lightly in the flour. In a skillet over medium heat, melt 1 tablespoon of the butter with 1 tablespoon of the olive oil. Brown the meatballs in the fat, removing them and setting aside when done.

Cover the dried mushrooms with hot water and set aside for 30 minutes to soften, then drain, reserving the soaking liquid. Rinse the mushrooms in running water to rid them of residual sand, then chop them coarsely. In the skillet in which the meatballs were fried, melt another tablespoon of the butter and gently fry the mushrooms for just long enough to release their fragrance, about 5 minutes. Strain the soaking liquid through a double layer of cheesecloth into the same pan and cook for 2 minutes to concentrate the juices. Add salt and pepper to taste and set aside.

Cut each chicken liver into 3 or more pieces. In the same skillet, in another tablespoon of butter, cook the livers over medium-low heat until they are thoroughly brown and firm. Add the Marsala, raise the heat, and cook briefly, scraping the pan, until the wine is reduced to a syrup. Remove and set aside.

Bring about an inch of lightly salted water to a boil in a small saucepan. Add the peas and cook for about 4 minutes. Add the prosciutto and another tablespoon of butter. Cook over high heat until the water has completely boiled away and the butter sizzles. Remove from the heat and set aside.

In the same skillet in which you cooked the livers, over medium-low heat, combine the carrot, celery, and onion with 2 tablespoons of the remaining olive oil and cook, stirring frequently, until the vegetables soften and take on a little color but are not browned. Add the tomatoes with their juice and raise the heat. Using the side of a spoon, break up the tomatoes and stir into the other vegetables. Cook, watching carefully that it doesn't burn, for about 5 minutes. The sauce should be very thick. Divide the sauce, setting aside about 1 cup for later use, the rest to be mixed with the rice.

Bring the broth to a slow simmer. Melt 1 tablespoon of the remaining butter and the last tablespoon of olive oil in a 2-quart saucepan over medium heat. Add the rice and cook, stirring, until the grains have turned opaque, about 3 minutes. Stir the reserved tomato sauce into the rice and cook until the sauce starts to bubble, then add about ½ cup of hot broth, stirring it in as for a risotto. Continue adding broth ½ cup at a time, as necessary, stirring continuously, cooking the rice for about 15 minutes in all. The rice will be slightly underdone and will finish cooking later. While the rice is cooking, dissolve the saffron in a tablespoon of hot water and add this to the rice just before removing it from the heat.

Away from the heat, stir 2 tablespoons of the remaining butter and the remaining grated cheese into the rice. Let it cool slightly, then add the remaining 2 whole eggs and stir to mix well. Taste the rice and add salt if necessary. Turn the rice out on a platter or a tray and leave it to cool thoroughly.

Make a besciamella: Heat the milk to just below boiling and set it aside. Melt 1 more tablespoon of butter in a saucepan over medium-low heat and, when it stops sizzling, add a tablespoon of flour. Cook, stirring with a wooden spoon, until the mixture thickens, about 3 minutes. Add the hot milk all at once, beating with a wire whisk, and continue to cook, stirring constantly, until the sauce is thick. Remove from the heat and season with salt, pepper, and a few gratings of nutmeg. Let the sauce cool slightly, then beat in the egg yolk. Set aside.

An hour before serving, preheat the oven to 350F.

Build the sartù: Butter the bottom and sides of a 2-quart charlotte mold or soufflé dish. Sprinkle with the bread crumbs, turning the dish so the crumbs adhere to the bottom and sides. Set aside about a cup of the rice mixture and use the rest to line the bottom and sides of the mold, pressing it against the sides. Fill the center with layers of meatballs, mushrooms, chicken livers, peas, mozzarella, and the reserved cup of tomato sauce. Top each layer with a little grated cheese and a few spoons of besciamella sauce. When all the ingredients have been used up, top with the reserved rice, sprinkle with the remaining bread crumbs, and dot with the remaining butter.

Transfer the sartù to the oven and bake for 30 minutes, or until the top has formed a golden crust. Remove from the oven and let rest for 10 minutes or so to consolidate. Run a knife around the sides, place a round serving platter upside down on top, say a prayer, and flip the mold over so that the sartù rests on the serving platter. Serve immediately. (If you don't want to risk this, serve the sartù directly from the dish in which it was baked.)

Tiella (Taieddha) di Patate, Riso, e Cozze

PUGLIESE BAKED RICE WITH POTATOES AND MUSSELS

A *tiella* (or *taieddha* or *teglia*) is one of a handful of dishes that define *la cucina pugliese*, the cuisine of Puglia. A structured, layered combination of several ingredients that often includes rice and almost always potatoes, tiella is often said to come from Spanish paella, brought to southern Italy during the long, harsh centuries of Spanish rule. But Spanish paella is a very different dish: Paella is always quick-cooked on top of the stove, where a tiella is always baked in the oven and once upon a time would have been baked in the ashes on the hearth, with the embers drawn up around the terra-cotta cooking vessel and piled over the top—an ancient Mediterranean cooking method. In fact, I believe the original tiella had nothing to do with rice or potatoes at all but was most likely made with that traditional Pugliese ingredient peeled wheat, *grano pestato*.

This is an adaptation of a recipe given to me by Paola Pettini, who had a well-known cooking school in Puglia's capital city, Bari. It is traditionally served as a first course, although it is so substantial that it can easily serve as a main course.

Be sure to warn guests that there are mussels in their shells in the middle layer of the casserole.

There are two tricks to success with this dish:

- Slice the potatoes very thin so that they will cook in the time allotted.
- Be sure to use a baking dish that is 12 inches in diameter; otherwise the layers will be too thick and by the time the potatoes are cooked the rice will be gummy.

MAKES 6 TO 8 SERVINGS AS A FIRST COURSE

¾ cup arborio or other short-grain rice for risotto

2 pounds mussels

5 tablespoons extra-virgin olive oil

¼ cup unseasoned dry bread crumbs

1 medium yellow onion, thinly sliced

½ cup chopped flat-leaf parsley

½ pound ripe red tomatoes, peeled and finely diced, or 1 cup drained canned tomatoes, coarsely chopped

2 pounds yellow-fleshed potatoes, such as Yellow Finn or Yukon gold, peeled and thinly sliced

2 medium zucchini, thinly sliced

¾ cup grated hard aged cheese: pecorino, parmigiano reggiano, or grana padano

Sea salt and freshly ground black pepper

1 small garlic clove, minced

1 pound ripe red tomatoes, thinly sliced

Preheat the oven to 425°F

Put the rice in a bowl and cover with water by 1 inch. Set aside to soak for at least 30 minutes.

Prepare the mussels as described on page 245, leaving the mussel meat attached to the half-shells. Discard the empty shells. Strain and reserve the mussel liquid. (If it's easier, you may steam the mussels in ½ inch of water just until they open, then discard the empty shells and strain the liquid left in the pan through a double layer of cheesecloth to get rid of any grit.)

Smooth a tablespoon of olive oil over the bottom and sides of a 12-inch round oven dish. Sprinkle 2 tablespoons of bread crumbs over the bottom and dribble another tablespoon of olive oil on top of the crumbs. Layer the onion slices over the crumbs, then scatter over them half the parsley and half the diced tomatoes. Layer half the potatoes and half the zucchini on top. Sprinkle with about ¼ cup of the grated cheese, along with salt and pepper to taste.

Layer the mussels in their half-shells on the potato-zucchini layer, the open part of the mussels facing up. Drain the rice thoroughly and distribute it in handfuls over the mussels. Sprinkle with another ¼ cup of the cheese and the remaining diced tomato and parsley. Add more salt and pepper and the minced garlic and dribble 2 tablespoons of olive oil over this layer.

Layer the remaining potatoes and zucchini on top of the rice. Sprinkle with the last ¼ cup of cheese, along with more salt and pepper. Use the sliced tomatoes as the final layer: They should cover the top completely. Dribble over them the remaining bread crumbs and olive oil, the reserved mussel liquid, and a little more salt.

Add 3 to 4 cups of boiling water to the oven dish to come halfway up the sides, then transfer the dish to the preheated oven. Turn the oven temperature down to 350°F and bake the tiella, uncovered, for 45 to 60 minutes, or until the potatoes are tender and the rice is thoroughly cooked.

May be served immediately but it is better if it's left to cool to slightly warmer than room temperature.

Migliaccio

CAMPANIA-STYLE POLENTA

Polenta, even under the best of circumstances, can be a bland and uninteresting dish. But given good, fresh cornmeal, not too finely ground, and a Campanian infusion of smoked provolone cheese and spicy salami, it turns into a primo piatto to delight the palate.

Most of the "imported Italian polenta" available in North America is not worth bothering with. It has been so long in transit that it has lost any freshness it might once have had. Much better to look for an American source of freshly ground cornmeal. If you have a say in the matter, ask for a coarse grind—it has more interesting texture. In Italian, this is called *polenta bramata*.

MAKES 6 SERVINGS

1½ cups stale bread, crusts removed, cut into ½-inch cubes	1 cup milk, at room temperature or warmer (optional)	1 cup (about ¼ pound) flavorful salami, cut into ½-inch cubes
¼ cup extra-virgin olive oil, plus a little for the baking dish	1 cup smoked provola or provolone cheese, cut into ½-inch cubes	Sea salt and freshly ground black pepper
1½ cups coarsely ground cornmeal (*bramata*)		

In a skillet over medium heat, gently cook the bread cubes in the olive oil until they are golden brown and crisp. Set aside on paper towels to drain.

Bring 5 cups of water to a rolling boil and slowly, a little at a time, stir in the polenta, using a wire whisk to get rid of any lumps. Lower the heat to simmer and cook for about 10 minutes, stirring frequently with a wooden spoon. Gradually add the warm milk, continuing to stir until the milk is fully incorporated. (If you prefer, substitute warm water for the milk.) Leave the polenta to cook for a total of 40 minutes, stirring occasionally. If the polenta starts to burn or stick to the bottom of the pan, turn the heat lower or use a Flame-Tamer to moderate the heat. You may also add a little more boiling water or hot milk if necessary to keep the polenta from sticking.

Preheat the oven to 400°F.

Use a little olive oil to grease the bottom and sides of a 9 × 12-inch oven dish.

200   CUCINA DEL SOLE

When the polenta is done, the grains will be thoroughly tender, yet with a little al dente bite at the center, a hint of texture, like al dente pasta. Add the croutons, cheese, salami, and salt and pepper, stirring to incorporate thoroughly into the polenta. Turn out into the oven dish and dribble olive oil liberally over the top. Set in the hot oven for 10 to 15 minutes, or until the top is brown. Remove from the oven and serve immediately.

Grano Pestato e Verdure/Cranu Pestatu e Foje

POUNDED OR PEARLED WHEAT WITH GREEN VEGETABLES

See the introduction to this chapter for information about grano pestato. Soaked overnight, then drained and steamed very slowly in fresh water until the grains are soft and tender, grano pestato can be served like pasta with a little tomato sauce and grated cheese. But it is also delicious cooked with legumes, or with vegetables as in this recipe. If you cannot find grano pestato, make this dish with farro, another species of durum wheat that also must be "pearled" or pounded (these days, by machine) to rid it of its husk.

MAKES 6 SERVINGS AS A FIRST COURSE

1 cup grano pestato or farro	2 tablespoons minced flat-leaf parsley	Sea salt
1 ounce pancetta, finely diced	1 teaspoon tomato extract, concentrate, or paste, diluted in 2 tablespoons hot water	Grated hard aged cheese—pecorino, caciocavallo, or parmigiano reggiano—for garnish (optional)
1 medium onion, finely chopped		
1 tablespoon extra-virgin olive oil		
2 cups diced green vegetables, such as celery, escarole, chard, zucchini, spinach, and/or chicory		

If you're using grano pestato, soak the grains in water to cover by 1 inch for 6 to 8 hours or overnight. When ready to cook, drain thoroughly. (This step may be unnecessary with farro.)

When ready to cook, bring water to a boil.

Combine the pancetta, onion, and olive oil in a heavy saucepan and gently toast the pancetta and onion over medium heat until the onion just begins to brown. Add the drained wheat and stir to mix well. Add about 2 cups of the boiling water, or enough to cover the grains by 1 inch. As soon as the water returns to a simmer, lower the heat, cover the pan, and cook very slowly, adding boiling water from time to time as the grains absorb the water in the pan. (Precise times and measurements depend on the age of the grain and whether you are using grano pestato or farro.)

Check the grains from time to time. When they start to get tender, add any or all of the diced vegetables. Stir in the parsley and tomato concentrate. Taste and add salt if necessary.

Continue cooking, covered, over low heat until the vegetables are cooked and the grain is very tender, about 15 minutes. Serve immediately, passing grated cheese if you wish.

VARIATION

In Basilicata, grano pestato is often served with a lamb ragù, similar to the Ragù del Pastore on page 137, or a ragù made with pork and sausages, tomatoes, and lots of peperoncini, hot red chilies.

I SECONDI

Main Courses

Fish and Seafood

Traveling in southern Italy, I have the sense always that I'm not very far from the sea. Even up along the forbidding heights of the Sila in Basilicata, where the Appenines that form Italy's long backbone culminate in peaks well above six thousand feet, I still discern the aroma, the charisma, you might call it, of the sea—as if these high, stony cliffs themselves were bathed improbably in the Mediterranean's luminous blue.

It is the sea, in fact, more than anything else, that has shaped the whole of southern Italy. It has carved out protected harbors and deep grottoes, defined shingle beaches and mythical headlands like Odysseus's dreaded Scylla and Charybdis on either side of the Messina straits or like Cape Palinuro where, Virgil tells us, Aeneas's helmsman, Palinurus, fell to his death. So close is the sea, so narrow the peninsulas, that in many places it's a mere thirty miles or less from one side to the other, from the Tyhrrenian to the Ionian, for instance, across Calabria, or from the Adriatic to the Gulf of Taranto in Puglia. (That's as the crow flies, of course; on donkey back or even in a speedy little Fiat, it's a good deal longer, miles and miles of switchback roads, up and down, over those mountains.)

Given the presence of the sea in their lives, it's no wonder that southerners consume more fish than any other Italians—more than sixty pounds per person in the last year of the twentieth century, which was the latest statistic I could find. Put that against Americans' paltry fourteen pounds each, and you see what we're up against in the international fish consumption stakes.

Curiously, though, the Mediterranean is not particularly rich in fish, certainly nowhere near as rich as the North Atlantic is or used to be. The dearth, as I've written elsewhere,* has to do primarily with geography and climate, although in the last half-century the human hand has weighed heavily on the sea's fragile ecosystem. In southern Italy, threats come from both industrial and tourist development, oil refineries along the southern and eastern coasts of Sicily and acres of campgrounds that disfigure broad sandy beaches south of Salerno in Campania.

Still, the most telling factor in the poverty of resource is the peculiar nature of the sea itself. Climate combined with the high threshold between the Atlantic and the Mediterranean keeps out great schools of deep-swimming cod, haddock, and halibut, such as there used to be in the North Atlantic. Instead, what proliferates are economically insignificant species—fish like anchovies, sardines, dogfish (a kind of shark), and big rays or skate, bony fish like gurnards and rascasse (good for flavoring fish stews but not much else), as well as octopus, calamari, and other cephalopods—all fish, it must be said in their defense, that local cooks use to dazzling effect.

That's not to say that the Mediterranean has nothing by way of an important fish resource. Tuna and swordfish migrate from the Atlantic into the Mediterranean to spawn,** and these big, valuable fish have provided economic stability for fishing communities in Sicily and southern Italy for generations, perhaps even for millennia. Ages ago, on a wall of a dark saltwater cave called the Grotta dei Genovesi on the island of Levanzo, one of the Egadi Islands off Sicily's west coast, a Paleolithic artist painted the shadowy figure of a giant tuna, evoking a little sympathetic magic to secure the success of the chase. Today the traditional tuna harvest, the mattanza, which was once as important culturally as it was economically, has almost disappeared; a group on nearby Favignana still performs the spring ritual, but it is more for television and tourist cameras than for the tuna, which are sadly depleted, too few in number, too small in size.

As for swordfish, much of what is harvested is also way too small. Juvenile fish, as a quick glance around the superanimated fish market in Catania on Sicily's east coast will confirm, are abundant, but swordfish do not spawn before they are three years old. Obviously, if they're caught before that, future generations will suffer. The juvenile fish harvest is illegal, but it goes on—like the harvest of a number of other protected species. A fisherman, after all, has to pay the rent, the taxes, the doctor's bill; has to feed his children and put gas in the car. And tourist hotels and restaurants demand smaller fish because they're easier to handle.

And it's the tourist market, as well as the foreign market (especially the Japanese market for prized Mediterranean bluefin tuna), that has put unsustainable pressure on the resource. Meanwhile, southern Italians, much as they esteem these high-status fish, continue to follow the culinary traditions of their forebears. What they actually eat is somewhat lower, sometimes very much lower, on the food chain.

---

*In *The Essential Mediterranean,* HarperCollins, 2004.
**But recent research suggests that the Mediterranean swordfish population may be genetically distinct from that in the Atlantic.

Lower on the food chain, but not without value, and sometimes considerable value, too. Take, for instance, the anchovies from the Cilento coast of Campania, *alici di menaica* as they're called in the local dialect. In the little fishing port of Marina di Pisciotta, which lies below the medieval hill town of Pisciotta in the curve of a bay just north of where Palinurus met his demise, the anchovies have been harvested, for as long as anyone can remember, by fishermen who go out at night in small boats to cast drift nets called *menaiche*. At dawn they return to their wives and girlfriends, who wait on shore with knives, salt, and a bevy of straight-sided, white-glazed earthenware jugs to transform the fish into salted anchovies. Because of the harvesting procedure, the anchovies are quickly bled at sea, an important point in getting plump, clean fish. Packed in salt in their ceramic jugs, they are set aside to mature and develop flavor—just like fine hams and sausages.

As with almost everything else in traditional food production, the work is hard and the economic benefits not great, although the anchovies are superb, well worth the effort. But only half a dozen or so fishermen are left who are willing to put up with it. Enter then two forces that in recent years have become instrumental in the effort to preserve Italian food traditions of all kinds. Slow Food's Foundation for Biodiversity, worldwide but based in Italy, has established a presidium for alici di menaica. This recognition is respected by consumers and the food press alike, but perhaps equally important, the presidium provides active support to help the remaining fishermen develop a smart, sensible market for their product. At the same time the *comune* of Pisciotta, through the Italian government, has applied to the European Union for a DO, an official denomination of origin, for alici di menaica. This will allow the traditional fishermen, and *only* the traditional fishermen, of the region to advertise and sell their wares as such—a move that has strong legal backing throughout Europe when and if it has to be enforced.

Throughout southern Italy, anchovy fishermen, or their wives, salt most of the catch, but they almost always set aside a few for eating fresh and virtually raw. The clean, bright flavor of the little fish is like the Mediterranean seaside on an early May morning. After slitting the bellies, cleaning the innards, and pulling out the backbones (but leaving the two sides of the fish attached at the tail), the anchovies are rinsed, drained, and put in a deep dish, then covered with the juice of several lemons and set aside to marinate for at least half an hour. After that the anchovies are drained once more and arranged on a serving dish. Seasoned with lots of chopped garlic, minced parsley, and crumbled red chili—not too hot so as not to overpower the fresh flavor of the fish—they're dressed with olive oil and more lemon juice. Treated like this, anchovies will keep, covered, in the refrigerator for up to a week, but they're more likely to be consumed immediately, as an antipasto or merenda; or they get mixed in a salad with strips of roasted, peeled red peppers. If you can find fresh anchovies—and they are occasionally available in high-class fish markets in North America—this is a great way to treat them.

A Word About Crudo

Recently in the United States, a preparation called *crudo* has become very popular in chic Italian restaurants. *Crudo* actually means "raw," but the reference is specifically to raw fish. Apart from very high-end restaurants where anything goes, Italians are not great consumers of raw fish, except for oysters. Except in Puglia. Down on the heel of the Italian boot, where four hundred miles of coastline have given seafood a prominent place in the diet, *antipasto alla barese* served in the fish restaurants of the great Adriatic port of Bari always includes fresh raw fish and shellfish: anchovies and anchovy fry (called *neonati,* or newborns, no more than an inch long, their eyes like pin dots, they're eaten by the spoonful in seawater with olive oil and a few drops of lemon juice); iodine-rich *ricci di mare* (sea urchins), their shells cracked to reveal the dark, seaweed-tasting, blood-red roe that you scoop out with nubbins of bread; pale raw clams, *telline* and *vongole verace,* served on the half shell; and raw oysters and black mussels from the aquaculture beds of the Taranto lagoon.

Another raw preparation, much appreciated in Puglia, is a tuna or swordfish carpaccio (*carpaccio di tonno o di pesce spada*), the fish sliced no more than 1/16 inch thick, the slices patted dry and chilled, then arranged like prosciutto slices on individual plates (for best results, the plates are also chilled in the refrigerator) and dressed with a combination of olive oil, lemon juice, chopped capers, minced parsley and mint, and, of course, salt and pepper.

Raw seafood of any variety should be consumed with caution, of course, in Puglia as much as anywhere else, but if you're certain of your resource, the primitive, briny, ocean flavor is both shocking and delicious. And it's probably the only taste in this modern world that has been handed down, unchanged, from our remotest ancestors. Yes! you think, this is how they ate in the Upper Paleolithic, and damned fine it was, too!

Sammurigghiu (Salmoriglio)

A LIGHT AND LEMONY SAUCE FOR GRILLED OR POACHED FISH

A Sicilian favorite, this simplest of sauces can be found elsewhere in the South too, wherever lemons are most flavorful—especially Campania and Calabria, where cooks typically add a pinch of their favorite crumbled red chilies to the sauce. Since this is a minimal sauce, to say the least, you will do well to seek out the very best ingredients—pungent wild Italian or Greek oregano, crisp Mediterranean sea salt, and of course the very finest and fruitiest olive oil, preferably from southern Italy. What does salmoriglio complement? Truthfully, almost any kind of grilled, broiled, or poached fish—a whole sea bass is ideal, big tiger shrimps are quite wonderful, but one of the finest uses for salmoriglio, curiously enough, is as a dipping sauce to accompany a whole steamed Maine lobster. It's a long way from the Mediterranean, but the two are almost perfect together.

The sauce is usually prepared and served apart, but sometimes it becomes a cooking medium in itself, imparting a good deal of flavor to the fish as it cooks—see the recipe on page 227.

MAKES 1 CUP; 6 to 8 servings

¾ cup extra-virgin olive oil	1 tablespoon dried oregano, crumbled	1 or 2 garlic cloves, finely minced (optional)
¼ cup fresh lemon juice		
Sea salt to taste	Freshly ground black pepper to taste	Crumbled dried red chili (optional)

Combine all the ingredients, including the optional ones if desired, and beat vigorously with a wire whisk or a fork to amalgamate. Serve immediately, spooning over prepared fish steaks, fish fillets, or whole fish cooked on the grill or roasted in the oven. Pass extra sauce to be added at the table.

Salsa di Pomodoro con Olive, Uva Secca, e Pinoli

TOMATO SAUCE WITH OLIVES, GOLDEN RAISINS, AND PINE NUTS

This sauce is served in Naples with batter-fried fish (chunks of salt cod are a favorite—see page 237), but it is equally delicious as an accompaniment to any simply grilled or sautéed fish or meat. Truth to tell, it's awfully good on a bowl of spaghetti too. (Or try it, instead of ketchup, with hamburgers—it's a revelation.)

MAKES ABOUT 1½ CUPS; 6 to 8 servings as a garnish

10 canned plum tomatoes, preferably imported San Marzano tomatoes (see page 127)	2 tablespoons pine nuts	2 tablespoons capers, preferably salt-packed, rinsed, drained, and chopped
2 tablespoons extra-virgin olive oil	2 tablespoons golden raisins, plumped in hot water and drained	Sea salt and freshly ground black pepper
2 garlic cloves, chopped	½ cup pitted black olives, coarsely chopped	

Drain the tomatoes, reserving about ¼ cup of their juice in case you need to add it to the sauce later. Chop the tomatoes coarsely and set aside.

Combine the olive oil and garlic in a saucepan over low heat. Cook the garlic until it is soft but not brown. Add the tomatoes, increasing the heat to moderate. Cook the tomatoes for about 15 minutes. Use the back of a fork to crush them as they cook down, adding a little of the reserved juice if necessary. The sauce, however, should be very thick.

Meanwhile, in a small skillet, toast the pine nuts over medium-low heat until they are golden, stirring constantly. Pine nuts burn quickly, so be attentive. Stir the toasted pine nuts into the sauce and add the drained raisins, olives, and capers. Add salt if necessary and pepper to taste. Serve the sauce warm or at room temperature.

FISH STEAKS OR FILLETS IN A DELICIOUS SAUCE

Ghiotta comes from the same Latin root as our English word *glutton,* so you have a pretty good idea of what it means in Italian. This is an epicurean dish, indeed, and a favorite way of preparing swordfish around the Sicilian port of Messina, where swordfishing is a major activity during the fish's spawning run through the straits of the same name in late May and June. It's also a tasty way to prepare tuna steaks when available. I like to have tuna steaks cut slightly thicker than swordfish—¾ to 1 inch—because tuna, to my palate, is always better when somewhat underdone. Other fish steaks—halibut and salmon come quickly to mind—are excellent given this treatment, as are thick fillets of haddock, cod, or monkfish.

MAKES 4 TO 6 SERVINGS

2 pounds fish steaks, about ½ inch thick, cut into 6 serving pieces	2 tablespoons golden raisins, plumped in hot water	6 canned plum tomatoes, drained
All-purpose flour for dusting the fish	2 tablespoons pine nuts	Sea salt and freshly ground black pepper
About ½ cup extra-virgin olive oil	2 celery stalks, finely chopped	3 or 4 bay leaves
1 medium onion, minced	2 tablespoons capers, preferably salt-packed, rinsed and drained	2 tablespoons fine dry bread crumbs
2 garlic cloves, minced	12 to 15 large green olives, pitted and coarsely chopped	

Dry the fish steaks with paper towels and dust lightly with flour. Put ¼ cup of the olive oil in a skillet set over medium heat. When the oil is hot, add the steaks and brown on both sides, about 3 minutes to a side. Transfer to an oven dish that will hold all the fish in one layer.

Preheat the oven to 350°F.

Add the remaining olive oil to the pan along with the onion and garlic. Lower the heat and cook, stirring occasionally, until the vegetables are very soft but not brown. Add the drained raisins, pine nuts, celery, capers, and olives and continue cooking, stirring occasionally, for about 10 minutes. The vegetables should continue to soften but not brown.

Chop the drained tomatoes or crush them in your hands and stir into the sauce. Continue cooking for 5 minutes or so, until the tomatoes are well incorporated. Remove from the heat, taste, and add salt and pepper. Spoon the sauce over the fish steaks. Tuck the bay leaves in among the steaks and sprinkle the bread crumbs over the top. Dribble with a little more olive oil.

Bake in the preheated oven for 20 minutes, or until the top is lightly browned and the sauce is sizzling. Remove from the oven and serve in the dish in which the fish was cooked.

You may also let this dish cool and serve it at room temperature. The sauce remains delicious, though you may have to add a little more salt before serving.

Pesce alla Stemperata

FISH STEAKS IN A SWEET-AND-SOUR SAUCE

The word *stemperata* refers to the "tempering" of the sauce by adding different ingredients at different times. At first glance, a *stemperata* looks very similar to the preparation called *alla ghiotta* (see the preceding recipe), but the two Sicilian treatments yield very different results, especially because of the marked presence of vinegar and sugar in the stemperata. This suggests, to me at least, that stemperata is a more antique recipe; indeed, the sweet-and-sour combination is often cited as an index of the Arab heritage that is so strong in Sicilian cuisine. But sweet-sour combinations, often called *agrodolce* in Italian, are much older than that; in fact, the Romans took great pleasure in similar combinations, using honey instead of sugar, as did the ancient Greek Sicilians, who were famed for their gastronomic pretensions at a time when the acme of Roman cuisine was boiled farro for supper on the banks of the Tiber.

You can use many different kinds of fish in this preparation—swordfish is traditional in Sicily, but tuna, halibut, or salmon steaks are good too. Just be sure to have them cut thick so that the flesh doesn't dry out with the additional cooking time.

A stemperata is traditionally served at room temperature, making it a good do-ahead preparation for a summer lunch or buffet.

MAKES 6 SERVINGS

2 medium carrots	½ cup chopped blanched almonds	¼ cup capers, preferably salt-packed, rinsed and drained
2 tablespoons extra-virgin olive oil	2 or 3 celery stalks, thinly sliced (½ cup)	¼ cup golden raisins, plumped in hot water and drained
6 fish steaks, at least 1 inch thick and about 5 ounces each	12 green olives, pitted and chopped	½ cup slivered fresh mint leaves
All-purpose flour for dusting the fish	2 tablespoons tomato extract, concentrate, or paste, diluted in ⅔ cup hot water	1 tablespoon sugar
2 garlic cloves, minced		2 tablespoons aged red wine vinegar
½ medium yellow onion, thinly sliced		Sea salt and freshly ground black pepper

Bring a small pan of water to a rolling boil and blanch the peeled whole carrots for 5 minutes, or until they start to soften but are not tender all the way through. Drain and rinse in cold water when done. Finely mince the carrots and set aside.

In a saucepan large enough to hold all the fish in one layer, heat the olive oil over medium heat. Pat the fish steaks dry with paper towels and lightly dust each one with flour on both sides. Brown the fish in the hot oil on both sides, just over a minute to a side. Remove the fish steaks as they brown and set aside on a platter or shallow serving dish.

Lower the heat under the saucepan and add the minced garlic. Cook, stirring frequently, until the garlic starts to soften and give off an aroma. Add the onion and cook, again stirring frequently, until the onion is soft, then add the almonds and continue cooking until the almonds start to turn golden, about 3 minutes. Stir in the carrots, celery, and olives and continue cooking. Once the celery starts to soften, stir in the tomato paste diluted in water. Let bubble and reduce slightly, for about 5 minutes, and finally add the capers, drained raisins, and mint, stirring to mix well.

Combine the sugar with the vinegar in a small bowl or cup and stir to dissolve the sugar. Add to the stemperata sauce in the pan, mix well, then taste and add salt and pepper as you wish.

Nestle each of the fish steaks into the stemperata sauce, spooning excess sauce over the top of each steak. If the sauce looks a little dry, add about ½ cup water and bring to a simmer. Cover the pan and cook over low heat for another 8 to 10 minutes, or until the fish steaks are thoroughly cooked but still moist. (If you are using tuna steaks, you may prefer to cook them less—not more than 5 minutes will give you tuna that is still rare in the middle.) Transfer the steaks to the serving dish and cover with the stemperata sauce. Set aside, lightly covered with plastic wrap, to cool to room temperature before serving. (You may, of course, serve this dish hot from the pan if you wish, but in Sicily it is usually served at room temperature.)

VARIATION

You may also bake the fish in a preheated 350°F oven. Omit the preliminary step of browning the fish steaks and simply set each one on a lightly oiled square of aluminum foil. Prepare the stemperata and spoon some of it over and around each fish steak. Draw up the sides of the foil to make a loose but firmly sealed packet around each steak. Set the packets on a cookie sheet or baking tray and bake in the preheated oven for 20 to 25 minutes, or until the steaks are cooked but still moist. This method retains a good deal of the moisture in the fish, although the pleasant flavor of browning is of course absent.

Pesce alla Marinara

FISH IN A WINE AND LEMON SAUCE

Have all your ingredients ready and measured ahead of time for this very quick and easy preparation that races along almost as fast as a Chinese stir-fry.

Good fish selections: Mackerel is traditional, but I have made this successfully with salmon fillets. It would also be good with bluefish in season or with drier fish like haddock or halibut. Adjust the cooking time to the thickness of the fish, but be careful not to overcook.

MAKES 4 TO 6 SERVINGS

2 tablespoons extra-virgin olive oil	2 garlic cloves, minced	Grated zest and juice of 1 lemon, preferably organic
1½ pounds mackerel or other fish fillets—at least 1 fillet per person for mackerel or bluefish	1 teaspoon crumbled dried red chili, or to taste	¾ cup dry white wine
	Sea salt and freshly ground black pepper	¼ cup mixed minced fresh basil and flat-leaf parsley

Set a skillet large enough to hold all the fish over medium heat and add the olive oil. While the oil is heating, pat the fish dry with paper towels.

Add the minced garlic to the oil and when it starts to sizzle, drop in the fish pieces. Sprinkle with red pepper flakes, salt, and pepper to taste. After about 1½ minutes, carefully turn the fish, using 2 spatulas if it's helpful, to brown the other sides. Sprinkle the grated zest over the top and add the lemon juice to the pan. Let cook for 1½ minutes, then add ½ cup of the wine to the pan along with half the minced herbs. Lower the heat to simmer, cover the pan, and cook for 4 to 5 minutes, or until the fish flakes easily with a fork.

Transfer the fish pieces to a warm platter and raise the heat under the pan. Add the remaining ¼ cup wine and cook rapidly, scraping up the brown bits. At the last minute, swirl in the remaining herbs, remove from the heat, and pour the juices over the fish on the platter. Serve immediately.

Spigola (Branzino) all'Acqua Pazza

SEA BASS IN CRAZY WATER

The crazy water is nothing more than a light court bouillon, flavored with the simplest aromatics—salt and pepper, parsley and garlic, a little white wine, some olive oil, and a few ripe tomatoes—but the simplicity is deceptive. Anything less than the finest ingredients will belie the minimal nature of the dish. If you have a fisher friend, try this with a freshly caught striper. In any case, use wild rather than farmed sea bass whenever possible.

The technique works well for many different firm-textured, white-meat fish, including porgies, breams, grouper, and hake.

Before you get ready to cook this (or any other) whole fish, be sure you have a skillet or shallow saucepan large enough to accommodate the length of the fish. I have sometimes improvised with a wide paella pan and aluminum foil to cover it.

MAKES 4 TO 6 SERVINGS

1 whole fish, preferably with the head, 2 to 3 pounds	2 garlic cloves, lightly crushed	3 or 4 fresh basil sprigs, slivered
Sea salt and freshly ground black pepper	½ cup dry white wine	1 bunch of flat-leaf parsley, coarsely chopped
¼ cup extra-virgin olive oil	4 or 5 ripe tomatoes, coarsely chopped	

Rinse the fish well, inside and out, and pat dry with paper towels. Sprinkle liberally inside and out with salt and pepper. Set aside.

In a skillet large enough to hold the whole fish, heat the olive oil over medium heat and, when hot, add the garlic. Cook, stirring, until the garlic starts to take on color, then remove the garlic and discard it. Immediately add the fish to the pan and sauté it in the garlic-infused oil, first on one side for about 5 minutes, then on the other.

Add the wine, tomatoes, basil, half the parsley, and about ½ cup hot water to the skillet so that the fish is surrounded but not covered by the tomato-wine broth. Bring to a simmer, lower the heat to keep it at a simmer, cover the pan, and simmer for 15 minutes. Then uncover the pan and raise the heat to high. Cook rapidly for another few minutes to reduce the juices and concentrate the flavors. Then remove and serve the fish, with its reduced stock, and the remaining chopped parsley as a garnish.

NOTE: *There is a fashion in North American restaurants for fish that often seems barely beyond the raw stage. Undercooking fish like this seems just as much a sin to southern Italian cooks as overcooking it. With some exceptions (tuna, for instance, and possibly salmon) fish should be cooked through, without a trace of pinkness, but not falling apart in the pan. When preparing pesce all'acqua pazza, it's good to keep a close watch on the fish and stop the cooking just as it's done. If necessary, remove the fish from the pan and set it aside on a warm platter while you reduce the stock.*

Farmed Fish or Wild?

I stress using wild sea bass for the preceding recipe because of its high quality compared to farmed bass. In taste and texture, the wild fish is way ahead. Although sea bass, *spigola* or *branzino* in Italian, is one of the most economically successful aquaculture enterprises in Italy (and in Greece, where it is even more widely farmed), the methods used are questionable. The use of overcrowded sea cages not only pollutes surrounding waters and endangers other fish but results in an inferior product in terms of both texture and flavor. (It doesn't have to be that way, but until sea farmers can organize to better police themselves, environmentalists and cooks alike will look askance at what they have to offer.) The Mediterranean may seem a long way from our North American shores, but most of the branzino and spigola (also daurade or bream) on U.S. restaurant menus comes from Italian and Greek aquaculture.

Of course, there are good substitutes for these. Snapper, wolffish, wild bream—almost any fish in the white-fleshed family—will be fine, but not oily or strong-flavored fish like mackerel or salmon.

Pesce al Finocchio

OVEN-ROASTED FISH WITH FENNEL

If you can find wild fennel, which grows along hillsides in California (and perhaps in other parts of the United States as well), use the feathery green tops for this dish; otherwise, use the tops of bulb or Florentine fennel, easily found in supermarket produce sections, often labeled *anise.* Boost the flavor of cultivated fennel with "wild fennel pollen," available from Zingerman's (see page 415) and other well-stocked gourmet markets.

MAKES 4 TO 6 SERVINGS

½ cup extra-virgin olive oil	1 cup chopped green fennel tops	1 lemon
1½ pounds white-fleshed fish fillets, such as haddock or halibut	1 tablespoon wild fennel pollen	2 tablespoons capers, preferably salt-packed, rinsed and drained
1 tablespoon fine sea salt	2 garlic cloves, minced	
Freshly ground black pepper	3 tablespoons fresh lemon juice	

Smear a little of the olive oil over the bottom of an oven dish large enough to hold all the fish in one layer. Pat the fillets dry with paper towels and set in the dish, sprinkling liberally with salt, pepper, fennel, fennel pollen, and garlic. Set aside for 1 hour to marinate. (If you wish, you can marinate for several hours, but the dish should be covered and refrigerated in that case.)

When you're ready to cook, preheat the oven to 350°F.

Pour the remaining olive oil and the lemon juice over the fish and transfer to the preheated oven to bake for 15 or 20 minutes, until the fish is almost done. (If the fish goes directly from the refrigerator to the oven, if may need an additional 15 to 20 minutes until done.)

While the fish is cooking, peel the whole lemon, leaving a small amount of the white in place. Cut off the ends and slice the lemon as thinly as you can.

Remove the fish from the oven and garnish with the lemon slices and capers. Baste with the pan juices and return to the oven for another 5 to 10 minutes, or until the fish is cooked through. Serve the fish directly from the oven dish, with the pan juices spooned over each serving.

Pesce al Forno alla Calabrese

OVEN-ROASTED WHOLE FISH FROM CALABRIA

When you find a whole fish, this is a quick and easy way to prepare it, one that retains all the flavors of the fish. Use any whole, firm-fleshed fish you can find; red snapper, sea bass, striped bass, Arctic char, and salmon are all good choices. A two-pound fish will easily serve four people and should fit an eighteen-inch baking pan; larger fish are fine too, but be sure you have a baking dish (and an oven!) large enough for the fish before you start to prepare it. The same treatment also works for smaller fish—one to a serving, for instance—but the baking time will obviously need to be adjusted for the size of the fish.

MAKES 4 TO 6 SERVINGS

1 whole fish, gutted and scaled but with head and tail on, weighing about 2 pounds	1 teaspoon crushed dried red chili	⅓ cup coarsely chopped flat-leaf parsley
¼ cup extra-virgin olive oil	1 teaspoon dried oregano	1 lemon, cut into quarters
	1 teaspoon sea salt	Juice of 1 lemon

Rinse the fish under running water, inside and out, and dry thoroughly with paper towels.

Use half the olive oil to oil the bottom of a roasting pan about 18 inches long (for a 2-pound fish). Combine the chili, oregano, and salt and rub the fish well all over, inside and out. Stuff the parsley into the opening, along with the lemon quarters. Set the fish in the pan and dribble the rest of the olive oil over the top. Cover lightly with plastic wrap or a towel and set aside for 30 to 60 minutes. (If you must refrigerate the fish, bring it back to room temperature before putting it in the oven or count on an additional 15 to 20 minutes of baking time.)

Preheat the oven to 425°F. Transfer the roasting pan to the preheated oven and bake for 15 to 20 minutes (for a 3-pound fish at room temperature when it is placed in the oven). Remove and immediately pour the lemon juice over the fish so that it sizzles slightly in the hot oven pan. Transfer the fish to a serving platter and spoon the pan juices over the top. Serve immediately.

Cernia con Patate allo Zafferano

BAKED WHOLE FISH WITH SAFFRON POTATOES

Cernia is grouper, but any large (at least 2 pounds) whole fish that you can find will be just fine here. See the note at the bottom of the recipe for a variation using fish steaks.

Saffron is used less in southern Italy than it once was—in fact, it's one of those flavors that seems to go in and out of fashion with almost predictable regularity. This recipe may start a swing of the wheel in a more positive direction.

MAKES 4 TO 6 SERVINGS

1 whole fish, cleaned and scaled but with head and tail on, about 2 pounds	1 yellow onion, chopped	4 medium waxy potatoes, peeled and thinly sliced
About ½ cup extra-virgin olive oil	1 garlic clove, chopped	Sea salt and freshly ground black pepper
Pinch of saffron threads	1 small dried red chili	
	⅓ cup dry white wine	
	2 tablespoons tomato puree or diced canned tomato	

Rinse the fish thoroughly in running water and dry inside and out with paper towels. Use a little of the olive oil to grease a rectangular or oval oven dish large enough to contain the fish. Set the fish in the dish.

Preheat the oven to 400°F.

Crisp the saffron by wrapping it in a clean white envelope (or fold a piece of clean white typing paper securely around the saffron). Set the paper in a dry skillet over medium heat. Toast, turning the paper with tongs, until it starts to turn a little golden, about 3 minutes.

Open the paper carefully and crumble the saffron. Sprinkle it over ¾ cup very hot water and set aside.

Heat ¼ cup of the olive oil in a skillet over medium-low heat and add the onion and garlic. Cook, stirring frequently, until the vegetables are very soft but not brown. Break the chili into the vegetables and mix well, then add the wine and bring it to a simmer. Simmer for a minute or two to burn off most of the alcohol. Stir in the tomato puree.

Distribute the potatoes around the fish in the oven dish. Spoon the onion-tomato sauce over the fish. Pour the saffron water over and around the potatoes. Sprinkle with salt and pepper and a few tablespoons of olive oil and transfer to the preheated oven. Bake the fish for 20 to 25 minutes, or until the fish is done all the way through, the potatoes are tender, and the sauce is quite dense. If the sauce seems too liquid, transfer the fish and potatoes to a heated serving platter and boil down the sauce in the dish (transferring it, if necessary, to a saucepan) until it is the desired consistency. Serve immediately.

VARIATION

Prepare inch-thick fish steaks in a similar manner, but blanch the potatoes in boiling water for 3 to 4 minutes before distributing them around the fish, to speed the cooking. The fish steaks should be done after 10 minutes in the oven.

Gianfranco Becchina's Pesce Arrosto

OVEN-ROASTED FISH

Gianfranco Becchina produces fine Sicilian olive oil on his estate in Castelvetrano. He is also a superb home cook, as evidenced by this recipe, for which he uses a whole cernia, or Mediterranean grouper.

Because it's difficult to find a whole fish in North American fish shops, I've adapted this recipe for fish steaks. Halibut steaks, cut about ¾ inch thick, are an excellent, if non-Mediterranean, choice. Half a halibut steak should be enough for each serving. If the potatoes aren't done when the fish steaks are, remove the steaks and hold them on a warm platter, then continue to cook the potatoes in the oven until they are tender.

MAKES 6 TO 8 SERVINGS

2 pounds potatoes, preferably Yellow Finn or Yukon Gold, peeled

2 pounds small, slender zucchini

¼ cup plus 2 tablespoons extra-virgin olive oil, preferably Sicilian

1 medium yellow onion, chopped

1 plump garlic clove, chopped

1 cup dry white wine

2 or 3 fresh plum tomatoes, peeled and chopped, or ⅔ cup chopped drained canned plum tomatoes

Crumbled dried red chili to taste (optional)

¼ cup capers, preferably salt-packed, rinsed and drained

4 halibut or other similar fish steaks, ¾ to 1 inch thick

½ cup black olives, preferably salt-cured, pitted

Salt and freshly ground black pepper

¼ cup fresh lemon juice

¼ cup minced flat-leaf parsley

Cut the potatoes into chunks, about 1½ inches to a side, and drop into a pan of rapidly boiling water. Return to a boil and cook for 5 minutes; drain and set aside. While the potatoes are cooking, trim the zucchini and cut in half lengthwise. Set aside.

Add ¼ cup of the olive oil to a sauté pan along with the onion and garlic and set over medium-low heat. Cook gently just until the vegetables soften, stirring occasionally. Raise the heat slightly and add the wine and tomatoes, along with a good pinch of crumbled red chili, if you wish. Cook rapidly, stirring, until the wine has reduced by about a third and the tomatoes are melting in the liquid. Remove from the heat and stir in the capers.

Preheat the oven to 325°F.

224   CUCINA DEL SOLE

Rub 2 tablespoons of olive oil over the bottom and sides of a roasting pan. Set the fish in the pan and arrange the blanched potatoes and the zucchini around the sides. Scatter the olives among the potatoes and zucchini. Spoon the prepared onion-wine sauce over the fish and vegetables and sprinkle with salt and pepper.

Transfer the pan to the oven and bake for 10 minutes; using tongs, turn the potatoes and zucchini and return to the oven for another 10 to 15 minutes, or until the potatoes are tender, by which time the fish will be cooked through.

Serve the fish directly from the roasting pan or transfer it to a heated serving platter, arranging the vegetables and olives around it. Stir the lemon juice and minced parsley into the pan juices and spoon over the fish. Serve immediately.

Pesce Spada al Limone

SWORDFISH IN A LEMON-CAPER SAUCE

Each year in late spring, when the swordfish are running through the Straits of Messina, the finest restaurants from Rome south to the tip end of Sicily add this simplest of preparations to their menus. The season is short, just a few weeks, and gourmands from the time of Archestratos in the late fourth century B.C.E. have delighted in this delicious offering. (Archestratos, a Sicilian Greek who is considered history's first great gastronome, esteemed the swordfish caught off Cape Pelorum—now Cape Faro—at the entrance to the Messina Straits, but I must admit that his first-place recommendation actually went to fish from the Bosporus.)

Italians generally like their swordfish sliced no more than ¼ inch thick, but, like most North Americans, I prefer a meatier slab. This is also a first-rate way to cook halibut or salmon steaks.

MAKES 6 SERVINGS

½ cup unbleached all-purpose flour	6 thick swordfish steaks, 5 to 6 ounces each	⅓ cup finely minced flat-leaf parsley
Sea salt and freshly ground black pepper	6 tablespoons extra-virgin olive oil	¼ cup capers, preferably salt-packed, rinsed and drained
	Juice of 2 lemons	

Combine the flour with salt and pepper to taste, tossing to mix well. Pat the fish steaks dry on both sides and dip them in the flour to coat lightly on all sides. It is important to dry and flour the fish; otherwise, it will steam and stay pale, rather than sauté and turn golden.

Heat ¼ cup of the olive oil in a sauté pan over medium heat. When it starts to shimmer, add the steaks, browning them well on both sides—about 4 minutes to a side. You may have to do this in 2 batches. As the fish finishes cooking, transfer it to a heated platter.

While the fish steaks cook, combine the lemon juice, parsley, and capers. When all the fish is done, discard the oil in the pan and add 2 tablespoons of fresh oil, along with the lemon-parsley-caper mixture. Bring just to a quick boil, then pour over the fish on the platter. Serve immediately.

Pesce Spada a' Sammurigghiu

BROILED SWORDFISH WITH LEMONY-OREGANO SALMORIGLIO

This Sicilian recipe is a good example of how salmoriglio is used in cooking, rather than as a sauce prepared and served apart (see page 211). The sauce here is both a marinade for the fish and a dressing to spoon over it as it cooks. The ingredients don't conceal the flavor of the fresh swordfish but rather exalt it.

Italians like their swordfish no more than ¼ inch thick. Like most North Americans, I prefer a thicker steak, at least ¾ inch, and that's what I've used in this recipe.

MAKES 6 SERVINGS

1½ pounds fresh swordfish steaks, ¾ inch thick	1 heaping teaspoon dried oregano, crumbled	Sea salt and freshly ground black pepper
½ cup extra-virgin olive oil	1 garlic clove, finely minced	Lemon wedges for serving
2 tablespoons fresh lemon juice		

Set the swordfish steaks on a flat platter or baking dish. Combine the olive oil, lemon juice, oregano, garlic, and salt and pepper to taste and beat vigorously with a fork or a small whisk. Pour all the salmoriglio over the swordfish and set aside, lightly covered, to marinate for at least 1 hour.

Preheat the oven broiler or grill as hot as you can get it. Arrange the steaks on a rack over a broiling or roasting pan. Paint them liberally with the marinade right before you put them in the preheated oven. Broil until the fish is opaque on top, but do not let the fish dry out—5 to 7 minutes should be sufficient. Or, if you have a stovetop grill, cook the steaks on the top of the stove. Turn the fish over and again brush liberally with the marinade. Return to the heat for another 3 minutes.

When the fish is done to taste all the way through, transfer to a serving platter and pour the hot pan juices over it. Serve immediately, with lemon wedges.

Involtini di Pesce Spada alla Messinese

STUFFED SWORDFISH ROLLS

For this recipe you'll need thin swordfish steaks, less than ¼ inch thick. If the fishmonger objects, ask him—very nicely and in advance—to freeze a larger section of swordfish for no more than an hour to firm it up, then to slice it on an electric slicer. You can also do this at home, although without an electric slicer, it is not easy to get slices that are consistent throughout.

When swordfish isn't available, or simply for variety's sake, try sandwiching the filling between two fillets of flatfish, such as sole or flounder. A flatfish sandwich, with a thin layer of filling, will cook more quickly than the involtini—10 minutes in a hot oven should be plenty of time.

MAKES 8 SERVINGS, at least 1 involtino per serving

2½ pounds thinly sliced swordfish	1 celery stalk, finely minced	3 tablespoons finely minced flat-leaf parsley
4 to 5 tablespoons extra-virgin olive oil	3 tablespoons finely minced yellow onion	1 egg
¾ cup fine dry bread crumbs	10 large green olives, pitted and finely chopped	4 small yellow onions, peeled and quartered
3 tablespoons capers, preferably salt-packed, rinsed, dried, and coarsely chopped	2 tablespoons golden raisins or black currants, soaked in hot water to plump	5 or 6 bay leaves, broken in half
3 tablespoons finely grated aged caciocavallo or parmigiano reggiano	2 tablespoons pine nuts	

Trim the swordfish steaks of their skin and any excess dark meat. Dry them well with paper towels. If the steaks are very large, cut them in two. Lay a steak (or half-steak) between 2 sheets of wax paper and very gently tap the steak all over to stretch it and make it even thinner. A rolling pin makes a dandy tool for this. The procedure is exactly the same as for making veal scaloppine but fish has a much more delicate texture; hence the caution. Set the steaks aside.

Preheat the oven to 400°F. Smear the bottom of a ceramic or glass oven dish with about a tablespoon of olive oil.

Set aside ¼ cup of the bread crumbs to use later. Mix the remaining ½ cup in a bowl with the capers, cheese, celery, minced onion, olives, raisins, pine nuts, and parsley. Add the egg and

2 tablespoons of olive oil and mix well. The mixture should be a slightly crumbly paste. Now place a swordfish steak on a cutting board and set 2 to 3 tablespoons of the bread crumb mixture at one end of the steak. Roll it up to make a snug roll, fastening the roll with toothpicks if it seems necessary. As you finish each roll, set it in the prepared dish. The rolls should fit snugly, without crowding. When all the rolls are in place, tuck the little onion quarters and the bay leaves around them. Sprinkle the rolls with the reserved bread crumbs and dribble them with more olive oil. Set in the preheated oven and roast for 15 to 20 minutes, or until the rolls are cooked through and turning a little golden on top. Remove and serve immediately with the roasted onion quarters.

La Mattanza

The mattanza, the annual slaughter of tuna that used to take place not just in Italy but in many areas of the Mediterranean, including Spain and Tunisia, has been described beautifully by Theresa Maggio in her book *Mattanza: Love and Death in the Sea of Sicily.* Maggio was lucky enough to experience, on many occasions, the historic mattanza on the island of Favignana, off Sicily's western coast, before the centuries-old, carefully prescribed ritual devolved into a spectacle for tourists. The last time I visited Favignana during the tuna season (generally May and June, when the big fish pass through the Canale di Sicilia on their way to their breeding grounds), the fishermen themselves were flexing their muscles in front of admiring girl tourists in the main piazza, just like small-town would-be rock stars, and the fishery itself seemed to take place exclusively for French television cameras.

In its essence, as Maggio and others have described it, the tuna hunt must have been very similar to the kind of organized mass killing that has provided humans with protein since the Paleolithic. And it is not the fault of the fishermen of Favignana and elsewhere that the hunt has become so debased—or not entirely their fault. The Mediterranean, like other parts of the global ocean, is an endangered resource, partly because of a constantly escalating demand for seafood on the world market and even more because harvesting methods are wasteful and destructive in the extreme. Overfishing, often by drift-netting, which is singularly damaging, has resulted in Mediterranean tuna, like swordfish, that every year are smaller in size and fewer in number. Not only that, but its impact on other fish in the sea is also injurious, almost to the point that recovery becomes questionable.

Tonno alla Marinara

OVEN-BAKED TUNA WITH A SAVORY TOPPING

1 fresh tuna steak, about ¾ inch thick (about 1 pound)

2 tablespoons extra-virgin olive oil

½ teaspoon sea salt

1 teaspoon crushed dried red chili

6 black olives, preferably salt-cured, pitted

1 tablespoon capers, preferably salt-packed, rinsed and drained

5 or 6 large fresh basil leaves

16 to 20 ripe cherry tomatoes, coarsely chopped

2 tablespoons fine dry bread crumbs

Preheat the oven to 350°F.

Pat the tuna steak dry. Spread a little of the olive oil over the bottom of an oven dish in which the tuna will fit comfortably and set the steak in the dish. Smear a little more oil over the top of the steak and sprinkle on the salt and chili.

Chop together the black olives, capers, and basil to make a coarse, crumbly mixture. Pile this on top of the tuna and then add the chopped tomatoes. Sprinkle the bread crumbs over the tomatoes and dribble the remaining oil over the top.

Transfer the dish to the preheated oven and bake for 15 to 20 minutes, or until the tuna is done to taste. (In southern Italy, tuna is almost always cooked well done, but Americans may prefer it with a streak of raw in the middle.)

Tonno al Pesto Trapanese

TUNA WITH A SAUCE OF TRAPANI PESTO

Just as the cuisine of Messina is always coupled with swordfish, from the fishery that takes place in the straits between Sicily and the mainland of Italy, so Trapani is associated with tuna because of the tuna harvest off the west coast of Sicily. Pesto Trapanese is quite different from the Ligurian pesto that most of us are used to because it uses almonds and tomatoes instead of pine nuts and basil.

MAKES 4 SERVINGS

4 tuna steaks, about ⅓ pound each	Pesto Trapanese, about ¾ cup (page 144)	½ cup fine dry bread crumbs
¼ cup extra-virgin olive oil		

Preheat the oven to 400°F.

Rinse and pat dry the tuna steaks. Use about a tablespoon of the olive oil to grease the bottom of an oven dish just large enough to hold all the tuna. Distribute some of the pesto over the bottom, then set the tuna steaks on top. Spread the remaining pesto over the tops of the fish, then sprinkle with the bread crumbs. Dribble any remaining oil over the crumbs and transfer the dish to the preheated oven. Bake for 12 to 15 minutes, or until the bread crumbs are crisp and golden and the tuna is done to your taste. Remove and serve immediately.

Sarde al Beccafico

SARDINES COOKED LIKE LITTLE BIRDS

Sarde al beccafico literally means "sardines in the guise of fig peckers." It's a Sicilian joke: The tails of the sardines, poking up above the bread crumbs, look just like the open mouths of little song-birds roasted in the oven. Or so they say. I, who have never roasted songbirds, take it on faith. If you find fresh sardines, this is a splendid if rather labor-intensive way to treat them.

MAKES 6 SERVINGS

About 2½ pounds sardines (24 small sardines)

1 cup bread crumbs

About 6 tablespoons extra-virgin olive oil

6 anchovy fillets, coarsely chopped

½ cup currants or golden raisins, plumped in warm water and drained

½ cup pine nuts

¼ cup capers, preferably salt-packed, rinsed and drained

¼ cup coarsely chopped pitted black olives

1 garlic clove, coarsely chopped

¼ cup coarsely chopped flat-leaf parsley

Sea salt and freshly ground black pepper to taste

2 tablespoons fresh lemon juice (from ½ lemon)

24 bay leaves

Prepare the sardines by cutting off the heads, slitting the bellies, and gutting them. Open each sardine like a book, leaving the two sides attached at the tail, and remove the backbone. Don't worry about getting every little bone out—sardine bones are very soft, and, in any case, we all need the extra calcium. Rinse the sardines and pat dry with paper towels.

In a saucepan over medium heat, combine half the bread crumbs with 2 tablespoons of the olive oil and toast the bread crumbs until they are crisp and golden. Remove from pan and set aside.

Add 2 more tablespoons of olive oil to the pan along with the anchovies. Cook the an-chovies, mashing them into the oil with a fork. When the anchovies are thoroughly melted into the oil, combine them with the toasted bread crumbs in a small bowl. Add all the remaining in-gredients except the bay leaves and the remaining ½ cup of bread crumbs.

Preheat the oven to 400°F. Use a little olive oil to lightly grease an oven dish that will just hold all the rolled-up sardines.

Take a butterflied sardine and spread it out, skin side down. Put about a teaspoon of the bread crumb mixture on the wide (head) end of the sardine and roll the fish up, jelly roll fashion, toward the tail. Set the sardine roll in the oiled oven dish with the tail sticking up. Continue with all the sardines. Then insert bay leaves in among them and sprinkle the remaining, untoasted bread crumbs over the top. Finally, dribble about a tablespoonful of olive oil over the top crumbs. Transfer the dish to the preheated oven and bake for 15 to 20 minutes, or until the bread crumbs are crunchy and golden.

Serve immediately.

Sarde Ammolicato

SMOTHERED SARDINES

In a part of the world where dozens of different small species of fish proliferate, every fishing port has a different way of dealing with them. This is one way that is quite typical all over southern Italy. If you can't find sardines, use other small whole fish as available. Depending on their size, the fish may also be filleted and dredged in the bread crumb mixture. Whether whole small fish or fillets of larger fish, some cooks prefer to grill or fry the fish, but baking them in the oven is easier, and it's a very tidy operation.

To butterfly sardines, cut off the heads, using a sharp knife, then slit open the bellies and pull out and discard the innards and the backbone, but leave the fish attached along the upper edge and at their tails. Don't feel you must remove every last little bone—sardine bones are very soft and easily digested, and the calcium is good for you too.

MAKES 6 SERVINGS

2½ pounds sardines, butterflied (4 per serving, or 24 sardines)	2 garlic cloves, finely chopped	½ teaspoon dried oregano
	¼ cup minced flat-leaf parsley	Sea salt and freshly ground black pepper
½ cup extra-virgin olive oil, plus a little oil for the top	⅓ cup dry bread crumbs	

Rinse the fish under running water and pat thoroughly dry with paper towels. Preheat the oven to 400°F.

Use a little of the olive oil to oil the bottom of a rectangular or oval oven dish large enough to hold all the fish in one layer without overlapping. Arrange the fish in the bottom of the dish.

Warm the rest of the olive oil in a small skillet over medium heat and add the garlic. Cook, stirring occasionally, until the garlic is soft but not brown. Add the parsley and stir just until it has softened, then stir in the bread crumbs. Cook, stirring, until the bread crumbs are crisp and golden. Crumble the dried oregano into the mixture and add salt and pepper to taste. Spoon this over the fish and dribble a little more olive oil over the crumbs before you put the fish in the oven.

Bake for 10 to 15 minutes, or until the crumb crust gets very crisp and dark golden. Remove and serve immediately.

Pesciolini in Scapece

PUGLIESE MARINATED FISH WITH VINEGAR AND MINT

Scapece or *escabeche,* often made with sardines or other small, throw-away fish, is found all over the Mediterranean in one form or another as a way of preserving fish for a short period of time. In Gallipoli, a bustling fishing port on the Ionian coast of Puglia, the fish used to be marinated in saffron vinegar and sold by street vendors called *scapecieri,* but home cooks are more apt to use garlic and crushed mint instead of the far more costly saffron. The meaty texture of sardines responds well to these strong flavors, but fresh sardines are hard to come by in North America, so I have occasionally made this with smelts instead. They have an entirely different flavor, but it's still an interesting dish. If you can find impeccably fresh sardines, though, firm textured and with a clean, briny fragrance, by all means use them.

In Venice, a similar preparation is called *pesce en saor,* and on Sicily's east coast it is *pesce di maloverso, maloverso* meaning a period of bad weather at sea, when fishing families must subsist on their share of a previous catch, preserved by this method. In the catalog of preserved fish, this is the simplest and roughest technique. But it makes an excellent first course or an antipasto for a summertime meal.

Serve the scapece with slices of crusty country-style bread, lightly toasted if you wish, for sopping up the juices.

MAKES 4 TO 6 SERVINGS

1½ pounds small fish, preferably sardines	1 tablespoon chopped fresh mint, or more to taste	½ cup fresh bread crumbs
4 or 5 garlic cloves, crushed	1 cup white wine vinegar	About ¼ cup unbleached all-purpose flour
	1 cup extra-virgin olive oil	

The fish should be gutted and the heads may be cut off, but otherwise they should be left whole. Rinse them quickly under running water and pat dry with paper towels. Combine the garlic and mint with the vinegar in a small saucepan over medium-low heat. As soon as the vinegar starts to boil, remove the pan from the heat, but keep the vinegar warm while the aromatics steep for at least 20 minutes.

In about a tablespoon of the olive oil, toast the bread crumbs in a small skillet over medium-high heat until they are golden brown and crisp. Remove from the heat and set aside.

Dredge each fish lightly in the flour. Add ½ cup of the remaining olive oil to a larger skillet over medium-high heat. When the oil is hot, brown the fish on both sides, about 3 minutes per side. Transfer the fish to a rack covered with paper towels to drain. When all the fish have been fried, discard the oil and wipe out the pan. Add the remaining clean olive oil to the pan and set over very low heat just to warm. Use a slotted spoon to extract the garlic and mint from the vinegar, but do not discard.

Layer the fish in a glass or ceramic dish, like a soufflé dish, sprinkling each layer liberally with toasted bread crumbs and the garlic and mint from the vinegar infusion. The topmost layer of toasted bread crumbs should completely cover the fish. Now combine the warm vinegar and warm clean oil and pour over the bread crumbs. Cover the dish with plastic wrap and set aside for several hours or up to 2 to 3 days in the refrigerator. If you refrigerate the fish, be sure to bring the dish back to room temperature before serving.

Baccalà Fritta alla Napoletana

BATTER-FRIED SALT COD FOR CHRISTMAS EVE

Neapolitans consider Baccalà Fritta to be essential for Christmas Eve, La Vigilia, which is traditionally a meatless feast. (See U Spaghett'Anatalina, page 146, for another Neapolitan Christmas Eve dish.) For Christmas the cod is usually served simply with lemon wedges to squeeze over it, but at other times of the year Baccalà Fritta may be served with a luxurious Tomato Sauce with Olives, Golden Raisins, and Pine Nuts (page 212). See page 238 for directions on freshening salt cod. If you don't wish to use salt cod, fillets of fresh cod, haddock, snapper, or similar firm-textured white-fleshed fish work very well with this recipe.

MAKES 10 TO 12 SERVINGS

½ teaspoon dry yeast	3 cups extra-virgin olive oil	Finely chopped flat-leaf parsley and lemon quarters for garnish
1½ cups unbleached all-purpose flour, plus about ⅓ cup for dredging the fish	3 pounds boneless salt cod, soaked out, or 4 pounds fresh cod, haddock, or similar fish fillets, cut into 2-inch pieces	
Sea salt		

Combine the yeast with ¼ cup very warm water in a medium bowl and let stand until the yeast is dissolved. Add 1½ cups of the flour, another 1½ cups of warm water, and salt to taste and beat the batter with a wooden spoon, until it is thick, smooth, and elastic. Cover the bowl with plastic wrap and set aside to rise in a warm place for about 30 minutes.

When ready to cook, set out a soup plate with the remaining flour in it. Have ready a rack spread with paper towels for draining the fish.

In a pan suitable for deep-fat frying, set the olive oil over medium heat and heat to around 360°F. (A small cube of bread will brown in about a minute, but use a frying or candy thermometer to be accurate. Batter-fried foods will absorb fat if cooked at a lower temperature.)

While the oil is heating, beat 3 tablespoons of water into the risen batter to loosen it to the consistency of heavy cream.

Pat the fish pieces dry with paper towels. Quickly dredge the fish pieces in the flour, shaking off the excess, then dip each piece in the batter, allowing any excess to drip off. Fry in the hot oil, turning the pieces once (use tongs to turn), until they are crisp and golden brown, about

6 minutes. Adjust the heat as necessary to keep the frying temperature constant. As the pieces brown, transfer them to the draining rack.

When all the fish is done, transfer the pieces to a heated platter and garnish with the parsley and lemon quarters. If you wish, pass a bowl of warm Tomato Sauce with Olives, Golden Raisins, and Pine Nuts to accompany the fish.

Salt Cod—Baccalà

It may seem surprising that in a seafood paradise like southern Italy cooks would use salt cod from the North Atlantic, but the tradition, which goes back over the centuries, is strong to this day. When a chef puts salt cod on the menu, the restaurant often runs out before the end of service, so popular is the demand. Most likely the tradition grew from the time when fish was the only "meat" allowed during Lent and other fasting periods. Lent comes at a time of the year when seas are rough and stormy and fishermen, if they can, prefer to stay safely in port. Thus, anyone who wanted fish during Lent, as many people did, had to make do either with *baccalà*, cod that has been cured by heavy salting and then dried, or with its close cousin, *stoccafisso* (stockfish), cod that has been air-dried without salting. Throughout Italy, when recipes call for baccalà, it is often stoccafisso that is used. Italian chefs vaunt the virtues of stoccafisso over baccalà, but I find the flavor of stoccafisso a bit high for North Americans, who prefer the milder taste of baccalà. (If you wish to try stockfish, you can often find it at West African or Caribbean groceries.)

Baccalà (or bacalao, its Spanish name) is available from good fishmongers, especially in Italian, Greek, or Portuguese neighborhoods. You can also find it online at Browne Trading and other dealers in high-quality seafood (see Where to Find It, page 415). I don't recommend the salt fish that comes in cute little wooden boxes, because the cod inside is not very good quality. Instead, I buy a whole side of boneless salt cod, weighing about three pounds, and soak it out in a large basin of cool water. Count on twenty-four to thirty-six hours of soaking, changing the water periodically, to freshen the cod. How do you know when it's ready? By the taste, which should be neither overly salty nor totally bland. Soaked-out cod will keep for several days in the refrigerator, so the soaking process can be carried out ahead of time for these recipes.

Baccalà con Peperoni alla Napoletana

SALT COD AND SWEET RED PEPPERS IN A NEAPOLITAN TOMATO SAUCE

Another favorite way of treating salt cod in the Terra di Lavoro, the fertile Casertano region north of Naples, this one takes advantage of summer peppers and tomatoes to make a dish that's perfect for farmworkers intent on getting their crops to market. Like other salt cod recipes, this one is quite acceptable made with any firm-textured white-fleshed fish, such as fresh cod. Note, however, that if you use fresh fish, rather than refreshed salt fish, the pieces must be dried thoroughly, then dredged lightly in flour just before being fried.

MAKES 6 SERVINGS

½ cup extra-virgin olive oil, plus 2 tablespoons, if necessary

1¼ to 1½ pounds refreshed salt cod (see page 238) or fresh fish

All-purpose flour for dredging fresh fish

2 medium onions, thinly sliced

1 pound ripe tomatoes, peeled, seeded, and chopped

1 tablespoon tomato concentrate, extract, or paste

3 sweet red peppers, roasted and peeled (see page 338)

½ small fresh hot green or red chili, roasted and peeled (see page 338)

2 tablespoons golden raisins, soaked in hot water to plump

Sea salt and freshly ground black pepper

2 tablespoons pine nuts

½ cup minced flat-leaf parsley

In a medium skillet, heat ½ cup of the olive oil over medium heat until it has reached frying temperature (360°F).

While the oil is heating, cut the fish into 1-inch pieces. Pat refreshed salt cod dry with paper towels. If you're using fresh fish, pat it dry, then dredge it lightly in flour, spread on a plate. (Do the drying and dredging right before you're ready to fry; otherwise the coating will get gummy.)

When the oil is hot, add the fish pieces to the pan a few at a time and fry briskly until golden on all sides, transferring the finished pieces to a rack spread with paper towels to drain.

When all the fish pieces are done, lower the heat to low. Discard the oil, wipe the pan out, and add 2 tablespoons of fresh olive oil. Add the sliced onions and cook gently over low heat, stirring occasionally, until the onions are very soft. Add the tomatoes, raise the heat slightly, and cook vigorously. As the tomatoes yield their liquid, stir in the tablespoon of concentrate. Continue to cook the tomatoes until they have disintegrated into a chunky sauce.

While the tomatoes are cooking, slice the peeled peppers into long ½-inch-thick strips. Chop the chili coarsely. Drain the soaking raisins.

Lower the heat under the tomato sauce again, then taste and add salt and pepper, keeping in mind that the salt cod may be very salty. Stir in the peppers, raisins, and pine nuts. Finally, fold in the pieces of fried fish. Cook the fish in the sauce over low heat for about 10 minutes to meld the flavors together, then serve immediately, garnished with the minced parsley.

How do I clean a squid? If you've never done this before, don't be alarmed: It's actually quite easy. Assuming you're right-handed, take the squid body in your left hand and the tentacles in your right. Give a gentle tug and the whole interior of the beast will slide out. Set the body or hood aside to be rinsed. Cut off the tentacles below the eyes and press out and discard the little bulb in the center of the tentacles where the mouth or beak is. Discard the beak and set the tentacles aside. The innards may be discarded, but if you care about it (and I do!), find and remove the little silvery sac that holds the squid ink. (You won't need it for this dish, but you can freeze it and use it later in Spaghetti al Nero di Seppia, page 181, for instance.) Be very careful not to puncture the sac itself. Put all the sacs together in a small bowl and cover with plastic wrap. Later on you should squeeze out the ink and either refrigerate it or freeze it, carefully covered.

Rinse the hoods inside and out. Some people believe you should take off the purple membrane clinging to the outside of the hood; others say it adds flavor to the dish. If you wish to remove it, it's easy, if a bit tedious, to do so. Rinse the tentacles. This may all be done several hours ahead of time and the squid refrigerated until ready to cook.

Seppie o Calamari Ripieni
STUFFED SQUID

Uncleaned whole squid with their tentacles still attached are not always easy to find. If you don't come across uncleaned squid, use the cleaned squid hoods and replace the chopped tentacles with a couple of ounces of peeled shrimp. It won't be as tasty, but it will still be pretty darned good.

MAKES 6 TO 8 SERVINGS

About 3 pounds uncleaned whole squid of uniform size (about 10 squid)	¾ cup finely chopped flat-leaf parsley	8 to 10 large green olives, pitted and coarsely chopped
1½ cups dry bread crumbs	2 to 3 tablespoons milk	3 canned plum tomatoes, drained and coarsely chopped
2 eggs, lightly beaten	About ½ cup extra-virgin olive oil	
3 garlic cloves, 2 chopped, 1 minced	Sea salt and freshly ground black pepper	½ cup dry white wine
1 medium onion, chopped	½ cup grated aged pecorino or parmigiano reggiano	Lemon wedges for garnish

Prepare the squid as described on page 241. Chop the tentacles into small pieces and transfer to a bowl. Add the bread crumbs and eggs. Combine the chopped garlic and onion and chop very fine. Add to the bread crumbs along with ½ cup of the parsley. Stir in the milk and 3 tablespoons of the olive oil. Add salt and pepper to taste, the cheese, olives, and tomatoes. Using your hands, mix everything together well. Fill the squid hoods loosely with the bread crumb mixture, keeping in mind that the filling will expand as it cooks. Reserve about ½ cup of the stuffing mixture to go in the bottom of the oven dish.

Preheat the oven to 375°F.

Now chop together the remaining ¼ cup of parsley and the minced garlic and place in a skillet with the rest of the oil. Cook gently, just until the aromas start to rise. Add the wine and bring it to a simmer. Spread a couple of tablespoons of the stuffing mixture over the bottom of an oven dish large enough to hold all the squid. Spoon a little of the oil-and-wine mixture on top. Arrange the squid bodies in the dish, then spoon the remaining oil-and-wine mixture over them. Cover loosely with aluminum foil and bake for 30 minutes, or until the squid and their stuffing are cooked through.

Remove from the oven and baste the squid bodies with the juices in the dish. Raise the oven temperature to 425°F and return the dish to the oven, uncovered, for another 5 to 10 minutes, to brown the tops of the stuffed squids. Remove from the oven and serve immediately, with lemon wedges and with the small amount of sauce left in the pan spooned over the squid.

VARIATIONS

Stuffed squid are served all over southern Italy, taking on various local colorations. If you want a more Calabrian dish, add a quantity of crumbled dried red chilies to the filling and a pinch of ground chili to the wine-and-oil mixture. If, on the other hand, you want a dish that tastes of Sicily, add pine nuts, soaked and drained raisins, and chopped black olives, together with a little finely grated lemon zest, to the filling.

Totani e Patate in Umido

BRAISED SQUID AND POTATOES

Italians have half a dozen different kinds of cephalopods—seppie, calamari, polpi (octopus), and moscardini (little octopus) among them. Totani are small squid, very sweet and tender. In this dish, the hoods (or bodies) of the critters are sliced into rings, and the tentacles are chopped and scattered over the rings. The yellow-fleshed potatoes absorb the flavor and fragrance of the sea. This dish makes a fine main course, although it's sometimes served as a first course or starter.

MAKES 4 SERVINGS

About ¾ pound small squid (calamari), cleaned (see page 241)

1 garlic clove, chopped

¼ cup extra-virgin olive oil, plus a little oil for the top

¼ cup dry white wine

3 medium yellow-fleshed potatoes, such as Yellow Finn or Yukon Gold, about ¾ pound, cut into ½-inch dice

12 to 16 cherry or grape tomatoes, halved

½ cup chopped flat-leaf parsley

1 teaspoon crushed dried red chili

Sea salt and freshly ground black pepper

¼ cup fine dry bread crumbs

2 tablespoons grated hard aged cheese: pecorino, caciocavallo, or parmigiano reggiano

Preheat the oven to 375°F.

Rinse the cleaned squid and pat dry with paper towels. Cut the hoods into rings ¼ to ½ inch thick. Slice the tentacles in half.

Combine the garlic and ¼ cup of olive oil in a deep skillet large enough to hold all the ingredients and cook over medium-low heat until the garlic is soft but not brown.

Add the squid pieces to the skillet, raise the heat slightly, and cook, stirring frequently, until the squid have lost their translucence, about 4 minutes. Stir in the wine and cook briefly, scraping up any brown bits on the bottom of the pan. Add the potatoes and ½ cup or so of hot water.

As soon as the liquid comes to a simmer, transfer the contents of the skillet to an oven dish such as an oval gratin dish. Cover the dish with aluminum foil and place in the preheated oven.

Bake for 25 minutes, or until the potatoes are very tender. Remove from the oven and stir in the tomatoes, ¼ cup of the parsley, the chili, and salt and black pepper to taste. Combine the remaining ¼ cup of parsley with the bread crumbs and cheese and sprinkle over the top of the potatoes and squid. Dribble a little olive oil over the top.

Return the dish to the oven and continue cooking, uncovered, for 20 minutes, or until the top is nicely browned. Remove from the oven and let sit for 5 to 10 minutes before serving.

Mussels

For those who think aquaculture was invented in the twentieth century, it will come as a surprise to learn that mussels and oysters have been cultivated in Puglia since Roman times, if not earlier. The Mar Piccolo, the broad lagoon of Taranto on the Ionian coast (the arch of the instep of the Italian boot), is famous to this day for the cultivation of mussels and oysters, which are said to be particularly tasty because of the freshwater springs, called *citri,* that occur naturally within the salty lagoon and keep the waters nicely brackish, just what oysters and mussels prefer. These are Mediterranean black mussels (*Mytilus galloprovincialis*), not the blue mussels (*M. edulis*) common to our shores and in our markets. If you can't find black mussels (they are grown in California and the Pacific Northwest), Maine blue mussels will do just fine in southern Italian mussel dishes.

Mussels, like clams, should be alive when purchased. Unless you are able to harvest your own (and never do that before checking with local authorities to make sure mussel beds are safe), farmed mussels, raised by aquaculture, are what is available. Most of them are very clean and need little more than a quick rinse under running water, scrubbing the shells together. Discard any with broken or gaping shells or any that feel suspiciously heavy—they may be full of mud. If mussels still seem gritty after cleaning, put them in a bowl of cool salted water into which you've stirred a spoonful of cornmeal and leave them for an hour or so. If the mussels have beards, use a paring knife to pull them away—but do this just before cooking, or, I am told, they will die.

To open raw mussels, cover your left hand (assuming you are right-handed) with a heavy workglove or towel to protect it and grip the mussel. Insert a small, strong, sharp oyster knife between the two shells at the point on the straighter edge where they are joined by a small muscle. Slide the knife back and forth to cut and loosen the muscle, then twist to separate the two shells. Do this over a bowl to catch the liquid in the shells—it's a tasty addition to any preparation.

But I'd be the first to confess that, when recipes require opening raw mussels, I usually cheat by steaming the mussels open first. I clean them, then put them in a deep wide saucepan with a couple of tablespoons of water or dry white wine, cover the pan, and steam them over medium heat just until the mussels start to open, making it easier to get at them. Don't worry if the mussels aren't thoroughly cooked—that will happen later in the process. But do discard any that fail to open after 8 or 10 minutes of steaming.

Pepata di Cozze

STEAMED MUSSELS WITH CRACKED BLACK PEPPER

You could crack the peppercorns simply by setting your pepper mill for a coarse grind, but cooks in Puglia crack them with a mortar and pestle for a more satisfying flavor.

In Pugliese kitchens, the mussels are cooked right in their peppery sauce, but if you're worried about grit in the mussels, cook them, as described here, separately from the sauce, then strain the mussel liquid to get rid of grit. Combine the mussel liquid, the mussels, and the sauce for a final simmer to bring the flavors together.

MAKES 4 SERVINGS AS A MAIN COURSE, 6 to 8 servings as a first course

4 pounds mussels	1 sweet green pepper, thinly sliced	1 teaspoon fresh lemon juice
1 celery stalk, including leaves, coarsely chopped	Zest of 1 lemon, preferably organic, thinly sliced	1 tablespoon freshly cracked black pepper, or more to taste
1 garlic clove, coarsely chopped	¼ cup extra-virgin olive oil	Pinch of freshly ground cinnamon
½ cup coarsely chopped flat-leaf parsley	½ cup dry white wine	

Rinse the mussels under running water and pick them over, discarding any with broken shells. Set aside.

Chop together the celery, garlic, and parsley. In a saucepan large enough to hold all the mussels in no more than 2 layers, combine the chopped vegetables with the sliced green pepper, lemon zest, and olive oil. Set over medium heat and cook, stirring occasionally, until the vegetables are soft but not brown. Add the wine and lemon juice and, as soon as the liquid comes to a boil, stir in the black pepper and cinnamon. Bring to a simmer and set aside.

Add the mussels to a separate pan and set the dry pan over medium heat. Cook, stirring and tossing, until all the mussels have opened. (If, after 10 minutes, there are still mussels that have not opened, discard them.) Remove from the heat, remove the mussels, and discard the empty shells. Strain the mussel liquid in the pan through a fine-mesh sieve or a linen or muslin cloth. Add to the pepper liquid in the first pan and turn in all the mussels. Return to medium heat and bring to a simmer, constantly stirring and tossing the mussels as you do so. The mussels need no further cooking—the moment the peppery sauce is hot is the moment to serve them.

Cozze alla Marinara

STEAMED MUSSELS IN A TOMATO SAUCE

This treatment, a favorite of legions of Neapolitan mussel lovers, is usually served over rounds of toasted bread, rubbed with garlic and dribbled with olive oil, but it is also a fine sauce for spaghetti, especially if you boil the pasta until it is not quite done, then let it finish cooking in the mussel-tomato sauce, a process Italian cooks call *saltando in padella*. Either way you serve it, the mussels are almost always intended as a generous first course.

MAKES 4 SERVINGS

4 pounds mussels	1½ cups finely chopped ripe fresh tomatoes or 6 to 8 canned tomatoes, drained	Sea salt and freshly ground black pepper
1 cup dry white wine		Slices of toasted bread, rubbed with garlic and dribbled with olive oil
2 tablespoons extra-virgin olive oil	1 teaspoon dried oregano	
2 garlic cloves, chopped	⅓ cup finely minced flat-leaf parsley	

Rinse the mussels under running water, discarding any with broken shells. Combine mussels and wine in a covered saucepan and set over medium heat. Cook until the mussels open, using tongs to remove each one. Discard unopened mussels after 10 minutes.

Shell the mussels, if you wish, or just remove the empty shell from each mussel pair, leaving the mussel attached to its half-shell. Strain the liquid through a fine-mesh sieve to get rid of any grit and set aside.

In a saucepan large enough to hold all the mussels with their sauce, combine the olive oil and garlic and set over medium-low heat. Cook until the garlic is meltingly soft but not brown. Add the tomatoes, raise the heat slightly, and cook rapidly until the tomato sauce starts to thicken. Stir in the oregano and parsley, then about 1 cup of the mussel cooking liquid, and finally the mussels themselves. Taste and add a little salt (mussels and their liquid can often be quite salty) and plenty of black pepper. The sauce should be quite thick, but you may add more mussel liquid if necessary or it seems too dense.

Put a slice of toasted bread in the bottom of each soup plate. Spoon the mussels and their sauce over the bread and serve immediately.

Vongole Saltate in Padella

CLAMS TOSSED IN A PAN

The clams used in southern Italy for this dish are small vongole verace, which are very clean since they are aquacultured. In North America I use widely available cockles or small brown Manila or mahogany clams to very good effect. Littlenecks and soft-shell clams, on the other hand, don't work in this recipe.

For linguine alle vongole verace, see note below.

MAKES 6 SERVINGS

2 pounds clean small cockles or Manila or mahogany clams	1 dried red chili, chopped if fresh, crumbled if dried	¼ cup finely chopped flat-leaf parsley
¼ cup extra-virgin olive oil	6 to 8 plump garlic cloves, chopped	1 slice toasted country-style bread for each serving (optional)
	¼ cup dry white wine	

Rinse the cockles or clams under running water and pick them over, discarding any with broken shells. Set aside.

In a wide pan deep enough to hold all the ingredients, heat the olive oil over medium-low heat and add the chili and garlic. Cook, stirring, just until the garlic starts to soften but is not browned. Add the wine and let it come to a boil. Add the cockles all at once and continue cooking, stirring and tossing, until all the cockles have opened. (Any that do not open after 10 to 12 minutes of cooking should be discarded.)

Sprinkle with chopped parsley and serve immediately. If you wish, set a slice of toast in the bottom of each soup plate and spoon the cockles and their juice over.

NOTE: *To make linguine alle vongole verace, bring a pot of lightly salted water to a rolling boil and drop in 1 pound of linguine. Use a slotted spoon to remove the cockles from their sauce as they open and set them aside in a warm place. When the pasta is almost done, drain it and turn it into the sauce remaining in the pan. Let the pasta finish cooking in the sauce, then transfer to a heated serving bowl and pile the cockles on top. Garnish with chopped parsley.*

Seafood Soups (Zuppe di Pesce)

You could wander like a nomad, from fishing port to fishing port, all down around the Italian peninsula, from Manfredonia in northern Puglia to Santa Maria di Leuca at the tip of the heel, up to Gallipoli and Porto Cesareo, then over the instep curve to Roseto and down to the toe, past ancient Crotone, then around the end and up toward Reggio and Scilla (of Scylla and Charybdis) and on to Tropea and Praia a Mare, then up past Acciaroli and Pisciotta and eventually to Napoli, where you could take a boat to Sicily and go from Palermo to Trapani to Mazara del Vallo and Sciacca and around to Siracusa and Catania, with its fabulous fish market, on the eastern end of the island, slipping past Messina and back toward Palermo with stops in Cefalù and Porticello. And in every harbor you would taste a different version of zuppa di pesce made by local cooks and distinguished from all others for its briny excellence. Or so the locals claim.

The differences are not always obvious—more or less parsley, basil, or oregano; fresh or canned or sun-dried tomatoes; fish alone, shellfish and crustaceans alone, or fish plus shellfish and crustaceans. White wine or red? Orange or lemon peel? Chilies? Bay leaves? Capers? Olives?

In fact the differences are mostly in the details. A strict structuralist interpretation of seafood soups and stews reveals not so much differences as startling similarities. Almost always you begin with a quick sauté of garlic, parsley, and chopped tomatoes, followed by a deglazing with white wine, the addition of seafood (finfish and/or shellfish, depending on what is available) and either fish broth or plain water in which to complete the cooking. The whole is then served over toasted slices of country-style bread, lightly rubbed with garlic and lavishly dribbled with olive oil. Like its close cousin bouillabaisse, zuppa di pesce is invariably said to have been created by fishermen (or their womenfolk) to use the leftovers of the day's catch, but as it gets more and more elaborate, with the addition of shrimps, langoustines, crabs, and even (Maine!) lobster, it seems to get farther and farther from the fishing fleet and closer and closer to a fancy resort hotel on the edge of the sea.

Still, cooked quickly, with impeccably fresh seafood, the combination of flavors is dazzling, the very fragrance of the Mediterranean itself mounting from the soup kettle to seduce assembled diners. Seated around the table on a winter night in, let us say, Ohio or Indiana, you will surely catch the fragrance, along with that of the stew, of the maquis, the dry aromas of stone pines, rosemary, wild thyme, and the briny tang from the edge of the sea. And you will almost surely hear in the distance the gentle break of waves and the high-pitched strum of cicadas as they shrill away a Mediterranean summer afternoon.

Brodo di Pesce

SEAFOOD BROTH

🌿 Most fish stews require several cups of Seafood Broth. This rich version adds distinction to any soup it graces. It requires the kind of small fish that Italian fishmongers practically give away and that are really hard to find in North America. If your fish market doesn't carry small trash fish like sea robins and the like, ask for heads and frames (backbones) of freshly cut cod, haddock, or any similar white-fleshed fish. (Oily fish like bluefish or salmon are never good choices for fish stock.) Add half a pound of shrimp in their shells, a few small crabs if available, possibly a small lobster chopped in half by the fishmonger—all to add flavor to the broth.

MAKES ABOUT 10 CUPS

2 tablespoons extra-virgin olive oil

1 medium yellow onion, thinly sliced

1 celery stalk, dark green if possible, chopped

8 garlic cloves, peeled and lightly crushed

2 pounds seafood suitable for broth—heads and frames, shrimp, crabs, etc. (see headnote for suggestions)

1 cup dry white wine

2 pounds ripe tomatoes, coarsely chopped

1/3 cup coarsely chopped flat-leaf parsley

Sea salt and freshly ground black pepper

OPTIONAL

1 small dried red chili

1 tablespoon tomato extract, concentrate, or paste, diluted in 1/4 cup hot water

1 big pinch of saffron threads

Combine the olive oil, onion, celery, and garlic in a heavy-duty stockpot over medium-high heat. Cook, stirring, until the vegetables are soft but not brown. Rinse the seafood, then add to the vegetables. As soon as the seafood starts to sizzle, add the wine, tomatoes, and parsley and raise the heat to high. Cook rapidly, stirring, until the tomatoes start to give off their liquid. Add salt and pepper and cook for about 5 minutes while you bring 6 to 8 cups of water to a boil. Add the boiling water all at once to the stockpot, along with any optional ingredients. Bring the stock to a simmer, lower the heat, cover, and simmer 30 to 45 minutes, or until all the ingredients are very soft.

Since the elements of the seafood broth will have given up most of their flavors, strain the broth through a couple of layers of cheesecloth and discard the solids. If you do not need to use this right away, the broth freezes very well and is good to have on hand for seafood pasta sauces, risotti, and, of course, soups.

Ghiotta di Pisci Siciliana

SICILIAN SEAFOOD STEW

I learned to make this Seafood Stew in Sicily, but in fact it is typical of many parts of southern Italy. Sicilians cut the fish into thick chunks, bones and all, because bones, they say, add richness to the broth. I prefer to use boneless chunks of fish and make the fish broth (Brodo di Pesce) separately (see page 250). The broth may be made several days in advance and refrigerated or frozen until ready to use.

For best results, use two or three different types of fish. Monkfish, haddock, snapper, halibut, and even swordfish are all good choices. This is the Seafood Stew that is often served with Trapani couscous (page 183).

MAKES 10 TO 12 SERVINGS

¼ cup extra-virgin olive oil, preferably Sicilian	1 fresh red chili, seeds removed, coarsely chopped, or ground or crumbled dried red chili to taste	4 pounds assorted white-fleshed fish, cut into chunks
1 medium onion, coarsely chopped	5 cups Brodo di Pesce (page 250)	Sea salt and freshly ground black pepper
5 garlic cloves, coarsely chopped	1 cup dry white wine	½ pound medium shrimp, peeled (optional)
1 celery stalk, coarsely chopped	1 cup drained canned whole plum tomatoes	Slices of toasted country-style bread, rubbed with garlic and olive oil, for serving (optional)
Pinch of wild fennel pollen (optional)	3 bay leaves	

In a heavy saucepan large enough to hold all the ingredients, heat the olive oil over medium-low heat and add the onion, garlic, and celery. Stir in the fennel pollen, if desired, and chili and cook for about 10 minutes, or until the vegetables are soft but not brown.

Bring the broth to a simmer.

Add the wine to the vegetables and raise the heat to medium. Cook briskly until the wine has reduced by about a quarter.

Stir in the drained tomatoes, breaking them up with the side of a spoon. Add the bay leaves and the chunks of fish. Stir gently to mix everything together without breaking up the fish, then add the simmering fish broth, making sure all the pieces of fish are covered with liquid (if necessary, add a little wine or hot water to cover the fish). Add salt and pepper to taste. As soon as the broth comes to a simmer, lower the heat, cover the pan, and cook very gently for about 10 minutes, or until the fish pieces are cooked through. (Be careful not to overcook to the point that the fish chunks fall apart.)

Remove the stew from the heat and immediately stir in the optional shrimp. Cover the pan again and set aside for 5 minutes, or until the shrimp are cooked through in the residual heat of the broth.

To serve, set a slice of toasted bread in the bottom of each soup plate and spoon the fish on top. Add one or two ladles of broth and serve immediately. Or serve with Trapani couscous (page 183).

VARIATIONS

A similar stew can be made from all sorts of seafood, even from just one or two varieties—monkfish, for example, is often cooked this way on its own or accompanied by mussels or clams. If you wish to use clams or mussels, cook them as described on page 245, strain the juices to get rid of any sand, and add the juices to the fish broth.

In Catania, on Sicily's East Coast, cooks might add green olives, golden raisins, and capers, mixing them into the tomatoes along with lots of slivered basil, before adding the fish broth.

Brodetto di Pesce con Spaghetti Tagliati

PUGLIESE FISH STEW WITH "BROKEN" SPAGHETTI

This recipe comes from Domenico Maggi, a fine Pugliese chef and professional cooking instructor who has headed up the Italian Culinary Olympics team for many years. Despite his classical chef's training, Chef Maggi has stayed close to the traditions of his native Puglia, where he spends time in his family trullo, a domed house built of limestone blocks, in the middle of the rolling hill country of the Murge. The best brodetto, he says, is made with whole fish, boned out and then the bones and heads used to make a basic fish broth, in which the rest of the fish is cooked. For most North American cooks, however, whole fish is hard to come by. Instead, I rely on cut fillets and/or steaks, cooked in Seafood Broth (page 250).

MAKES 8 SERVINGS

2 pounds firm-textured white-fleshed fish, such as cod, haddock, red snapper, or monkfish	½ cup packed flat-leaf parsley leaves, plus finely chopped parsley for garnish	1 pound spaghetti, broken into pieces about 2 inches long
About ¾ pound medium shrimp, peeled	2 medium ripe fresh tomatoes, coarsely chopped, or 3 canned plum tomatoes, drained and chopped	Freshly ground black pepper
Sea salt		Finely chopped zest of ½ lemon, preferably organic
One 1¼-pound live lobster	½ cup extra-virgin olive oil	Grated hard aged cheese: caciocavallo, pecorino toscano or sardo, parmigiano reggiano, or grana padano
½ pound crabmeat	6 cups Brodo di Pesce (page 250)	
4 garlic cloves, coarsely chopped		

Cut the fish and shrimp into bite-sized pieces and set aside in a bowl. To cook the lobster, bring an inch of water to a rolling boil in the bottom of a pot large enough to hold it. Add a small handful of salt and then the lobster. Boil until the lobster changes color to bright red. Remove instantly and run under cold water. Crack the shells and remove the meat from the claws and the tail. Cut into bite-sized chunks and set aside in a separate bowl.

Combine the garlic, parsley, tomatoes, and olive oil in a saucepan or soup kettle large enough to hold all the ingredients. Set over medium heat and cook, stirring constantly, until the garlic is soft and the tomatoes have partially melted into the oil, about 15 minutes. Add the broth. As soon as the liquid simmers, cover and reduce the heat to low. Simmer for 15 to 20 minutes, then add the broken spaghetti. Cook for 4 minutes, then add the fish pieces. Cook for 2 minutes, then add the shrimp pieces. Cook for 1 minute, then add the lobster and crabmeat. Let the brodetto return to a simmer, adding plenty of black pepper.

Check to be sure the pasta is done, then turn off the heat and taste the soup, adjusting the seasoning. Serve immediately, garnishing with the parsley and lemon zest and passing the grated cheese at the table.

Meat and Poultry

Chi nun pô avé 'a porpa, s'attacca all'osso.
Those who can't get meat must stick to the bone.
—Neapolitan proverb
(With thanks to Kyle Phillips)

As in other Mediterranean regions, meat seldom plays a starring role in the daily diet of southern Italians. Even in wealthy households, meat is presented, if at all, in small portions, a serving of plain meat (or fish or poultry, for that matter) usually being no larger than a deck of cards. This is not true in restaurants, which is why travelers in the South, expecting a typical Mediterranean diet with loads of vegetables and very little meat, are so often confounded by huge portions of meat—or of fish—and very few vegetables on the menu. But if you ask, you'll often find there are several vegetable offerings, based on what the cook found in the market that morning, only they neglected to include them on the list.

At home, as a rule, meat appears as an ingredient in a dish more frequently than as the focus of a meal. It can form part of a larger dish (in a pasta sauce, for instance, such as a ragù made from a cheap cut of meat simmered for hours in a tomato bath until its juices and much of its flavor have been absorbed into a sauce that will then serve far more people than the meat would on its own). Or meat might be ground and mixed with a variety of other ingredients that stretch the meat to make more food—tasty meatballs, for example, either for a pasta sauce or to have on their own in the kind of sweet-and-savory blends that are typical of the South. Involtini, or braciolone, are another example of this thrifty way with meat—a lean piece of pork, beef, or veal is pounded and stretched thin, then wrapped around a tasty filling, based on bread crumbs but livened with ingredients like red chilies, fresh green herbs, olives, cheese, or pine nuts. The point is to expand the offering of meat to fill more bellies, but to fill them in a most agreeable manner.

Because many North Americans had their first experience with Italian food through the exuberant traditions of the Italian-American kitchen (I often think Italian America should be considered the twenty-first region of Italy), we sometimes have a misguided sense of the abundance of the southern Italian table. Abundance, *l'abbondanza,* was something assimilated in America (and in Australia, Argentina, and other parts of the world to which Italians emigrated as well). Particularly as far as meat is concerned, so solidly did abundance become adopted and expected that Sunday meals from the Old Country became everyday fare in the new, while once-in-a-lifetime feasts (weddings, christenings, first communions) started to appear regularly for every family's Sunday lunch.

But back in the Italian South, the Mezzogiorno from which so many immigrants departed, the old habits never died completely. It's true that, with increasing prosperity, more meat has crept into the Italian diet as a whole (and health statistics are starting to show the results), but still, compared to the North American average, overall Italian meat consumption is low—about 180 pounds a year (and in southern Italy even lower) as opposed to the annual 228 pounds per capita in the United States. More interesting, I think, is the fact that for Italians meat is still governed by the seasons—beef and pork are winter foods, as is horsemeat, which is rarely consumed in summertime; lamb and goat (kid) are for spring feasting, especially for Easter, while summer is largely given over to rabbits and poultry of one sort or another, *animale da cortile* in Italian, meaning the animals that come from the farmyard rather than from the fields.

So most of the recipes in this chapter are for special-occasion dishes to be served for celebrations—weddings, baptisms, Christmas or Easter dinner, or just Sunday lunch with the whole multigenerational family. Even when I describe a dish as coming from a tradition of extremely limited resources, such as the rabbit dish from the island of Ischia on page 297, it is festive food, Sunday food, and decidedly not everyday.

There are also a number of meat dishes from the Mezzogiorno that I have deliberately not included in this chapter, primarily because they are made from parts of the animal that are either illegal to sell (blood or lungs, for instance) or nearly impossible to find (intestines) in North America. But adventurous eaters, traveling through the Italian South, will want to seek out these dishes in country restaurants, at market stalls, and along well-traveled highways where cooks set up temporary shop with the specialty of the day. I remember a little hole-in-the-wall osteria next to an obscure stop on the rail line that runs from Palermo to Caltanisetta. Traveling by car, we had stopped to use the public rest rooms, but the aromas from the kitchen, where the signora was frying up rolled packets of lamb's liver wrapped in the same creature's intestines, was irresistible and drew us to a paper-covered table where her husband poured thick tumblers of viscous red wine to eat with the delicacies, which were crisp and crackling on the outside, creamy and unctuous within.

In Calabria, an adventurous traveler will look for *marro,* an ancient dish—one might say a Homeric dish and one that reminds us once again of how closely the traditions of the rural Italian South are tied to those of classical Greece. Marro is made by chopping the liver, kidneys, heart, and lungs of a recently slaughtered goat or kid, then wrapping them with cheese, pancetta, parsley, and garlic in the caul fat of the animal to make a little package that is then tied with a length of intestine and cooked in a saucepan or grilled over an open fire. Content with the mere fragrance of grilled meat, Olympian gods and goddesses inhaled blissfully as the aromatic smoke of cooking fires rose toward heaven, but we mortals are more fortunate. On the rare occasions when I've been present at this delicious mess, it has taken a great act of self-control to keep from inhaling the entire platter as it's served up from the grill. In Calabria they make much ado about all these innards—another specialty is *morzèddru,* the liver, heart, lungs, and tripe of a slaughtered animal, blanched, then fried in oil with garlic to which a good deal of tomato sauce and lots of hot red chilies are added and the whole thing tucked inside a round pitta bun to be consumed as a midmorning snack or merenda.

In Sicily, two of Palermo's greatest and most renowned street foods belong in the awesome offal category. *Pane co' la meusa* is a rather soft (by southern standards, that is) sesame-strewn muffoletta roll, filled, like Calabrian morzèddru, with a lush amalgam of spleen, lungs, and other interior parts that have been blanched and roasted in lard; often garnished with ricotta or grated caciocavallo, it is as much a delight to consume as it is to watch others consuming it, especially a group of fur-coated and bejeweled Sicilian matrons greedily consuming the greasy sandwiches at the Antica Focacceria San Francesco, which has apparently been making these . . . delicacies for close to two hundred years. *Stigghiole* is another Palermitano street food, and this you often find along the highways leading into Palermo, just at dusk as cooks set up their grilling stations to capture the evening traffic of hungry truckers, commuters returning home, and the occasional tourist—like a little group of Americans who surprised one another a couple of years ago by chowing down enthusiastically on several skewers of crisp, meaty, fatty, delicious intestines, hot off the grill.

I should also mention snails, since they too are meat (although they seem not to be forbidden during Lent, so perhaps they qualify as fish). Fish or flesh, however, snails are an example of the kind of free-for-the-taking delicacy that delights frugal southern hearts. Foraged after a rain, purged for several days or even weeks, they are boiled until the little creatures can be extracted from their shells, then transferred to a spicy tomato sauce, made by stewing tomatoes and a little garlic with plenty of chili and perhaps a good pinch of dried oregano. Stew the snails in this sauce until the sauce is thick and the snails are very tender. If you can find a good source of snails (don't gasp—I have seen them sold on Ninth Avenue in Manhattan, and surely they exist in other places as well), you might try the recipe, though the above is as far as I'm willing to go.

In writing up these recipes, I have given quantities for what Americans expect to eat—if the recipe says "Makes 4 servings," it will serve four normal North American eaters. If you wish to serve in a more southern Italian style, you will precede the *secondo,* whether of meat or fish, with a *primo*—usually pasta, although it could also be a vegetable dish or a soup—and in that case you may well find that the meat dish will serve more people. Another difference from North

American customs is in what "goes with" the meat course. Often in southern Italy it is nothing at all, sometimes it's potatoes, rarely rice or a vegetable, but never, ever, is it pasta, which, like vegetables, is treasured enough to merit a place of its own on the menu. There's no law, of course, that says you have to present a meat dish in this fashion, but it is a fine way to honor pasta, vegetables, and meat, by separating them and giving them each a distinctive role to play on the menu.

NEAPOLITAN POT ROAST OF BEEF WITH ONIONS

This is one of the most celebrated Neapolitan treatments for a cut of beef that isn't as tender as one might wish, specifically, the rump, or *lacerto* as it's called in Napoli—*girello* in the north of Italy. The preparation and its use will inevitably remind you of ragù, the rich, tomato-based sauce that is, or was, an inevitable part of Sunday lunch in Italian-American homes, just as it is, or was, in Italy. The biggest difference between the two preparations is the disproportionate quantity of onions in the Genovese and the lack of any form of tomato. Some cooks, it's true, may add a few chopped tomatoes or a tablespoon of tomato paste, but this is a minor addition and in no way essential; others swear that the presence of tomatoes in a Genovese is incontrovertible evidence of corruption.

Why is it called *Genovese* if it comes from Napoli? There are many theories. Neapolitans like to claim that it was cooks from Genoa who introduced the sauce, and there may be some truth to it. But perhaps not much.

Although rump is called for in traditional Italian recipes, it's a dry cut of meat and less successful than a blade or chuck pot roast, which I have used on the advice of my butcher.

MAKES 6 TO 8 SERVINGS

2 to 3 pounds boneless beef chuck or blade (pot roast), rolled and tied	1 thick green celery stalk, chopped	2 pounds yellow onions, halved and thinly sliced
1 tablespoon pure pork lard or unsalted butter	3 or 4 fresh sage leaves, chopped	2 cups meat or chicken broth
1 tablespoon extra-virgin olive oil, plus more if necessary	2 fresh marjoram branches, chopped	Sea salt and freshly ground black pepper
1 medium carrot, chopped	2 ounces pancetta, diced	1 cup dry white wine

Dry the beef thoroughly with paper towels so that it will brown nicely. Set a heavy saucepan just large enough to hold the meat over medium-high heat and melt the lard or butter in the olive oil, then add the meat and brown on all sides to a nice dark color.

While the meat is browning, chop together the carrot, celery, herbs, and pancetta to make a fine mince.

When the meat is browned thoroughly, remove it from the saucepan and set aside. Lower the heat to low and add the onions to the pan, along with another tablespoon of oil if necessary.

Cook the onions very slowly, stirring frequently to prevent burning, until they are thoroughly melted and golden, 20 to 30 minutes.

Once the onions are melted almost to a puree, stir in the minced mixture, raise the heat slightly, and cook very briefly, just until the vegetables start to soften. Return the meat to the pan, nestling it into the onion-vegetable mixture, then stir in the broth and salt and pepper to taste. Lower the heat so that the liquid is just barely simmering and cook, uncovered, very gently for 2 to 3 hours, turning the meat every 30 to 45 minutes so that it cooks evenly. As the liquid in the pan evaporates and is absorbed by the meat, add the wine, a little at a time. Once the wine has been absorbed, add up to a cup of boiling water, again a little at a time.

At the end of the cooking time, remove the meat and set aside on a warm platter. If the sauce in the pan is very liquid, raise the heat and cook rapidly to reduce.

When ready to serve, set aside ½ to 1 cup of the dense sauce to garnish the meat. Use the rest to dress a first course of pasta (ziti are traditional) and serve the meat, sliced, with the remaining pan juices spooned over, as a second course.

Stufato di Manzo

SPICED BRAISED BEEF

This Sicilian recipe for slow-cooked braised beef is a typical way to render the toughest meat almost meltingly tender, and since much of the beef traditionally available in the South was from work animals, it was always necessary to find a way to soften the meat without giving up any of its goodness. The subtle spicing of cinnamon and cloves, instead of the more usual soffrito of garlic and parsley, gives an exotic flavor to the sauce.

In Sicily, and throughout the South, a beef stew like this would be served traditionally with slices of coarse-textured country-style bread, either plain or toasted or fried to a crisp in olive oil. If you prefer, you could also serve it with new potatoes, steamed or rubbed with olive oil and roasted in the oven.

When ripe fresh tomatoes are not in season, use a good quality of canned tomatoes, well drained and chopped.

A fine point: Tie the cinnamon, cloves, and bay leaves loosely in a cheesecloth bag to make it easier to remove them before serving.

MAKES 6 TO 8 SERVINGS

1 pound small white onions (8 to 12, depending on size)	2 garlic cloves, crushed with the flat blade of a knife	1 teaspoon dried oregano
¼ cup extra-virgin olive oil	½ cup full-bodied red wine	Sea salt and freshly ground black pepper
2 pounds stewing beef, cut into 1- to 2-inch pieces	1 cinnamon stick, about 2 inches long	About ⅓ cup chopped flat-leaf parsley
2½ cups chopped peeled tomatoes	8 to 10 cloves	
	2 bay leaves	

Peel the onions, but leave them whole. In a heavy skillet, heat the olive oil over medium heat and brown the onions on all sides. Remove with a slotted spoon and transfer to an ovenproof saucepan or casserole large enough to hold all the ingredients.

Dry the beef pieces thoroughly with paper towels. Add the meat to the oil in the skillet and cook over medium heat, browning the meat on all sides. As they finish browning, transfer to the casserole. Add the tomatoes and set the casserole over medium-low heat.

Preheat the oven to 300°F.

Add the garlic and wine to the casserole, cover, and bring to a simmer, then stir in the cinnamon, cloves, bay leaves, and oregano. Transfer the covered casserole to the preheated oven and leave to cook for 3 to 4 hours, or until the meat is fork-tender and the onions have practically dissolved in the sauce. Check the casserole after 3 hours. Add salt and pepper to taste and, if necessary, remove the cover for the last hour of cooking to concentrate the juices.

Before serving, remove the spice package. Serve in the casserole or transfer to a platter, garnishing with the parsley.

Bracioline di Manzo o Vitello alla Pugliese

BEEF OR VEAL ROLLED AROUND A PIQUANT STUFFING

In northern Italy, a *braciola* is a chop, usually a pork chop, but in the South it's synonymous with a piece of lean meat pounded thin and rolled around a savory stuffing. The meat is usually cut from what we would call the top round or from a flank steak. These meat rolls are called *braciolone* when they're large and *bracioline,* as in this recipe from Puglia, when they are small enough for two of them to make a single serving. In Puglia, the meat used is apt to be deliciously flavorful and very tender horsemeat. Since that's pretty much unavailable in North America, I've made these with beef instead, although you could substitute veal if you can find an acceptable source for it.

MAKES 4 SERVINGS

8 thin boneless beef or veal cutlets or scaloppine (about 1½ pounds)	⅓ cup coarsely grated pecorino, caciocavallo, or provolone	¼ cup dry red wine
8 very thin slices savory baked ham, prosciutto, or pancetta	¼ cup extra-virgin olive oil	2 cups coarsely chopped drained canned whole tomatoes
2 tablespoons finely chopped flat-leaf parsley	2 tablespoons (about 2 ounces) minced pancetta	1 small dried red chili or ½ teaspoon crushed dried red chili
3 tablespoons finely chopped fresh basil	1 medium yellow onion, finely chopped	Sea salt and freshly ground black pepper
1 garlic clove, minced with the parsley and basil	1 garlic clove, chopped with the onion	Finely minced fresh basil or flat-leaf parsley for garnish
1 heaping tablespoon capers, preferably salt-packed, rinsed and drained	1 carrot, finely chopped	

An obliging butcher should pound the beef or veal cutlets thin for you, but if he won't, it's easy enough to do yourself. Put a cutlet between 2 sheets of wax paper and gently but firmly pound it all over, using a meat pounder or a heavy rolling pin. The cutlets should be as thin as you can make them without tearing them—⅛ inch or less.

Lay a slice of ham on each cutlet, then sprinkle with a teaspoon or so of the herb-garlic combination, a few capers, and about a scant tablespoon of grated cheese. Roll each cutlet up over the filling and secure with a toothpick or tie with a little piece of kitchen twine.

In a skillet over medium-high heat, brown the beef rolls on all sides in the olive oil. Remove the rolls as they brown and set aside.

Add the minced pancetta to the skillet, along with the chopped onion and garlic and the carrot. Lower the heat to medium-low and cook, stirring, until the vegetables are quite soft but not brown. Add the wine, raise the heat slightly, and cook, scraping up any brown bits. When the wine has reduced by about half, add the tomatoes and continue cooking for 5 to 10 minutes, until it is all reduced to a thick sauce.

Crumble the chili and stir it in, then return the beef rolls to the pan, spooning the sauce over them to cover. Add salt and pepper to taste and cover the pan. Lower the heat to simmer and continue to cook for about 25 minutes, or until the beef rolls are thoroughly impregnated with the flavors of the sauce.

You may serve the beef rolls with the sauce or, to be more traditional, use some of the sauce to dress pasta as a first course, reserving just a few spoonsful to garnish the beef rolls as the second or main course. Sprinkle with the minced basil and or parsley just before serving.

Polpettine in Agrodolce

SICILIAN MEATBALLS IN A SWEET-SOUR TOMATO SAUCE

Beef in southern Italy typically comes from less than prime animals, so it's often ground or minced to make it more tender. These little meatballs are often part of a celebration table, because it's easy both to stretch the meat to feed more hungry guests and to make it festive by adding more opulent flavors. Similar preparations exist all over the South, but the sweet-and-sour tomato sauce marks this one as classically Sicilian.

You will notice a lot of room for variety in the quantities listed. Use your hands to mix the meat with the other ingredients and pay attention to the texture of the mixture. Too dry will fall apart in the frying pan; too wet will collapse under its own weight. If you're uncertain, make a small meatball and test it, then adjust the mixture by adding more bread crumbs to make it drier or more olive oil or another egg to make it wetter.

MAKES 6 TO 8 SERVINGS

1½ pounds lean ground beef	⅓ to ½ cup fine dry bread crumbs	**FOR THE SAUCE**
2 garlic cloves, minced	About 2 tablespoons extra-virgin olive oil, plus oil for deep-fat frying (½ to 1 cup)	2 cups Basic Tomato Sauce (page 125)
¼ cup capers, preferably salt-packed, rinsed, drained, and chopped		½ cup red wine vinegar
	Sea salt and freshly ground black pepper	¼ cup sugar
¼ cup minced fresh basil, flat-leaf parsley, or a combination	Unbleached all-purpose flour for rolling the meatballs	Pinch of ground red chili (optional)
1 or 2 eggs		⅓ cup blanched toasted almonds, slivered

Combine the beef, garlic, capers, and basil in a bowl and mix together very well, using your hands. Add an egg and mix it in, then add about ⅓ cup of the bread crumbs and 2 tablespoons of olive oil. Mix well, using your hands, and adjust the texture, adding another egg or another tablespoon of oil or more bread crumbs. When the texture is right, add salt and pepper to taste.

Spread a little flour out on a plate. Shape the ground meat into small meatballs, no larger than a walnut. Roll each ball in the flour, shaking off any excess.

In a heavy skillet, heat about ¼ inch of olive oil over medium heat. Add the meatballs and brown them quickly on all sides, removing them as they finish cooking.

Meanwhile, in a saucepan large enough to hold the meatballs and their sauce, bring the tomato sauce to a simmer. In a separate, smaller saucepan, heat the vinegar to boiling and immediately stir in the sugar. When it comes to a boil again, add about ½ cup of the tomato sauce and cook to a dark brown, about 8 minutes. Stir the sweet-sour mixture into the pan of simmering tomato sauce and, if you wish, add the chili. Now stir the meatballs gently into the sauce, mixing carefully to coat them thoroughly with the sauce. Let cook briefly to thicken the sauce, then set aside until ready to serve.

When ready to serve, reheat the meatballs in their sauce if necessary, then transfer to a heated serving dish. Top with the slivered almonds and serve immediately.

VARIATION

In Naples, about ½ cup of grated cheese, preferably well-aged provolone, may be added to the meat mixture. Instead of the tomato sauce, the meatballs are served with the following:

6 anchovy fillets	1 teaspoon fresh lemon juice or white wine vinegar, or more to taste	2 tablespoons capers, preferably salt-packed, rinsed and drained
1 garlic clove, chopped		
2 tablespoons extra-virgin olive oil		¼ cup finely minced flat-leaf parsley

Combine the anchovies, garlic, olive oil, and lemon juice in a blender or food processor and process briefly, just long enough to combine well. Taste and add more lemon juice if you wish.

Chop the capers coarsely and combine with the parsley. Stir into the anchovy mixture and set aside, covered with plastic wrap, for 30 minutes or so to let the flavors develop, then serve poured over meatballs that have been lightly sautéed.

NOTE: *Don't be tempted to add the capers and parsley to the food processor to puree them. The sauce is tastier and much prettier if these 2 ingredients are left more intact than the rest of the pureed sauce.*

Vitello con Salsa di Acciughe

POT ROAST OF VEAL WITH AN ANCHOVY-CAPER SAUCE

Eleanora Consoli is a fine gourmet and food writer who gives cooking classes, in Italian and in English, from her home in Viagrande, a pretty village tucked under the slopes of Mount Etna in eastern Sicily. The deliciously savory sauce, which is made separately and then combined with a reduction of pan juices, contrasts beautifully with the gentle flavors of young milk-fed veal, but it could be used with other, stronger-flavored meats—roast chicken, lamb, or pork, for instance—as well.

Some people don't eat veal because of the way so much veal is raised in this country. They object, and with good reason, to inhumane practices that often require heavy doses of medication to keep the animals alive. I try to buy veal from a farmer I can trust to raise the meat humanely and without medication; if you don't have access to this kind of meat, you could easily substitute a rump or blade roast of beef, boned and tied, for the veal.

MAKES 8 TO 10 SERVINGS

¼ cup extra-virgin olive oil, plus more if necessary

1 medium yellow onion, finely chopped

Leaves from 2 fresh rosemary sprigs, chopped

2 fresh sage sprigs, chopped

1 tablespoon instant flour

Sea salt and freshly ground black pepper

1 boneless shoulder roast of veal, about 3½ pounds

4 whole cloves

FOR THE SAUCE

1 garlic clove, chopped

2 tablespoons extra-virgin olive oil

4 anchovy fillets, chopped

2 tablespoons capers, preferably salt-packed, rinsed and drained

2 tablespoons red wine vinegar, or more to taste

Leaves from 4 or 5 fresh mint sprigs, slivered, plus mint for garnish

In a heavy saucepan large enough to hold the veal roast, warm the olive oil and gently cook the onion and herbs over medium-low heat until the onion is very soft but not brown.

Meanwhile, combine the flour with a pinch of salt (keeping in mind that the anchovies in the sauce will add salt to the finished dish) and pepper to taste. Dry the veal thoroughly with paper towels and rub it all over with the savory flour.

Use a slotted spoon to remove the onions and herbs from the pan, leaving the oil behind. Set the onion mixture aside. Add oil to the pan if necessary to make about ¼ cup, then raise the heat to medium-high and add the veal. Brown the meat all over, including the ends, turning frequently. When the meat is nicely browned with a caramel crust, remove it from the pan. Discard the burned oil in the pan and set the meat back in it, surrounded by the onion-herb mixture. Add the cloves and about ¾ cup of hot water. Bring to a simmer, then lower the heat, cover the pan securely, and cook very gently, using a heat diffuser if necessary, for 1½ to 2 hours or until the meat is thoroughly cooked. Turn the meat over at least once during the cooking time and, if necessary, add a little more boiling water to the pan.

When the meat has reached an internal temperature of 180°F, remove the roast from the pan. The pan juices should be concentrated and thickened to about 1½ cups. If necessary, degrease the pan juices by setting them aside until the fat rises to the top; put the juices in a bowl and set it in the freezer to make the fat easier to remove. (Degreasing should not be necessary, however, with veal.)

Meanwhile, prepare the sauce: Gently cook the garlic in the olive oil in a small skillet until it is soft but not brown. Stir in the anchovies, pressing with a fork to mash the anchovies into the oil. Add the capers and vinegar and, as soon as the mixture starts to simmer, stir it into the reduced pan juices and return to a simmer. Taste and adjust the seasoning, adding more vinegar or salt if necessary.

Slice the veal and arrange the slices on a warm serving platter. Add the slivered mint to the sauce and spoon it over the meat. Garnish with more mint and serve immediately, passing any extra sauce to be added at the table.

SPRINGTIME LAMB WITH ARTICHOKES

Abbacchio refers to very young baby lamb, often so small that a boned leg might weigh just two to three pounds—perfect for this dish, a springtime favorite from Napoli. The sweet and delicate flavor of the lamb acts as a counterpart to the slight bitterness and astringency of the artichokes. Except in Greek and Italian neighborhoods at Eastertime, North American butchers on the whole sell much older lamb, young mutton in the Italian view. Lamb shoulder should be your first choice because the interlacing of fat and lean makes the meat moist; otherwise, use boned leg of lamb, the smaller the better.

MAKES 6 TO 8 SERVINGS

2¼ pounds boneless young lamb, cut into large pieces	3 garlic cloves, minced	Sea salt and freshly ground black pepper
2 tablespoons extra-virgin olive oil	¼ cup minced flat-leaf parsley	Pinch of dried oregano, crumbled
1 medium yellow onion, minced	1 cup dry white wine	6 to 8 small globe artichokes
	1 cup chicken or light meat stock	1 or 2 lemons

Preheat the oven to 300°F.

Pat the pieces of lamb dry with paper towels. Heat the olive oil over medium heat in an oven dish large enough to hold all the lamb. Brown the lamb on all sides, removing the pieces as they brown and setting them aside.

Add the onion, garlic, and parsley to the oven dish, lower the heat, and cook, stirring frequently, until the vegetables are soft. Return the lamb to the dish and add the wine and stock. Bring to a simmer and add salt and pepper to taste, as well as the crumbled oregano.

Once the liquid is simmering thoroughly, set the dish, uncovered, in the preheated oven and cook for about 3 hours, checking every 30 to 40 minutes to make sure the liquid has not boiled away. If it has, add some boiling water—there should always be at least an inch of liquid in the bottom of the dish.

Meanwhile, prepare the artichokes, using the lemons, as described on page 305. If the artichokes are very large, cut them in half. Remove the spiny chokes.

About 30 minutes before the end of the cooking time, remove the dish from the oven and arrange the drained artichokes over the top, again checking to make sure there is at least an inch of liquid in the bottom. Cover the top with a lid that fits tightly—or with a lid supplemented with aluminum foil—and return it to the oven for a final half hour of cooking, after which the artichokes should be tender and the lamb falling apart.

Serve, if possible, in the same dish in which it was cooked.

NOTE: *This dish can also be prepared on top of the stove, but the heat should always be very, very gentle so that it cooks slowly.*

VARIATION

Calabrian cooks often prepare the dish with young goat, boneless and cut into large serving pieces, just like the lamb. Goat is not often available, but when you find it (usually in the spring, in butcher shops in Greek or Italian neighborhoods), it's an extremely tasty meat.

Spezzatino di Agnello al Marsala

LAMB BRAISED IN MARSALA

Marsala, a fortified wine from the town of the same name on the west coast of Sicily, may be Sicily's best-known wine, but like its cousins port and Madeira, it has declined in popularity in recent years and is often recommended only as a cooking wine, to the despair of makers of fine Marsala like Marco de Bartoli. At its best, Marsala is a deeply flavored, rich, and complex after-dinner wine, one to be treasured and reserved for special occasions.

But there are also plenty of lesser Marsalas on the market that add an elusive hint of sweetness and spiciness in the kitchen, as in this very simple recipe, which comes from Marsala itself. Be sure to use a dry Marsala, however, as a sweet one will be overpowering. The dish is often made with young goat, but lamb will do just as well and is a lot easier to find in North American meat markets.

In Sicily, this stew would be served on its own, without accompaniment, but you can, if you wish, serve it with steamed or roasted potatoes or a combination of root vegetables—potatoes, carrots, and parsnips (practically unknown in southern Italy) would be a fine mix, their sweetness bringing out the sweetness of the Marsala sauce.

MAKES 6 SERVINGS

2½ to 3 pounds lean boneless lamb, cut into 1- to 2-inch pieces for stewing 1 cup dry Marsala	2 garlic cloves, coarsely chopped 2 tablespoons extra-virgin olive oil	1 medium onion, halved and thinly sliced Sea salt and freshly ground black pepper ¼ cup minced flat-leaf parsley

Set the lamb in a bowl and add the Marsala. (If the Marsala does not cover the meat, add a little water.) Add one of the garlic cloves and set aside to marinate for an hour or two.

When ready to cook, combine the second clove of garlic with the olive oil in a heavy saucepan and cook very gently over medium-low heat until the garlic is softened. Stir in the onion slices and cook until soft, about 20 minutes. Meanwhile, strain the lamb pieces from the marinade, reserving the marinade, and dry very well with paper towels. Use a slotted spoon to remove the vegetables from the oil and set them aside. Raise the heat to medium-high and brown the lamb pieces quickly, turning to brown them all over.

Stir the onion back into the pan with the meat and pour in the Marsala. Bring to a boil, turn the heat down to a bare simmer, and cook, covered, for 45 minutes, or until the meat is very tender. If the sauce becomes too dry, add a very little water, but there should not be a lot of sauce with this dish and what there is should thickly nap the pieces of meat.

Taste for seasoning, adding salt and pepper to taste. Just before removing from the heat, stir in the minced parsley. Serve immediately.

Agnello all'Aceto

LAMB BRAISED IN AGED WINE VINEGAR

In Calabria, the home of this surprisingly simple recipe, cooks use a whole shoulder or leg of baby lamb. In North America a lamb shoulder, boned and tied, is the best choice of all. Otherwise, use a boned piece of leg.

The vinegar will reduce and blend with the cooking juices to make a tasty sauce for the braised lamb.

MAKES 8 TO 10 SERVINGS

2 ounces pancetta	2 or 3 tablespoons extra-virgin olive oil	Big pinch of dried oregano
3 garlic cloves		½ cup aged wine vinegar, preferably white
1 boned and rolled lamb shoulder or leg roast, 2½ to 3 pounds	Sea salt and freshly ground black pepper	

Preheat the oven to 325°F.

Cut the pancetta into lardons ⅛ to ¼ inch wide and about ½ inch long. Slice the garlic very thin. Using the sharp point of a knife, make incisions all over the surface of the meat, pushing a garlic sliver or a pancetta lardon into each incision. Don't worry if you don't use all the garlic and pancetta—they can be added to the sauce later on.

Rub the surface of the meat with a tablespoon of the olive oil. Then sprinkle with salt, pepper, and oregano. Set aside to rest for an hour or so—refrigerate the meat if you want to let it sit in its flavorings overnight.

Set a heavy-lidded flameproof oven dish over medium-high heat and add another tablespoon of olive oil. When the oil is hot, add any leftover garlic or pancetta, then add the meat and brown it on all sides, turning frequently, until it is a beautiful dark color all over, about 15 minutes. Remove from the heat and, if the oil is burned, which it may well be, tip it out and add a fresh tablespoon of olive oil. Add the vinegar and ¼ cup of water to the lamb in the pot and return the pot to medium heat. As soon as the liquid starts to simmer, cover the pot and transfer it to the preheated oven. Braise the lamb for about 2 hours, or until it is fork-tender. From time to time, turn the meat over and check to be sure the liquid has not evaporated—if it has, add a little more boiling water.

When done, you should have just a very small amount of savory sauce in the bottom of the pan. Remove the meat and set aside for 15 to 20 minutes to allow the juices to retreat into the meat. Meanwhile, pour the pan juices into a bowl or measuring cup and refrigerate until the fat has congealed on top and can be removed (the freezer is the fastest way to do this). Reheat the defatted pan juices, letting them simmer a little to concentrate, then slice the lamb and serve with the pan juices spooned over.

Agnello Cacio e Uova

NEAPOLITAN EASTER FRICASSEE OF SPRING LAMB

Made all over southern Italy at Eastertime, agnello cacio e uova, with its lush napping of eggs and cheese, is usually served on Easter Monday, Pasquetta or Lunedi dell'Angelo (Monday of the Angel), a day for picnics in the spring sunshine. The greens change, depending on where you are and whether Easter falls in mid-March or late April. In the Albanian communities the dish is called *verdhet* and is made with wild spring greens; in Bari it's typically called *verdetto* or *bredette* and made with wild asparagus or cardoons. And in Naples it's often made with fresh green spring peas as here.

MAKES 8 TO 10 SERVINGS

4 pounds boneless lamb shoulder or leg, cut into pieces about 2 inches square	2½ cups shelled fresh peas	Leaves from 1 bunch of flat-leaf parsley, coarsely chopped
½ cup extra-virgin olive oil	3 eggs	Juice of ½ lemon, plus lemon slices or quarters for garnish
4 medium onions, thinly sliced	1 cup grated hard aged cheese: caciocavallo, grana padano, or parmigiano reggiano	Salt and freshly ground black pepper
1 cup dry white wine		

Rinse the pieces of lamb and dry them well. Place the olive oil in a flameproof casserole over medium-high heat and brown the lamb pieces, setting them aside when they are done. Lower the heat, add the onions and stir them into the juices in the pan. Cover the pan and cook, stirring occasionally, until the onions are very soft, almost melting into the oil, and golden but not brown, about 30 minutes. If the onions look like they're browning, add a little water from time to time.

Add the browned lamb back to the onions with about ½ cup of the wine. Continue cooking the stew over very low heat, uncovered, for 30 minutes, or until the wine is mostly evaporated. Add the remaining wine, along with ½ cup of water and the peas. Cover the pan and cook over low heat for 30 minutes, or until the peas are very tender.

Remove the lamb, onions, and peas from the casserole and set aside on a warm platter in a warm place while you make the sauce.

Set the casserole over very low heat so that the pan juices are barely simmering. Beat the eggs well and mix in the grated cheese. Add a ladleful of hot pan juices to the eggs, beating well as you dribble it in. Continue beating in meat juices until the egg mixture is quite warm. Then carefully beat the egg mixture into the juices in the casserole. Continue beating over very low heat until the sauce is thick enough to coat a spoon. *Do not let the sauce come to a boil*, or you will scramble the eggs. If the sauce appears to be at the boiling point, remove from the heat immediately, beating to cool it down as rapidly as possible.

Remove the sauce from the heat and beat in the parsley and lemon juice. Add salt and pepper to taste. Spoon the sauce over the warm lamb and peas, garnish with lemon, and serve immediately.

Almond-Stuffed Leg of Lamb with Chickpea Puree

This is adapted from a dish on Chef Ciccio Sultano's menu at Ristorante Il Duomo in Ibla, the twin town that sits on a hilltop facing Ragusa in southeastern Sicily. For presentation purposes, Chef Ciccio forms the chickpea puree into quenelles, but a looser pureed cream of chickpeas forms a nice base for the sliced leg of stuffed lamb.

The lamb has to be tied once it has been stuffed, so make sure you have kitchen or butcher's twine on hand.

MAKES 8 SERVINGS

1 tablespoon peppercorns	**FOR THE STUFFING**	2 firm green celery stalks, including leaves, chopped
1 teaspoon coarse sea salt	¾ cup chopped blanched almonds	1 medium onion, chopped
2 tablespoons chopped fresh sage	1 teaspoon extra-virgin olive oil	¼ cup extra-virgin olive oil
1 boned leg of lamb, about 3 pounds	½ cup dry bread crumbs	Leaves from 4 large fresh mint branches
	1 medium yellow onion, finely chopped	1½ cups dried chickpeas, soaked overnight
	5 garlic cloves, chopped	1 teaspoon fine sea salt
	1 medium carrot, chopped	Slivered fresh mint leaves for garnish (optional)

In a mortar, pound the peppercorns, coarse salt, and sage together to the texture of coarse crumbs. Rub the mixture all over the outside of the lamb and set aside to marinate for at least 30 minutes and up to 3 hours.

Make the stuffing: Combine the almonds and olive oil in a skillet over medium heat and toast the almonds, stirring frequently, until golden, being careful not to burn them. Transfer the almonds to a food processor. Add the bread crumbs to the skillet and toast them, stirring constantly, until they are crisp and light brown, then combine with the almonds. Process very briefly, pulsing, then add the finely chopped onion and process again to make a fine mince. Be careful not to overprocess and grind the nuts to a paste. They should still have a good deal of texture.

Set aside about ½ cup of the filling. Lay the meat out on a board with the inside (where the bone was) facing up. Smear the remaining filling over the surface of the meat. Roll the leg and tie it with kitchen twine to hold it together.

Preheat the oven to 400°F.

In a pan just large enough to hold the lamb and vegetables, combine the garlic, carrot, celery, and chopped onion with 2 tablespoons of the olive oil and set over medium-low heat. Cook gently, stirring frequently, until the vegetables are soft but not brown, about 30 minutes. Push the vegetables out to the edges of the pan and add the lamb to the middle. Raise the heat slightly and brown the lamb on all sides, about 15 minutes.

When the lamb is thoroughly browned, stir half of the reserved filling (¼ cup) into the vegetables, then add water to come about three-quarters of the way up the meat. Bring to a simmer, add the mint, cover the pan, and set in the preheated oven. Reduce the heat to 325°F.

Roast until the lamb is done to taste—1¼ to 1½ hours. When the lamb has cooked for about 30 minutes, add the remaining ¼ cup of filling to the sauce, stirring it in.

While the lamb is cooking, drain the chickpeas and transfer to a saucepan. Cover with water, bring to a simmer, and cook until they are very soft—about 1 hour. Add the salt in the last few minutes of cooking. Drain the chickpeas, reserving their liquid, and process to a soft puree, adding some of the reserved cooking water if necessary—that is, if the puree is hard and sticky. With the motor running, add 2 tablespoons of olive oil to the puree. Set aside but keep warm.

When the lamb is done, remove it from the roasting pan and set aside to firm up the texture. Set the roasting pan over medium-low heat and boil the sauce left in the pan to concentrate the flavors.

To serve the lamb: Spread the chickpea puree over a serving platter. Slice the lamb and arrange the slices over the puree. Spoon the lamb sauce over the meat. Sprinkle with a few slivers of mint, if you wish, and serve immediately.

Agnello della Nonna/Agunu da' Nanna

GRANNY'S SLOW-COOKED LAMB WITH WILD MUSHROOMS

This old Calabrian recipe relies on wild mushrooms to add a bosky flavor to lamb cooked very, very slowly for a very, very long time. Once upon a time, the terra-cotta casserole in which the lamb should cook would have been set in the family bread oven (or sent to the village baker) to cook in its dying heat. Nowadays, even in Calabria, most cooks rely more on electricity or gas—a loss in flavor, perhaps, but a considerable saving on the cook's time and energy.

The mushrooms can be any variety of wild mushroom. Most typical would be either porcini or cardoncelli, as oyster mushrooms are called in southern Italy, but I have made this very successfully in late summer with fresh black trumpets.

You may also use dried mushrooms, reconstituting them by soaking them for about thirty minutes in very warm water. Once the mushrooms have softened, strain them through a fine-mesh sieve, reserving the mushroom water. Rinse the mushrooms under running water to get rid of any specks of soil. Strain the soaking liquid through a fine-mesh sieve lined with paper towels and use that flavorful liquid to replace some of the wine in the recipe.

Have the butcher chop the lamb shoulder into serving-sized pieces, but keep the bones attached as they lend considerable flavor to the dish. If you cannot find lamb with the bone on, use 3 to 4 pounds of boneless shoulder or leg.

MAKES 8 TO 10 SERVINGS

½ pound fresh wild mushrooms	1 lamb shoulder on the bone, about 6 or 7 pounds, cut into serving-sized pieces, or 3 to 4 pounds boneless lamb shoulder or leg, cut into large chunks	2 or 3 fresh rosemary branches
¼ cup extra-virgin olive oil		2 cups dry white wine
1 cup light chicken broth		1 dried red chili or 1 teaspoon crumbled dried red chili
1 tablespoon unsalted butter		
Sea salt and freshly ground black pepper	4 garlic cloves, sliced	

Rinse the mushrooms quickly and slice, trimming away any bruised spots. (Small mushrooms may be left whole.)

Transfer the mushrooms to a skillet with 2 tablespoons of the olive oil. Set over medium-low heat and cook, stirring occasionally, until the mushrooms start to give off some of their liquid. Raise the heat slightly and continue cooking, adding the broth ¼ cup at a time. When all the broth has been added and the mushrooms are tender, stir in the butter and salt and pepper to taste. Set the mushrooms aside.

Preheat the oven to 475°F.

Add 2 more tablespoons of olive oil to a deep oven dish and set over medium heat. Dry the pieces of meat very well with paper towels and add them to the hot oil. Brown the meat on all sides. Toward the end of the cooking time, add the garlic and rosemary, along with more salt and pepper. Turn the mushroom "sauce" over the lamb, stirring to mix well, and set the oven dish, uncovered, in the preheated oven for 15 minutes.

Warm the wine to just below boiling.

Remove the meat from the oven, lowering the oven temperature to 300°F, and pour the warm wine over the meat in the dish. Add the chili and cover the dish with aluminum foil and then with its lid. Return the dish to the oven to bake for about 2 hours longer, or until the meat is very soft and tender.

When the lamb is done, the juices in the pan should have reduced considerably. If not, transfer the pieces of meat to a serving dish and boil the juices down over high heat on top of the stove. Spoon the juices with the mushrooms over the meat and serve immediately.

Costolette di Capretto ai Pomodorini

BABY GOAT CHOPS WITH LITTLE TOMATOES

Baby goat, or kid, is not easy to find, but you may get lucky in the springtime, especially in ethnic neighborhoods (Greek Queens, Italian South Philly, Latino/Hispanic Chicago, for instance) in metropolitan areas. It is a wonderful meat, with all the tender meaty qualities of young lamb but without the dominating mutton flavor that some people (not I!) dislike.

The tomatoes used in this recipe, which originated with Dora Ricci, the guiding spirit of Ristorante da Ricci in Ceglie Messapico, Puglia, are small cluster tomatoes typical of Puglia. Called *pomodorini appesi*, or "hanging tomatoes," and about the size of large cherry tomatoes, they are harvested when ripe in the autumn and then hung from a beam in a cool, shady, dry spot. Incredibly, they keep this way all through the winter, gradually wrinkling and drying and concentrating their sweet flavor. I substitute ripe fresh tomatoes, preferably the ones called *grape tomatoes,* which are usually quite sweet, even when raised in hothouses.

MAKES 6 SERVINGS

2 tablespoons extra-virgin olive oil	2 cups dry white wine	24 small sweet ripe tomatoes, such as grape tomatoes
18 rib chops from a baby goat or young lamb	Sea salt	2 tablespoons finely chopped flat-leaf parsley
1 medium yellow onion, coarsely chopped	2 bay leaves	
	1 small dried red chili	
	2 garlic cloves, crushed with the flat blade of a knife	

Add the olive oil to a deep skillet or saucepan large enough to hold all the little chops and set it over medium-low heat. When the oil is hot, add the chops and cook, turning the chops, until they are brown on both sides, about 10 minutes to a side. Remove from the pan and set aside.

Lower the heat and add the onion to the pan. Cook, stirring, until the onion is soft. Add the wine along with salt to taste. Simmer until the wine has reduced to about ½ cup. Add the bay leaves, cover the pan, and continue cooking for 5 to 10 minutes, then stir in the chili, garlic, and tomatoes. Return the chops to the pan. Cover and cook another 5 to 10 minutes. The chops should be very tender and the juices in the pan reduced to a syrupy liquid.

Transfer the chops and their juices to a serving platter and sprinkle with the chopped parsley. Serve immediately.

Costate di Maiale Ripiene/Cuòsti Chini

SICILIAN STUFFED PORK CHOPS

In the town of Chiaramonte Gulfi, which clings to a hillside north of Ragusa in Sicily, there is a renowned restaurant called da Maiore, where the menu consists of pork, pork, and more pork. I doubt that a piece of lamb or beef has ever been served there, and as for vegetarians—well, they just have to find another place to eat in town. Not that there are many vegetarians in Chiaramonte Gulfi. On the wall of the restaurant hangs a plaque that reads " *Qui si magnifica il porco*"—here pork is glorified.

One of da Maiore's glories, for which I always try to arrange a stop when I'm in the neighborhood at lunchtime, is *liatina* (*gelatina*), a deliciously firm and tasty aspic enclosing chunks of delectable pork. A simpler treat from da Maiore, one that is easier to produce in a home kitchen, is stuffed pork chops. The stuffing or filling used at da Maiore includes equal parts of ground pork and minced pork liver. I can't recommend eating pork liver in North America unless you have raised the pig yourself or know who has, so I often use only ground pork to mix with the other ingredients. But if I happen to have a couple of chicken or rabbit livers in the freezer, I may throw them into the mixture.

If you can't get a good caciocavallo cheese, use provolone, but the cheese should be young and fresh, rather than aged and hard.

MAKES 6 VERY GENEROUS SERVINGS

6 pork rib chops, at least 1 inch thick	⅓ cup grated young caciocavallo	1 medium yellow onion, finely chopped
About ½ pound ground pork	1 hard-cooked egg, chopped	2 tablespoons extra-virgin olive oil
1 chicken (or rabbit) liver, if available, chopped	¼ cup fine dry bread crumbs	1 cup meat or chicken stock
2 ounces salami, finely chopped	½ cup dry red wine	
	Sea salt and freshly ground black pepper	

Each pork chop should have a pocket cut in it, so that it can be stuffed but is still attached at the bone.

Mix together the ground pork, liver, salami, cheese, egg, and bread crumbs to make a paste. If the stuffing seems very dry, stir in a tablespoon or so of the wine. Season the mixture well with lots of freshly ground black pepper. Add a little salt, but not too much (the salami and cheese may be salty enough). To be sure, fry a teaspoonful of stuffing in a little olive oil and taste for seasoning.

Open each pork chop and fill with 2 or 3 tablespoons of the stuffing. You may close the pork chops with a couple of toothpicks or do as they do at Maiore and sew big basting stitches along the edge with kitchen twine.

In a skillet large and deep enough to hold all the chops, combine the onion and olive oil and set over medium-low heat. Cook, stirring occasionally, until the onion is soft. Push the onion out to the sides of the pan, raise the heat to medium, add the pork chops, and carefully brown on both sides. When the chops are golden, after about 10 minutes on each side, add the remaining wine and cook over medium heat for about 5 minutes to reduce and concentrate the wine a little; then add stock—the liquid should come about halfway up the chops. If not, add a little boiling water. Bring the liquid in the pan to a steady simmer, cover, and cook for about 30 minutes, then carefully turn the chops. Continue cooking another 30 minutes, by which time the pork should be tender all the way through and the liquid in the pan considerably reduced.

Transfer the pork chops to a heated platter. If the pan juices are not sufficiently concentrated, raise the heat and boil rapidly until you have a sauce that is thick and will nap the chops. Spoon the sauce over the chops and serve immediately.

NOTE: *At da Maiore, the chops are served with a dish of rice dressed with some of the juices that have been cooked down with a combination of sugar and vinegar to make a typical Sicilian agrodolce (sweet-sour) sauce.*

PORK BRAISED IN RED WINE WITH CHOCOLATE

A dish similar to this, pork cooked with red wine and chocolate, is served at Palermo's historic restaurant, the Antica Focacceria di San Francesco, which, despite its name, is an only-in-Sicily combination of bakery, friggitoria or fry shop, and full-fledged restaurant specializing in traditional Sicilian cuisine. (It is also one of the best places to sample the great Palermitano street sandwich, pane cu'la meusa, soft buns stuffed with a savory stew of beef spleen.) San Francesco's proprietor, Vincenzo Conticello, told me the dish comes from the monzù tradition. That is quite possible, but I suspect its lineage goes back to Spain and ultimately to Mexico, where the Spanish learned to add a little unsweetened chocolate to give body and robust flavor to many sauces.

Use the best chocolate you can find for this. My personal favorites are Valrhona and Scharffen Berger.

Note that you'll need an oven dish large enough to hold all the pork slices, overlapping slightly.

MAKES 6 TO 8 SERVINGS

1 pound yellow onions, halved and very thinly sliced	Sea salt and freshly ground black pepper	1 tablespoon thick tomato extract, concentrate, or paste
¼ to ½ cup extra-virgin olive oil	1½ cups full-bodied red wine, preferably Sicilian	1 or 2 ounces unsweetened chocolate, coarsely grated
About 2¼ pounds boneless pork loin, cut into 8 to 10 slices 1½ inches thick		

Preheat the oven to 300°F. Bring a kettle of water to a boil.

In a medium skillet over low heat, gently cook the onions in ¼ cup of the olive oil, stirring frequently, until they are a rich golden brown. (This may take 20 to 30 minutes.) Transfer the onions to an oven dish large enough to hold all the ingredients comfortably.

Add more oil to the skillet if necessary. Turn the heat up to medium. Pat each pork slice dry with paper towels and quickly brown the slices on each side, transferring them as they brown to the oven dish. Sprinkle the pork with salt and pepper to taste.

Add the red wine to the pan and, as it starts to simmer, stir in the tomato extract and the grated chocolate. Cook, stirring, just until the tomato and chocolate have dissolved in the sauce. Pour the sauce over the pork and add enough boiling water to barely cover the meat.

Transfer to the preheated oven and bake for 1 hour, adding a little more boiling water from time to time as the sauce cooks away. There should always be enough sauce in the dish to barely cover the meat.

When done, remove the pork slices and arrange on a heated serving platter. If the liquid in the oven dish is not thick enough (it should have the consistency of very heavy cream), boil it down on top of the stove, then spoon the oniony sauce over the pork slices and serve immediately.

NOTE: *This rich sauce is great with a simple dish of plain polenta. If you have leftovers, chop the meat and mix into the sauce to serve as a ragù over polenta, tagliatelle, or other pasta.*

Salsicce al Vino Rosso

PORK SAUSAGES BAKED IN RED WINE WITH ONIONS AND BAY LEAVES

At Regaleali, the Tasca family wine estate in central Sicily, dinners are sometimes elaborate affairs, drawing on the resources of the aristocratic monzù traditions. (Until his recent retirement, Monzù Mario was the head of the Tasca family kitchen.) But Anna Tasca Lanza, who gives cooking classes in her comfortable farmhouse in a corner of the vast estate, is more apt to produce an uncomplicated dish like this one when she relaxes at home. It comes straight out of the Sicilian countryside and is as simple as can be imagined. What makes it special is, first of all, the quality of the sausages (which should be the best you can find and not too lean, because flavor and texture come from sausages that are a little on the fatty side) and, second, the quality of the wine in which they're cooked and that is served with them—in both cases, a bottle of the prize-winning, deep-flavored ruby-red Rosso del Conte, made from nero d'Avola grapes, an autochthonous varietal grown on the estate.

MAKES 4 TO 6 SERVINGS

8 to 10 fresh Italian-style pork sausages flavored with fennel	6 to 8 small yellow onions, quartered 6 to 8 bay leaves	2 cups nero d'Avola or similar red wine

Preheat the oven to 425°F.

Set the sausages in an oval or rectangular oven dish in which they will just fit. With the sharp point of a paring knife, prick each sausage in several places so they don't burst while cooking. Tuck the quartered onions and the bay leaves, broken in two, around the sausages. Bring the wine to a simmer in a small saucepan on top of the stove and pour about two-thirds of it over and around the sausages.

Transfer the baking dish to the preheated oven and cook for 30 minutes, then turn the sausages and onions over, using tongs. If the wine boils a way before the sausages are done, add more from the saucepan, first heating it again so it doesn't lower the temperature of the sausages. Cook for another 15 to 20 minutes, or until the winy sauce has reduced considerably and the sausages are brown. Remove from the oven and serve immediately.

Pollo al Limone

LEMON AND GARLIC CHICKEN

The Sorrento Peninsula, between Naples and Salerno, is justifiably famous for the quality of its lemons. Along narrow terraces called *macere* that climb the steep south-facing hills above Amalfi, Ravello, and Maiore, the lemon trees grow, often propped up by stout chestnut stakes and protected by overhanging nets. Many of these are the feminello variety, probably the most prized lemons in the world. Not surprisingly, these lemons are key ingredients in local dishes, and their deeply flavored zest is the critical element in limoncello (page 408). I smiled recently when I read that California growers, responding to demands from the hard-to-please gourmet produce sector, are rushing to market feminello lemons, as if variety alone produces that incomparable flavor. Indeed, so rich is the soil of the Sorrento Peninsula, so beneficent the climate, that even the thistles that grow by the roadsides taste better than anywhere else.

MAKES 6 SERVINGS

2 fresh lemons, preferably organic	⅓ cup extra-virgin olive oil	Sea salt and freshly ground black pepper
1 head of garlic	3 or 4 bay leaves	12 to 16 small new potatoes, partially peeled
1 roasting chicken, about 4 pounds, cut up, or 4 pounds chicken legs and thighs	2 fresh rosemary sprigs	

Preheat the oven to 350°F.

Rinse the lemons and chop them, skin and all, into about 8 pieces each. Smack the head of garlic on a board to separate the cloves, then smash each one lightly with the flat blade of a knife to loosen the peel. Remove and discard the peels.

Rinse the chicken parts and dry thoroughly with paper towels.

Smear a couple of tablespoons of the olive oil all over the bottom of a roasting pan, then arrange the chicken pieces in the dish. Add the lemon sections to the dish, squeezing each one slightly to release the juice and pressing them down in among the chicken. Scatter the garlic cloves, bay leaves, and rosemary among the chicken pieces. Dribble the rest of the olive oil over the chicken and sprinkle it quite liberally with salt and pepper.

Transfer to the preheated oven and bake for about 20 minutes.

Meanwhile, bring a large pot of water to a rolling boil and add the potatoes. Cook for about 15 minutes, just long enough to tenderize the potatoes slightly. Drain the potatoes and set aside.

After 20 minutes, remove the chicken from the oven and raise the oven temperature to 425°F. Turn each piece of chicken over and add the potatoes to the pan, stirring to coat them well with olive oil. Return the dish to the oven and roast for 30 to 40 minutes longer, or until the chicken and the potatoes are crisp and brown.

Remove and serve immediately.

The best capers are produced on islands off Sicily, either Pantelleria, which is halfway between Sicily and Tunisia, or Salina, one of the Aeolian islands north of the big island. There capers are harvested laboriously, one by one, then dried in the sun and packed in salt. If you can't find salted capers from Pantelleria or Salina, use the kind packed in vinegar or brine, but rinse them very thoroughly in running water before adding them to the pot. (The vinegar flavor is important in this dish, but you want to be certain it's a good-quality vinegar, not always true with the vinegar in which capers are packed.)

MAKES 4 TO 6 SERVINGS

1 medium onion, finely chopped	3 to 4 pounds chicken parts (legs, thighs, wings)	Sea salt and freshly ground black pepper
¼ cup extra-virgin olive oil, plus a little more if necessary	3 tablespoons white wine vinegar	¼ cup finely minced flat-leaf parsley
	⅓ cup capers, preferably salt-packed, rinsed and drained	

Combine the onion and olive oil in a sauté pan and cook, stirring frequently, over low heat until the onion is softened but not turning brown. Using a slotted spoon, remove the onion from the pan and set aside.

Dry the chicken pieces thoroughly with paper towels. Add a little more oil to the pan if necessary, raise the heat to medium, and brown the chicken thoroughly on all sides. As the pieces brown, transfer them to the dish with the onion.

Add the vinegar to a cup measure, then add water to fill to the 1-cup mark. As soon as all the chicken is done, stir the vinegar-water and the capers into the pan and cook rapidly, scraping up any brown bits. Return the chicken and onions to the pan and add salt and pepper to taste. Stir in the parsley.

Cover the pan and turn the heat down very low. Cook at a bare simmer for 1 hour. The chicken with its vinegar-caper sauce may also be transferred to an oven dish and baked in a preheated 350°F oven for 1 hour.

Remove from the heat and serve immediately, with the pan juices spooned over each serving.

VARIATIONS

✿ Pollo ai Capperi is delicious on its own, but to make an easy one-dish meal, add an appropriate vegetable for the last 20 to 30 minutes of cooking time. Lightly browned wedges of potato are an obvious choice, but eggplant, salted, rinsed, dried, then browned in good olive oil, makes a more unusual dish; zucchini, cut into chunks and briefly sautéed just to brown the edges, are also good. Or chargrill and peel red peppers (see page 338), cut them into quarters, and add for the last 5 minutes since they barely need any cooking at all.

Spezzatino di Pollo al Peperoncino

CALABRESE BRAISED CHICKEN WITH CHILIED TOMATO AND GREEN OLIVES

Add as much or as little dried red chili to this dish as you wish. In some parts of Calabria, especially around Diamante, chicken is served with a decidedly hot sauce, but in other parts of that mountainous region you'd be hard put to say exactly what it is that gives a nice but barely discernible heat to the dish.

You could make this with a chicken cut into parts—legs, thighs, breasts, wings. Or, if you prefer, make it with all legs or thighs or breasts.

MAKES 4 TO 6 SERVINGS

2 garlic cloves, finely chopped	1 dried red chili or 1 teaspoon crumbled dried chili, or more to taste	½ cup dry red wine
1 medium onion, chopped		½ cup mixed minced flat-leaf parsley and fresh basil
¼ cup extra-virgin olive oil	One 4-pound chicken, cut into 8 serving pieces, or 3 to 4 pounds chicken parts	
2 sweet red peppers		Sea salt and freshly ground black pepper
1 pound ripe tomatoes, peeled and chopped, or 1 cup chopped well-drained canned tomatoes	Unbleached all-purpose flour for dredging	1 cup coarsely chopped pitted green olives

Combine the garlic, onion, and 2 tablespoons of the olive oil in a saucepan or deep skillet large enough to hold all the ingredients and set it over low heat. Cook gently until the onion is soft but not brown.

Meanwhile, use a vegetable parer to peel the red peppers, then slice them lengthwise into thin strips. Add the peppers to the pan with the onions and stir to mix. Cook the peppers until soft, then stir in the tomatoes and chili.

Dry the chicken pieces thoroughly with paper towels. Spread the flour on a plate and dredge the chicken in the flour.

Heat the remaining 2 tablespoons of olive oil in a separate skillet over medium-high heat and cook the chicken pieces until golden brown on both sides, about 10 minutes per side. As they finish cooking, transfer them to the tomato sauce.

Add the wine to the skillet in which the chicken cooked and cook quickly, scraping up any brown bits. Add the wine to the tomato sauce, along with the herbs and salt and pepper to taste. Reduce the heat to low, cover the pan, and cook slowly for about 20 minutes. Then stir in the green olives, cover again, and cook for 15 minutes longer. Prick the chicken with a fork to test for doneness. If the juices run clear yellow, it is done. Otherwise, let it cook for another 10 minutes or so. If there is a lot of juice in the pan, leave the lid off to boil down and concentrate the juices. Serve immediately.

Coniglio alla Stimpirata

SICILIAN BRAISED RABBIT IN A SWEET-AND-SOUR SAUCE

Take a look at the recipe for Pesce alla Stemperata on page 215 and you'll see that this is a variation on the theme, using rabbit instead of fish. It's especially popular in the southeastern corner of Sicily, around Ragusa. When people talk about the complex flavors of Sicilian food, they call on this dish, with its rich ingredients and intricate balance of sweet-and-sour flavors as a brilliant illustration. Easy to prepare, Coniglio alla Stimpirata is also stunning enough to serve as the focus of a dinner party.

MAKES 4 TO 6 SERVINGS

1 fresh rabbit, weighing about 4 pounds, cut into 6 pieces	1 dark green celery stalk, coarsely chopped	1 cup light chicken or meat stock
Unbleached all-purpose flour for dredging	½ cup green olives, pitted	1 tablespoon tomato extract, concentrate, or paste
Sea salt and freshly ground black pepper	¼ cup capers, preferably salt-packed, rinsed and drained	Pinch of ground cinnamon (optional)
½ cup extra-virgin olive oil	¼ cup pine nuts	½ cup red wine vinegar
1 medium yellow onion, thinly sliced	⅓ cup golden raisins, soaked in hot water to plump and drained	1 tablespoon honey
2 garlic cloves, coarsely chopped		

Rinse the rabbit pieces and pat dry with paper towels. Spread the flour on a plate, toss in salt and pepper to taste, and dredge the rabbit pieces in the flour, shaking to remove excess. In a skillet large enough to hold all the rabbit pieces in one layer, heat ¼ cup of the olive oil over medium heat. Add the rabbit and brown slowly on all sides, turning frequently, about 20 minutes in all. Remove the rabbit pieces as they brown and set them aside.

When the rabbit is done, empty the pan of the burned oil and wipe it out with paper towels. Add ¼ cup of fresh oil and return the pan to medium-low heat. Stir in the onion, garlic, and celery and cook, stirring, until the vegetables are soft.

Meanwhile, bring a small pot of water to a rolling boil and drop in the olives. Bring to a boil and simmer for about 1½ minutes, then drain. (This will reduce any saltiness considerably.) Chop the olives coarsely.

Stir the chopped olives, capers, pine nuts, and raisins into the softened vegetables. Cook for about 5 minutes, then add the rabbit pieces back to the skillet, stirring to mix everything together well. Add salt and pepper to taste, along with the stock. Dilute the tomato extract in a cup of very hot water and add to the pan, stirring to mix everything together well. If you wish, add a small pinch of ground cinnamon. The rabbit pieces should fit in the pan, and the sauce and its ingredients should lap up over the rabbit. Cover the pan, lower the heat, and simmer the rabbit for about 35 minutes, or until it is cooked all the way through. (Test the rabbit for doneness by pricking with a fork. The juices should be clear.)

Combine the vinegar and honey in a small saucepan and bring to a simmer. Cook gently until the liquid has reduced by half. After the rabbit has cooked for 35 minutes, add the sweet-sour mixture to the sauce. Raise the heat to medium and cook, uncovered, for 10 minutes, or until the sauce thickens and coats the rabbit pieces nicely. Taste and adjust the seasoning.

Serve immediately, spooning the syrupy sauce over the rabbit pieces.

Rabbit / Coniglio

Why do Americans so resist rabbit, that wonderfully tasty yet low-fat, low-cholesterol meat? Beats me, but I have to say, those who avoid it don't know what they're missing. In fact I confess that I have sometimes served rabbit to the unknowing, who consume it happily, thinking it's just another kind of chicken.

Most rabbit recipes can, in fact, be made with chicken, but the firm texture of rabbit contributes greatly to the appeal of these dishes. If you insist on chicken, be sure to get a free-range bird with firmer flesh (and better flavor) than the industrially manufactured chickens most supermarket meat counters provide. (These are not, in fact, very good to eat under any circumstances.)

Coniglio a Calabresi / Conigliu a Calavrisi

COUNTRY-STYLE RABBIT FROM CALABRIA

A mixture of hot and sweet flavors, of wild and domestic herbs and the great Calabrese favorite chili, marks this tasty, tangy rabbit dish.

MAKES 4 TO 6 SERVINGS

---

1 rabbit, weighing about 4 pounds, cut into 6 pieces

FOR THE MARINADE

1 medium yellow onion, thinly sliced

½ cup coarsely chopped flat-leaf parsley

2 fresh rosemary branches, coarsely chopped

2 garlic cloves, smashed with the flat blade of a knife

⅔ cup wine vinegar mixed with ⅓ cup water

4 garlic cloves, chopped

1 medium yellow onion, chopped

¼ cup chopped fresh basil, plus a little basil to finish

¼ cup chopped flat-leaf parsley, plus a little parsley to finish

Pinch of dried oregano

Pinch of fennel seeds or wild fennel pollen (see page 415)

2 bay leaves

1 small fresh red chili

2 ounces pancetta, finely diced (¼ cup)

1 tablespoon extra-virgin olive oil

¼ cup grappa or other strong distilled liquor

2 pounds ripe fresh tomatoes, peeled, or 2 cups chopped well-drained canned tomatoes

Sea salt

Place the rabbit pieces in a bowl along with the onion, parsley, rosemary, and garlic. Pour the vinegar-water over the rabbit and marinate, refrigerated, overnight, turning the rabbit pieces from time to time in the marinade.

When ready to cook, remove the rabbit from the marinade and dry the pieces carefully with paper towels. Mince together the chopped garlic, onion, basil, parsley, oregano, fennel, bay leaves, and chili.

In a saucepan, preferably terra-cotta, gently cook the pancetta in the olive oil over medium-low heat until the fat starts to run. Add the minced mixture and continue cooking, stirring, until the vegetables have softened. Using a slotted spoon or spatula, remove the vegetables and set aside.

Raise the heat to medium and add the rabbit pieces to the fat remaining in the pan. Brown on all sides, turning frequently, about 20 minutes in all. Add the grappa and let it bubble up. As the grappa starts to cook down and evaporate, return the reserved vegetables to the pan, along with a cup of water. Turn the heat to low, cover the pan, and cook very gently for about 45 minutes. Stir in the tomatoes and cover again, leaving the sauce to simmer for another 15 minutes. At the end of this time, if the sauce is too liquid, remove the rabbit pieces and set aside on a warm serving platter. Raise the heat and cook the sauce down rapidly until it is thick enough to coat the rabbit with a thick sauce. Stir in more minced basil and parsley along with salt to taste and spoon the sauce over the rabbit on the platter. Serve immediately.

RABBIT BRAISED IN WHITE WINE FROM THE ISLAND OF ISCHIA

Ischia, the largest of the islands in the Bay of Naples, is a fashionable destination for Euro-trendsetters these days, but not too long ago it was, like many islands, a remote and impoverished outpost in the Mediterranean where fishing families lived on limited resources. In addition to fish, however, the Ischitani had rabbits, which they fattened in deep ditches, and thus evolved Ischia's great contribution to Italian gastronomy, this very simple recipe for Coniglio all'Ischitana.

MAKES 4 TO 6 SERVINGS

1 rabbit, about 4 pounds, cut into 6 pieces	1 cup dry white wine	1/3 cup slivered fresh basil
Sea salt and freshly ground black pepper	1 pound ripe fresh tomatoes, peeled, seeded, and chopped, or 1 cup well-drained canned tomatoes	Leaves from 2 fresh rosemary branches
1/4 cup extra-virgin olive oil		

Dry the rabbit pieces thoroughly with paper towels. Sprinkle with salt and pepper to taste. In a deep skillet over medium heat, brown the rabbit in the olive oil, turning frequently, until it's a nice golden color all over, about 20 minutes in all. Add the wine and raise the heat. Boil the wine to reduce by about half.

Stir in the the chopped tomatoes. Set aside a tablespoon or so of basil to garnish the finished dish and stir the rest into the tomatoes, along with the rosemary leaves. Lower the heat and cook for about 20 minutes, until the tomatoes have started to disintegrate and form a sauce. At this point, add 1½ cups boiling water, and as soon as the liquid in the pan has returned to a boil, reduce the heat to a simmer, cover the pan, and cook for 1 hour to 1½ hours, or until the sauce has reduced once more and the rabbit is very tender.

Transfer the rabbit to a heated platter. If the sauce is thin, raise the heat and boil it in the skillet until it has reduced and thickened. Taste for seasoning and, if necessary, add more salt and pepper. Spoon the sauce over the rabbit and sprinkle with the reserved slivered basil.

VERDURE E INSALATE

Vegetables and Salads

Respected all over the Mediterranean, vegetables are regarded with something down-right close to veneration here in Italy's Mezzogiorno. You won't find many true vegetarians in the Italian South, although Pythagoras, that early promoter of vegetarian diets, did some of his best thinking at the Greek city of Crotone on Calabria's Ionian coast. But you will find many, many people who eat almost nothing but vegetables, and happily so, often with just a little meat stirred into the dish. Meat on its own is for feast days, fish for days of obligation, but vegetables are what we eat every day.

Nonetheless, there is nothing commonplace about vegetables in the South. Handled with respect, even with love, they are evidence of a skillful farmer's green thumb as much as of a cook's vaunted talents. You notice this immediately when you wander through one of the rum-bustious open-air markets that still abound—the teeming Ballarò in Palermo, for instance, or the pretty, palm-shaded Piazza Vittorio market in Monopoli on Puglia's Adriatic coast, or dozens of neighborhood markets all over Napoli. For a North American, used to shopping in supermarket produce sections, where much of the food comes already wrapped and in any case was harvested days, if not weeks, earlier in far distant parts of the world, these markets are star-tling. The sights and sounds, the rhythm of call and response, the daily dramas enacted with a wily eye to the audience, the barely concealed double entendres and sly word games as mer-chants and salesmen toy with housewives who feign prissy discomfiture, are all part of the play. But the stars of the show, front and center, are the fruits and vegetables, flamboyant colors massed in vivid contrasts, glossy black eggplants piled next to the architectural complexity of artichokes, brilliant oranges and lemons beside somber, earthy potatoes, tomatoes in dozens of shapes from deeply ridged costolutos to big pearlike drupes, particolored borlotti beans and fleshy green favas, garlic and onions, red, white, and yellow, in braided ropes. And along with the sights go the market smells—pungent basil, acrid dark green celery, and the sharp, sudden, sensual impact of a bright mandarino or a dark-red tarocco blood orange, split open and of-fered as a sample to a skeptical customer.

For that American shopper, accustomed to rather limited choices—lettuce that is either red leaf or green, iceberg or romaine, potatoes that are floury for baking or waxy for boiling, or-anges that are labeled "juice" or "eating," and lemons that are . . . well, lemons—the variety on offer at any given time of the year is simply staggering. Sweet red onions from Tropea in Cal-abria are famous all over Italy, as are the prized Sorrento lemons from the Amalfi coast north of Salerno. But what about lemons from the island of Procida off Naples or pink, torpedo-shaped Acquaviva onions from Puglia? Or pesche tabacchiere, snuff-box peaches from the slopes of Mt. Etna, slightly squashed and with a suggestion of roses in their flavor, to be found only in markets in eastern Sicily and only in July? Or velvet-textured Sarconi beans and crisp Senise red peppers, fresh or dried, but available only near where they grow, in the remote Agri and Sinni River valleys of Basilicata? And this is but a tiny sampling of the choices available—not all at once, by any means, but in season, in the territories where they are cultivated.

The Italy-based Slow Food organization has moved mountains to bring attention to this precious cargo of vegetables and fruits. Through locally based groups called *presidia,* Slow Food brings attention to varieties that have disappeared, are in danger of disappearing, or simply have noncommercial but nonetheless valuable qualities. Slow Food organizes growers and pro-ducers to establish standards on the one hand and, on the other, through its awards and pro-grams, educates the public and makes these products known in the marketplace, both national and European, so that consumers become aware of their rare qualities. The list of Slow Food presidia in Italy, a long one indeed, includes a great number of products from the South—violet-colored artichokes from Castellammare di Stabia south of Naples, for example, Bronte pistachios from Mt. Etna, bergamot lemons from the Ionian coast of Calabria, cucumbers from Polignano on Puglia's Adriatic, and more than fifty other varieties—and each year worthy con-tenders are added to the list.

But vegetables are not valued solely on the farm and in the marketplace. At the table, too, they are given pride of place, a slot of their own apart from the pasta, soup, or main dish, a course to be relished independently, for its own sake, without competition from meat, fish, or potatoes. Served like this, vegetables are glorified as seasonal specialties. When artichokes come to market in early winter, enthusiasts can enjoy the purity of artichokes in all their glory, stuffed and baked, diced and stewed, crisply fried, even raw as a salad. Ditto tomatoes or sweet peppers in summer or fresh green peas or fava beans in spring—each has its unique place, savored and appreciated for its individual merits.

Travelers in Italy will recognize this when handed a restaurant menu. Instead of the Ameri-can focus on piling each main-course item with additional foodstuffs, Italian restaurant offer-ings are more sober, with vegetables coming near the end, just before the dolce, as a separate entry called *contorni.* The word *contorno* means, literally, "trimming" or "dressing," something to go with the protein, but a vegetable that is the icon of the moment is more often served strictly on its own, to be savored for its individual virtues.

Having said that, I also have to add that vegetables play many other roles on the Italian table, showing up throughout the meal. Most soups, most pasta sauces, even when they include meat or fish, are centered on vegetables, whether the ubiquitous tomato sauces or something like the splendid pasta sauce from the Terra di Bari made with broccoli rabe and anchovies. Or Easter lasagna made with artichokes, peas, and wild mushrooms. As for main dishes, thumb through the pages of any southern Italian cookbook and you will be hard put to find a preparation that doesn't begin with a trio or more of vegetables—garlic, onions, parsley (the flat-leaf parsley that Italians love, not the curly English variety), perhaps a stout carrot, or a flavorful dark-green rib of celery, or a few wild mushrooms—that make up what's called the *battuto* or *soffrito,* the aromatic mixture of minced vegetables and herbs that is sautéed in olive oil or pork fat to start the cooking process.

Vegetables are often served as an antipasto too. It might be as simple as a mash of savory beans topping crisp crostini or as complex as thin wafers of eggplant rolled around a garlicky, herby ricotta filling and braised in an aromatic tomato sauce. And in Puglia, vegetables even take the place of dessert. I'm not joking: Served raw at the end of a meal, whether singly or together on a platter, they're called *sopratavola*, meaning an addendum to the table or the meal, and include anything crisply sweet and seasonal—fennel, celery, sweet red-tinged carrots, raw fava beans or peas, fresh cucumbers, radishes, lettuce, or the tender chicory called *catalogna.* Try it sometime, one of these alone or several in combination, utterly plain, no oil, no lemon, perhaps just a touch of sea salt—it's a crisp, delicious, and effective digestive.

The reason behind all this hortophilia is simple and incontrovertible: Vegetables are better in southern Italy than almost anywhere else in the world, a fact that, as with so much of southern Italian food, comes down mostly to geography and climate but also to a long history of gardening know-how. The bright summer sun, the soft winter rain, the mineral-dense soil—whether we're speaking of the volcanic runoff from Vesuvius and Etna or of Puglia's limestone plateau—all combine with an attentive agriculture, the result of farmers who have been working the same pieces of land generation after generation for thousands of years, and cultivating the same crops, if not for millennia, at least for several centuries. Techniques are handed down, father to son, mother to daughter, refined and improved on, sometimes with more up-to-date equipment or knowledge, sometimes by going back to the old ways after a period of experimenting with the new.

The sweet violet-colored artichokes from Castellammare in Campania provide a good example of this traditional know-how. Like many Italian varieties of artichoke, they lack the tough cluster of spiny prickles that covers the heart (the base or foundation of the fruit, where all the leaflike bracts come together) of artichokes grown in America. That "choke" is not always easy to remove and can cause a lot of grief if ingested by mistake. Why Italian artichokes should be spineless was a mystery to me until I discovered that in Castellammare—and elsewhere in Italy too—artichokes are traditionally cultivated as annuals, even though they are in fact perennials. Clones or shoots, called *carducci,* that grow up around the mother plant in the spring are removed and transplanted to make new plants for the next season, unlike in California, where the same plant provides a harvest year after year for as many as ten or twelve years—but a harvest of big, fat, globe artichokes with all the prickly thistle bits intact. No one could tell me when the growers of Castellammare developed this technique—"We've always done it that way" was the universal, and predictable, response.

If the range of cultivated vegetables is astonishingly wide, it is almost matched by the use of foraged greens and other wild and semiwild foods. In the mountains of Basilicata, where there are Albanian (Arbëreshë) communities that date from the fifteenth century, a study in the year 2000 of one such village found that at least 120 wild food and medicinal plants were still being actively foraged—or a good half of all the food plants consumed in the community. The wild things ranged from familiar chicories (like dandelion greens) to poppy greens, wild clematis, goosefoot or lamb's quarters, wild fennel, wild asparagus, mallows, nettles, hop vines, borage, herbs like mint and oregano, and wild alliums. Next door in Puglia, where a similar taste for foraged foods obtains, wild hyacinth bulbs (called *lampascione*) are so popular that they are actually imported from North Africa—an anomaly, given that part of the appeal of wild food is the fact that it's free for the picking.

So it's no wonder if this paradise of vegetables (and fruits, I hasten to add, lest the lemons, oranges, almonds, plums and grapes, apricots and peaches go unrecognized) is also the heartland of the Mediterranean diet. Such a high consumption of vegetables, along with grains, legumes, and olive oil, and such a low consumption of meat, especially red meat, has been directly correlated by research scientists to the low incidence of coronary heart disease, diabetes, and certain types of cancer among southern Italians. Like Pythagoras, the late Dr. Ancel Keys, who was one of the principal and earliest researchers behind these theories, got much of his inspiration from the time he spent in his home away from home in Pioppi, south of Salerno along the Cilentano coast of Campania.

And this is still the greatest lesson that southern Italians can offer to the rest of the world: eat your vegetables. But start off, as the people of the Mezzogiorno do, by paying strict attention to quality—buy locally, buy seasonally, then follow the simple no-fuss (for the most part) recipes of southern Italian cooks.

Artichokes / Carciofi

Artichokes are subspecies in the *Cynara* genus of thistlelike vegetables. Their great-great-grandparent is the wild thistle that proliferates in sandy soils all around the Mediterranean. The artichoke you buy in a produce market is a big, unopened bud that, if left to flower, would look very much like the purple-blue flowers of thistles—beautiful but cruelly thorny.

The artichokes commonly available in North America all seem to come from the same growing region around Castroville, California, a town whose boosters call it, with little justification, the artichoke capital of the world (even Egypt produces more artichokes than California, while Italy is the world's leading producer). These big globe artichokes suffer from an over-abundance of what plant botanists call "prickly phyllaries," meaning that tough, indigestible bunch of thorns at the center of the fruit (the "choke"), which must be removed if one is to enjoy eating the thing. More recently, something called "baby artichokes" have appeared in our markets. These are not really immature but rather small, mature artichokes that are cultivated for size and with a less developed spiny center.

Artichokes usually must be trimmed before cooking. Note that the cut surfaces will blacken on contact with air. To prevent that, add the juice of half a lemon to a bowl of cool water and use the other lemon half to rub the cut surfaces as you work. When you finish with each one, toss it into the acidulated water. The tough outer bracts (leaves) should be removed, and the stem should be cut back—depending on how the artichoke will be used, either cut the stem flush with the base or leave an inch or two protruding. Protruding stems should be peeled of the rough outside skin.

Once you have removed enough of the outer bracts to reach the paler, more tender inside, cut the top of the artichoke back about an inch or so and, if the remaining bracts are very prickly, use scissors to cut the tops off each one. If the artichokes are very large, with well-developed chokes, you can usually push the inner leaves aside and use a serrated grapefruit spoon to scrape out the prickly thistles, or choke. Otherwise, cut the artichoke into quarters and discard the thistles.

This simplest of all artichoke recipes works well with young, very fresh artichokes, something difficult for many of us to come by. If you must use large artichokes, with their spiny centers, trim them very thoroughly, cutting away the tough, spiny chokes and rubbing the cut surfaces with lemon to keep them from darkening.

Baby artichokes are also fine for this dish. You will need four for each serving—twenty-four artichokes to serve six. Baby artichokes should be prepared like larger globe artichokes, but because they lack the thistles in the center, they may be cooked either whole or cut in half.

MAKES 6 SERVINGS

2 lemons, preferably organic	2 garlic cloves, finely minced	½ cup extra-virgin olive oil
24 baby artichokes, or 6 large ones	½ to ¾ cup chopped flat-leaf parsley	Sea salt and freshly ground black pepper

Peel the zest from one of the lemons and set it aside. Add the juice of that lemon to a bowl of cool water large enough to hold all the artichokes. This acidulated water will keep them from blackening on their cut surfaces. Prepare the artichokes as described on page 305, cutting the stems to within 1½ inches of the base, rubbing the cut surfaces with a lemon half. Cut large artichokes into quarters and, if necessary, remove the choke from each quarter. As the artichokes are done, toss them into the bowl of acidulated water.

Mince the reserved lemon zest and combine it with the minced garlic, chopped parsley, and olive oil. Set aside.

Drain and dry the artichokes. Transfer them to a heavy saucepan or soup kettle along with the oil mixture. Set over medium heat and cook briefly, stirring until the artichokes start to brown, then turn the heat down to low. Spoon the savory olive oil all over the artichokes. Sprinkle on salt and pepper, add 2 or 3 tablespoons of water, and set over low heat. Bring to a simmer, cover the pan, and cook for about 15 minutes, or until the artichokes are tender—the larger the artichoke, obviously, the longer it will take to cook. Transfer the artichokes to a serving platter, spooning the hot juices over them. Add the juice of the remaining lemon half and serve immediately.

Carciofi in Tortiera

CALABRIAN ARTICHOKE AND POTATO PIE

MAKES 6 SERVINGS

6 tablespoons extra-virgin oil	1 pound yellow-fleshed potatoes, such as Yellow Finn or Yukon Gold, peeled and sliced ¼ inch thick	⅓ cup grated aged pecorino or caciocavallo
½ cup fine dry bread crumbs		1 or 2 garlic cloves, coarsely chopped
2 lemons		
4 large globe artichokes, or 16 to 20 baby artichokes	Sea salt and freshly ground black pepper	

Preheat the oven to 375°F. Rub the insides of a 1½- to 2-quart soufflé dish or a similar round oven dish with about a tablespoon of olive oil, then sprinkle with about 3 tablespoons of bread crumbs. Set aside.

Use the lemons to prepare the artichokes as described on page 305, cutting the stems to about an inch in length. If using large artichokes, cut them into quarters and scrape out the spiny central chokes, then divide each artichoke quarter in half, so that you have 8 pieces from each whole artichoke. If using baby artichokes, cut them in half. Drop the prepared artichoke pieces into the acidulated water.

Layer half the potato slices over the bottom of the prepared oven dish. Cover with half the artichoke pieces. Sprinkle with salt and pepper, then half the grated cheese. Scatter about half the chopped garlic over the cheese and dribble over it 2 tablespoons of olive oil. Layer the remaining artichokes, potatoes, salt, pepper, cheese, and garlic. Top with the remaining bread crumbs and dribble with the remaining olive oil. Add about ¼ cup of boiling water, dribbling it around the edges of the dish.

Lightly cover the dish and transfer to the oven. Bake for 20 minutes, then remove the cover and bake for another 20 minutes, or until the vegetables are tender throughout and the top is browned. Serve immediately or, if you prefer, set aside to cool to just above room temperature before serving.

Carciofi sott'Olio

ARTICHOKES PRESERVED IN OIL

Baby artichokes, if you can find them, are ideal for this recipe. If they're unavailable, use large globe artichokes and cut them into quarters. Like other *sott'olii,* these are often part of a mixed antipasto.

MAKES 2 PINTS

2½ lemons	1½ cups white wine vinegar	8 to 10 cloves
8 or 9 globe artichokes, or 36 baby artichokes	3 bay leaves	Extra-virgin olive oil
	1 teaspoon black peppercorns	1 garlic clove, slivered

Use 1½ lemons to prepare the artichokes, following the directions on page 305. As each artichoke is finished, toss it into a bowl of acidulated water.

In a saucepan large enough to hold all the ingredients, mix the vinegar with 2½ cups water. Add the bay leaves, peppercorns, and cloves. Slice the remaining lemon and add the slices to the pan. Bring the liquid to a boil. Drain the artichokes and add to the boiling liquid. Return to a boil and cook the artichokes for 5 to 10 minutes, or until they are tender but not mushy. Remove from the heat and drain, discarding the lemon slices.

Transfer the artichokes to clean pint or half-pint canning jars, distributing the bay leaves, peppercorns, and cloves among the jars. Cover with olive oil and top each jar with a few slivers of garlic. Screw down the jar lids and store in a cool place, but not refrigerated, for 2 weeks. For longer keeping, use sterilized jars and process the jars for 20 to 30 minutes, following the instructions on page 129.

Cabbages and Greens/Broccoli, Cavoli, Cavolfiore, Cime di Rape, ecc.

Cabbages, both crinkly-leaved savoy and smooth green drumheads; sprouting broccoli like what's called broccoli rabe or rapini in North America, and *cime di rape* (which really means, confusingly, turnip greens) in Italy; creamy white and purple cauliflowers; the beautiful jade-green *broccoli romanesco* (often called green cauliflower in North America) with a spiral of flower clusters that come to a peak in the center—the range of cabbage-family vegetables, Brassicas or Cruciferae, eaten in southern Italy is so extensive that it may be easier to say what is not used than what is. What is not used, then, includes, curiously enough, Brussels sprouts and many kales, especially lacinato or Tuscan kale. Broccoli itself is rare except for romanesco, and often in old cookbooks, when broccoli is specified, what we call cauliflower is clearly what is meant. Apart from those few restrictions, however, every village, every secluded valley, seems to have developed its own autochthonous varieties, like *friarielle,* a kind of extra-spicy broccoli rabe available only in Neapolitan markets and not to be confused with the peppers called *friarielle* from the Cilento, a little to the south. In fact, when it comes to recipes, almost any member of this broad family can be substituted for any other, and I have even had success with certain related Chinese vegetables, like Chinese sprouting broccoli and bok choy. For many of the following recipes, I have made suggestions for vegetables that would not appear on a southern Italian table but that profit mightily from a southern Italian treatment in the kitchen.

Cime di Rape o Cavalfiore Stufati

BRAISED BROCCOLI RABE (RAPINI) OR CAULIFLOWER

In this dish from Puglia's Alta Murgia, the high rolling grassland west of Bari, broccoli rabe or cauliflower is stewed in a small amount of liquid along with onions, tomatoes, little hot chilies, and black olives. I have also found it to be very successful with broccoli, the head broken into florets—in fact a combination of cauliflower and broccoli works well and looks terrific. Traditionally this is served with a topping of grated cheese to make a great vegetarian main course, but if you plan to serve this as a contorno, or accompaniment, to fish or meat, the cheese topping seems a bit excessive.

MAKES 4 TO 6 SERVINGS

1½ pounds broccoli rabe (rapini), or 1 pound cauliflower or broccoli

1 medium red onion, thinly sliced

3 tablespoons extra-virgin olive oil, plus a little more oil if using cheese

1 dried red chili, crumbled

Sea salt

15 to 20 cherry or grape tomatoes, halved

15 to 20 black olives, pitted and coarsely chopped

⅓ cup grated hard aged cheese: pecorino, caciocavallo, or parmigiano reggiano (optional)

Rinse and trim the broccoli rabe and discard any yellow or wilted leaves. Cut into 2-inch lengths. If you're using broccoli or cauliflower, rinse and cut into florets.

Combine the onion with the olive oil in a pan that will not suffer when put under the broiler. Set over medium-low heat. As the onion starts to sizzle, add the chili and salt to taste. Stir in the vegetable pieces, halved tomatoes, and black olives. Add about ¼ cup boiling water, then cover the pan, lower the heat, and cook for about 10 minutes. Check the vegetables for tenderness, piercing the thick parts with the point of a knife. If they need to cook a little longer, you may wish to add a little more boiling water to keep the vegetables from scorching.

Meanwhile, if you're using the cheese topping, turn the broiler on to high. When the vegetables are done, sprinkle the cheese over the top, dribble on a little more olive oil, and run under the broiler just long enough to melt the cheese. Remove and serve immediately.

Cime di Cavolfiore Gratinate

GRATIN OF CAULIFLOWER

Try this also with Brussels sprouts but parboil them for about 10 minutes, or even longer if they are very large.

MAKES 4 TO 6 SERVINGS

3 tablespoons extra-virgin olive oil	2 cups canned plum tomatoes, with their juice	3 tablespoons dry bread crumbs
1 garlic clove, chopped	Sea salt	⅓ cup coarsely grated hard aged cheese: caciocavallo, pecorino, toscano, grana padano, or parmigiano reggiano
1 medium yellow onion, chopped (about 1 cup chopped onion)	Ground or crumbled dried red chili, to taste	
	¼ cup finely chopped or slivered basil	
3 to 4 anchovy fillets, chopped, or 1 teaspoon anchovy paste	2 pounds cauliflower, trimmed and broken into florets	3 to 4 tablespoons finely chopped blanched almonds

To make the tomato sauce, combine 1 tablespoon of the olive oil with the garlic and onion in a saucepan or skillet and set over medium-low heat. Cook, stirring, until the vegetables are very soft but do not let them brown. When the vegetables are soft, stir in the chopped anchovies and cook, using the back of a fork to press the anchovies into the oil in the saucepan.

Add the tomatoes with their juice and raise the heat to medium. Simmer the tomato sauce until thick, about 20 minutes, stirring occasionally and breaking up the tomatoes with a cooking fork or big spoon. Add salt to taste and a good pinch of chili. When the sauce has reached the right thickness, remove from the heat and stir in the basil.

While the sauce is cooking, preheat the oven to 425°F. Bring about 2 inches of lightly salted water to a rolling boil in another saucepan and add the cauliflower florets. Cover the pot and let cook 5 to 7 minutes, or until the cauliflower is just tender all the way through. Drain the cauliflower and set aside.

Rub another tablespoon of olive oil over the bottom and sides of an oval gratin or other oven dish. Sprinkle 1 tablespoon of the bread crumbs over the bottom and sides of the dish. Arrange the cauliflower in the oven dish and spoon the tomato sauce over the cauliflower. Combine the grated cheese, almonds, and remaining 2 tablespoons of bread crumbs and sprinkle over the tomato sauce. Dribble the remaining tablespoon of oil on top and transfer the dish to the pre-heated oven. Bake until the top is brown—about 15 minutes.

Serve immediately, or if you prefer, set aside until the dish is just a little warmer than room temperature before serving.

Cavolfiore in Padella

CAULIFLOWER WITH A SPICY SAUCE

As with many recipes that call for cauliflower or broccoli, you may in fact use one or the other in this almost embarrassingly simple recipe. Simple, yes, but a remarkable illustration of how southern Italian cooks can make tasty dishes with not much time and very few ingredients. The trick is to have all the prep work done in advance so you can fly through the recipe at the last minute.

MAKES 4 SERVINGS

1½ pounds cauliflower (1 medium head)	1 tablespoon pine nuts (optional)	1 teaspoon white wine vinegar, or 1 tablespoon fresh lemon juice
Sea salt	2 garlic cloves, chopped	
3 tablespoons extra-virgin olive oil	6 anchovy fillets, chopped	1 teaspoon ground red chili, or more or less to taste

Rinse, core, and trim the cauliflower, but leave it whole. Set it in a saucepan that is just large enough to fit, adding water to barely cover. Remove the cauliflower and set the pan, covered, over medium-high heat. When the water has reached a rolling boil, add 1 or 2 tablespoons of salt and the entire head of cauliflower, stem end down. Bring to a boil again and cook for 5 minutes, or until the cauliflower is just tender. Use a slotted spoon to remove the cauliflower from the water and set it aside to drain.

In a small saucepan, heat the olive oil over low heat. If you're using pine nuts, add them and cook until golden, then remove and set aside. Add the garlic to the oil and cook gently, just until tender but not brown. Add the anchovy pieces and use a fork to mash the anchovies and the tender garlic into the olive oil. Add a ladleful (about ¼ cup) of the cauliflower cooking water and the vinegar and let come to a rolling boil while you separate the cooked cauliflower into florets.

Transfer the cauliflower florets to a serving bowl. Away from the heat, add ground red chili to the liquid in the pan and swirl to combine it well. Return the toasted pine nuts to the hot liquid and pour over the cauliflower. Use 2 forks to toss the florets and coat them well. Serve immediately.

VARIATIONS

🌿 Substitute 2 or 3 tablespoons diced pancetta for the anchovies; the pancetta should be browned in the oil and removed before the garlic is added. If the pancetta releases a good deal of fat in the pan, remove all but 3 tablespoons before adding the garlic. Add the pancetta dice to the hot liquid with the pine nuts.

🌿 This also makes a good sauce for pasta. Cook the cauliflower in a large quantity of water, then cook pasta in the same cooking water. Chop the cooked cauliflower into smaller pieces before pouring the cooking liquid over, then mix the whole with the pasta before serving. If you wish, pass grated pecorino toscano or parmigiano reggiano cheese. For a more colorful dish, substitute broccoli florets for half the cauliflower.

Lanugghje e Verza

BRAISED CABBAGE AND SAUSAGE

This is a wonderful example of how thrifty southern cooks can take a small amount of meat and use it as an ingredient rather than the focus of the meal. Stretched with vegetables, zesty pork sausages become a savory addition, to deepen and enrich the crisp flavors of winter cabbage—and, of course, to feed more people than the sausages would if served on their own. Serve this Calabrian dish as the main course, preceded by a pasta or a hearty soup, and you'll see that it's plenty for all.

The lanugghje from Calabria is actually a tripe sausage; I have substituted ordinary Italian-style fresh pork sausages, either hot or sweet, depending on your taste. Or mix the sausages—a couple of hot ones and a couple of sweet ones. If you can find crinkly-leaved savoy cabbage, it is much preferred for this dish; otherwise, use the ordinary round drumhead cabbage.

MAKES 8 SERVINGS

1 medium yellow onion, halved and finely sliced	4 small ripe fresh tomatoes, peeled and chopped, or canned plum tomatoes, well drained and chopped	Sea salt and freshly ground black pepper
2 tablespoons extra-virgin olive oil		2 or 3 tablespoons grated hard aged cheese—pecorino, caciocavallo, grana padano, or parmigiano reggiano—for garnish (optional)
4 fresh Italian-style sausages, sweet, hot, or a mixture	2 pounds cabbage, preferably savoy, trimmed	

Combine the onion and olive oil in a large skillet and cook very gently until the onion has softened. Meanwhile, remove the sausage meat from the casings. Break up the meat and add it to the skillet when the onion is soft. Raise the heat to medium and continue cooking until the sausage meat is thoroughly browned. Stir in the tomatoes and about ¼ cup of water. Lower the heat and leave to stew gently while you prepare the cabbage.

Quarter the cabbage and discard the core. Sliver each quarter as fine as you can. Bring water to a rolling boil in a pot large enough to hold all the cabbage. Add a big pinch of salt and then the cabbage slivers. Return the water to a boil and, as soon as the cabbage is boiling vigorously, drain it.

Taste the seasoning in the sausage mixture and adjust, adding salt if needed and several grinds of pepper.

Stir the cabbage into the sausages and continue cooking for about 5 minutes longer. The cabbage should be tender but a little crisp and still more green than pale. (Southern Italian cooks would cook the cabbage for 20 to 30 minutes, but this crisp-tender stage is more to North American tastes.)

Remove from the heat and serve immediately, garnishing the dish with grated cheese.

VARIATION

🌿 For a more robust supper dish, add along with the cabbage about 1½ cups of white beans that have been soaked overnight, then cooked until tender with a little garlic and perhaps a red chili.

Friarielle in Padella

CHILI-BRAISED GREENS

Friarielle are Neapolitan, but in fact a similar treatment is accorded spicy cabbage or chicory greens all over the South. Neapolitan friarielle are a type of broccoli rabe, but Chinese sprouting broccoli or bok choy would also be good choices.

MAKES 4 TO 6 SERVINGS

1½ pounds broccoli rabe (rapini)	2 garlic cloves, chopped	Crushed dried red chili
Sea salt	2 tablespoons extra-virgin olive oil	

Rinse the greens and cut into short lengths. Bring a pan of lightly salted water to a rolling boil and drop in the greens. Cook just until the greens are somewhat tender but not fully cooked, about 7 minutes. Drain well.

Meanwhile, melt the garlic in the olive oil in a skillet over low heat. When the garlic is very soft, add the drained greens, stirring to mix well. Cover the pan and cook gently until the greens are very tender, shaking the pan from time to time. There should be plenty of moisture in the greens to keep them from catching, but if necessary, add 1 or 2 tablespoons of boiling water.

When the greens are done, add salt and crushed red chili to the pan, stirring to mix well. If there's a lot of liquid in the pan, raise the heat and boil rapidly, uncovered, to concentrate the juices. Serve immediately.

Spinaci Saltati

SAUTÉED SPINACH

A simple recipe, this is one of the easy kitchen secrets I learned from Gianfranco Becchina, a fine Sicilian cook. Most recipes for spinach call for steaming it, draining it, and then sautéing it in olive oil, like the greens in the preceding recipe. But Gianfranco skips the steaming and draining and simply sautés washed and dried spinach in his own olive oil, Olio Verde. "With a vegetable as tender as spinach," he said, "it doesn't make any sense to cook it twice." Plan on preparing the spinach for cooking well in advance so that you can dry it as thoroughly as possible. The actual cooking goes very quickly.

Keep in mind that spinach is the most reductive of greens, meaning it reduces so much that it practically evaporates in front of you as you cook it. For four people, you will need at least four pounds of spinach and, when cooked this way, probably more because it's so good.

MAKES 4 SERVINGS

4 pounds fresh spinach, trimmed	¼ cup extra-virgin olive oil Sea salt	Juice of ½ lemon

Pick over the spinach and wash it very carefully in several changes of water to get rid of any residual earth. Spin it in a salad spinner to get rid of excess water, then spread the spinach out on clean kitchen towels and cover with more towels. The goal is to get the spinach as dry as possible before starting to cook it. Do this well in advance and transfer the washed and dried spinach to a big colander so that it can dry further.

When ready to cook, add the olive oil to a large, heavy saucepan over medium heat. When the oil is hot, add the dried spinach. Add a sprinkle of salt, and, as the spinach cooks, turn it with kitchen tongs. When the spinach is well coated with oil, cover the pan and leave the spinach to cook, stirring occasionally, until done to your taste—in Sicily they like it very well done, soft and tender; North Americans tend to like their spinach a little closer to the raw material. All you need at this point is a spritz of lemon, and the spinach is ready to serve.

Carrots/Carote

Carrots are often considered less a vegetable in their own right than a flavoring, an aromatic, or *odore*, in southern Italian cooking. They are almost always included in the battuto or soffrito that is the foundation of so many sauces, ragùs, and minestre.

Nowadays, most carrots in southern markets are the familiar bright orange ones, but occasionally I've come across old-fashioned carrots that are very pale, almost white, although with the same full, sweet flavor as modern carrots—modern carrots, that is, when they are properly raised and quickly brought to market. I find an extraordinary difference in flavor between carrots available at farmers' markets and those wrapped in cellophane in supermarket produce sections.

Carote al Marsala

MARSALA CARROTS

Carrots are sometimes served raw in a winter salad, but this recipe is one of the few preparations I've come across for cooked carrots served on their own. Although the use of butter marks it as a decidedly nontraditional recipe, it is delicious and worthy of inclusion.

MAKES 4 TO 6 SERVINGS as a side dish with grilled or roasted meat

1 pound carrots	3 tablespoons unsalted butter	⅓ to ½ cup dry Marsala
1 tablespoon extra-virgin olive oil	Sea salt and freshly ground black pepper	

Peel the carrots if you wish and slice them rather thick.

Combine the olive oil and butter in a skillet over medium-low heat. When the butter starts to foam, toss in the carrot slices. Add salt and pepper to taste and cook, stirring and tossing, until the carrots are thoroughly coated with butter. When the carrots start to soften, add the Marsala. Continue to cook and stir. As the Marsala cooks down, add ½ cup of water. Turn the heat down to low, cover the pan, and cook until the carrots are tender, 15 to 20 minutes.

Uncover the pan. If a lot of liquid is left, raise the heat to high and cook down until you have just a few tablespoons of syrupy liquid. Serve immediately, spooning the liquid over the carrots.

Eggplant/Melanzane

The quality of eggplant available in North American supermarket produce sections is often less than thrilling, even when several different varieties—long and skinny, short and round, green striped, white, and basic black—are displayed. An eggplant may look good, it's true, and feel hefty in the hand, which is supposed to be a sign of freshness. But when I cut it in half, all too often I find the inside filled with seeds, the mark of eggplant well past its prime.

What to do? As with other fruits and vegetables, shop locally or at least regionally, and if you must buy eggplant that has been raised commercially in some distant part of the world, let the manager of your supermarket produce section know it when you find an example that is not up to par.

In New England, I find the best eggplants at farmers' markets, during the brief weeks of late summer when local eggplants are ripe and ready to harvest. Above all, avoid eggplant that is soft, dented, or wrinkled on the surface—the skin should be taut and shiny.

Eggplant, *melanzana,* is almost as much a signature of the southern kitchen as the ubiquitous tomato. Traditional southern Italian recipes usually call for the vegetable to be sliced or cubed and then either heavily salted and drained or immersed in brine for thirty minutes or so. This is said to reduce the bitterness, although modern eggplant varieties have had much of that bitterness bred out of them. Keeping that in mind, I'm often tempted to avoid this step, but I almost always regret it, especially whenever eggplant is fried. Eggplant that has been salted ahead of time, then rinsed and dried, absorbs much less fat than untreated eggplant. Moreover, the texture of eggplant, once it has been salted, is firm and compact rather than spongy. It adds extra steps and time to any eggplant recipe, but I think the results are worth it.

Involtini di Melanzane al Forno

OVEN-ROASTED EGGPLANT ROLLS WITH A RICOTTA-HERB FILLING

Thin eggplant slices rolled around a filling based on ricotta cheese are a southern classic, often presented as part of a mixed antipasto. But if you're in a hurry or just don't feel like fiddling with the rolls, you can use the flat slices, topped with the ricotta mix and cheese, overlapping in the oven dish like tiles on the roof of a Calabrian farmhouse. If you can find ricotta made from ewe's or goat's milk (try a nearby farmers' market), it will make a more flavorful dish.

Any number of fresh green herbs work well for the filling, even just plain parsley. But if you have fresh basil or herbs like borage, lovage, or dill (the last two unknown to southern Italian cooks), they will add an extra spark.

MAKES 6 TO 8 SERVINGS

2 or 3 long dark eggplants (about 1½ pounds) Sea salt Extra-virgin olive oil	2 cups whole-milk ricotta cheese, drained in cheesecloth for at least 30 minutes ⅔ cup chopped mixed fresh herbs Freshly ground black pepper	¾ cup grated hard aged cheese: pecorino, caciocavallo, parmigiano reggiano, or grana padano 1½ cups Basic Tomato Sauce (page 125)

Peel the the eggplants and slice them the long way into ⅛-inch-thick slices. Stack the slices in a colander, salting liberally between the layers. Set a plate on top with a weight and put the colander in the sink to drain for 30 to 60 minutes.

Preheat the oven to 375°F. Lightly oil a baking sheet.

Rinse the eggplant slices thoroughly and dry them with paper towels. Lay them on the oiled baking sheet and brush each slice with a little more olive oil. Set in the preheated oven to brown on both sides, turning once, 5 to 10 minutes to a side. When golden on both sides, remove. Raise the oven heat to 425°F.

Mix the ricotta with the chopped herbs, adding black pepper to taste. Spread a little olive oil over the bottom of an oven dish large enough to hold all the eggplant slices. As soon as they are cool enough to handle, spread each slice with some of the ricotta mixture, then sprinkle with a little grated cheese. Roll each slice up to make a little bundle and set the bundles snugly in the oven dish. (Or leave the eggplant slices flat, spread with the ricotta and grated cheese, and layer them, overlapping, in the oven dish.)

When all the slices are done, spoon the tomato sauce over the top, sprinkle with more grated cheese, and dribble with a little more oil. Set in the preheated oven for 20 minutes or so, until the tomato sauce is bubbling on top and starting to brown around the edges.

Remove and set aside to cool slightly before serving.

VARIATION

The filling in the main recipe comes from Sicily, but every southern Italian region has its own way of stuffing involtini. Here's a filling used by Concetta Cantoro, a fine Pugliese home cook and former restaurant chef.

2 heaping tablespoons capers, preferably salt-packed, rinsed, drained, and chopped	2 heaping tablespoons golden raisins, soaked in hot water to plump and drained	Sea salt and freshly ground black pepper
2 heaping tablespoons lightly toasted pine nuts	6 or 8 anchovy fillets, finely chopped	
	½ cup fine dry bread crumbs	

Mix all the ingredients together in a small bowl and spread on the eggplant slices. Roll the slices and bake as described.

Melanzane Abbottonate

WHOLE STUFFED EGGPLANTS, SICILIAN STYLE

Use whatever fresh herbs are at hand for this and don't be too fussy. For a truly Sicilian flavor, however, you'll want parsley and mint for sure, and wild fennel if you can get it, but not sage, as its flavor is too strong. Lovage and savory, apparently unknown in Sicily, add a fine complexity to the mixture, and chives or scallion tops can contribute as well.

MAKES 4 SERVINGS

4 small long eggplants	½ cup chopped fresh herbs: flat-leaf parsley, basil, mint, wild fennel tops, thyme, savory	½ cup Basic Tomato Sauce (page 125)
Sea salt		1 tablespoon capers, preferably salt-packed, rinsed and drained
3 garlic cloves, chopped	Extra-virgin olive oil	

Rinse the eggplants, but leave them whole. Using a small sharp paring knife, cut long slits, from top to bottom, every inch or so around each eggplant. Do not cut through at the top or the bottom. When done, each eggplant should hold together, but with long openings. Force small handfuls of sea salt into each opening and set the eggplants aside for about an hour to purge them of their juices.

When ready to continue cooking, chop the garlic cloves with the herbs to make a fine mince. Preheat the oven to 350°F.

Rinse the eggplants of their salt and dry them well. Into each slit, stuff as much of the garlic-herb mince as you can fit.

In a large skillet, heat ¼ cup of olive oil over medium heat. When it is hot, add the stuffed eggplants and brown them well on all sides. (You may have to do this in 2 batches.) Some of the stuffing will fall out, but don't worry—it will all come together in the end. As the eggplants brown, transfer them to a baking dish. Add the tomato sauce and capers to the oil in the skillet and stir just to heat the sauce to boiling. Pour the sauce over and around the eggplants and transfer to the preheated oven. Bake for 30 to 40 minutes, or until the eggplants are very tender and collapsed.

Remove from the oven and let cool slightly, for about 10 minutes, before serving.

Parmigiana Bianca

"WHITE" PARMIGIANA

A "white" recipe in Italian usually means simply that the dish in question has no tomatoes. This is the simplest kind of parmigiana, one that can be put together easily for a family supper, and it's rich enough with cheese to make it a *piatto unico,* a one-dish meal, with a salad to go with it and some fruit to come after. But it could also work as a vegetable side dish, or contorno, to accompany a very plain grilled steak, for instance, or, served in small quantities, as an antipasto before the first course.

If you have access to a charcoal or wood-fired grill for browning the eggplant slices, it will add a pleasant flavor to the dish; otherwise, brown them in the oven. (If you wish, you could also fry the eggplant slices in olive oil, but it will add a considerable amount of oil to the dish, more than most modern cooks would find acceptable.)

MAKES 4 TO 6 SERVINGS

1 pound eggplant, preferably the fat, round variety	About ¾ pound fresh mozzarella, sliced	Freshly ground black pepper
Sea salt	⅓ cup grated pecorino toscano or other hard aged cheese	⅓ cup finely minced flat-leaf parsley or mixed parsley and fresh basil
½ cup extra-virgin olive oil		
⅓ cup fine dry bread crumbs		

Slice the eggplant about ¼ inch thick and stack the slices in a colander, sprinkling each layer with salt. Weight the layers and set the colander in the sink to drain for at least 30 minutes.

If using a charcoal or wood-fired grill, prepare it well ahead. Preheat the oven to 400°F.

Rinse the eggplant slices to rid them of salt and pat each one dry with paper towels. Paint both sides of the slices with olive oil and either grill them until brown on both sides or set them on a cookie sheet and transfer to the preheated oven for about 15 minutes, turning once, until brown on both sides.

Use about a tablespoon of olive oil to grease the bottom and sides of a 1½-quart soufflé dish or other oven dish deep enough to hold at least 2 layers of eggplant and cheese. (You should have at least two layers of eggplant in the dish, but three or more will be more sumptuous.) Scatter a tablespoon of bread crumbs over the bottom of the dish.

Line the bottom of the dish with some of the eggplant slices and top with some of the mozzarella slices. Scatter bread crumbs, grated cheese, very little salt (because the eggplant will have absorbed some salt while draining), plenty of black pepper, and some of the minced herbs over the top. Continue layering the ingredients, ending with a layer of bread crumbs, cheese, and herbs. When done, dribble another tablespoon or so of olive oil over the top and transfer to the preheated oven. Bake for about 20 minutes, or until the top is brown and crisp and the cheese is bubbling.

Remove from the oven and let sit for 10 minutes or so before serving.

About Parmigiana

The name *parmigiana* is used all over southern Italy for a dish of vegetables (eggplant, artichokes, zucchini, etc.) layered with tomato sauce and cheese and baked in the oven, traditionally in a terra-cotta oven dish called a *tortiera*. Complex, multilayered dishes like these used to be prepared early in the day and sent to the village oven to be cooked in the residual heat left after the baker finished the morning's bread. A servant girl or a small child would be sent to pick it up in time for the family lunch, which usually didn't take place before midafternoon in the South. Any leftovers were then consumed at leisure, and at no damage to the finished result, in the cool of the evening.

Despite its name, this southern Italian favorite has nothing at all to do with the northern city of Parma except possibly the use of parmigiano reggiano cheese between the layers of eggplant. But even that is a recent innovation, while earlier cooks most likely used local pecorino or caciocavallo. Parmigiana di melanzane (sometimes mistakenly called *melanzane alla parmigiana,* which really does mean "eggplants in the style of the woman from Parma") was one of the great dishes Italian emigrants carried with them out into the world. It has long been a staple of old-fashioned Italian-American restaurants in North America, where, like most immigrant foods, it gets decked out with an abbondanza that belies its appealingly simple origins.

The cheese used? Usually it was a grated aged sheep's milk pecorino, or a scamorza or caciocavallo made from cow's milk, or some other cheese typical of the South. Only in recent decades, with the spread of parmigiano reggiano all over the country, has that become the cheese to use—but traditionalists still argue that it gives entirely the wrong flavor to a proper southern parmigiana.

The following recipe is the simplest, and you'll note immediately that it has no tomatoes. Following that are recipes for more elaborate dishes.

Parmigiana di Melanzane Pugliese

PARMIGIANA OF EGGPLANT

🌿 This may seem complicated at first reading, but if you make the tomato sauce ahead of time, it's really just a matter of browning the eggplant and assembling the ingredients. Since the dish is served more often at room temperature than hot from the oven, the whole thing is usually prepared in the morning to present at dinner that evening.

The recipe is from Puglia, where cooks coat the eggplant slices with egg and bread crumbs before browning them in oil. In Naples, on the other hand, the slices are fried without further embellishment—making a version that is less rich, more digestible, and simpler to put together. If you wish to do so, by all means leave out the egg-and-bread-crumb coating. Nothing else in the recipe will change. And for an even simpler preparation with less oil, follow the instructions in the preceding recipe for Parmigiana Bianca, baking the eggplant slices in the oven before assembling the dish.

MAKES 6 SERVINGS AS A FIRST COURSE

2 medium to large eggplants (at least 2 pounds)	Extra-virgin olive oil for frying	⅔ cup freshly grated aged cheese: parmigiano reggiano, grana padano, pecorino, or caciocavallo
Sea salt	½ cup finely chopped fresh basil	
1 egg	½ cup finely chopped flat-leaf parsley	½ pound fresh mozzarella, finely diced
½ to ¾ cup unbleached all-purpose flour	2 cups Basic Tomato Sauce (page 125)	Freshly ground black pepper
¾ cup fine dry bread crumbs		

Slice the eggplant lengthwise into ¼-inch-thick slices. Stack the slices in a colander, sprinkling the layers generously with salt, set a weight on top (a can of tomatoes on a plate), and let stand for 30 minutes; then rinse the slices in running water and dry them well with paper towels.

Meanwhile, use a fork to beat the egg with 2 tablespoons of water in a soup plate. Place the flour in another soup plate and the bread crumbs in a third.

Put ½ inch of olive oil in a frying pan over medium heat and heat to 360°F (when a little cube of bread turns golden and crisp in about a minute). Lightly dip each dried eggplant slice in flour, then in beaten egg, then in the bread crumbs, coating them well on both sides. Fry the slices, turning them once, until golden brown on both sides, about 2 minutes to a side. Drain the slices on a cake rack covered with paper towels.

Heat the oven to 425°F.

Mix the chopped herbs into the tomato sauce. Spoon a little of the sauce over the bottom of a 2-quart ceramic or earthenware baking dish and layer the eggplant slices in the dish, scattering over each layer plenty of grated cheese, more tomato sauce, a handful of diced mozzarella, and black pepper. You should have at least 2 layers, but 3 or more is better. On the top layer of eggplant, spread an abundance of tomato sauce and a scattering of grated cheese. If you have any diced mozzarella or herbs left, add them to the top layer.

Dribble a tablespoon or more of olive oil on the top of the dish and transfer to the preheated oven. Bake, uncovered, for 45 minutes. Remove from the oven and set aside to cool to room temperature before serving.

VARIATION: PARMIGIANA DI MELANZANE CON POLPETTINE

For a more elaborate and even richer presentation, to make a centerpiece for a festive meal, Pugliese cooks add tiny meatballs to the dish. Follow the preceding recipe, but make the meatballs ahead and distribute them over each layer of eggplant slices.

½ cup fine dry bread crumbs	1 egg yolk	Sea salt and freshly ground black pepper to taste
½ pound finely ground lean veal or pork or a mixture	¼ cup finely minced flat-leaf parsley	2 tablespoons extra-virgin olive oil
¼ cup freshly grated hard aged cheese: pecorino, caciocavallo, parmigiano reggiano, or grana padano	2 tablespoons finely minced fresh basil	

Thoroughly combine the bread crumbs with all the other ingredients except the olive oil. Dampen your hands with a little water and form the mixture into small meatballs about the size of marbles. Heat the oil in a sauté pan over medium heat and quickly brown the meatballs all over. Add the meatballs to each layer of eggplant slices in the dish.

Fresh Legumes: Favas, Green Beans, and Peas/ Fave, Fagiolini, e Piselli

Like wheat and barley, like lentils, all staples of the southern kitchen, fava beans and peas are among the oldest of Mediterranean food crops, their cultivation going back to the beginning of the Neolithic, some eight thousand years ago. In southern Italy they're early spring crops, especially peas, since, as gardeners know well, they don't like the extreme heat and drought of a southern summer. Favas are either the last crop of the old season or the first crop of the new season, depending on your point of view: Planted in December, right after the olives are in and the pig has been slaughtered, they stay in the ground comfortably, then start to grow with the increasing warmth and sunlight and are ready to harvest by early April. Beans, on the other hand, love summer's heat just so long as they get enough water. So the three together make a good fresh vegetable resource from the *orto,* or family garden, one following the other, just as spring follows winter and summer follows spring.

These legumes (for they are indeed legumes, though we're talking now about cooking and eating them in their fresh green state) are also valuable because they can be dried easily and successfully, making a year-round source of valuable protein.

Fagiolini al Pomodoro e Basilico

GREEN BEANS BRAISED IN TOMATOES AND ONIONS

A simple recipe, such as you find all over the South, this relies on the freshness and youth of green beans. They could be pencil-thin and slender or the flat wide beans called *romano* that Italians love; whichever they are, they should be freshly harvested, as close to the garden as possible.

MAKES 6 SERVINGS

¼ cup extra-virgin olive oil	3 ripe tomatoes, chopped	Sea salt and freshly ground black pepper
1 or 2 medium fresh spring onions, preferably red, chopped	1 pound fresh green beans, topped and tailed	

Combine the olive oil, onions, and tomatoes in a pot large enough to hold all the ingredients and set it over medium-low heat. As soon as the onions start to sizzle and the juice of the tomatoes begins to run, add the beans and cover the pot with a tight-fitting lid. Cook for about 5 minutes, then uncover and stir the ingredients all together, adding a good pinch of salt and lots of black pepper. Cover again and cook for another 10 minutes, by which time the beans should be tender but not overly so and napped with the tomato-onion sauce. Serve immediately or set aside and serve just above room temperature.

Fave o Piselli con Prosciutto o Pancetta

FAVAS (BROAD BEANS) OR PEAS BRAISED WITH PROSCIUTTO OR PANCETTA

From Rome south, this is a favorite way of treating fresh young broad beans or peas and, to my mind at least, the finest possible expression of all their sweet goodness.

Peas, of course, must be shucked before being cooked. Broad beans should be shucked, although I often leave slender, very young pods whole, just topping and tailing them as I would green beans and cutting them into one-inch lengths. Don't feel you must peel individual fava beans. This is a restaurant technique, developed in France, where broad beans are harvested when they're a good deal more mature than what would sell in southern Italian markets. If the individual beans need peeling, we feel, they're too old to eat fresh and should be kept for drying.

MAKES 4 SERVINGS

¼ cup finely diced yellow onion	4 pounds tender young fava beans or 3 pounds young peas, shelled	Sea salt and freshly ground black pepper
⅓ cup extra-virgin olive oil	1 cup light chicken stock or water	1 tablespoon minced flat-leaf parsley
2 or 3 slices prosciutto or 2 ounces pancetta, diced		1 teaspoon minced fresh mint

In a heavy saucepan over low heat, gently cook the onion in the olive oil until it is meltingly soft but not brown. Add the prosciutto or pancetta and stir just until the fat starts to run, then add the beans or peas and stir to coat them well. Pour in the stock and add salt and pepper to taste.

Raise the heat to medium and cook quickly, without covering, so that the beans or peas retain all their bright color and fresh flavor. By the time the vegetables are tender, there should be just a few spoonsful of rather syrupy liquid in the bottom of the pan. Stir in the parsley and mint, remove from the heat, and serve immediately.

Fagioli Freschi alla Napoletana

FRESH SHELL BEANS WITH A SPICED TOMATO SAUCE

The beans used in Napoli are borlotti, but in America they're called cranberry beans, presumably because their lovely shells or pods, like the beans inside, are the color of ivory liberally streaked with cranberry red. In any case, in either place, they are used both as fresh shelled beans in summer and as dried beans in winter. Old farmwives in America sometimes called them shell or shucky beans, and you might find them still referred to by that name.

MAKES 4 TO 6 SERVINGS

2 pounds fresh cranberry beans (borlotti), shelled

2 tablespoons extra-virgin olive oil, plus oil to finish

⅓ cup finely minced flat-leaf parsley

1 celery stalk, thinly sliced

1 pound ripe fresh tomatoes, peeled, seeded, and coarsely chopped

1 garlic clove, chopped

Pinch of dried oregano (optional)

Pinch of ground dried red chili (optional)

Sea salt and freshly ground black pepper

Slices of country-style bread, toasted, for serving (optional)

Put the beans in a soup pot, preferably of terra-cotta, and add cool water to cover by 1 inch. Set over medium-low heat and bring to a simmer. Add the olive oil, parsley, celery, tomatoes, garlic, oregano, and chili, if desired. Cover the pot and cook very slowly until the beans are tender—this may take 30 to 45 minutes.

At the end of the cooking time, uncover the pan and raise the heat to boil down some of the juices and concentrate the flavors. After 5 minutes of boiling, you should have a small amount of concentrated liquid in the bottom of the pan. Taste and add salt and pepper at this point. Serve the beans as is, or if you wish, spoon them on top of slices of toasted bread, with more olive oil to dribble over the top.

Mushrooms/Funghi

Wild mushrooms are among the great body of foraged foods that form such an important part of the traditional diet in the Mezzogiorno. Most of those foods—poppy greens, wild fennel, hop vines, nettles—are simply unavailable to North American cooks, but occasionally, through our own efforts or through fine produce and farmers' markets, we do have access to good wild mushrooms. (At my farmers' market on the coast of Maine, for instance, one enterprising mushroom forager has throughout the season chanterelles, black trumpets, oyster mushrooms, porcini, and hen of the woods, to mention just a few.) Most southern Italian mushroom recipes are eminently adaptable so that if, for instance, you don't have oyster mushrooms available, you can certainly substitute porcini (*Boletus edulis*) or wild agarics, similar in shape, but not in flavor, to ordinary supermarket mushrooms.

Funghi Cardoncelli Mollicati

BREAD-CRUMBED OYSTER MUSHROOMS

Cardoncelli, or oyster mushrooms, grow all over the Alta Murgia in Puglia and have become a sort of symbol of traditional cuisine and traditional ways of life. There's even an organization, the Association of the Friends of the Cardoncello Mushroom, to which I proudly belong. This is a recipe from that region. Although members of the association insist that cardoncelli are not the same as oyster mushrooms, I am hard put to tell the difference.

MAKES 4 SERVINGS

1 pound oyster mushrooms, cleaned and trimmed	2 tablespoons grated aged pecorino or parmigiano reggiano	¼ cup finely minced flat-leaf parsley
2 to 3 tablespoons extra-virgin olive oil	1 or 2 garlic cloves, finely minced	Sea salt and freshly ground black pepper
2 to 3 tablespoons fine dry bread crumbs		

Preheat the oven to 425°F.

Pick over the mushrooms, making sure they are very clean and free of twigs and, perish the thought, bugs. Remove the stems and chop them very fine.

Use a little of the olive oil to oil the bottom and sides of an oval gratin dish large enough to hold all the mushrooms in one layer. Set the mushrooms, caps down, in the dish. Sprinkle the mushrooms thoroughly with the finely chopped stems, the bread crumbs, grated cheese, garlic, and parsley. Sprinkle with salt and pepper to taste. Dribble more olive oil over the tops (actually the bottoms) of the mushrooms and transfer the dish to the oven. Bake for 15 to 20 minutes, or until the mushrooms are cooked through and sizzling and the bread crumbs are browned. Serve immediately.

Funghi e Patate

WILD MUSHROOM AND POTATO GRATIN

Use any kind of wild mushrooms available to you—chanterelles, porcini, oysters, black trumpets.

MAKES 4 TO 6 SERVINGS

½ pound wild mushrooms, carefully trimmed and cleaned

¼ cup finely minced yellow onion

½ garlic clove, finely minced

2 to 3 tablespoons extra-virgin olive oil

Sea salt and freshly ground black pepper

1 pound yellow-fleshed potatoes, such as Yukon Gold or Yellow Finn, peeled and thickly sliced

1 cup light chicken or meat broth

Preheat the oven to 400°F.

Cut the mushrooms into thick slices and combine with the onion, garlic, and 2 tablespoons of the olive oil in a sauté pan. Set over medium-low heat and cook, stirring, until the onion is soft and the mushrooms have given off their liquid, about 8 minutes. If necessary, add another tablespoon of oil during the cooking. Add salt and pepper to taste and stir to mix well.

While the mushrooms are cooking, bring a pot of lightly salted water to a rolling boil. Add the potato slices and cook for 5 to 7 minutes, or until they are tender but not falling apart. Drain the potatoes and combine with the mushrooms in the pan, stirring carefully so the potatoes don't break up. Add the broth and bring to a simmer.

If the sauté pan is not ovenproof, transfer the mushroom-potato mixture to a gratin or other shallow oven dish and set in the oven. Bake for 20 to 25 minutes, or until the top is nicely browned and the stock has been mostly absorbed by the potatoes. Serve immediately.

Onions and Garlic/Cipolle e Aglio

Garlic and onions are the stars of the *Allium* genus, at least in southern Italy, where other members, such as leeks and shallots, are not used much. Garlic is not universal, however, and indeed the whole of the Salentino in southeastern Puglia claims to be a region where garlic is added only sparingly to local dishes. I find garlic almost indispensable, no matter what I'm cooking, and tend to add it even to dishes from the Salentino.

Garlic is best in June and July, when it is fresh, a fact to which most Americans are indifferent because we don't have the sense of garlic as a seasonal vegetable except in occasional farmers' markets. But June garlic has a sweetness that is lacking the rest of the year. If you are a garlic-timid cook, try to find some young, freshly harvested garlic in early summer—the difference is striking.

Sweet red onions, from Tropea in Calabria or from Acquaviva in Puglia, with their deep pink to almost violet colors and their lovely torpedo shapes, are much in demand in southern Italy, especially for salads and eating raw; for cooking, dried yellow onions are more apt to be used. In Puglia, a special early onion called *sponsale* or *cipolla porraia* (leek-onion) is much sought after in the early spring. Since none of these onions is available in North America, I have suggested various substitutes.

Cipolle sotto Cenere

EMBER-BAKED ONIONS

This is not so much a recipe as it is a simple instruction. You must have a fireplace, or at least a fire, to do this. Try it at the beach when you build a bonfire. Or try it in your living room fireplace if you're lucky enough to have one.

Use large yellow onions, the kind that come with thick dark-yellow to brown skins. Let the fire burn down to a pile of embers and bury the onions, unpeeled, just as they are, right down in the live embers, piling more embers on top of them. Leave them like this for an hour or so, by which time they should be cooked through. Remove the onions and, as soon as you can handle them, peel away the outer burnt layers. Slice the insides on a plate, dress with some fine extra-virgin olive oil, sprinkle with sea salt, and serve.

In southern Italy these would be red onions, but sweet red onions are generally not available in the United States, so use Vidalia, Walla Walla, Maui, or other sweet onions. If you're unable to find sweet onions of any color, use ordinary yellow onions and add about ½ teaspoon of sugar to the bread crumbs sprinkled over each onion top.

MAKES 6 SERVINGS

6 large sweet onions, peeled	Ground dried red chili (optional)	½ cup dry bread crumbs
Extra-virgin olive oil		Red wine vinegar
Sea salt and freshly ground black pepper		

Preheat the oven to 375°F.

When you trim the onions, make a flat cut along the root ends so they will stand up in the baking dish. Cut a cross about ½ inch deep in the other end of each onion and press the onion lightly to open the cross.

Use a little olive oil to lightly grease the bottom of an oven dish just large enough to hold all the onions. Rub each onion well with oil and set in the dish. Sprinkle with salt, black pepper, and chili if you wish. Sprinkle about a tablespoon of bread crumbs over the top of each onion, then dribble more oil—about a tablespoon for each onion—over the top. Hold your index finger over the top of the vinegar bottle and sprinkle a few drops of vinegar around each onion.

Transfer to the preheated oven and bake for about 1 hour, or until the onions are tender and brown on top. If necessary, sprinkle with a little more oil and/or vinegar during the cooking time.

Remove and allow to cool to room temperature before serving.

Cipolline in Agrodolce

SWEET-AND-SOUR BABY ONIONS

Whenever I see these delicious little onions on a restaurant's display of antipasti, I head straight for them. Traditionally they were cooked in a mixture of lard (*strutto*) and oil or all lard. Because good lard is really hard to come by in North America, I have substituted unsalted butter, but if you find a good source of lard that has not been treated with preservatives, by all means use it instead of the butter.

Serve these as a contorno, or accompaniment, to a meat dish (they are delicious with any pork) or as part of an antipasto spread.

MAKES 6 TO 8 SERVINGS

2 pounds whole baby onions (cipolline) or white pickling onions	1 garlic clove, crushed	2 tablespoons extra-virgin olive oil
	½ medium yellow onion, chopped	Sea salt
1 or 2 slices prosciutto, including the fat	2 tablespoons unsalted butter	Aged wine vinegar

Peel the baby onions, but leave them whole and—very important—do not cut away the roots, which will hold the onions together as they cook.

Chop together the prosciutto, garlic, and the yellow onion to make a fine mince.

In a medium skillet over medium-low heat, melt the butter in the olive oil, then add the minced mixture and cook, stirring, until it starts to give off a nice aroma. Add all the baby onions and raise the heat slightly. Cook the baby onions, turning them to color them on all sides. Add a good pinch of salt and water to come halfway up the baby onions—measure the water as you add it because you will need to add a similar quantity of vinegar later.

Now lower the heat and cook the onions, gently, gently, uncovered, until the liquid has almost completely cooked down and evaporated, about 30 minutes. Turn the onions over to cook the other sides and add vinegar in the same amount as the water. Cook, again gently, gently, until the onions are completely tender and the liquid is reduced to a syrupy glaze. If the liquid starts to cook down too much before the onions are tender, add more water.

Serve immediately if you wish, but this dish is even better at room temperature.

Sweet Peppers and Chilies/Peperoni e Peperoncini

Like tomatoes, capsicum peppers, both sweet and hot, arrived in Italy sometime after the Spanish brought them back from the Americas, but peppers were greeted much more enthusiastically than tomatoes. Hot chilies were especially welcome to replace black pepper, imported from India at considerable expense and prized for its supposed medicinal virtues as much as for the fact that it made bland food tastier. Chilies could be planted in the family garden, harvested, and dried to keep through the winter, much better than waiting for the precious cargo to arrive from the East, and they cost a lot less, too. "A democratic spice," Italians call them, reflecting these plebeian origins. Travelers are more likely to encounter chili-spiced food in Calabria and Basilicata, where cooks use hot peppers with greater abandon than elsewhere in the South—especially chili-spiked sausages like Calabrian *'nduja,* a soft, spreadable sausage colored deep red with chilies. In Diamante, a pretty little fishing village and beach resort on the Calabrian coast, peperoncino enthusiasts, members of the Accademia Nazionale del Peperoncino, stage an annual hot chili festival during the first weekend in September.

It's sometimes necessary to roast and peel sweet peppers, whether using them raw or cooking them further. The process, which softens the peppers, also sweetens them and brings out a richness of flavor that isn't always there with plain raw peppers. The most effective way to do this is over a charcoal or wood fire. Simply set up a grill and put the rinsed peppers on it. Turn them, using tongs, until they are thoroughly blackened and blistered on the outside. If you don't have a charcoal or gas grill, or a convenient fireplace, you may also roast them over a gas flame on top of the stove. Pierce a single pepper at the stem end with a barbecue or other long-handled fork and, holding the fork, turn the pepper directly in the flame until the skin is blackened and blistered. The peppers will be soft but not really cooked. As you finish with each pepper, place it in a paper bag. When all the peppers are done, set the bag aside for 30 minutes or so. This makes the peppers easier to peel.

(If you don't have any other source of heat, you will have to roast the peppers in an electric oven under a broiler, but this is the least satisfactory method and requires fairly constant attention to keep the peppers from burning.)

After thirty minutes of rest in the paper bag, use a small sharp paring knife to scrape away the thin outside skin or pellicle; it should lift and come away easily. Don't be too finicky about this as a few little black spots simply add to the appeal of the roasted peppers. And don't rinse the peppers any more than is necessary as running water will rinse away the flavor. Once this is done, you can trim and slice the peppers any way you wish.

Peperoni Imbottiti

STUFFED PEPPER ROLLS

A delicious and colorful addition to a platter of antipasti, these rolls of sweet peppers stuffed with currants, pine nuts, and other savories are also often served as a contorno to go with grilled or roasted lamb or pork. If you want to go all out, make one of the stuffed eggplant dishes, like Involtini di Melanzane al Forno (page 321), and present the two vegetables together on the same platter. You can make them both well ahead to avoid last-minute distress and disorder.

MAKES 4 TO 6 SERVINGS

4 large green, red, or yellow sweet peppers or a combination of colors	2½ tablespoons capers, preferably salt-packed, rinsed and drained	¼ cup currants or raisins, plumped in hot water and drained
½ cup fine dry bread crumbs	2 tablespoons finely minced flat-leaf parsley or mixed parsley and basil	¼ cup pine nuts
3 or 4 tablespoons extra-virgin olive oil		15 black olives, pitted and coarsely chopped
6 anchovy fillets		

Roast and peel the peppers (see page 338). Cut each pepper in half lengthwise, draining its juice into a bowl.

Mix together the bread crumbs, 2 tablespoons of the olive oil, and 2 tablespoons of the reserved pepper juice. Chop together the anchovy fillets, capers, and parsley to make a coarse paste. Add to the bread crumb mixture, along with the drained currants and the pine nuts. Use a small amount of the remaining olive oil to oil a gratin or other oven dish large enough to hold all the pepper rolls in one layer. Preheat the oven to 375°F.

Set a pepper half, skin side down, on a board or countertop. Put about a teaspoon of stuffing at the widest end of the pepper half and roll it up toward the narrow end, then set it in the gratin dish with the open end of the pepper roll down. Continue with all the peppers. If you have any stuffing left over, sprinkle it over the tops of the pepper rolls. Scatter the chopped olives over the top and sprinkle the remaining olive oil over all. Set in the oven and bake for 20 to 30 minutes, until the peppers are starting to brown a little on top.

Remove and serve immediately, or they may be set aside and served at room temperature.

Peperonata con Patate e Peperoncino

SWEET PEPPER, HOT PEPPER, AND POTATO STEW

The hill town of Venosa, renowned as the birthplace of the great Roman poet Horace, was once an important crossroads of the South, guarded militarily by a fortress and spiritually by a famous Benedictine abbey. One late autumn afternoon, after exploring the remains of the first and the ruins of the second, we dined in Venosa on a local pasta called *strascinati,* made with dark flour from *gran'arso,* or burnt grain (see page 165), and followed it up with this splendid dish of peppers and potatoes, a meal straight out of the peasant kitchen but as carefully composed as anything to be found in a Michelin-starred restaurant. One indication of that care: The peppers were peeled with a vegetable peeler rather than roasted beforehand. Roasting softens peppers and cooks them slightly; they are delicious, but raw peppers, cooked in the pan with the other ingredients, are what is needed in this dish.

Peperonata is found all over rural Italy. What marks this as from Lucania, as Basilicata is also known, is the presence of hot red chilies.

MAKES 4 SERVINGS AS A MAIN COURSE, 6 to 8 servings as a side dish

2 medium yellow onions, halved and thinly sliced	Sea salt and freshly ground black pepper	1 pound ripe fresh tomatoes, diced, or 1 cup chopped drained canned plum tomatoes
⅓ cup extra-virgin olive oil	6 sweet peppers, preferably red and yellow	
2 medium potatoes, peeled and sliced or cut into chunks		1 fresh or dried red chili, or more to taste

Combine the onions and olive oil in a skillet large enough to hold all the ingredients and set over medium-low heat. Cook, stirring occasionally, until the onions start to soften, then stir in the potatoes along with salt and pepper to taste and continue cooking and stirring for about 10 minutes, until the potatoes are tender enough to pierce with the point of a knife.

Meanwhile, peel the sweet peppers, using a vegetable peeler to remove the thin filament on the outside. Cut the peppers into long, inch-wide strips.

Add the pepper strips to the pan, stirring carefully to mix well without breaking up the potatoes. Cook for about 15 minutes, or until the peppers are beginning to soften, then stir in the tomatoes. (Note that because the peppers are raw, they will take longer to soften than roasted peppers would.) Cut the fresh chili in half, discard most of the seeds and white membrane, cut it into very thin slices, and add to the pan; if using a dried chili, break it, shaking out and discarding most of the seeds (which is where a lot of the heat is located) and crumble into the pan. Stir once more and cook for another 15 minutes, until the tomato sauce is thick and all the vegetables are very soft. If there is still a lot of liquid in the pan, raise the heat and boil rapidly until the liquid is reduced to a syrupy sauce.

Remove from the heat and serve immediately. Peperonata is also often served at room temperature.

VARIATION

To make a heartier dish, to serve as a main course at supper for instance, break 5 or 6 eggs into a bowl and beat them lightly with a fork. When the vegetables are tender, pour the beaten eggs over them and cook briefly, stirring and lifting the vegetables to let the egg slide underneath. If you wish, run the skillet under a preheated broiler to brown the top of the frittata lightly before serving.

Although this appears at first glance to be quite labor intensive, the labors are spread out over several days and the result is well worth any effort. Do make this when peppers in the market are fresh from local farms and gardens, not shipped in from far away. The flavors will be that much better and more intense.

The balance of sweet and hot peppers is really up to you: If you have mildly spicy peppers, like New Mexico or Anaheim peppers, for instance, make Pepone with those on their own; but if, on the other hand, the only chiles available are fiercely hot—like Scotch bonnets—you might want to cut down on the quantity of chilies and increase the amount of sweet peppers.

MAKES 4 PINTS

6 pounds green and red sweet peppers	2 medium carrots, peeled	1 quart white wine vinegar
15 fresh hot red chilies	1 large white onion	2 cups extra-virgin olive oil
3 celery stalks	4 plump garlic cloves	
	2 tablespoons sea salt	

Wash and thoroughly dry the peppers and chiles, then cut them in half, discarding the seeds and white internal membranes. Chop the peppers, chiles, celery, carrots, onion, and garlic rather coarsely by hand. Transfer the chopped vegetables to a bowl and add the salt. Set aside for 24 hours, but do not refrigerate. The vegetables will give off quite a lot of liquid. At the end of that time, turn into a colander, rinse the salt off thoroughly under running water, and set aside to drain. Transfer to a bowl, cover with the vinegar, and set aside for another 24 hours.

Have ready 4 pint (or 8 half-pint) sterile canning jars (see page 129).

Drain the vegetables in a colander, but do not rinse. Fill the jars with vegetables, then with olive oil, which should completely cover the chopped vegetables. Push a table knife down into the jar in several places to get rid of any air bubbles. Screw down the lid and proceed with the remaining jars.

Process the jars for 20 minutes, following the directions on page 129. Remove from the heat and let cool. Then remove the jars from the canning kettle. Set aside in a cool, dark place. The Pepone will be ready to use in 2 weeks. Use as a condiment for any meat or fish dish.

Olio Santo

HOT CHILI "HOLY" OIL

The hot chilies will overpower any complexity or subtlety in a fine oil, so this is one time when an inexpensive extra-virgin olive oil is called for. Used in small quantities—a drop or two at a time until you get used to its impact—Olio Santo adds a kick to many pasta sauces and soups. In Puglia, where this recipe originates, the chilies used are tiny fiery ones, called *diavolicchi,* or "little devils." Why is it called "holy"? Presumably because it anoints the food like a baptism of fire.

Patience Gray, a great food writer who lived for many years in the Salentino, deep in the south of Puglia, told me that the Pugliese have been addicted to chilies since they were introduced centuries ago by the Turks. The Turks were counting on chili consumption to kill off the locals. Instead, they took to chilies with a passion, "but," Patience added, "there is a very high incidence of stomach problems in consequence."

MAKES 1 PINT

Handful of dried red chilies, the hotter the better	2 cups extra-virgin olive oil

In a saucepan over medium heat, combine the chilies and ¼ cup water. Bring to a boil and cook until the liquid evaporates completely, about 15 minutes. (This will rid the chilies of any contaminants that might spoil the oil.) Toward the end, be very careful not to let the chilies burn. When the water has evaporated, transfer the chilies to a sieve and shake them dry, then set aside to continue drying. They should be perfectly dry before you proceed.

When the chilies are completely dry, transfer them to a pint-sized sterile glass canning jar (see page 129). Add the olive oil, seal the lid, and set the jar aside at room temperature for 2 days before using, shaking the jar from time to time.

Olio santo should be stored at room temperature or colder (but not refrigerated). It should keep well for up to 6 months.

Potatoes/Patate

When southern Italians cook potatoes, they almost always indicate a preference for potatoes with what they call *pasta gialla,* or "yellow flesh"—really rather creamy gold in color. Potatoes like these are quite commonly available in North American produce markets, although not always in the specific varieties used in the Mezzogiorno. To use in recipes from the region, look for Yellow Finn, Yukon gold, or, at farmers' markets especially, any of the large numbers of fingerling potatoes, such as rattes or Russian bananas. These are waxy potatoes that hold together well when cooked. Our mealy potatoes, like big Idaho russets, are better for baking and not really suitable for southern Italian recipes.

Patate e Cipolle al Forno

GRATIN OF POTATOES AND ONIONS

A simple favorite from the Alta Murgia plateau of Puglia, this may be served with plainly grilled meat or fish; or increase the amount of grated cheese, sprinkle the cheese between layers, and you'll have a fine vegetarian main course.

MAKES 6 TO 8 SERVINGS

1¼ pounds yellow-fleshed potatoes, such as Yellow Finn or Yukon Gold	Sea salt and freshly ground black pepper	¼ cup toasted bread crumbs (see page 139)
¼ cup extra-virgin olive oil	3 or 4 peeled fresh or canned tomatoes, coarsely chopped (optional)	¼ cup freshly grated hard aged cheese: pecorino, caciocavallo, or parmigiano reggiano
2 medium yellow onions		

Preheat the oven to 400°F.

Scrub the potatoes well, peel them partially, and slice them about ¼ inch thick. Spread a thin layer of olive oil in the bottom of a gratin or other oven dish. Layer half the potatoes over the bottom of the dish.

Peel and thinly slice the onions. Layer half the onions over the potatoes. Add a sprinkle of salt and pepper and the tomatoes, if you're using them. Make another layer of the remaining potatoes, then the remaining onions, sprinkling again with salt and pepper. Top with the bread crumbs and grated cheese. Dribble the rest of the olive oil over the top and add a small amount of boiling water to the dish—about ½ cup.

Cover the dish with aluminum foil and place in the oven for 25 to 30 minutes, or until the potatoes are tender. Remove the foil and continue to bake, uncovered, for another 10 minutes to brown the top before serving. Serve immediately.

Tortino di Patate e Cipolle

POTATO AND ONION TORTE FROM BASILICATA

Potatoes and onions, onions and potatoes—the combination appears with great frequency on humble country tables throughout the South—and no wonder, for every garden boasts at the very least a potato patch and a swaying grove of onion plants, both being vegetables that will keep through the winter and into the early spring before anything new and fresh comes up. Imaginative cooks have been challenged to produce dozens of variations on the basic combination to entice diners through those lean weeks of the year. This treatment is like a potato pie; hence its name—a little pie.

MAKES 4 TO 6 SERVINGS

Butter for the oven dish

2 tablespoons extra-virgin olive oil, plus a little oil for the top

4 anchovy fillets, coarsely chopped

½ pound yellow onions, finely chopped (about 1½ cups)

1 tablespoon capers, preferably salt-packed, rinsed and drained

4 canned plum tomatoes, well drained and coarsely chopped, plus 2 tablespoons of the liquid

2 pounds yellow-fleshed potatoes, such as Yukon Gold or Yellow Finn

¼ cup whole milk, at room temperature, or a little more if necessary

1 egg

3 tablespoons grated hard aged cheese: pecorino, caciocavallo, parmigiano reggiano, or grana padano

12 to 15 black olives, pitted and coarsely chopped

Sea salt and freshly ground black pepper

Unbleached all-purpose flour, if necessary

1 to 2 tablespoons fine dry bread crumbs

Preheat the oven to 400°F. Use a little butter to grease the bottom and sides of an oval gratin dish about 14 inches long.

Combine 2 tablespoons of the olive oil and the anchovies in a small skillet over medium-low heat. Cook gently, pressing the anchovies into the oil with the back of a fork. When the anchovies are melted into the oil, add the onion and continue cooking gently until very soft but not brown, 20 to 30 minutes. Stir in the capers and add the tomatoes and liquid. As soon as the liquid begins to simmer, remove from the heat and set aside.

Boil the potatoes in lightly salted water until very tender—20 to 30 minutes, depending on size. While still warm, peel and mash them, using a food mill with a disk set at fine holes. (You may also use a potato masher but it is difficult to get a smooth puree; do not use a blender or food processor, which will turn the potatoes to glue.) Beat the milk with the egg and stir into the warm potato puree, adding the grated cheese. Stir in the black olives. Taste and add salt and pepper. (If the cheese and olives are very salty, you may not need to add any salt.) If the potato puree is very liquid, add a little flour; if too solid, add a little more milk.

Use about two-thirds of the potato puree to cover the bottom of the gratin dish. Distribute the onion-tomato mixture over the top and cover it with the remaining potatoes. Sprinkle the top layer with a tablespoon or so of bread crumbs and dribble a little olive oil over the top. Transfer to the preheated oven and bake for 20 minutes or so, until the top is golden brown. Remove and let sit for 10 minutes before serving.

Squash and Zucchini/Zucca e Zucchine

The *Cucurbit* genus, which includes pumpkins, hard winter squash, tender summer squash, and zucchini, is held in high regard by southern Italian cooks, at least in part because pumpkins and other hard varieties keep well throughout the cold months of the year, providing a welcome source of bright color and vitamins on winter plates.

The kinds of squash used in southern Italy are not always readily available in North America, but other varieties are easily substituted, while zucchini, as every gardener knows, are abundant. If you have your own garden, just two or three zucchini plants are enough to keep most families supplied throughout the summer with young green fruits as well as blossoms for stuffing and frying.

As for pumpkins, an old-fashioned kind with a tan skin called cheese pumpkin or the deep red variety called *rouge vif d'Etampes,* both available at good farmers' markets, are better for cooking than the varieties meant for jack-o'-lanterns—nothing wrong with Halloween, but pumpkins sold for carving are bred for sturdiness and size rather than flavor.

One Sicilian "squash" is very special in that it isn't really a squash at all but more properly a gourd. Called zucca longa (long squash) or cucuzza, it's a long, pale-green, smooth-skinned, summer fruit that may be the same as the so-called snake gourd used in Indian cuisine. Cucuzza (the proper botanical name is *Lagenaria longissima*) is not easy to find but more and more seed catalogs carry it, and I'm sure it will become more widely available in farmers' markets in the next few years—something to watch for.

Franco Crivello's Zucca Marinata or Scapici di Zucca

MINT-MARINATED HARD WINTER SQUASH OR PUMPKIN

Franco Crivello, chef/owner of a lively seafood restaurant in the little fishing port of Porticello, tucked in behind the peninsula east of Palermo, is a former fisherman and a great seafood cook. But he is as much a connoisseur of vegetables as of fish. For this dish, he uses a hard winter squash similar to our Hubbard blue squash, but you could also use pumpkin.

MAKES 6 TO 8 SERVINGS

About 2¼ pounds hard winter squash or pumpkin	2 medium yellow onions, very thinly sliced	½ cup slivered or coarsely chopped fresh mint
¾ cup extra-virgin olive oil	¼ cup wine vinegar, preferably white	1 teaspoon sea salt, or to taste

Cut the squash into slices ½ to ¾ inch thick. Trim away the rind and set the slices on a rack in a cool place to dry for several hours or overnight. If the slices are not dry enough to brown well when it comes time to fry them, dry them with paper towels just before frying.

Add ½ cup of the olive oil to a large skillet over medium heat and, when the oil is hot, add the squash slices, frying them until they are brown and blistered on one side, then turning to brown on the other. As the slices finish, transfer them to a serving platter.

When the squash is done, discard the oil and wipe the pan with paper towels. Add ¼ cup of fresh olive oil to the pan and stir in the onion slices. Set over low heat and cook the onions very gently, stirring frequently, until soft and melting in the pan, 20 to 30 minutes.

Meanwhile, combine the vinegar with an equal quantity of water in a small saucepan and bring to a boil. Boil until reduced by half—until you have ¼ cup once more.

When the onion slices are done, raise the heat to medium and immediately stir in the mint and reduced vinegar. Cook, stirring vigorously, just until the liquid comes to a simmer, then remove from the heat and pour over the squash slices, covering them completely with onions and mint. Sprinkle with salt to taste.

Set the squash aside to cool to room temperature. You may serve it at this point, but it will be even better if you wait at least 24 hours before serving. Cover the squash with plastic wrap and keep in a cool place, but do not refrigerate.

Minestra di Cucuzza o Zucchina alla Ghiotta

SICILIAN SUMMER SQUASH BRAISED IN OLIVE OIL

If you can't find the pale green Sicilian favorite, cucuzza, also called zucca lunga, use yellow summer squash.

This is a recipe from the Becchina family, producers of olive oil in Castelvetrano on the south coast of Sicily. Enza, the family cook, calls it *zuppa,* or soup, though it is less a soup than a vegetable stew, with just enough liquid to soak up chunks of delicious pane nero di Castelvetrano, bread made from a local variety of durum wheat. Overcome by a sense of the utter ordinariness of the dish, so everyday that it's almost unmentionable, Enza had a hard job describing it to me—"you can cook it as long as you want to," a local saying goes, "and it's still cucuzza." But it is made glorious by a big dollop of olio nuovo, extra-virgin oil from the most recent harvest.

The dish can be served hot from the stove, but on warm summer days it's apt to be served at room temperature, as the centerpiece of a refreshingly simple lunch. Sometimes the minestra is turned into a zuppa with the addition of a handful of ditalini pasta with a little of the water in which the pasta cooked. In this case, it is always served hot, and fresh pecorino cheese is shaved over the top.

MAKES 4 SERVINGS

2 cucuzza squash (18 to 24 inches long), or 4 to 6 medium yellow summer squash (about 2 pounds)	Leafy tops of 2 celery stalks Leaves from 1 bunch of fresh basil	2 ripe tomatoes, about 1 pound, peeled, seeded, and thinly sliced
1 pound yellow-fleshed potatoes, such as Yellow Finn or Yukon Gold	½ cup extra-virgin olive oil, preferably Sicilian, plus oil for garnish	Sea salt ½ pound ditalini or other short pasta (optional)
1 fresh red chili, seeded and chopped	1 large red onion (about ½ pound), halved and thinly sliced	Grated or shaved young pecorino or parmigiano reggiano (optional)

If you can find long, slender cucuzza squash, cut it into chunks about 6 inches long. Peel the chunks and quarter each one lengthwise. Cut away most of the seeds, then slice the quarters into pieces about 1½ inches long. If you cannot find cucuzza, use regular tender-skinned yellow summer squash, but do not peel or seed them—simply slice into 1½-inch-long chunks, cutting the chunks in half if they are very fat.

Peel the potatoes and cut into pieces about the same size as the squash. Coarsely chop together the chili, celery, and basil—you should have about ½ cup of chopped aromatics.

Cover the bottom of a deep, heavy saucepan with the olive oil, then add the onion, followed by the potatoes, the chopped aromatics, the squash chunks, and finally the tomatoes. Sprinkle with salt to taste, cover the pan, and set it over low heat to cook for about 15 minutes, or until the vegetables are sizzling in the oil. Bring water to a boil and add ½ cup to the pan. Cover again and cook just until the potato slices are tender, another 5 to 10 minutes. There should be sufficient liquid in the pan to keep the vegetables from scorching, but if not, add a few more tablespoons of boiling water as needed.

When the potatoes are tender, everything else should be fully cooked. Remove the pan from the heat and either serve immediately or set aside to cool to room temperature before serving. Garnish each portion with a dollop of olive oil when you serve. If you want to turn the minestra into a zuppa, cook the ditalini in salted water until just tender and add it with about ½ cup of its cooking water, to the vegetables, stirring gently. As soon as the liquid returns to a boil, serve the zuppa in deep soup plates, sprinkled with grated or shaved young pecorino cheese (mature cheese will interfere with the fresh flavors of the vegetables) and with a spoonful of extra-virgin olive oil on top.

VARIATION

For a totally un-Sicilian but delicious change, add the kernels cut from two or three ears of fresh sweet corn during the last 10 minutes of cooking.

Zucchine alla Poverella/Zucchine a Scapece

POOR COOK'S ZUCCHINI/MARINATED ZUCCHINI

Zucchine alla poverella, sometimes called *zucchine a scapece,* is a first cousin once removed to the Zucca Marinata that Franco Crivello makes at his restaurant on the Sicilian coast east of Palermo (recipe, page 349). Such preparations, like pesce a scapece, are in the ancient tradition of escabeche or scapece, a method of short-term pickling, preserving extra food for several days. Food historians say the technique comes from Middle Eastern Jewish and Arab cuisines.

Any one of these marinated vegetables makes a fine antipasto, or, for a more sumptuous presentation, make both zucchini and orange squash—and serve them together on a handsome platter that shows off their bright colors. Anything *a scapece* should be made well ahead of time and served at room temperature, never cold from the refrigerator.

The zucchini slices must be quite dry before being fried so they'll turn an appetizing golden brown. You can flour them lightly, but a cleaner presentation results if you simply pat each slice with paper towels just before dropping it into the hot oil. Southern cooks often lay slices on a rack to dry for several hours in the sun, but that's not always feasible.

MAKES 4 TO 6 SERVINGS

2 pounds medium dark green zucchini	Salt and freshly ground black pepper	2 tablespoons slivered fresh mint
2 plump garlic cloves	1 small dried red chili, crumbled (optional)	2 tablespoons white wine vinegar
6 tablespoons extra-virgin olive oil		

Slice the zucchini about ¼ inch thick, discarding the ends. Lay the slices on paper towels on a rack and set aside to dry for a couple of hours.

Slice one of the garlic cloves very thin and combine with ¼ cup of the olive oil in a medium skillet. Set over medium-low heat until the garlic is a little golden but not brown. Remove the skillet from the heat and leave the garlic to steep in the oil while the zucchini slices are drying. Remove and discard the garlic before cooking the zucchini.

When ready to cook, return the skillet to medium heat and add the zucchini slices, a handful at a time, patting them gently, if necessary, between paper towels. The zucchini will not brown well if there is a lot of moisture on the surface. Let the slices cook briskly on both sides until they are golden brown and blistered. As the slices brown, remove them from the skillet using tongs and transfer to a serving platter.

Mince the second clove of garlic, and as soon as you have a layer of fried zucchini on the platter, sprinkle it with the minced garlic, salt, pepper, chili, if you like, and mint. Sprinkle each layer of zucchini as you go along.

When all the zucchini is done and all the garnishes have been used up, discard the frying oil and wipe the skillet out with paper towels. Add 2 tablespoons of fresh olive oil and the vinegar to the skillet. Bring to a simmer over medium heat, then pour over the zucchini slices.

Cover lightly with plastic wrap and set aside at room temperature to marinate for at least 30 minutes before serving.

Fritelle di Fiori di Zucca o Zucchine

DEEP-FRIED ZUCCHINI BLOSSOMS

The fresher the zucchini flowers, the better this treatment will be. Buy bright-looking blossoms without a trace of wilt or slime. Best of all are those that come from your own garden, just minutes before it's time to fry them. (Zucchini is very easy to grow, even on a city terrace, and amazingly prolific with blossoms.) I am told that one should pick only the male blossoms, leaving the females to grow into fruits. I confess to an inability to tell the difference, so I just pick them all. I know of no one who has ever suffered from a poverty of zucchini.

Are other types of squash blossoms suitable for this treatment? Yes indeed, but smaller is always better, so think finger food. Some blossoms are so large you'd have to eat them with a knife and fork.

These are addictive. You may find guests and family members simply stand around the stove, scarfing up zucchini blossoms as fast as they come out of the fryer.

MAKES 4 TO 6 SERVINGS

40 fresh zucchini blossoms	Sea salt and freshly ground black pepper	Extra-virgin olive oil for deep-fat frying
½ cup unbleached all-purpose flour	½ cup finely minced flat-leaf parsley (optional)	

Rinse the blossoms carefully, leaving the stems attached, and gently shake them dry.

Put the flour in a small bowl and add salt and pepper to taste. Use a fork or wire whisk to beat in tepid water, a little at a time, until you have a batter that is about the consistency of heavy whipping cream. Add parsley to the batter if you wish.

Add 2 inches of olive oil to a deep frying pan and heat to about 360°F (a small cube of white bread will sizzle and turn golden in about a minute). Have ready a rack covered with paper towels. Dip a zucchini blossom in the batter and hold it over the bowl to drip—you should have just enough batter to coat the blossom lightly. Drop the blossom into the hot fat and let it sizzle and turn golden, using tongs to turn the blossom once to crisp it all over. When done, transfer to the paper towel–covered rack. Depending on the size of your pan, you can fry 4 or 5 blossoms at once, but be careful not to crowd the pan. It's important to keep the frying temperature up; otherwise the blossoms will absorb oil instead of forming an instant crisp defense against it.

Serve immediately, while still hot, sprinkling the blossoms with more salt if necessary.

VARIATION

Some cooks like to tuck a little piece of anchovy or mozzarella inside each blossom before dipping it into the batter.

Tomatoes/Pomodori

Over the course of the last five hundred years or so, tomatoes have become probably the single most significant element in la cucina del Mezzogiorno, but it wasn't easy getting started. As in many other parts of Europe, tomatoes were regarded with suspicion when they were brought back as botanical specimens after the Spanish conquest of Mexico. Not until 1692 do we find the first real tomato recipes anywhere in Europe. Significantly, those first recipes come from a Neapolitan cookbook, *Lo scalco alla moderno* by Antonio Latini, who was steward to the Spanish governor of Naples. Significantly, too, they are for tomato sauces "in the Spanish style." Despite these recipes, tomatoes appear not to have been common in Neapolitan cooking before the early nineteenth century.

I wrote about the quality of Neapolitan tomatoes, especially those grown in the mineral-rich volcanic soil below Vesuvius on page 127, but sammarzanos are hardly the only delicious tomatoes in Italy, a country that abounds in the flavorful fruit. Pachino tomatoes, from the southernmost tip of Sicily, farther south even than the city of Tunis, are highly regarded, especially the deeply ridged costolutos and the ciliegini, like fat, succulent cherry tomatoes. Then there are *pomodori a pennula,* small cluster tomatoes that are harvested when barely ripe and hung by the cluster in a dry, airy pantry to mature slowly as the sweet juices concentrate and the flavor deepens throughout the long months of winter. (I didn't believe it the first time I heard about it, but in Puglia these fragrant tomatoes are a staple of the wintertime kitchen, lasting well into spring.) Along with *la pomarola*, tomato sauce put up in glass jars or bottles (see page 129), and tomato extract (*stratto* or *conserva di pomodoro*), *pomodori a pennula* are used in countless sauces and pizzas and as garnishes to spark dull winter palates.

One other tomato point that sometimes surprises North Americans: Italians in general, and not just in the South, prefer underripe tomatoes for most salads (Insalata Caprese, page 366, is an exception to the rule), so underripe that we might consider them too green to be eaten raw. The slightly acerbic flavor, they say, is preferable in a salad to the full sweetness of a ripe red tomato.

Pomodori Ripieni Piu Semplice

THE SIMPLEST BAKED STUFFED TOMATOES

Look for ripe, but not overripe, red fruits that are still firm enough to stand up to the heat of the oven. Good varieties to use are any of the ridged tomatoes—Zapotec, Brandywine, Marmande—that are large and round but with flattened tops and bottoms.

This is the simplest way to stuff a tomato, reminescent of a classic treatment from Provence. Serve these with grilled meat or fish or on their own as an antipasto.

MAKES 4 SERVINGS

Extra-virgin olive oil	⅓ cup chopped flat-leaf parsley	Sea salt and freshly ground black pepper
4 ripe but firm round tomatoes, about ½ pound each	⅓ cup fine dry bread crumbs	½ teaspoon dried oregano, preferably Greek or Sicilian
1 tablespoon chopped garlic		

Preheat the oven to 425°F. Lightly oil a baking dish large enough to hold 8 tomato halves.

Cut each tomato in half and gently squeeze out the seeds and juice. Set the tomato halves, cut side up, in the dish.

Chop together the garlic and parsley and combine with the bread crumbs, salt and pepper to taste, the oregano, and about ⅓ cup olive oil. Use this mixture to stuff the holes left in the tomatoes and smear lightly over the top of each tomato half.

Transfer the dish to the preheated oven and bake for 40 to 50 minutes, or until the tomatoes are bubbly and the tops are starting to brown.

Serve immediately, let cool slightly before serving, or serve at room temperature, perhaps as part of a lunch buffet.

VARIATION

For Pumaruolo o'Grattè, the Neapolitan version of baked stuffed tomatoes, add to the filling some finely diced salami, chopped anchovies, and a good handful of capers.

Pomodori Ripieni di Formaggio

CHEESE-BAKED TOMATOES

A slightly richer and more complex recipe, this is still very easy to throw together at the last minute, assuming you have all the ingredients on hand. As usual, I have substituted soft goat's milk cheese for the fresh cow's milk cheese that would be used in parts of southern Italy.

Because of the rich filling, these are better as an antipasto than as a contorno. Minus the anchovies, they might also make a vegetarian main course for a light lunch.

For suggestions of varieties to use, see the preceding recipe.

MAKES 6 SERVINGS

6 ripe round but firm tomatoes, about ½ pound each	¼ cup minced fresh basil	1 garlic clove, minced
Sea salt	2 tablespoons minced flat-leaf parsley	3 tablespoons fine dry bread crumbs
¼ cup extra-virgin olive oil	2 tablespoons capers, preferably salt-packed, rinsed and patted dry	6 anchovy fillets, each one cut in half
½ cup soft goat cheese		
3 tablespoons grated hard aged cheese: pecorino, caciocavallo, grana padano, or parmigiano reggiano	1 small or ½ medium onion, minced	
Freshly ground black pepper		

Cut the top off each tomato at the stem end. Make the cut wide enough so that you can gently press or scrape out much of the liquid and seeds. Sprinkle the insides with a little salt and set upside down on a rack to drain for 15 or 20 minutes.

Preheat the oven to 375°F. Spread 2 tablespoons of the olive oil over the bottom of a gratin or other oven dish large enough to hold all the tomatoes comfortably.

Mix the cheeses together and add a little black pepper, the basil, and the parsley. Chop the capers coarsely, and add to the cheese mixture along with the onion and garlic. Use this to fill the tomatoes, pushing the mixture down into the tomatoes as much as you can without breaking the sides. When all the tomatoes are done, set them side by side in the oven dish.

Sprinkle the bread crumbs generously over the tops of the tomatoes, then cross two halves of an anchovy on the top of each one. Dribble the remaining olive oil over the tops.

Transfer the oven dish to the preheated oven and bake 30 to 40 minutes, or until the tomatoes are soft and the tops are crisp and golden. Remove from the oven and serve immediately.

VARIATIONS

Recipes for stuffed tomatoes, either baked or served raw, abound in southern Italy. You could, for instance, add some partially cooked rice or small pasta shapes to the above recipe and let the rice or pasta finish cooking in the tomatoes. Or you could substitute canned tuna for the cheese, and serve the tomatoes raw with a dollop of homemade mayonnaise instead of the bread crumb mixture on top.

Pomodori Schiacciati

SQUASHED TOMATOES

The simplicity of this Calabrian dish is stunning, and for that reason there is no point in even thinking about it until that time in late summer when utterly ripe, red, and flavorful garden tomatoes are in season—preferably from your own or a neighbor's garden. That's where the flavor lies—there and in the use of fine extra-virgin olive oil, good crunchy sea salt, a zesty dash of hot red chili, and, of course, the charcoal fire on which the tomatoes are set to roast. Toast the bread over the charcoal embers after you finish the tomatoes, so it will be crisp but not tough and hard.

Use smaller tomatoes for this—cluster tomatoes are great, even very small ones like Sweet 100s or grape tomatoes, but make sure they don't slip through the grill. Note that you could also cook the tomatoes on a stovetop grill or even under an oven broiler.

Serve Pomodori Schiacciati as a primo, either with toasted bread or pasta.

MAKES 6 SERVINGS

2½ pounds fresh tomatoes, fully ripe but firm to the touch Extra-virgin olive oil	Sea salt and freshly ground black pepper Ground or crumbled dried red chili	6 slices country-style bread 1 garlic clove (optional)

Have ready a charcoal fire or glowing wood embers in a fireplace. Set up a grill. Rinse and dry the tomatoes and set them on the grill about 3 inches above the coals. Grill or roast until they have softened and the skins are starting to split open. Remove the tomatoes, using tongs, before they turn totally soft and slip through the grill. Transfer the tomatoes to a serving dish and squash them lightly with a fork so that the juices run out a little. Immediately dress them generously with olive oil, salt, black pepper, and chili and mix the dressing into the tomato juices.

Toast the bread slices, over the embers if possible. If you wish, rub a cut clove of garlic over each slice. Set the toasts on plates, spooning the tomato sauce on top. Serve immediately.

VARIATION

It doesn't take a lot of imagination to see that this "sauce" would be just as good on pasta—short, stubby pasta shapes are best—as it is on toasted bread.

Ciaudedda o Stufato di Verdure

A BRAISE OF EARLY SPRING VEGETABLES

A dish from mountainous Basilicata, this is a hearty preparation meant to sustain countryfolk in their labors. It could easily be a main course, particularly for vegetarians—just omit the pancetta and add a little more olive oil. Or serve as a first course instead of pasta.

MAKES 4 SERVINGS AS A FIRST COURSE, 2 to 3 servings as a main course

4 to 6 small (baby) artichokes or 2 to 3 globe artichokes	2 tablespoons extra-virgin olive oil	Sea salt and freshly ground black pepper
1½ lemons	2 medium yellow-fleshed potatoes, such as Yellow Finn or Yukon Gold, sliced or diced	1¼ pounds fava beans, shucked
4 small yellow onions, thinly sliced		
⅓ pound pancetta, diced		

Trim the artichokes as described on page 305, using one of the lemons to rub the cut surfaces. Drop the trimmed artichokes into acidulated water. Cut each baby artichoke into 4 pieces; if you're using larger globe artichokes, cut into 4 pieces to remove the choke. Then cut into smaller bite-sized pieces.

Combine the onions and pancetta with the olive oil in a saucepan large enough to hold all the vegetables comfortably. Set over medium-low heat and cook until the onions are soft. Add the potatoes and stir, sprinkling with salt and pepper. As the potatoes soften, add the drained artichokes and the fava beans, stirring carefully to mix without breaking up the potatoes.

Add about ¼ cup hot water to the vegetables, cover the pan, and continue cooking until all the vegetables are done. Check from time to time to see if more hot water should be added—there should always be a small quantity of liquid in the bottom of the pan but never so much that the vegetables are boiling. When done, add the juice of the remaining lemon half and taste for seasoning. Serve immediately or set aside and serve at a little above room temperature.

Ciambotta Cilentano/Ciammotta Lucana

A LATE SUMMER VEGETABLE MIX

A mixture of late summer's bounty, ciambotta (or ciammotta as it's called in Basilicata) can be made richer by the addition of a topping of beaten eggs and grated cheese, but the simplicity of the dish on its own, without the enrichment, is also very appealing, with its contrasting flavors and textures, between the well-done potatoes and eggplant and the barely cooked tomatoes.

If you can't get good eggplant, substitute zucchini. Some cooks add coarsely chopped yellow onions, sautéing them with the garlic toward the end, before adding the tomatoes. Note that the quantities used are not important. If you have more peppers or fewer potatoes, it won't make a big difference. What *is* important for the peak of flavor, however, is that the vegetables be fresh, preferably from a nearby farm or garden.

MAKES 8 TO 10 SERVINGS

1 large or 2 medium eggplants (about 1½ pounds), cut into 1-inch cubes

Sea salt

¾ cup extra-virgin olive oil, or more if necessary

1 pound yellow-fleshed potatoes, such as Yellow Finn or Yukon Gold, peeled and cubed

2 large red, yellow, or green sweet peppers, roasted and peeled (see page 305), cut into wide strips

2 garlic cloves, coarsely chopped

12 to 15 very ripe cherry or grape tomatoes, halved

Handful of slivered fresh basil

Freshly ground black pepper

1 cup grated aged pecorino or parmigiano reggiano (optional)

4 large eggs (optional)

Set the eggplant cubes in a colander and sprinkle liberally with salt, tossing to coat them. Set a plate, with a weight, on top and place the colander in the sink to drain for 30 to 60 minutes. Prepare the other vegetables while the eggplant cubes are purging.

Heat about ⅓ cup of olive oil in a heavy skillet over medium heat. Add the potatoes and cook, stirring and tossing, until they are tender and starting to brown. Transfer to a bowl, leaving the oil behind.

Add more oil to the pan—you should have about ½ inch in the bottom. While the oil is heating, rinse the eggplant cubes well and dry with paper towels. Add the eggplant to the hot oil and cook, stirring and turning, until the cubes are brown and tender, about 5 minutes. Remove with a slotted spoon and add to the potatoes. (If you need to add more oil, keep in mind that eggplant absorbs oil like a sponge unless the oil is hot enough to brown the eggplant very quickly. If you add more, do it when the pan is empty and heat the oil before adding more eggplant.)

When the eggplant is done, add the roasted peppers to the pan, along with the garlic and a little more oil, no more than 2 tablespoons, if necessary. Cook until the garlic is tender but not brown, then add the tomatoes and cook until they give off enough juice to make a syrup in the bottom of the pan. (The tomatoes should be soft but still retain their shape.) Stir in the basil and transfer the contents of the pan, with all the syrupy liquid, to the vegetables in the bowl. Cover the bowl with aluminum foil until ready to serve—the tomatoes will continue to soften in the residual heat.

When ready to serve, stir gently to combine everything well. Taste and add salt if necessary and a few grinds of black pepper. The dish may be prepared to this point ahead of time and served as it is, at room temperature.

If you wish to add the egg and cheese topping, you may refrigerate the vegetables before continuing, but be sure to allow time to bring the dish back to room temperature before finishing.

Preheat the oven to 425°F. Transfer the vegetables to a lightly greased oven dish—a soufflé dish is fine for this.

Set aside 2 tablespoons of the grated cheese. Beat the eggs together with a fork, adding the remaining grated cheese a little at a time. Pour the egg mixture over the top of the vegetables, then sprinkle with the reserved cheese. Transfer to the oven and bake for 20 minutes, or until the topping is firm and golden on top. Remove and serve immediately.

CAPONATA OF EGGPLANT, TOMATOES, AND PEPPERS

WITH A TOUCH OF CHOCOLATE

Caponata is often described as Italy's answer to French ratatouille, but the addition of "Arab" ingredients like raisins, capers, pine nuts, and olives, along with the vinegar and sugar in the sweet-sour tomato sauce, gives this all-time favorite an unmistakably exotic touch. Like ratatouille, caponata is often served on the antipasto tray, but it makes a perfectly fine first course for summer dining. It's a more refined dish than the rustic ciambotta and combines the complex flavors typical of Sicilian cuisine.

This recipe has evolved from years of watching and learning from Sicilian cooks. The most striking caponata I've ever seen was presented at an early autumn lunch by Eleonora Consoli, a talented cooking teacher who lives north of Catania on the slopes of Mount Etna. She served the caponata on a handsome round majolica platter, the whole thing topped by a dome of chocolate studded with pine nuts. "It's the way our family monzù always did it for special occasions," she said modestly. To make the dome, she had inverted an aluminum bowl, covered it with plastic wrap, then laboriously painted layer after layer of dark melted chocolate over it, waiting for each layer to harden before adding the next. After the final layer was added, but before it had solidified, she studded it with pine nuts. When the whole thing was ready, she slid it off the bowl, removed the plastic wrap, and carefully set it over the caponata. To serve it, she broke through the chocolate dome at the table so that each portion came with bits of chocolate and pine nuts on top.

MAKES 6 TO 8 SERVINGS

2 pounds eggplant, cut into large cubes

Sea salt

6 tablespoons extra-virgin olive oil

2 medium yellow onions, chopped

1 anchovy fillet, chopped

2 green celery stalks, including leaves, sliced ¼ inch thick

1 pound ripe tomatoes, peeled and chopped

2 tablespoons tomato extract, concentrate, or paste, or 4 sun-dried tomatoes, plumped in hot water, drained, and chopped

¼ cup red wine vinegar

2 tablespoons sugar

2 tablespoons finely grated dark unsweetened chocolate

2 red sweet peppers, roasted and peeled (see page 338) and thinly sliced

2 tablespoons capers, preferably salt-packed, rinsed and drained

2 tablespoons golden raisins

2 tablespoons pine nuts

12 to 14 green olives, pitted and coarsely chopped

Freshly ground black pepper

¼ cup mixed finely minced flat-leaf parsley and fresh basil for garnish

Set the eggplant cubes in a colander and sprinkle heavily with salt. Set a plate on top of the eggplant and weight it. Set the colander in the sink to drain for at least 30 minutes, then rinse the eggplant cubes thoroughly in running water and pat very dry.

Heat ¼ cup of the olive oil in a large skillet, add the dried eggplant cubes, and cook until until they are golden on all sides, about 8 minutes. You may have to do this in several batches. As the eggplant cubes brown, transfer them to a bowl.

Lower the heat to low and add the onions and anchovy to the oil in the pan, first adding a little more olive oil if necessary. Cook the onions very gently so they melt in the oil rather than sizzle and fry. When the onions are very soft, add the celery and tomatoes and raise the heat to medium. Cook, stirring frequently, until the tomatoes have given off their liquid and start to soften into a sauce.

Add the tomato extract or sun-dried tomatoes and stir into the sauce. Add the vinegar, sugar, and chocolate, stir well, and simmer for about 5 minutes, during which time the sauce will thicken and darken. Now stir in the remaining ingredients except the garnish, with plenty of black pepper as well as the reserved eggplant cubes. Mix everything together very well, coating the eggplant cubes with the sauce. Transfer to a serving platter and garnish with the chopped herbs.

Serve immediately or set aside to serve later at room temperature. Caponata is one of those dishes that improves in flavor if kept overnight, but if you must refrigerate it, be sure to allow time for it to come back to room temperature before serving. It loses a lot of complexity when served chilled.

NOTE: *In some regions, cooks garnish the caponata with a sprinkling of minced fresh mint leaves instead of basil—a nice touch.*

Salads/Insalate

Seldom does a meal in southern Italy end without at least a bite of salad, the very simplest kind of salad imaginable—sweet lettuce or fresh bitter chicory or radicchio or spicy rughetta (arugula), possibly with a few slices of sweet red or white onion or a couple of chunks of cucumber, dressed with lots of good olive oil, a sprinkling of sea salt, and a light spritz of vinegar or lemon. In springtime the salad might be composed of wild greens, in summer it might have a few wedges of firm, underripe tomatoes, but otherwise it's as plain as can be imagined, deliberately so because its whole reason for being is to clear the palate and help digest the meal.

But more elaborate salads—still usually restricted to no more than three or four primary ingredients—are apt to be served as an antipasto to start the meal off. And for chic, modern southern Italians, concerned about setting a bella figura and watching their waistlines, a salad like Insalata Caprese, with its delicious combination of ripe tomatoes, mozzarella, and fresh green basilico, might well serve as the main course for a light lunch, especially during the August holidays at the seaside.

Insalata Caprese

SALAD OF MOZZARELLA, TOMATOES, AND BASIL FROM THE ISLE OF CAPRI

Insalata Caprese must have been "invented" on the lovely, mountainous Sorrento peninsula, the graceful southern arm of the Bay of Naples, and named for the island of Capri, which looms like a blue mountain on the horizon off the peninsula's tip end. Ideally, I'm told, the tomatoes should come from the terraced hills above Vico Equense; the mozzarella should be, in fact, fior di latte, from the milk of Agerolese cows that graze high on those hillsides; and the oil to dress the salad should be from Massa Lubrense, the best being that produced by Vittoria Brancaccio at her *olivetto* in Sant'Agata sui Due Golfi, with trees that some say go back to the times of the Emperor Tiberius. This combination of flavors is so right, so perfect, that it seems divinely ordained.

In recent years Insalata Caprese has become popular all over Italy. Its tricolor of red tomatoes, green basil, and white mozzarella is a true expression of Italian patriotism, appropriately enough in food. But even when Insalata Caprese is made far from Sorrento, it's a wonderful combination of summer flavors.

This, by the way, is one time when Italians agree that the tomatoes should not be the usual underripe salad tomatoes—crisp-textured and streaked with green—but rather lush, fully ripe, red and juicy tomatoes, rushed from the garden to the plate where their sweet-tart juices mingle with the oil and the vinegar. A very pretty presentation results if you use two or three different varieties of heirloom tomatoes—some golden, some red, and some of those beautiful green zebras that, even when fully ripened, look like tomatoes carved in jade.

Be sure that the mozzarella, either cow's milk (*fior di latte*) or buffalo-milk, is freshly made.

MAKES 4 TO 6 SERVINGS AS AN ANTIPASTO, 2 to 3 servings as a main course

½ pound fresh mozzarella	1 tablespoon aged wine vinegar	8 to 10 fresh basil leaves, slivered
1 pound ripe tomatoes		
¼ cup extra-virgin olive oil	Sea salt and freshly ground black pepper	

Cut the mozzarella and tomatoes into slices of equal thickness—about ¼ inch. Arrange them, overlapping, on a serving platter or on individual salad plates.

Mix together the olive oil and vinegar and pour over the cheese and tomatoes. Sprinkle with salt and pepper, then distribute the slivered basil over the top. Set aside to let the flavors develop for about 30 minutes, then serve.

VARIATIONS

Leave the basil leaves whole and insert them in between the slices of mozzarella and tomato.

A version popular in Naples includes 2 or 3 anchovy fillets, pounded to a paste and mixed with the oil and vinegar. This combination of ingredients also makes a splendid sandwich, served on thin slices of country-style bread.

Insalata di Rinforzo

NEAPOLITAN CHRISTMAS VEGETABLE SALAD

Rinforzo means "reinforced"—and there's a story behind this name: Since the salad is served in Naples throughout the Christmas season, always on the family or festive table, it is in constant need of topping up, or reinforcing. In Napoli, the reinforcing usually comes in the form of more *giardiniera* vegetables—vegetables that have been pickled and preserved in vinegar and olive oil. Unfortunately, to my taste at least, the result is a dish in which every ingredient tastes like almost every other ingredient. In my own adaptation of this Christmas tradition, I marinate the carrots and celery beforehand, then mix them with the rest of the vegetables and leave the mixture to meld for several hours before serving.

The chilies used in Naples are definitely spicy but not burning hot. If you can't find a fresh red chili, use a fresh green one; otherwise use a mild dried red chili, such as ancho chili, crumbled into the salad.

Insalata di Rinforzo is usually served as an antipasto, but it might also be offered as a merenda to guests who drop by during the holidays.

MAKES 6 TO 8 SERVINGS

2 medium carrots, peeled and cut into julienne strips	1 medium cauliflower (about 1 pound)	2 tablespoons capers, preferably salt-packed, rinsed and drained
1 crisp green celery stalk, cut into julienne strips	1 small fresh mild flavored red or green chili, or 1 small dried red chili	6 anchovy fillets, coarsely chopped
2 tablespoons wine vinegar, plus more to taste	12 large black olives, pitted and coarsely chopped	¼ cup finely chopped flat-leaf parsley
1 teaspoon salt, plus more to taste	6 large green olives, pitted and coarsely chopped	2 tablespoons extra-virgin olive oil
1 sweet red pepper		

Combine the julienned carrots and celery with 2 tablespoons of the wine vinegar and the teaspoon of salt in a small bowl. Toss to mix well and set aside, covered, to marinate for several hours or overnight.

Roast and peel the sweet red pepper (see page 338). Cut the pepper into long, thin slivers. Break the cauliflower into small florets. Bring a saucepan full of lightly salted water to a rolling boil, add the cauliflower, and cook until it is just barely tender, 7 to 10 minutes, then drain thoroughly. Combine the peppers and cauliflower in a salad bowl.

If you're using a fresh chili, cut it in half and discard the seeds and white membranes, thinly slice, and add to the cauliflower, along with the olives, capers, anchovy fillets, and parsley. Add the olive oil and stir in the carrots and celery, along with any juices that have accumulated in the bottom of the bowl. (If you're using a dried red chili, crumble it over the salad at this point.) Stir carefully to mix well without breaking things up. Taste and adjust the seasoning, adding more salt, vinegar, or olive oil if you wish. The salad should be more piquant with vinegar and salt than an ordinary green salad. Cover the bowl with plastic wrap and set aside for at least several hours before serving.

VARIATION

Finely chop a couple of hard-cooked eggs and sprinkle over the salad just before serving.

Insalata di Acciughe e Peperoni

ANCHOVY AND RED PEPPER SALAD

Another Christmas tradition, like the preceding Insalata di Rinforzo, this salad, when traditionally made, also includes lots of pickled and preserved vegetables. But over the years I've found that I prefer the fresh, immediate taste of bright red sweet peppers to contrast with the salty anchovies. The optional oil-packed tuna and olives make this a more substantial dish. To make a lighter antipasto, keep it simple: just peppers and anchovies. At Christmastime, this would be made with canned peppers or peperoni sott'olio, but when fresh red peppers are available (as they are just about year-round in North America), they are a better choice.

No salt is added since the anchovies contain plenty.

MAKES 6 SERVINGS

6 sweet red peppers, roasted and peeled (page 338)	One 6-ounce can oil-packed tuna, drained and flaked (optional)	Freshly ground black pepper
18 anchovy fillets		1 tablespoon aged wine vinegar
18 large black olives, pitted and coarsely chopped (optional)	¼ cup extra-virgin olive oil	

Slice the roasted peppers into long strips about ½ inch wide. Arrange the pepper strips on a deep serving plate or platter. Arrange the anchovy fillets in a lattice on the top. If you wish to use the chopped olives and flaked tuna, distribute them over the top.

Combine the olive oil with plenty of black pepper and the vinegar, beating with a wire whisk to mix well, then pour over the ingredients in the dish. Cover with plastic wrap and set aside for several hours—but do not refrigerate—before serving.

Insalata Estiva

SICILIAN SUMMER SALAD

This summery salad is often served at Tenuta Pignatelli, a rose-walled villa outside Castelvetrano that is the home of the Becchina family, makers of Olio Verde, one of Sicily's finest olive oils. The hearty salad is part of summer buffets in the villa garden, but it could be a first course for a dinner party, and of course it also makes an excellent main course all on its own for lunch.

MAKES 4 TO 6 SERVINGS

1 pound yellow-fleshed potatoes, such as Yellow Finn or Yukon Gold	6 anchovy fillets, coarsely chopped	1 teaspoon dried oregano or 2 tablespoons minced fresh basil
Sea salt	12 to 15 olives, black, green, or both, pitted and coarsely chopped	1 tablespoon fresh lemon juice, or to taste
¼ cup extra-virgin olive oil, preferably Sicilian	1 tablespoon capers, preferably salt-packed, rinsed and drained	2 hard-cooked eggs, sliced
1 pound green beans, cut into 2-inch lengths	1 medium red onion, halved and thinly sliced	
1 large slightly underripe tomato, seeded and diced		

Peel the potatoes and slice them ¼ inch thick. Bring a large pan of lightly salted water to a rolling boil and drop in the potato slices. Boil rapidly until the potatoes are just tender—about 5 minutes.

While the potatoes cook, mix the olive oil with about a teaspoon of salt in the bottom of a salad bowl. As soon as the potatoes are tender, drain them and turn into the bowl, stirring gently with a wooden spoon to coat the slices with the oil.

Bring more lightly salted water to a rolling boil and add the green beans. Cook rapidly until the beans are just tender, about 5 to 7 minutes. Drain, rinse under cold running water to preserve their color, then toss dry and add to the potatoes, stirring gently so as not to break up the potato slices.

Add the tomato, anchovies, olives, capers, and onion. Sprinkle with oregano, crumbling it in the palm of your hand to release its aroma. Turn the salad ingredients very gently, adding the lemon juice as you do so. Taste and adjust the seasoning, adding more salt, herbs, or lemon juice, if you wish. Finally, distribute the egg slices over the top.

Set aside for 15 to 30 minutes to let the flavors meld, then serve.

VARIATIONS

To make a heartier salad, toss in finely diced fresh white cheese or mozzarella, or flaked oil-packed tuna or mackerel, and serve the salad with toasted crostini—rubbed with garlic and olive oil. Or present the salad on a bed of fresh greens, in which case arrange the dressed salad on top of the greens, then distribute the egg slices over the top.

Insalata di Funghi con Formaggio di Grana o Parmigiano

FRESH MUSHROOM SALAD WITH FLAKED GRANA OR PARMIGIANO CHEESE

Altomonte is one of Calabria's loveliest medieval hill towns, sitting high on a spur of the great range of the Monte Pollino national forest. The dense forests and grassy meadows of the park are home to an enormous variety of wild mushrooms, many of them edible. Each year in autumn, the restaurant in Altomonte's Hotel Barbieri hosts a magnificent mushroom festival to celebrate this bounty. This salad is one of many mushroom-based dishes on the menu.

If you gather wild mushrooms, be sure you know what you're dealing with! Even the easily distinguished boletes include some questionable members. Or play it safe and buy mushrooms from a reputable and trusted source. Porcini (*Boletus edulis,* sometimes called *cèpes* from the French, but usually known as *boletes* in English) are the best and most typical variety for this recipe, but there are many other types of firm-textured wild mushrooms that could be substituted.

To flake parmigiano reggiano, or its less expensive cousin grana padano, use a vegetable ruler and shave off short strips of the grainy, crumbly cheese.

MAKES 4 TO 6 SERVINGS

1 pound fresh wild porcini mushrooms (*Boletus edulis*) ½ pound grana padano or parmigiano reggiano	¼ cup extra-virgin olive oil 2 tablespoons finely minced flat-leaf parsley	Sea salt and freshly ground black pepper Fresh lemon juice

Clean the mushrooms well, using a soft brush to brush away any earth or dried leaves that cling to them. Since they absorb a great deal of water, it is better not to wash porcini, particularly if they are to be used, as in this recipe, raw. Instead, use a damp kitchen towel to clean off any stubborn grit. Cut away any soft parts or bits that look wormy or otherwise undesirable.

Often mushroom stems are very soft and flabby. If so, discard them or freeze them to use for flavoring next time you make stock. If the stems are nice and firm and free of worm holes, slice them lengthwise no more than ¼ inch thick. Slice the caps similarly. Transfer to a salad bowl.

Use a paring knife or a vegetable peeler to scale the cheese into thin irregular chunks. Scatter the cheese over the mushrooms.

In a small bowl, combine the olive oil, parsley, salt and pepper to taste, and a teaspoon or so of lemon juice. Taste for seasoning, then beat with a fork or wire whisk and immediately pour over the mushrooms and cheese. Toss the mushrooms gently so as not to break them up.

Let the salad sit, lightly covered, for an hour or so before serving.

VARIATION

Some cooks like to add a handful of julienned crisp celery to the mushrooms, making a nice texture contrast.

INSALATA DI CARCIOFI E GRANA

Replace the mushrooms with young, impeccably fresh artichokes, all the hard bits cut away and discarded (rubbing the cut surfaces with lemon as you trim; see page 305) and the tender core thinly sliced. An insalata di carciofi will benefit if the artichokes marinate in the dressing for a couple of hours before being served, and you will probably want to boost the amount of lemon juice to a tablespoon or so.

Insalata di Arance, Cipolle Rosse, e Finocchio

SICILIAN ORANGE, RED ONION, AND FENNEL SALAD

Blood oranges are prized for their distinctive acid-sweet flavor balance and their dark ruby flesh, flecked with crimson highlights like a well-aged wine. *Tarocco* is the most esteemed Sicilian variety, but two others, almost as good, are called *moro* and *sanguinello*. Any of these varieties will make a superb, deep-garnet-colored juice that is rich with flavor—and vitamins.

Blood oranges grown in Florida and California are not always widely available, the quality is not always what it should be, and they are usually absurdly expensive. If you cannot find acceptable blood oranges, use ordinary juice oranges, but taste before using. Tangy, acidic oranges are preferred, but if sweet navels are all you can get, add a spritz of lemon juice to the orange juice on the plate.

MAKES 4 SERVINGS

4 small oranges, preferably Sicilian tarocco or other blood oranges	12 to 16 black olives, preferably salt-cured, pitted and halved	3 tablespoons extra-virgin olive oil
1 or 2 fat fennel bulbs, trimmed and very thinly sliced	6 anchovy fillets	Freshly ground black pepper
4 very thin slices red onion	1 tablespoon fresh lemon juice, if necessary, or more to taste	

Peel the oranges, cutting away the white pith as well as the membrane that covers it. Slice the oranges as thinly as you can manage on a plate that will catch the juices.

Arrange the orange slices in a circle on a serving dish or on individual salad plates. *Do not discard the juice left behind on the slicing plate.*

Distribute the fennel slices over the top of the oranges, then the red onion slices, and finally arrange the black olives and anchovy fillets on top.

If the oranges you are using are very sweet, add lemon juice to taste to the orange juice on the slicing plate. Pour the juice over the top of the salad, holding back any seeds. Dribble the olive oil over the salad, then sprinkle with pepper.

Cover lightly with plastic wrap and set aside at room temperature to let the flavors develop for at least 30 minutes before serving.

Insalata di Grano Pestato o di Farro

GRANO PESTATO OR FARRO SALAD

Grano pestato means "pounded grain" and refers to an old-fashioned strain of durum wheat still grown in Puglia and other parts of the Italian South. Because each berry or grain of this wheat is covered with an indigestible pellicle, the wheat must be dampened, then pounded in a mortar to get rid of that outer skin. This traditional process is similar to that used for cleaning farro, and the strain of wheat used in Puglia may well be a type of farro.

This is a very old method of food processing that doubtless goes back to the Greeks of Magna Graecia, since the words for the mortar (*stompu*) and the pestle (*stompatura*) both come from Greek. (The pounded grain, in Pugliese dialect, is sometimes called *cranu stumpatu*.) It was probably one of the earliest methods of preparing grain for human consumption. Nowadays both grano pestato and farro are mechanically prepared, but there are still a few old people in Puglia who know how to pound the wheat, gently, gently, to clean it—they are considered national treasures.

Peeled wheat, grano pestato, can sometimes be found in Italian delicatessens and groceries, especially around Easter since it is obligatory in the Neapolitan Easter sweet, pastiera di grano (page 401). Or see Where to Find It, page 415. If you can't find grano pestato, however, substitute the more easily available farro, which is similar enough to work fine for this salad.

Note that grano pestato must be soaked for several hours before being cooked.

MAKES 6 SERVINGS

1½ cups grano pestato or farro	About ½ cup coarsely chopped fennel	Zest of ½ lemon, preferably organic
Sea salt		
1 small red onion, very thinly sliced	¼ cup coarsely chopped flat-leaf parsley	3 to 4 tablespoons extra-virgin olive oil
1 medium underripe tomato, coarsely chopped	¼ cup thinly sliced celery	About 2 tablespoons fresh lemon juice

Rinse the grain quickly under running water, then transfer to a bowl and cover with 1 inch of water. Set aside to soak for several hours or overnight. (If you are using farro, presoaking is not usually necessary, but check the package to be certain.)

Drain the grain and transfer to a heavy saucepan. Add water to cover by 1 inch and a good pinch of salt. Bring to a simmer, cover, and simmer for 40 to 60 minutes, or until the grain is tender but still has a little bite in the center. Drain thoroughly and transfer to a salad bowl.

Add the onion, tomato, fennel, parsley, celery, and lemon zest, stirring to mix well. Add olive oil and lemon juice to taste. Mix again, then cover the bowl with plastic wrap and let the salad sit for 30 minutes or longer at room temperature to develop the flavors.

The salad may be made well ahead of serving, but if it must be refrigerated, be sure to allow plenty of time to bring it back to room temperature before serving.

Insalata di Riso Campanese

RICE SALAD FROM CAMPANIA

In Campania, I was told to use a risotto type of short-grain rice—arborio or vialone nano—for this insalata di riso. In fact, however, I find that long-grain carolina rice works much better in a salad. Watch the rice carefully as it cooks—it should be tender but with a little bite in the center of each grain.

To toast the pine nuts, simply put them in a small skillet and set over medium heat. Cook, stirring occasionally, until they turn golden—but be careful because they go very quickly from golden to burnt. Remove from the heat as soon as they are the right color and scrape them into a bowl to cool slightly.

MAKES 4 TO 6 SERVINGS

1½ cups long-grain rice	2 tablespoons pine nuts, lightly toasted	1 tablespoon fresh lemon juice, or more to taste
Sea salt	2 tablespoons minced flat-leaf parsley	Freshly ground black pepper or ground red chili to taste
3 sweet peppers, preferably green, yellow, and red, roasted and peeled (page 338)	2 tablespoons currants or golden raisins, soaked in warm water to plump and drained	Slivered fresh basil for garnish (optional)
⅓ cup cooked green peas	3 to 4 tablespoons extra-virgin olive oil	
2 ounces pitted black or green olives, chopped (about ¼ cup)		

Combine the rice in a saucepan with 2½ cups water and a good pinch of salt. Set over medium heat and bring to a boil, then turn down to a simmer, cover the pan, and cook until the rice is tender, 15 to 20 minutes.

Meanwhile, dice the peppers and prepare the other ingredients. As soon as the rice is done, drain it and transfer to a salad bowl. Add the diced peppers along with the peas, olives, pine nuts, parsley, and drained currants. Add the olive oil and stir to mix well, coating all the rice with the oil. Add the lemon juice, then taste and add more lemon juice or salt if necessary. Stir in the black pepper or red chili.

The salad may be served immediately, but it is also good at room temperature. If you must refrigerate it, be sure to allow plenty of time for it to come back to room temperature before serving. Sprinkle the salad with slivered basil before serving.

DOLCI

Sweets

Scattered across the landscape of southeastern Sicily is a trio of hill towns—Noto, Modica, Ragusa-Ibla—that are acclaimed for the enchanting, floridly Baroque architecture of churches, chapels, and palazzi, an exuberant display of arches, volutes, cherubs, delightful demons, and mythological creatures carved in stone. The style evolved in this region after a devastating earthquake in 1693 and is so particular and peculiar that the whole Val di Noto, as the region is called, has been named a UNESCO World Heritage site.

But while the architecture is grand, these towns are noted for other things too: Ragusa for its fragrant aged cheese, called *ragusano* and made from the milk of local modicana cows; Noto for the high-quality fruit-based jams, jellies, and ice creams made there; and Modica for its chocolate, specifically the old-fashioned, grainy chocolate made by small family operations like Antica Dolceria Bonajuto, established 125 years ago by Francesco Bonajuto. Today the Bonajuto chocolate *laboratorio* and shop are supervised closely by Francesco Ruta, great-grandson of the original Francesco, whose shy, serious demeanor belies his enthusiasm for his products. Modica chocolate, Franco Ruta explained to me as we sampled his wares in the front of his modest establishment in the lower part of the historic town, is made by a cold process, originally developed by the Aztecs and brought back to Europe by Spanish conquistadors. "Only here and in Catalonia," Franco said, "perhaps also in Mexico, is chocolate still made this way." Because the chocolate is not heated, as it is in most modern chocolate making (a process called *conching* that also involves kneading the chocolate for as long as three days), the resulting small bars, flavored with cinnamon, vanilla, or hot chili peperoncini, have a pleasantly grainy, crunchy texture and retain a lot of the natural bitterness of chocolate that is offset but not concealed by the added sugar. The full bittersweet complexity of chocolate itself is the most apparent flavor.

There are other sweets for which the Antica Dolceria is noted as well. The strangest and most intriguing that we sampled that afternoon was *'mpanatigghi,* little baked ravioli filled with a mixture of chocolate, crushed almonds, sugar, honey, pounded cinnamon and cloves, and finely minced lean beef. And no, that's not a misprint—chocolate and meat together make a flavor combination that is odd, dark, and mysterious, something out of the distant past—as indeed this is, for the name is clearly derived from Spanish (*empanadilla*) and the recipe itself, Franco told me, is Spanish in origin, once made with meat from wild animals, boar or deer, he said, for which modern chocolatiers like himself substitute lean sirloin of beef.

I mention this because Modicana chocolates and Sicilian 'mpanatigghi are just two among a variety of southern Italian sweets that are as odd to the North American palate as can be imagined. Another is represented by a whole range of sweet dessert tortes and cakes, dense with dried fruits and nuts, that derive their richness and their thick texture from pig's blood, collected when the animal is slaughtered and quickly transformed into a winter pudding or budino called *sanguinaccio,* meaning "blood pudding."

Arab culinary influences are behind many southern Italian sweets—although obviously, I hasten to add, not sanguinaccio since Arabs, like Jews, don't consume blood, and certainly not pig's blood. Sweetness came with the Arabs, naturally enough, since it was Arabs who brought sugar cultivation into the Mediterranean, especially to island states like Sicily. Many of these sweets are as simple as mixing nuts or seeds, almonds or sesame seeds, with sugar, stirring the mixture over heat until the sugar caramelizes, then letting it harden into a brittle candy. When made with almonds, hazelnuts, or pistachios, this is often called *torrone,* and it's made and sold all over the South for the long Christmas season, which extends from the Feast of the Immaculate Conception on December 8 to La Befana, or Epiphany, on January 6. Torrone may have come into Sicily directly with the Arabs, or it may have come indirectly, from the Arabs but via Spain, since a similar and equally tempting candy exists to this day in Spain.

Another source of these sweet confections was in convent kitchens, where women with a good deal of time on their hands could spend hours over a hot stove, patiently stirring cauldrons of hot syrup. Another combination of sugar and blanched almonds that may have originated with Arab cooks but reached its apotheosis in convent kitchens is *pasta di mandorle* or *pasta reale* (almond or "royal" paste), which we would call marzipan. Made by pounding the nuts and sugar together to a fine white paste, pasta di mandorle has the consistency of modeling clay, and indeed it is most often used to model small, intricately detailed fruits and vegetables that are painted with vivid vegetable dyes to mimic their real-life counterparts. In the medieval village of Erice, perched on a mountaintop in western Sicily, the delightful Maria Grammatico, who herself was raised in a convent, is an astute and gifted practioner of the art, but she is not alone. In the convent of San Giovanni Evangelista in Lecce, at Eastertime the nuns still make extra cash for their needs by modeling pasta di mandorle lambs, hearts, and doves, which they then fill with thick, pale pear marmalade (page 413).

These more elaborate and costly sweets were not, of course, for everyone. In country kitchens and peasant farmhouses, such things were rare, even unknown, and sweets, such as they were, were more apt to consist simply of fresh fruit in season—figs, melons, peaches, cherries, even the odd and, to my palate, unappetizing *fichi d'India,* or prickly pears, harvested cautiously from spreading groves of prickly pear cactus, another American import. Other fruits were dried for a wintertime treat, especially figs, which, once dried, are often stuffed with a chopped mixture of almonds, grated orange zest, and hazelnuts, then dusted with fine sugar to keep them from sticking together. In Calabria, the Colavolpe family has been making and marketing similar confections for three generations; the filling for their figs includes a delicious syrup made from a secret formula that is guarded closely by the three members of the present generation, Giulia, Nicola, and Gerardo, each one of whom has been entrusted with just one-third of the formula, thus guaranteeing no sibling rivalry, or at least none that would interfere with the production of their *crocette.* (Colavolpe-stuffed fig crocette are imported by Manicaretti; see Where to Find It, page 415)

Finally, one can't really talk about sweets in the south of Italy without mentioning mosto cotto or vincotto. If sugar is a "modern" and expensive import, if honey was restricted to monastery production (a by-product of beeswax for church candles) and thus to the elite, what did the common folk do for sweetening? *Mosto cotto,* cooked must, was the answer: When grapes were pressed in autumn, a certain amount of juice was set aside and, rather than being fermented into wine, boiled down to make a thick syrup, as sweet as molasses but with a slightly acidic bite. Mosto cotto, sometimes called *vincotto* (cooked wine), is also available in gourmet shops, imported by Manicaretti and others.

The reader will note that the title of this chapter, Dolci, does not translate as "desserts" but rather as "sweets." That's because most of the time in the Mezzogiorno of Italy, as in the rest of the Mediterranean, sweets are not eaten as dessert except for rare celebratory occasions. On the everyday table—and this holds for restaurants and private homes, rich and poor alike—the dessert course is usually nothing more than a piece of seasonal fruit, if that. Sometimes the fruit will be served plain, sometimes tricked out with a little lemon juice and sugar or an appropriate liqueur. The northern European and American habit of eating large quantities of sweet, chocolaty, creamy cakes and so forth at the end of a filling meal is baffling in the extreme.

The fact is southern Italians adore their sweet traditions, but they consume them at a different time of day, most often in the late afternoon, accompanied by little cups of strong, sweet coffee or glasses of sweet wines and ratafias. Whether associated with specific holidays, like the Easter pastiera, a rich ricotta torte from Naples, or simply evoking the idea of celebration, like the elaborately constructed Sicilian cassata, these tend to be consumed away from the meal, even away from the dining table. But as Italians bend, with barely concealed ill will, to the more workaholic habits of the European Union, this custom of the late-day pause for sugar and spirit is unfortunately dying out. Perhaps in the future food historians will read a book like this for a glimpse of a vanished past, wherein one of the marks of a civilized life was precisely that unwillingness to let work trump pleasure. In the meantime, you will find in the recipes that follow both the simple, straightforward, fruit-based sweets that Italian cooks offer at the end of a meal and more complex fantasies, often associated with specific holidays, especially Christmas and Easter, that have evolved out of the intricate braid of traditions from Arab kitchens, aristocratic banquets, and cloistered convent halls—and that, today, are more often the output of professional pastry kitchens.

Arance al Marsala

SLICED ORANGES WITH SUGAR AND MARSALA

The simplest kind of fruit dessert, this is a good example of what southern cooks expect to serve at the end of a meal—and what southern diners expect to find.

Use oranges with a good tart-sweet balance—blood oranges, when you find them, are best, but other oranges can be good too, as long as they aren't overly sweet. You'll need an orange for each serving, more if they are very small.

MAKES 6 SERVINGS

6 to 8 oranges, preferably blood oranges	Superfine sugar to taste	Dry Marsala

Peel each orange, cutting away the pith and the membrane that covers it. Using a sharp knife, segment the orange directly into a bowl by cutting between the membranes that separate each segment. Squeeze what's left in your fist, letting the juice fall into the bowl. (You could also slice the oranges horizontally and arrange the slices on individual serving dishes.)

Sift a little sugar over the oranges—how much sugar depends on how tart the oranges are and is a matter of personal taste. Spoon a little dry Marsala on top—not too much, because the Marsala is there to complement the oranges, not vice versa.

NOTE: *If you can't find a dry Marsala, other dessert wines could be substituted, but do stay away from excessively sweet wines. A dry Tuscan vin santo should be very good.*

Torta di Mandorle

ALMOND CAKE

Although this recipe comes from Calabria, a similar cake, pleasantly dry and not terribly sweet, can be found all over Italy. Very often cakes like these are served at breakfast as a special treat, but they're also delicious at tea time or at the end of a meal—especially for people who don't like to finish dinner with a great wallop of sugar.

Almond cake is traditionally made with blanched almonds. I recommend lightly toasting the almonds to boost the almond flavor. You could also use almond extract in place of the vanilla, but to my taste it lends an unpleasant chemical flavor to the cake.

MAKES 8 TO 10 SERVINGS

Unsalted butter and all-purpose flour for the pan	½ cup cake (pastry) flour	5 eggs, separated
1 cup blanched almonds	1½ teaspoons baking powder	¾ cup whole milk
1 cup granulated sugar	½ teaspoon sea salt	Confectioners' sugar for the top (optional)
1½ cups unbleached all-purpose flour	½ pound (2 sticks) unsalted butter, at room temperature	

Preheat the oven to 350°F. Butter and flour a 9-inch round cake pan.

Spread the blanched almonds in a single layer on a cookie sheet and set in the preheated oven. Toast for 10 to 15 minutes, or until the almonds are a pale golden color. Remove from the oven and let cool slightly, then transfer to a food processor. Add 2 tablespoons of the granulated sugar and process the almonds, pulsing, until they are a uniform small grain, like coarse cornmeal. Do not overprocess; the almonds should not become a pasty almond butter. (You could also chop the almonds, without the sugar, on a wooden board.)

Combine the flours, baking powder, and salt with half of the remaining granulated sugar and toss with a fork to mix well. Add the almonds.

Set aside another 2 tablespoons of the sugar and transfer what is left to a mixing bowl. Add the butter and beat to a thick cream, then beat in the egg yolks, one after another. Continue beating for about 5 minutes to get a thick, light-lemon-colored batter.

Fold about a third of the flour-almond mixture into the batter, then fold in a third of the milk. Continue alternating dry and liquid ingredients until all the flour and all the milk have been folded in.

In a separate bowl, using clean beaters, beat the egg whites to soft peaks. Add the reserved 2 tablespoons granulated sugar and continue beating to stiff peaks. Stir about a quarter of the egg whites into the batter, then fold in the remaining egg whites.

Turn the batter into the prepared cake pan and transfer to the preheated oven. Bake for 40 to 60 minutes, or until the center is firm and springy and the sides pull away from the pan slightly.

Remove from the oven and let cool slightly on a cake rack before removing from the pan. If you wish to sift confectioners' sugar over the cake, invert it and remove the pan, then sift the sugar over the flat bottom of the cake—which is now the top.

Delizia di Limone

LEMON DELIGHT

Delizia di limone is a delicate and delicious lemon cake, made in the pastry shops of the Amalfi coast in towns like Amalfi and Maiori. The lemons, of course, are those famously flavor-packed feminello lemons from the Sorrento Peninsula. This is just one of a variety of lemon tarts and cakes made in the pasticcerie of the region. This recipe and the one that follows are based on familiar pastry-shop treats, simplified for home cooks.

The cakes are usually sold as small individual cupcakes covered with a lush lemon cream and topped with grated lemon zest and sugar-coated lemon leaves. Because it's a little tricky to ice individual cupcakes, I usually make this as a traditional two-layer cake and serve it sliced into wedges. This is a perfect teatime treat, but quite addictive.

You can find commercial limoncello in a well-stocked liquor store, but homemade limoncello (page 408) is much preferred. However, don't expect to make it in a day—it can take a good thirty days to make limoncello, and it gets even better the longer you leave it.

You will need a 9½-inch tube pan (an angelfood cake pan), preferably one with a removable bottom.

MAKES 10 TO 12 SERVINGS

FOR THE SPONGE CAKE	FOR THE LEMON SYRUP	FOR THE LEMON PASTRY CREAM
6 large eggs, at room temperature	⅓ cup sugar	2 cups whole milk
¾ teaspoon cream of tartar	Zest of ½ lemon, preferably organic	1¾ cups whipping cream
1¼ cups sugar	2 tablespoons limoncello (page 408)	⅔ cup sugar
1½ cups unbleached all-purpose flour		Grated zest of 1 lemon, preferably organic
1 teaspoon baking powder		6 egg yolks
Pinch of sea salt		¼ cup cornstarch
1 lemon, preferably organic		2 tablespoons limoncello (page 408)

First, make the sponge cake: Preheat the oven to 375°F.

Separate the eggs into 2 bowls. Add the cream of tartar to the whites and beat to soft peaks. Gradually beat in ¾ cup of the sugar until stiff peaks form. Set the beaten whites aside.

Combine the flour, remaining ½ cup sugar, the baking powder, and salt and toss with a fork to mix well.

Grate the zest of the lemon. Squeeze the lemon juice into a cup measure and add cool water to make ½ cup liquid. Add the zest to the liquid.

In the second bowl, without rinsing the beaters, beat the yolks, then add about a third of the dry ingredients and about a third of the liquid. Beat to mix, then continue alternating between flour mixture and liquid, beating after each addition, until both are all mixed in.

Stir about a quarter of the beaten egg whites into the yolk mixture, then fold in the remainder of the whites. Transfer the cake batter to a tube pan and set in the preheated oven. Bake for about 35 minutes, or until the surface of the cake is dry and the sides are pulling away from the cake pan.

Remove from the oven and invert over a cake rack. Leave to cool thoroughly before removing the cake pan. While the cake is cooling, make the lemon syrup and the lemon pastry cream.

To make the lemon syrup, combine in a small saucepan the sugar and ½ cup water. Add the lemon zest and bring to a boil. Boil gently for 5 minutes, then remove and set aside to cool. When cool, add the limoncello. Let the syrup sit until ready to use, but remove the lemon zest before using.

To make the lemon pastry cream, combine the milk, 1 cup of the whipping cream, and ⅓ cup of the sugar in a saucepan. Bring to a boil and remove immediately from the heat. Stir in half the grated lemon zest.

Beat the egg yolks with the remaining ⅓ cup sugar and the cornstarch. When the yolks are thick, add a small amount of the hot milk mixture, beating as you do so. Continue to add hot milk to temper the egg mixture, beating continuously. Add the remaining lemon zest and transfer to the top of a double boiler. Set over (but not in) boiling water in the bottom part of the double boiler and cook over simmering water, stirring constantly, for 7 to 10 minutes, or until the mixture has thickened to a soft pudding consistency. Remove from the heat and set aside to cool down. When slightly cool, beat in the limoncello. You will have about 2 cups of pastry cream.

When the cake is cool, slice it horizontally into 2 layers and open the layers with the cut sides facing up. Pierce each layer with a wooden skewer in 8 or 10 places (this encourages the syrup to dribble down into the cake) and spoon the prepared syrup over each layer. Use about 1 cup of the pastry cream to spread all over the bottom layer, then set the top layer over it, cut side down. Set the cake in the refrigerator for at least 30 minutes.

Beat the remaining ¾ cup whipping cream to stiff peaks, then fold it into the remaining pastry cream. Use this to ice the top and sides of the cake. If you wish, sprinkle the top with more finely grated lemon zest. Refrigerate the cake until ready to serve.

MAKES 8 SERVINGS

Unsalted butter and all-purpose flour for the pan	½ teaspoon baking soda	¼ cup fresh lemon juice
1½ cups unbleached all-purpose flour	1 teaspoon sea salt	¼ cup extra-virgin olive oil
	4 large eggs	1 teaspoon pure vanilla extract
½ cup cake (pastry) flour	1 cup sugar	Confectioners' sugar for the top
1 teaspoon baking powder	Finely grated zest of 4 lemons, preferably organic	

Butter and flour a 9-inch round springform cake pan. Preheat the oven to 325°F.

Combine the flours, baking powder, baking soda, and salt in a mixing bowl and toss with a fork to mix well.

Separate 3 of the eggs. Combine the yolks with the remaining whole egg, ½ cup of sugar, and the lemon zest. Beat until the batter is thick and forms a ribbon falling from the beaters.

Combine the lemon juice, olive oil, and vanilla.

Using a rubber spatula, fold about a third of the dry mixture into the egg batter, then about a third of the liquid mixture; continue alternating between dry and liquid until everything has been incorporated.

Using clean beaters, beat the egg whites to soft peaks. Continue beating, adding the remaining ½ cup of sugar, a little at a time, until stiff peaks form.

Stir about a quarter of the egg whites into the batter, then fold in half of the remaining egg whites and finally the rest of the whites. Turn the batter into the prepared cake pan and transfer to the preheated oven. Bake for 40 to 50 minutes, or until the cake is firm but springy in the center and pulls away slightly from the sides of the pan.

Remove from the oven and invert over a cake rack. Leave to cool thoroughly before removing the cake pan. If you wish, sift confectioners' sugar over the top before serving.

Torta di Noce

OLIVE OIL CAKE WITH WALNUTS

This makes a simple, not very sweet cake—the kind to be served at home to women friends in the late afternoon, with a cup of tea or coffee or, for the more daring, with a glass of sweet wine. In southern Italy it's often flavored with homemade grappa or another household liqueur, for which I have substituted dark rum. If you wish, a handful of golden raisins could be folded into the batter at the end. Powdered sugar is sprinkled over the top after the cake has been removed from its pan and cooled slightly.

MAKES ONE 9-INCH CAKE; 8 generous servings

Unsalted butter and all-purpose flour for the pan	Scant ¾ cup granulated sugar	½ cup roughly chopped walnuts
2½ cups cake (pastry) flour	3 eggs	¼ cup whole milk
2 teaspoons baking powder	1 tablespoon grated lemon or orange zest, preferably organic	⅓ cup golden raisins (optional)
½ teaspoon sea salt		Confectioners' sugar for the top
5 tablespoons extra-virgin olive oil	¼ cup dark rum	

Lightly butter and flour a 9-inch round cake pan. Preheat the oven to 350°F.

Combine the cake flour, baking powder, and salt in a bowl, and toss with a fork to mix well.

In a mixing bowl, beat the olive oil and granulated sugar together, then beat in the eggs, one at a time, mixing well after each addition. Sift about a third of the dry ingredients over the egg mixture, then sprinkle the citrus zest over the flour. Use a spatula to fold the flour, zest, and egg mixture gently together. Add the rum and walnuts and fold. Sift another third of the dry ingredients over and fold. Add the milk and fold. Finally, sift the rest of the dry ingredients and fold so that all the ingredients are well blended. If you're using raisins, fold them in at this time.

Turn the batter into the prepared cake pan and bake in the preheated oven for about 25 minutes, or until the cake pulls away from the sides of the pan and springs back when pressed lightly in the center. Remove from the oven, turn out onto a cake rack, and let cool. Sprinkle with confectioners' sugar before serving.

The name for this famous Neapolitan rum-drenched sweet cake, pronounced ba-BAH, comes from the equally famous French cake known as *baba au rhum.* You will not find its ilk anywhere else in Italy, north or south, but in Napoli it's a favorite, not least because it's a nostalgic reminder of the King- dom of the Two Sicilies and the French royal house of Bourbon that ruled from Napoli over all the Italian South. These soft cakes drenched in rum syrup are worth every minute of the time spent preparing them, and they keep well so they can be made ahead for a dinner party.

Travelers to Napoli (like travelers to Paris) can find special small babà molds for these little cakes, but similar ones are available at well-stocked kitchen supply stores such as Bridge Kitchenware in New York City (see Where to Find It, page 415). You could also make these in rather deep muffin tins. Yet an- other option is to make one large babà in a ring mold or tube pan, rather than small ones.

Long beating at a slow speed using the paddle attachment of an electric mixer is what gives these cakes their light texture.

MAKES 20 SMALL CAKES; 20 servings

One ¼-ounce envelope dry yeast	4 large eggs	**FOR THE SYRUP**
½ cup warm milk	8 tablespoons (1 stick) unsalted butter, at room temperature, plus more for the molds	1 teaspoon pure vanilla extract
¼ cup sugar		1 cup sugar
2¼ cups unbleached all-purpose flour		Zest of 1 lemon, preferably organic, or ½ teaspoon pure vanilla extract
	Pinch of sea salt	4 or 5 tablespoons dark Jamaican rum
		Vanilla-flavored whipped cream for garnish

In a large mixing bowl, combine the yeast with the warm milk and ¼ cup warm water. Let it dissolve, 5 to 10 minutes, then stir in a tablespoon of the sugar and ¼ to ½ cup of the flour. Mix to a thick slurry, cover the bowl, and set aside to rise until the sponge has doubled.

While the sponge is rising, sift the remaining flour.

Add to the doubled sponge, about a quarter of the sifted flour, a tablespoon of the remaining sugar, and one of the eggs. Using the paddle attachment of an electric mixer, beat at slow speed to mix thoroughly. Add another fourth of the flour, another tablespoon of sugar, and another egg. Continue until all the ingredients have been incorporated, beating after each flour-sugar-egg addition. Continue beating while you add half the softened butter, then the remaining butter. Finally, add a pinch of salt and continue mixing, with the paddle attachment on the slowest speed, for about 15 minutes, until the dough is very light. When the dough is ready, it will be elastic and pulling away from the sides of the mixing bowl.

Cover the bowl with plastic wrap and set aside in a warm (but not hot) place to rise until doubled in size.

Thoroughly butter twenty 2-inch round babà molds.

Shape the dough into 20 small balls, one for each mold. (If you have a scale, weigh the balls—they should weigh about 2 ounces each.) Set them in the well-buttered molds and cover loosely with a kitchen towel. Set aside to rise again for about 1 hour.

While the dough is rising, prepare the rum syrup: Bring 2 cups water to a boil and add the vanilla, sugar, and lemon zest. Boil for about 15 minutes, until it has condensed to a thin syrup, then set aside to cool down. When the syrup is cool, add 2 or 3 tablespoons of the rum. Have the syrup ready in a wide pan in which you can soak the cakes.

Preheat the oven to 350°F.

When the cakes have risen, transfer them to the preheated oven and bake for 20 to 25 minutes (25 to 30 minutes for a single large babà), or until they are golden on top. Remove and let cool, then turn the babas out directly into the rum syrup, turning them over and over until they have fully absorbed the syrup. If you pierce each little cake in 2 or 3 places, it will absorb the syrup more readily.

When you are ready to serve, spoon a little more straight rum on top of each babà and garnish it with a dollop of vanilla-flavored whipped cream.

Zeppole di San Giuseppe

SAINT JOSEPH'S DAY ZEPPOLE

The feast day of St. Joseph (San Giuseppe) on March 19 is celebrated enthusiastically through-out the south of Italy with special foods made for the occasion. Zeppole have been called "Italian doughnuts," although they also exist in a version that's more like *bombolone* or cream puffs, filled with a sweet custard cream.

MAKES 24 TO 30 ZEPPOLE

1 cup unbleached all-purpose flour	2 eggs	Oil for deep-fat frying, preferably extra-virgin olive or canola
2 teaspoons baking powder	1 cup whole-milk ricotta	
Pinch of sea salt	½ teaspoon pure vanilla extract	1 tablespoon ground cinnamon, or to taste
1½ tablespoons sugar, plus ½ cup for coating	Grated zest of 1 lemon, preferably organic	

Combine the flour, baking powder, salt, and 1½ tablespoons of the sugar in a bowl and toss with a fork.

In another bowl, beat the eggs, then beat in the ricotta, vanilla, and lemon zest. Fold the dry ingredients into the egg-ricotta mixture.

Put 1½ to 2 inches of oil into a frying pan or deep skillet. Set over medium heat and heat the oil to 360°F (a small cube of bread will brown in about a minute). Have ready a rack spread with paper towels.

When the oil is hot enough for frying, drop the batter by tablespoonsful into the hot oil. Fry 4 or 5 zeppole at a time, no more, to prevent the oil temperature from dropping. Keep an eye on the temperature and adjust to maintain it at around 350°F. The zeppole will quickly brown and rise to the surface of the oil, though you may need to nudge them a little with a long-handled fork or a pair of tongs. As the zeppole fry, try to pierce each one with a wooden skewer—it will make them crisper. Cook the zeppole until they are a deep nut-brown color, then remove with a slotted spoon and transfer to a rack to drain and cool slightly. When all the zeppole are done, combine the cinnamon with ½ cup sugar in a bowl. Roll each zeppole in cinnamon sugar and stack in a bowl for serving.

About Ricotta

Fresh ricotta right off the fire—clumps of soft, creamy, white curds, fragrant with woodsmoke and bathed in whey that is still warm from the cauldron in which it cooked—is a rare pleasure, one you won't come across in any restaurant. To sample this exceptional treat, you must be in the dairy after the morning milking, at the very moment that the cheesemaker—who is often the shepherd or the shepherd's wife—dips into the cloudy bath to extract a dipperful of cheese and whey that is then poured over crumbled pieces of yesterday's bread. You consume it, if you're in the dairy, standing up, shifting from foot to foot to keep warm in the morning's chill, absorbing the sweet, milky flavors of the cheese, the grainy energy in the crumbled bread. It is an archaic, primitive, primordial treat—easy to imagine Homer's rustics, even one-eyed Polyphemus himself, tucking into similar fare at the dawn of a new day.

It's not always understood that ricotta is not so much a cheese as a by-product of cheesemaking. That means any kind of cheesemaking, from the rich milk of goats, cows, ewes, even buffalo. But for authentic southern Italian flavors, the best ricotta to use is sheep's milk ricotta, *ricotta di pecora*. Unfortunately that's the one that's hardest to find in North America. Every now and then in some American farmers' market I come across a sheep's milk cheesemaker who's willing to go the next step and make ricotta from the whey. Then I buy as much as I can handle and carry it home to delight family and friends.

The process of making it could not be simpler: After the cheese curds have been drained, the leftover whey is gently reheated (*ri-cotta* means "cooked again"), often some fresh milk is added, and residual proteins blossom from the whey, rising and clustering to form the familiar creamy blooms of ricotta, white flowers floating on the surface of the whey. The curds are collected with a strainer and set in woven baskets (these days woven of plastic) to drain further.

Ricotta is at its best as fresh as possible. Sometimes a little olive oil is poured over it and it's sprinkled with black pepper; at other times it's served as a sweet course, with honey or mosto cotto, the boiled-down and thickened juices of grape or fig must, or just with cut-up fruit. Most often it's used in other recipes, both sweet and savory, to add richness.

Ricotta can also be salted and kept for two months to mature—in which case it's called *ricotta salata*—and it can be baked in a wood-fired oven, until a golden crust forms on the outside. This is called *ricotta infornata* (see the following recipe) and is delicious when lightly sweetened and fragrant with vanilla or other aromas.

When buying ricotta in America, look for whole-milk ricotta, preferably made from sheep's or goat's milk, otherwise from cow's milk; get the freshest available. For eating straight up, as it were, you'll want the ricotta to be moist, but for cooking it's best to drain for a good twenty-four hours in a fine-mesh sieve or a colander lined with cheesecloth to keep the dish from being watery.

Ricotta Infornata

BAKED RICOTTA (FLOURLESS RICOTTA CAKE)

This Pugliese treatment of ricotta results in something more like a pudding than a proper cake. It is very light and delicious when served with seasonal fruits—strawberries in spring are a natural, as are peaches in summer. In winter, you could poach some pears in a sugar syrup and serve them with the ricotta infornata, strewn with crisp toasted walnuts.

MAKES 8 TO 10 SERVINGS

2 pounds whole-milk ricotta	1 cup superfine sugar	Almond oil or very light olive oil for the pan
1/3 cup whipping cream	Grated zest of 1 lemon, preferably organic	
1 teaspoon pure vanilla extract		
3 eggs	1 teaspoon fresh lemon juice	

The day before you plan to make the cake, set the ricotta to drain in a fine-mesh sieve or a colander lined with cheesecloth. Let it drain for at least 24 hours, refrigerating it if your kitchen is very warm.

When you're ready to bake, preheat the oven to 350°F.

Remove about 3 cups of the ricotta (there may not be much more than that in any case once the ricotta has drained) and put it in a mixing bowl. Add the cream and beat vigorously to a smooth cream, about the texture of yogurt. Beat in the vanilla and then the eggs, one after the other, beating after each addition. Finally, beat in the sugar, a little at a time. When all the sugar is incorporated, fold in the lemon zest and juice.

Lightly oil the bottom and sides of a loaf pan measuring 8½ × 4½ × 2½ inches. Transfer the ricotta cream to the prepared pan and smooth the top with a narrow spatula or palette knife. Cover with a piece of foil and set the pan in a larger roasting pan. Fill the roasting pan with boiling water to come about 1½ inches up the sides of the loaf pan. Carefully transfer to the preheated oven and bake for 1 hour. Remove the foil and raise the heat to 400°F. Let the ricotta continue to bake for 35 to 40 minutes, or until it is firm and golden on top.

Remove from the oven and set aside to cool. To serve, cut a slice from one end of the cake and slide a long spatula or palette knife under the cake. Lift it out of the pan and transfer to a serving dish. Spoon the fruits or sauce around the dish and serve. You may refrigerate any leftovers, but the ricotta infornata is really best at room temperature.

Torta Ricca di Ricotta

RICH RICOTTA TART OR CHEESECAKE

An ornate and egg-rich cheesecake, this is something a Pugliese cook might prepare for Easter or for a special occasion like an elaborate lunch to celebrate the baptism of the newest arrival in the family.

The ricotta should be drained for several hours or overnight in a fine-mesh sieve to get rid of the remaining whey. Otherwise, the filling may ooze liquid—an unattractive prospect.

To toast the almonds, spread them on a cookie sheet and put in a preheated 350°F oven, stirring occasionally, until they are golden, 10 to 15 minutes.

MAKES ONE 10-INCH TART; 10 to 12 servings

FOR THE PASTRY	FOR THE FILLING	
1½ cups unbleached all-purpose flour, plus a little flour for the board	2 pounds whole-milk ricotta, preferably sheep's milk, well drained	½ cup candied citron or peel
¼ cup dry white wine	12 eggs, separated	½ cup golden raisins, plumped in hot water
4 tablespoons (½ stick) unsalted butter	¾ cup sugar	½ cup toasted slivered almonds
2 tablespoons sugar	Grated zest of 2 lemons, preferably organic	

Make a pastry crust with the flour, wine, butter, and sugar, working the ingredients together well until they resemble coarse meal. Gather the pastry into a firm ball, wrap it in plastic wrap or foil, and refrigerate for 1 hour.

Preheat the oven to 375°F. Roll the chilled pastry out between 2 sheets of wax paper and use it to line the bottom and sides of a 10-inch round straight-sided pan, like a quiche pan. Cover the crust with wax paper or aluminum foil and weight it to keep it from rising and bubbling while it bakes. (I keep a tin full of old dried beans in my pantry for this purpose, though there are also commercially available pie weights from mail-order houses like Williams-Sonoma.) Set the pan in the preheated oven and bake for 12 to 15 minutes. Remove from the oven and, when cool enough to handle, remove the beans and discard the wax paper.

Put the well-drained ricotta through a food mill or sieve to get rid of any lumps. In a large mixing bowl, beat the egg yolks with the sugar until the mixture is very thick and lemon colored, then beat in the sieved ricotta. Fold in the lemon zest and candied citron. Drain the raisins and fold them in along with the slivered almonds.

Beat the egg whites until they are stiff but not dry. Fold the beaten whites gently into the ricotta mixture, turn the whole thing into the pie shell, and bake for about 1 hour, or until the top of the tart is golden brown.

Remove and let cool just to room temperature before serving.

Probably the most loved of all the great Sicilian sweets, the one that Sicilians and Sicilian-Americans always mention when asked about their traditions, cannoli are simple but a little tricky to make—tubes of crisply fried sweetened dough filled with ricotta cream or with a *crema pasticcera* (pastry cream). The best cannoli I ever had came from the small, symmetrical town of Grammichele—the whole town is laid out like a series of gradually expanding pentagons—in the Sicilian heartland west of Mount Etna. In the main piazza at the Bar Central, next to the headquarters of the Partito Democratico della Sinistra, the Democratic Party of the Left, Francesco the barista fills his cannoli to order, a must if one wants to avoid the soggy crust that results so often when the crisp pastry rolls are filled in advance. Whenever I'm in Sicily, I try to arrange a stop in Grammichele for one of Francesco's cannoli.

This recipe is a traditional Sicilian recipe, similar to the cannoli served at the Bar Central. Be sure to drain the ricotta well through a fine-mesh sieve lined with cheesecloth; even if it appears to be dry, you may be surprised at the amount of liquid it gives off. To make cannoli, you will need special cannolo tubes, available from good kitchen supply houses such as Bridge Kitchenware in New York (see page 415).

MAKES 10 CANNOLI

FOR THE PASTRY ROLLS
1¾ cups unbleached all-purpose flour
2 tablespoons sugar
½ teaspoon freshly ground cinnamon
2 tablespoons pure pork lard or unsalted butter
1 tablespoon sweet white wine
1 tablespoon honey

Extra-virgin olive oil or pure pork lard for deep-fat frying
1 egg, beaten with 1 teaspoon water, for sealing the tubes

FOR THE FILLING
1½ pounds whole-milk ricotta, drained for 24 hours and sieved to remove lumps
1 to 1½ cups superfine sugar
1 teaspoon pure vanilla extract
Grated zest of 1 lemon, preferably organic
Candied fruit
Bitter chocolate, chopped into bits
Confectioners' sugar for dusting

Mix together the flour, sugar, and cinnamon, tossing the dry ingredients with a fork. Add the lard or butter and blend it into the dry ingredients. Add the wine and honey and mix to a dry crumble. Now stir in up to ¼ cup of cold water until the mixture reaches the consistency of pasta or piecrust dough. (You may also do this in a food processor.) Knead the dough briefly, then shape into a ball and cover with plastic wrap. Set it aside for at least 30 minutes to rest.

When ready to make the cannoli, add 2 inches of olive oil to a deep frying pan and set over medium heat. Heat the fat to 360°F (a small cube of bread will brown in about a minute). Have ready the egg and water beaten in a small bowl.

Lightly flour a wooden board and roll out the cannoli dough as thin as you can make it—almost transparent, say Sicilian cooks. Cut the dough into 4½- to 5-inch squares. Set a cannolo tube at the corner of a pastry square and roll it diagonally toward the other corner, smearing a little of the beaten egg along the sides of the square so it will adhere. Press the edge gently to seal the rolled-up dough. (Be careful not to get egg on the tube; otherwise it may be difficult to extract the tube from the finished cannolo.) Trim the pastry tubes so that they are a little shorter than the cannolo tubes.

When the oil is hot, add the cannolo tubes with the pastry and fry until the dough is crisp and golden on the outside. Use a slotted spoon or skimmer to remove the tubes from the hot fat and set them aside on a rack to drain. When cool enough to handle, slide the tube gently out of the cannolo. Cannoli can be made a day ahead and kept in a dry place; they should not be filled until just before serving. When ready to serve, use a pastry bag with a wide hole to fill each cannolo with ricotta cream.

To make the ricotta cream, mix the ricotta with the sugar and vanilla, beating with a hand beater to make the mixture as creamy and homogenous as possible. Using a spatula, fold in the grated lemon zest and the candied fruit, then fold in the chocolate bits. I have not indicated quantities of fruit and chocolate, leaving that up to individual taste.

Once all the cannoli are prepared, sprinkle them with a fine dusting of confectioners' sugar and serve immediately.

NOTE: *Sicilian pastry makers garnish each cannolo with a green or red candied cherry at each end. To me, this seems like carrying exuberance to an unnecessary degree, but if you wish to be totally authentic you will want to do so.*

Pastiera di Grano

NEAPOLITAN RICOTTA AND PEELED WHEATBERRY PIE FOR EASTER

Pastiera di Grano is a Neapolitan tradition that used to be available only during the Easter season but is now on offer pretty much year-round. Traditionalists, however, still insist on eating it *only* during Easter week. And they are right to do so, for this pastiera, its rich, sweetened ricotta filling studded with symbolic grains of wheat and pine nuts, goes straight back to the great spring fertility festivals of the old Mediterranean religion, festivals that evolved gradually into Christian Easter.

The peeled (or hulled) whole wheatberries, *grano pelato* or sometimes *grano pestato* (meaning "pounded wheat") that are used in this and a few other traditional dishes also represent a sort of cultural memory. Archaic varieties of hard durum wheat, like emmer (more commonly known to modern gourmets by its Italian name *farro),* retain, even after threshing, an indigestible pellicle that must be removed to make the wheat palatable. These days the grain is cleaned by machinery, but in an ancient process that is sometimes still used in country districts of Puglia and other parts of the South, the grain is dampened and then gently pounded in a deep mortar made from a tree stump until the pellicle is broken but the grain itself remains intact.

Peeled wheat (grano pestato) is available at Italian markets such as Manganaro's on Ninth Avenue in Manhattan or D'Angelo Brothers on South Philadelphia's Ninth Street. It is supplied by Sunnyland Mills (see Where to Find It, page 415), who may be able to give you a local source for the product. Farro, another variety that is also peeled of its indigestible outer husk (but less thoroughly than grano pestato), could be substituted. Barley might also be used—and, since the ancient Greeks tended to favor barley over wheat, that would take you right back to the origins of the preparation in the Greek cities of Magna Graecia. You could also use ordinary wheat berries, widely available at health food stores, but they must be soaked much longer—up to three days, changing the water from time to time. Whatever grain you choose, it's best to try a sample a week or so before you intend to make the pastiera, to determine whether or not it needs long soaking and how much time it will need to be cooked to be made tender.

Pure pork lard adds considerably to the flavor of this dish, especially to the crust. If you can't get it, however, substitute unsalted butter.

Fiori di Sicilia is a citrus essence, imported from Italy. It is available from The Baker's Catalogue (see page 415). If you can't find it, add the grated zest of one organically cultivated orange to the ricotta cream, along with the grated lemon zest.

Toast the pine nuts carefully—they burn easily—in a skillet over medium-low heat until they are lightly golden.

Use a deep tart or quiche pan for this recipe, preferably one with a removable bottom so you can easily transfer the pie to a plate once it is done.

MAKES ONE 9- TO 10-INCH PIE; 10 to 12 servings

¾ cup peeled wheat (see above)	4 tablespoons (½ stick) unsalted butter, at room temperature	Grated zest of 2 lemons, preferably organic
1 tablespoon pure pork lard or unsalted butter	¼ cup pure pork lard, at room temperature	1 tablespoon fiori di Sicilia essence or orange-flower water
2½ cups whole milk, heated	½ cup cake (pastry) flour	1 teaspoon pure vanilla extract
½ cup granulated sugar	Grated zest of 1 lemon, preferably organic	5 egg yolks
FOR THE PASTA FROLLA DOUGH	Unsalted butter and all-purpose flour for the tart pan	⅓ cup finely slivered or diced candied orange peel
2 eggs	**FOR THE FILLING**	½ cup lightly toasted pine nuts
½ cup sugar	¾ pound whole-milk ricotta, drained of its whey for several hours	3 egg whites
2 cups unbleached all-purpose flour		Granulated sugar for the top

Soak the peeled wheat for 3 to 4 hours to soften it, then drain and combine with the lard and hot milk in the top of a double boiler. Cook, uncovered, over boiling water for 1 to 1½ hours. In the end, the wheat should be soft and in separate grains, like rice, neither gluey nor hard. If at any point the wheat seems too dry, add about ⅓ cup more hot milk and stir well. From time to time, check the water in the bottom of the double boiler, adding more boiling water if necessary. Once the wheat is soft, stir in the sugar and continue cooking for 30 minutes. Cover the wheat and set it aside to cool. The milk will continue to be absorbed as the wheat cools, but if there is still a lot of liquid left after 30 or 40 minutes of cooling, drain the wheat.

Make the pastry dough: Separate one of the eggs. Reserve the yolk to brush the pastry before you put the pie in the oven. Combine the white with the whole egg in a food processor. Add the sugar and process, pulsing, to a smooth cream. (You could also do this with an electric mixer.) Add about ¼ cup of the all-purpose flour and pulse to mix.

In a small bowl, use the back of a spoon to cream together the butter and lard. Add the mixture, a little at a time, to the egg mixture, pulsing or beating after each addition. Pulse in the remaining all-purpose flour and the cake flour. Finally, add the lemon zest, pulsing just enough to mix smoothly. Shape a third of the dough into a ball, wrap it in plastic wrap, and set aside. This will be rolled out later and cut into strips to make a lattice to cover the pie.

Lightly butter and flour the bottom and sides of a 9- to 10-inch tart or quiche pan. Roll out the remaining dough between 2 sheets of wax paper to fit the bottom and sides of the pan. Work quickly as the dough becomes crumbly if it is overhandled. Set the piecrust in the pan, cover it with plastic wrap, and refrigerate for at least 1 hour.

While the crust is chilling, beat the ricotta to a smooth cream using a food processor or an electric mixer. Add the lemon zest, flavorings, and, one after another, the egg yolks. Beat to a cream, then, using a spatula, fold in the candied peel and the drained wheat.

Preheat the oven to 300°F.

Beat the egg whites until they are very stiff. Stir about a quarter of the whites into the ricotta mixture to soften it, then fold in the remaining whites. Pour the mixture into the chilled piecrust. Roll out the reserved dough between 2 sheets of wax paper and cut into lattice strips to fit the top of the tart. Beat the reserved egg yolk with a little water and use it to paint the top of the tart, then sprinkle the top with a little granulated sugar.

Transfer the pastiera to the oven and bake for 1½ to 2 hours, checking from time to time to make sure the tart is baking evenly and not getting too brown on top. If it starts to brown too much, cover lightly with aluminum foil. The tart is done when the ricotta mixture is firm but springy to the touch. The top should be golden brown. Once the tart is done, and the ricotta mixture is cooked all the way through, turn off the heat but leave the tart in the oven with the door ajar, to cool. Serve at room temperature or just barely warm.

VARIATION

Some cooks add lightly toasted chopped almonds to the ricotta cream.

Crostata di Pesche

A crostata is the simplest and homiest kind of dessert imaginable. Because it's so simple and easy, it is often made by country housewives for a family treat after Sunday lunch. All you really need for a satisfying crostata is a little piecrust, enriched with egg and, if you wish as in this recipe, some crushed almonds or hazelnuts. Often grated lemon or orange zest is added to the crust for extra flavor.

Fill the crust with fresh seasonal fruit or, simplest of all, with delicious fruit jam, preferably home-made, then pop it into the oven and there you have it.

MAKES ONE 10-INCH TART; 8 to 10 servings

FOR THE PASTRY	½ cup ground toasted almonds	FOR THE FILLING
8 tablespoons (1 stick) unsalted butter, plus a little butter for the pan	½ cup granulated sugar	4 medium ripe peaches, peeled
	1 egg	½ cup superfine sugar
1¾ cups unbleached all-purpose flour	Pinch of sea salt	Juice of ½ lemon

Use a little butter to grease the bottom and sides of a 10-inch straight-sided cake or torte pan, preferably a springform pan.

Toss together the flour, almonds, and sugar. Cut the butter into the dry mixture, using 2 table knives or a pasty blender, until it is the consistency of fine bread crumbs. Add the egg and salt and mix well, kneading slightly. If the mixture seems too dry, knead in a tablespoon or two of cold water. (You may also do all of this, including the kneading, in a food processor, but be careful not to overwork the dough.) When the pastry comes together nicely, shape it into a ball, cover it with plastic wrap, and refrigerate for 30 to 60 minutes.

Slice the peaches. Add the sugar and lemon juice and toss to mix well. Cover with plastic wrap and set aside (do not refrigerate) for 30 to 60 minutes.

When you're ready to assemble the pie, preheat the oven to 350°F. Remove the dough from the refrigerator. It will still be quite soft. If you can, roll it out between 2 sheets of wax paper to fit the pie pan; if it's too difficult to roll out, shape the ball into a disk using your hands and then fit it into the pie pan, pushing the dough out and up the sides of the pan. It should be no more than about ⅛ inch thick. Trim off any excess and set aside.

Drain the peaches, reserving the syrup that will have accumulated in the bowl. Arrange the peach slices over the piecrust. Bring the syrup to a boil in a small saucepan and boil for about 5 minutes to thicken somewhat, then pour the syrup over the peaches. Transfer the pie pan to the preheated oven and bake for about 40 minutes, or until the dough is crisp and golden and the peaches are starting to brown a little on top.

Remove from the oven and set aside for 15 to 20 minutes before serving.

NOTE: *If you wish, use any excess dough, rolled out, to make a lattice topping for the pie—or roll the dough out and use a cookie cutter to cut out amusing figures to arrange on top.*

VARIATION

Many other kinds of fruit are suitable for this, including apples, pears, and plums. I've even had crostate made with a filling based on sweetened green (unripe) tomatoes. To make a crostata di marmellata di arance (orange marmalade pie), strew chopped bits of bittersweet chocolate over the crust, then top with a ½-inch-thick layer of fine orange marmalade. Because the fruit is already cooked, a marmalade pie needs less baking time—25 minutes should be sufficient to brown the crust.

Granita di Caffè

COFFEE GRANITA

🌿 A *granita* is really nothing more or less than an old-fashioned water ice, deeply refreshing at almost any time of day in the extreme heat of a southern summer. *Granite* are a little like *sorbetti* in that they're composed of water, sugar, and flavoring, but unlike *sorbetti* (sorbets or sherbets), they are frozen in a tray and the crystals are stirred up with a fork every thirty minutes or so to give them a properly grainy texture. A sorbetto, on the other hand, is made like ice cream or gelato in a constantly churning ice cream maker that yields a softer, creamier consistency. Granite don't keep very well in the freezer; they tend to get hard. You can compensate for that somewhat by removing the tray and letting it thaw slightly, then starting the freezing and stirring process all over again, but the sweet is really best consumed within a few hours of completing the original process.

In Sicily, to my surprise and delight, I was often served *granita di caffè* or *granita di limone,* coffee or lemon granita, for breakfast. The idea is to take a freshly baked warm brioche and fill it with the icy confection, then consume the two together.

MAKES 6 CUPS; 6 to 8 servings

1½ cups finely ground coffee	½ cup sugar	1 teaspoon pure vanilla extract (optional)

Have ready a double boiler with water simmering in the bottom part.

Separately bring 5 cups of water to a rapid boil.

In the double boiler top, combine the coffee and sugar, stirring to mix well. Add the 5 cups of boiling water, pouring it over the coffee-sugar combination, stirring to mix very well. Add the optional vanilla. Set the top over the bottom of the double boiler and let the coffee mixture steep for 30 minutes over simmering water. Then remove from the heat and strain through a fine sieve to get rid of the coffee grounds (you could also pour it through a paper coffee filter).

Transfer to a bowl, cover with plastic wrap, and set the bowl in the refrigerator to chill thoroughly. Then set the bowl, still covered, in the freezer and freeze for about 3 hours, stirring up the crystals with a fork every 30 minutes or so.

Granita di Limone

This could just as easily be a lime or orange granita. Or try the recipe with other juicy fruits, such as strawberries or plums; if you have a juicer, that's easy to do. Otherwise you'll have to puree the fruits, then strain out the pulp.

MAKES ABOUT 5 CUPS; 6 servings

1¼ cups sugar	Grated zest of 2 lemons, preferably organic	Juice of 5 lemons, preferably organic

Combine 2 cups water, the sugar, and grated zest in a saucepan over medium heat. Cook carefully until the sugar has melted, but do not let the water come to a boil. Remove from the heat and let cool to room temperature.

Strain the cooled syrup and combine with the strained lemon juice. Transfer to an ice tray or metal bowl and freeze for about 3 hours, stirring up the crystals with a fork every 30 minutes or so.

Limoncello

LEMON LIQUEUR

Long a southern Italian favorite, especially along the lemon coast, the Sorrentino Peninsula south of Naples, limoncello was discovered by foreign tourists a few years ago, and word of it spread quickly all over the world—including all over the rest of Italy. With good reason—it's a refreshing digestif served very cold after dinner, and it's dead easy to make at home. In fact, this and other similar liqueurs, called *rosolii,* are still made by country housewives in order to have something strong, sweet, and reinforcing to offer guests at the end of a meal. Fragrant with mint, bay leaves, basil, coffee, citrus, or green walnuts, these rosolii are the pride of the housewife's larder, often displayed in crystal decanters laid out on a sideboard. The decanters, along with the recipes that fill them, are passed down from mother to daughter over generations. This recipe comes from the father of Concetta Cantoro. When I first met her, she was the most famous restaurateur in Lecce. Now retired, she still makes limoncello every year when the lemon crop is at its peak.

It's not easy to find grain alcohol in America, although there are several websites that offer a 190-proof brand called Everclear for sale. But it's a potentially dangerous product, so I use 100-proof vodka instead.

MAKES ABOUT 1½ QUARTS

8 large lemons, preferably organic	1 fifth (750 ml) 100-proof vodka 3 cups spring water	1½ cups sugar

Rinse and dry the lemons, then carefully peel off the yellow zest in very thin strips, leaving behind the white pith. (You won't need the lemon juice for this recipe. If you have no other use for it, squeeze the peeled lemons and freeze the juice—in ice cube trays for convenience.)

Put the lemon zest and vodka in large glass jars, screw down the lids, and set aside in a cool dark place (but not refrigerated) for 7 to 10 days.

At the end of this time, strain the vodka through a sieve, discarding the lemon zest. Bring the spring water to a boil and dissolve the sugar completely in the water. Cool to room temperature, then mix with the strained vodka. Bottle in canning bottles or jars or in rinsed-out wine bottles. Cork tightly and set aside for 24 hours. Then refrigerate for 15 to 20 days.

Serve the limoncello, well chilled, in tiny glasses after dinner.

Semifreddo al Torrone

SOFT ICE CREAM WITH ALMOND BRITTLE

The first step of this recipe will produce torrone or almond brittle, which is delicious in its own right if you don't wish to go on with the ice cream itself. Caramelizing the almonds requires constant attention: Be careful working with hot sugar, which burns painfully if it spills.

MAKES 6 TO 8 SERVINGS

½ pound whole almonds, with their skins on	Bland oil, preferably almond oil to oil a marble countertop	Pinch of sea salt
½ pound superfine sugar	3 eggs	½ cup confectioners' sugar
		1 cup whipping cream

Combine the almonds and superfine sugar in a saucepan and cook over medium heat, stirring constantly, until the sugar has caramelized. It will liquefy and turn golden, then a richer brown. At this point, turn the almonds out onto a marble surface that has been lightly oiled and spread them in a sheet to dry and cool completely. When the almonds are thoroughly cooled, crush them to a coarse crumble. This is easiest in a food processor, pulsing in brief spurts. Be careful not to overprocess. You should have about 2 cups of crushed almonds.

Separate the eggs into 2 bowls. Beat the whites with a pinch of salt and about a third of the confectioners' sugar until they form stiff peaks.

In the second bowl, beat the yolks with about a third of the confectioners' sugar until they thicken and form a ribbon falling from the beaters.

In a third bowl, beat the cream with about a third of the confectioners' sugar until it is very thick.

Delicately, using a rubber spatula, fold the almonds into the egg yolks, then fold in the whites. Turn the cream into this mixture and, again working delicately, fold it into the egg-almond combination. The resulting cream should be foamy but quite firm.

Turn into a mold or ice trays and set in the freezer for at least 24 hours; before serving, transfer to the refrigerator for 1 hour to soften gently.

Coviglia al Caffè
FROZEN COFFEE PUDDING

Another in the repertoire of simple, coffee-flavored, frozen or chilled desserts that are favorites in the Italian South, this one is somewhere between a *semifreddo* and a frozen soufflé. A *coviglia* is actually the little dessert cup in which this delicate sweet was traditionally served. I use little soufflé dishes about 3 inches across that hold no more than ¼ to ½ cup, which is plenty for a single serving. Coviglie should not be served frozen hard, so, if you must keep them in the freezer longer than two to three hours, be sure to transfer them out of the freezer and into the refrigerator for several hours to loosen up before serving.

You can buy ready-ground espresso coffee but for a richer flavor, grind espresso-roast beans yourself just before using them. Grind them to a very fine texture—much finer than you would use in most coffee makers.

MAKES 6 SERVINGS

1 cup whole milk	½ cup sugar	½ cup strong brewed black coffee
2 teaspoons very finely ground espresso coffee	4 egg yolks	1 cup whipping cream
2 teaspoons all-purpose flour	1 teaspoon pure vanilla extract	2 egg whites

Put the milk in a saucepan over low heat. Warm the milk until it is just above body temperature—hot to the touch—but do not let the milk come to a boil.

Combine the ground espresso and flour in a small bowl, tossing with a fork to mix well. Set aside.

Add the sugar to the egg yolks in a mixing bowl and beat until the mixture is light-colored and thick enough to form a ribbon falling from the beaters. Continue beating as you slowly pour the warm milk into the eggs. Add the vanilla and the coffee and then the mixture of ground espresso and flour, beating constantly.

When everything is well combined, transfer the mixture to a heavy saucepan and set it over low heat. Cook, stirring continuously, until the mixture thickens to a cream. Note that it's important to watch the mixture and stir constantly because if comes to a boil, it will curdle as the eggs start to cook. (If that starts to happen, all is not totally lost. Immediately pull the pan off the heat and cool it down by setting the base of the pan in cool water. You can then strain the mixture through a sieve to get rid of any curdled/cooked bits and continue with the remainder.) In the end, the mixture should be as thick as very heavy cream. When it has reached that consistency, remove the pan from the heat and set aside to cool.

Beat the cream until it forms soft peaks, then fold the whipped cream into the coffee mixture. Rinse the beaters and beat the egg whites to stiff peaks, then fold them into the coffee cream.

Transfer the coffee cream to individual serving dishes or, if you wish, put it all in a serving bowl. Set in the freezer for about an hour, then stir the mixture, which should be half-frozen, and return to the freezer for another hour before serving.

Gelo di Caffè

These jellies are favorite desserts in Sicily, where their lightness and simplicity are much appreciated after a heavy meal. Note that these are not gelatins—instead they are thickened with starch. Sicilian cooks use wheat starch, but cornstarch, more readily accessible here, is just as appropriate. A coffee jelly like this one is served at the Planeta winery, an outstanding estate located in a stunning landscape of rolling vineyards north of Menfi in southwestern Sicily. Make the coffee ahead of time, using one and a half times as much coffee as you normally would to obtain a really strong brew.

MAKES 8 SERVINGS

1 tablespoon finely grated lemon zest, preferably from organic lemons	3 tablespoons cornstarch	Vanilla-flavored whipped cream for garnish
2 cups freshly made hot, strong-brewed coffee	1 cup sugar, or to taste	

Add the lemon zest to the hot coffee and set aside to steep for 15 to 20 minutes, keeping it hot. Then pour the coffee through a fine strainer or a paper filter to get rid of the lemon zest and any remaining coffee grounds.

Combine the cornstarch and sugar in a saucepan, mixing well so there are no lumps, only a smooth powder. Add about ½ cup of the hot, strained coffee, stirring as you pour. Keep adding coffee by ½-cup increments, stirring all the while.

When all the coffee has been added, set the saucepan over low heat and bring to a simmer, stirring constantly. As soon as the mixture starts to simmer, let it cook for 2 minutes, stirring all the while, or until it is as thick as cream. Pour it into individual serving glasses and chill in the refrigerator for 2 to 3 hours. Serve the gelo when it is completely chilled. Add a dollop of vanilla-scented whipped cream on top if you wish.

VARIATION

Some cooks like to add a tablespoon of unsweetened cocoa powder to the cornstarch and sugar mixture.

Marmellata di Pere

PEAR MARMALADE

At the convent of Saint-John the Evangelist in Lecce, the nuns make a famous sweet, originally for Easter but now available year-round. It's an almond-paste (marzipan) confection, in the shape of a fish or lamb, beautifully detailed with the curls of lambs' wool or fish scales. The interior of each figure is filled with pear marmalade. You don't have to make a marzipan fish to enjoy the marmalade, however— it's brilliant on breakfast toast or a croissant.

MAKES 4 OR 5 HALF-PINT JARS

2 pounds ripe but firm pears, peeled and cut into small pieces	1⅓ cups sugar

Mix the fruit and sugar together thoroughly. Cover the bowl with a kitchen towel and set aside for at least 3 hours to let the juices start to run. Transfer to a large nonreactive saucepan and cook over moderate to medium-low heat for about 45 minutes, stirring with a wooden spoon to prevent sticking. Remove from the heat when the mixture is dense.

Have ready 5 sterilized half-pint canning jars and their lids (see page 129).

Turn the hot marmalade into the clean dry jars, screw down the caps, and seal. If you are planning to keep the marmalade for more than a few weeks, it's safer to take a little extra time to seal the jars in a boiling water bath, processing them for 10 minutes.

The Baker's Catalogue (King Arthur Flour Company), P.O. Box 876, Norwich, VT 05055. 800-827-6836; shop.bakerscatalogue.com; kingarthurflour.com. An excellent mail-order source for baking supplies, grains and flours, seasonings, and many other ingredients and equipment, not just for baking.

The Bridge Kitchenware Company, 711 Third Avenue (45th Street), New York, NY 10017. 212-688-4220; bridgekitchenware.com. The best shop for fine professional and home kitchen products, including hard-to-find pots and pans, Italian mezzalune (half-moon choppers), and so forth.

Browne Trading Company, 260 Commercial Street, Portland, ME 04101. 800-944-7848; browne-trading.com. Excellent salt cod (baccalà) as well as imported and domestic fresh seafood.

Chefshop.com. 877-337-2491; www.chefshop.com. Good online service primarily (there's a small retail shop in Seattle) for a variety of interesting food products, many from southern Italy.

D'Angelo Brothers, 909 South Ninth Street, Philadelphia, PA 19147. 215-923-5637; dangelobros.com. Good source for Italian cuts of meat, sausages, lard, and so on.

Di Palo's, 206 Grand Street, New York, NY 10013. 212-226-1033; A historic New York City outlet for high-quality Italian imports, di Palo's also makes its own fresh mozzarella daily.

A. G. Ferrari Foods, 14234 Catalina Street, San Leandro, CA 94577. 877-878-2783; agferrari.com. Imported Italian food products of the highest quality; also with a chain of retail specialty shops in the Bay Area, plus mail order.

Formaggio Kitchen, 244 Huron Avenue, Cambridge, MA 02138. 888-212-3224; formaggiokitchen.com. Fine cheeses, olive oils, pastas, honeys, and other products, many imported from Italy. Retail shop with mail-order service, catalog available.

Gustiamo.com. 718-860-2949, 877-907-2525; gustiamo.com. Excellent mail-order resource for fine Italian products such as Miracolo di San Gennaro San Marzano tomatoes, bottarga, farro, cicerchie beans, Sicilian estratto di pomodoro, and more.

Manicaretti. manicaretti.com. An excellent source for fine Italian ingredients, Manicaretti is a wholesaler but the website can provide information about retail outlets.

P. G. Molinari & Sons, 1401 Yosemite Avenue, San Francisco, CA 94124. 415-822-5555; molinarisalame.com. Producers of a number of fresh and dried Italian-style sausages that are very close to the real thing—which is, of course, otherwise unavailable in the United States.

Murray's Cheese, 254 Bleecker Street, New York, NY 10014. 212-243-3289; murrayscheese.com. A first-rate source for hard-to-find Italian (and other) cheeses.

Sunnyland Mills, 4469 E. Annadale Avenue, Fresno, CA 93725-2221. 559-233-4983; sunnylandmills.com. Suppliers of *grano pestato,* also known as peeled wheat, used in southern Italian dishes such as pastiera di grano from Napoli.

Todaro Brothers, 555 Second Avenue, New York, NY 10016. 877-472-2767; todarobros.com. First-rate Italian and other imported food products; retail and mail order.

Zingerman's Deli, 422 Detroit Street, Ann Arbor, MI 48104. 888-636-8162; zingermans.com. Fine cheeses, olive oils, pastas, honeys, and other products, many from southern Italy. Retail shop with mail-order distribution; catalog available.

*

Sur La Table. 800-243-0852, 866-328-5412; surlatable.com.

Williams-Sonoma. 877-812-6235; williams-sonoma.com.

Both of these sources are well known for catalog sales and many retail outlets around the United States, with specialty cookware such as couscoussières.

Food and travel go hand in hand. What better way to understand the dialect of another cuisine than by experiencing it directly, on the spot and in the mouth? Like language, cuisine can be truly understood only in the place where its soul is at home. But is it really safe to travel in the Italian South?

Once upon a time, it seems, the cities of the Mezzogiorno were ruled by thugs and hoodlums, *la malavita* in Italian, while the southern countryside was legendary for bandits and cutthroats ready to fall upon unsuspecting tourists and denude them of their cash, their jewels, and, for the most unfortunate, their lives. Thankfully that time, if it ever really existed, is long past. For many years the traveler in southern Italy has been as safe as anywhere in the world, and a lot safer than in many places. Yet much of Italy's South still suffers from an undeservedly scary reputation. Of course pickpockets exist, as they do in every major city and tourist mecca around the world, but, apart from petty thievery (which admittedly feels unpetty to its victims), crime, where it exists, is not aimed at tourists. Stay alert to your environment, just as you would in New York, Chicago, Paris, or London, and you should be as safe and comfortable as you would in any major city in the world.

And some of the greatest cities in the world are in the south of Italy. Places like Napoli, Palermo, Catania, and Bari are home to the Mediterranean's oldest and deepest cultures; whether you're looking for ancient ruins or modern discos, these are places of tremendous fascination. In the hearts of these old towns you'll find lively street life and thriving markets, vibrant with the daily drama of give-and-take, and no less so for the foods to be had, from the double-crusted savory pies issuing from bakeries in Bari to the fragrant traditional pizzas of Napoli to the deep-fried rice balls called *arancini* in the *friggitorie,* the fry stalls, of Palermo. Apart from these splendid street traditions, some of the Mezzogiorno's greatest restaurants are also located in these cities, both grand establishments replete with crystal and crisp linens and humble neighborhood *trattorie* where you dine on butcher's paper and the wine is poured into scratched tumblers.

But don't forget the countryside, too, when traveling in the South. It's a curious thing that differentiates southern European restaurant culture from that of North America that many of the finest, most interesting, and most innovative restaurants are not in fact located in cities at all but out in the country, often deep in the country—in tiny, unpromising villages, perhaps, or down narrow, dusty, apparently endless lanes. But wherever you go, even far from fine restaurants with Michelin stars and guidebook acclaim, you'll find that it's hard to get a really bad meal in the Italian South. At the very least you can expect just picked local vegetables, farm-raised chickens, eggs, and rabbits, or fish fresh from the sea, and good wine and olive oil. And if you don't find that, just head for the nearest market to assemble a selection of local cheeses and well-cured salami, bread and wine, along with tomatoes or oranges, cherries, pomegranates, or persimmons, depending on the season, then look for a mountain glade or a sandy stretch of beachfront to enjoy a picnic lunch al fresco, Italian style.

Open-air markets are great places to get a feel for local food and local customs. I think of the crowded Ballarò and Capo markets in Palermo or the daily market at the beginning of the ancient island district of Ortygia in Siracusa, of the many small, vibrant neighborhood markets that pepper the backstreets and squares of Napoli, of the bustling marketplace in the main piazza of Monopoli south of Bari, or the open-air fish market of Catania, where you truly feel the beat of the heart of this great city. In the bustle and commotion of markets like these, you'll find mostly what's strictly seasonal since few stalls sell imported foodstuffs apart from bananas. Wherever you go, the market philosophy in general is: if it's from here, if it's in season, it's bound to be good; if it's not from here, if it's not ripe yet, we don't need it. So it's prickly pears, wild mushrooms, and table grapes in late October, foraged snails after a period of rain, artichokes and a whole plethora of spicy wild and cultivated greens in winter, asparagus, peas, and sweet, fresh fava beans in springtime, then drifting from spring to summer, through all the wonderful stone fruits and hot-weather vegetables, red and yellow peppers, black and purple eggplants, and of course tomatoes in dozens of different sizes, shapes, and colors. Here, too, you'll find that seafood follows the seasons, although it may not be so obvious—with pearly pink and moist swordfish, deep crimson tuna, octopus, and squid in as many varieties as you can imagine, freshly cultivated mussels, clams, and oysters, so alive their shells wink open and shut, and anchovies and sardines that seem to sing with sweet flavor. There may be a stout countrywoman on a corner steaming stuffed artichokes for shoppers to take home or an old gent hunched over a stick fire in a converted oil drum in which he roasts the season's first chestnuts for munching as you stroll through the market stalls. Inevitably there will be African youths, wares spread on plastic sheets, selling knockoff Rolexes and Vuitton bags along with genuine boxes of Kleenex and bootlegged CDs of favorite Afro singers, as if we were in Freetown or Accra instead of the Mezzogiorno italiano. In any case, markets like these are all about flavor, color, fragrance, the passionate cries of market vendors, about intensity—about life itself.

When should you go to southern Italy? Summers are hot and winters can be dreary with icy rain. Springtime is lovely, with rolling green fields of wheat and wildflowers blossoming along roadsides; Easter, the ancient Mediterranean festival of returning life, is celebrated with a power and passion like nowhere else in the world. But autumn is my all-time favorite season. The weather has cooled measurably from summer's heat but is still pleasant enough for only a light cardigan during the day, and the hordes of Italian and northern European tourists, whose goal in life seems to be to acquire a deep tan while consuming quantities of beer and Coca-Cola, have thankfully departed. Moreover, autumn is the harvest season. The grape harvest extends from late August through October, while the olive harvest begins in mid-October and lasts in some areas till Christmas. Summer fruits and vegetables are still available, and autumn ones are coming on. The first artichokes show up in market stalls along with bosky wild mushrooms, fichi d'India (prickly pears), and persimmons, while bitter wild asparagus is still appearing on restaurant menus.

Carrying food products back home to share with those left behind is part of the thrill for food lovers when they travel. There is a certain amount of mythology afloat about what can and cannot be taken back to the United States. To set the record straight: Under no circumstances

---

In general, the wines of southern Italy have suffered for years, perhaps for centuries, from a poor reputation. Much of the wine produced in this prolific area is still what Australians call *plonk*. Traditionally, lots of southern hot-country wine was shipped north in bulk to boost the strength of northern wines. (Lecce in southern Puglia is known as the Florence of the South, in part because it's a beautiful town but not least because wines from the surrounding Salento were regularly sent north to Tuscany to add oomph to flaccid chiantis.) Recent years, however, have seen a surge in production of high-quality wines, both reds and whites, throughout the Mezzogiorno, most notably in Sicily and Campania, as winemakers have responded to consumer demand with new technologies and new plantings, many of them the international chestnuts chardonnay, cabernet, and merlot.

But the great strength of the South is in its abundance of local varieties, autochthonous and traditional vines, many with very distinguished ancestry—*aglianico* is said, on uncertain authority, to be a corruption of *ellenico,* indicating a vine that was brought by the first Greek settlers back in the mists of time. Modern consumers, bored with the same old cabs and chards that taste alike from Napa to Barossa and back again, are increasingly turning to southern Italy for more exciting and interesting aromas and flavors. Red varieties like Puglia's negro amaro and Sicily's nero d'Avola, whites like fiano and greco, both grown primarily in Campania, along with the great aglianico and dozens of others—uva di Troia and primitivo from Puglia, Sicily's white inzolia and catarrato, Calabria's red magliocco canino—are all capable of producing interesting wines and often, given greater care in the vineyard and up-to-date technology in the winery, even great wines.

can any meat products, including cured sausages and hams, be taken home, even when cry-ovacked; nor can fresh produce, fruits and vegetables alike, be carted back in any form. On the other hand, cheese—if it's obviously for your own consumption—is completely legal, even un-pasteurized cheese, if it's clearly for your own use and not for resale. Dried pasta is fine, and so are various packaged food products, including dried wild mushrooms, canned tomatoes, and tomato paste or estratto di pomodoro. Wine is limited but not banned, and if you find a bargain in a fine wine and want to bring back more than the two-bottle limit, you will simply declare it and pay the duty—and most likely it will still be a bargain.*

For my money, however, the best use of the returning traveler's euros as well as baggage allowance is not to spend it on wine, unless you come across a truly great and rare bottle or two, but rather to spend both euros and allowance on olive oil, especially if you are in Italy during the harvest season and have the opportunity to buy straight from a *frantoio*, or mill. Purchase at a hardware store (*ferramenteria*) or housewares shop (*casalinga*) a five- or ten-liter bidone (a plastic jug with a screw top), rinse it thoroughly and let it dry, then take it to the mill and have it filled with fresh oil. You may curse as you drag the thing through DeGaulle or Heathrow, but you will bless yourself a thousand times over once you get that incomparable oil back in your own home kitchen.

The following are names and other relevant information about people, products, and places, those mentioned in this book and also a few that I lacked space to include in the text. Several places I've listed are agriturismi. For readers unfamiliar with the term, this indicates a working farm (more or less) that has rooms, sometimes even apartments, often quite elaborate and comfortable, for paying guests. Breakfast is always included, and often arrangements can be made for an evening meal as well. Agriturismi are usually a good deal cheaper than hotels, and although lacking in some amenities (concierge, phone in the room, television), they may otherwise be well equipped. Often the food, ideally based on farm products, is very good indeed.

In Campania

SANT'AGATA SUI DUE GOLFI, MASSA LUBRENSE (NAPOLI): Ristorante Don Alfonso 1890, Corso Sant'Agata 11; 081-878-0026; donalfonso.com. Chef Alfonso Iaccarino and his wife, Livia, produce some of the best food in Campania, if not in all of Italy; innovative, yes, but deeply rooted in tradition. Awarded two stars by the Michelin guides, Don Alfonso is one of a handful of southern Italian restaurants to have received this accolade. Five comfortable guest suites are attached to the restaurant. If it's convenient, ask for a tour of the restaurant's organic gardens, Le Peracciole, out on the end of the Sorentino Peninsula with a view of Capri.

*Under current (new) restrictions, no liquids may be carried onto U.S.-bound flights.

SANT'AGATA SUI DUE GOLFI, MASSA LUBRENSE (NAPOLI): Agriturismo Le Tore; 081-808-0637; letore.com. A comfortable agriturismo (farm-stay hotel) high up on the Sorentino Peninsula, Le Tore offers a very different experience from Don Alfonso. Owner Vittoria Brancaccio produces high-quality extra-virgin olive oil from centuries-old trees, as well as wine, apples, nuts, fruits, jams, and honeys, all organically, and all served at the farmhouse table, which is open only to guests.

PAESTUM (SALERNO): Agriturismo Seliano, loc. Borgo Antico, via Seliano; 0828-724-544, 0828-723-634; agriturismoseliano.it. Just outside the stunning Greek temple complex of Paestum, this comfortable agriturismo also functions as a water-buffalo ranch. The farm's herd supplies the table with mozzarella, ricotta, and other buffalo-milk products, as well as buffalo veal for delicious main-course stews and ragù: Meals are served only to guests staying at the farm. Cooking classes may be arranged.

NAPOLI: Antica Pizzeria da Michele, via Cesare Sersale, 1–3; 081-553-9204. Located in the heart of Napoli (Spaccanapoli), da Michele offers what to my mind are the best, the most authentic, and the most traditional Neapolitan pizzas. For a fuller description, see page 45.

NAPOLI: La Cantina di Triunfo, Riviera di Chiaia 64; 081-668-101; closed Sundays. The Cantina functions as a wine shop in the daytime, but at night it comes alive as a restaurant, where Tina Nicodemo prepares dishes that are deeply rooted in the finest Neapolitan traditions. Not surprisingly, there is also a very complete wine list, overseen by Tina's husband, Carmelo.

NAPOLI: Mimi alla Ferrovia, via Alfonso d'Aragona 21; 081-553-8525. Near the Napoli train station, this is a famous old Neapolitan bistro that continues to serve a fine, robust, traditional cuisine. At lunchtime the place is bustling with lawyers and businessmen, which, in Italy, is often the mark of a really great kitchen.

PIETRAVAIRANO (CASERTA): La Stalla della Caveja, via SS. Annunziata 10; 0823-984-824; closed Sunday evenings and Mondays. Berardino Lombardo runs this country-style restaurant with a good selection of local dishes and products, many of them—olive oil, cured meats, and excellent bread from a wood-fired oven—produced specifically by or for the restaurant. Simple, clean rooms make this a good stop for travelers heading south on the A-1 autostrada; it's near the Caianello exit.

Food Products to Look For in Restaurants or Shops

MOZZARELLA DI BUFALA: The real thing, this is almost as symbolic of Campanian cuisine as pizza alla napoletana. Caseificio Vannulo in the town of Capaccio Scalo near Paestum (0828-724-765) is an especially interesting buffalo farm along with a sparkling clean dairy, open to the public, where mozzarella and other cheeses, along with ice cream and yogurt, are made from the milk of the farm's large herd of darkly beautiful *bufale*.

PROVOLONE DEL MONACO: Another fine cheese, this is made by the pasta filata (stretched curd) method from the raw milk of agerolese cows on the Sorentino peninsula. Fratelli Fusco, via Santa Maria 45, in Agerola (081-879-1339) makes a very fine provolone that is aged in caves below the dairy.

LA COLATURA: Cetara, west of Salerno at the beginning of the Amalfi coast, is home to this curious condiment, made from the amber-colored juice expressed by anchovies as they cure. The modern equivalent of ancient Roman garum, the fermented fish sauce is as strange and addictive as Vietnamese nuoc mam, which it closely resembles. Try spaghetti alla colatura at Ristorante Acquapazza, Corso Garibaldi 38, in Cetara (089-261-606); closed Mondays.

AMALFI LEMONS: Famous throughout Italy for their characteristic sweet, yet intensely aromatic fragrance, these are grown on steep, south-facing terraces to absorb maximum sunlight, while soft sea breezes keep the lemon trees cool. Sfusato amalfitano and feminello are the two varieties that make the best limoncello, a product that has become something of a cliché in Italy recently but that, at its best, as it is here, can be a delightful revelation.

PASTA: In Gragnano and Torre Annunziata, two towns just south of Naples, it's the water quality, they say, that makes the pasta so special. Any pasta made in this mini-region is bound to be good; a personal favorite is Setaro from Torre Annunziata, a pasta that is also available on a limited basis in North America.

ACCIUGHE DELLA MENAICA: A deeply traditional method of harvesting anchovies, still practiced at the tiny fishing port of Marina di Pisciotta in the Cilentano south of Salerno, produces exceptionally fine anchovies because of the nature of the nets used. A fleet of small craft practices this sustainable fishery in season, and the fishermen's wives salt the anchovies and pack them in ceramic containers.

OLIVE OIL: Campania boasts three areas of protected denomination of origin for extra-virgin olive oil—DOP Cilento, DOP Colline Salernitane, and DOP Penisola Sorentino.

WINES: Locally grown white varietals include fiano, which was almost extinct when the Mastroberardino winery brought it back to life some fifty years ago. Fiano makes a distinguished white wine (and Mastroberardino's Radici Fiano di Avellino is perhaps the most distinguished) with elegant honey and tropical fruit flavors; other white varieties include greco (best known as Greco di Tufo), coda di volpe (fox tail), and falanghina. Reds include piedirosso, which wine authority Ian d'Agata says may be related to grenache, and the all-star aglianico, the grape responsible for Taurasi, the region's only DOCG, which produces elegant red wines, rich and full-bodied with plenty of dark fruit fragrance (plums, black cherries), especially when planted in the volcanic soils in which the South abounds. D'Agata includes twenty-one important producers of red and white wines in Campania, among them Mastroberardino, Terredora (which evolved out of an acrimonious dispute within the Mastroberardino family), Feudi di San Gregorio, and Marisa Cuomo's Gran Furore on the Amalfi coast.

In Puglia

CEGLIE MESSAPICO (BRINDISI): Al Fornello da Ricci, Contrada Montevicoli; 0831-377-104; ricciristor@liebro.it; closed Monday nights and Tuesdays. In the country outside the town of Ceglie Messapica, Dora and Angelo Ricci established this stylish restaurant some years ago; now the kitchen is primarily under the supervision of daughter Antonella and her husband, Vinobha Sookhar, while another daughter, Rossella, helps run the dining room. The Riccis' adherence to local products and local traditions is still firmly in place while the younger generation has brought a stylish, modern touch to the classic dishes of the region.

GRAVINA IN PUGLIA (BARI): Osteria di Cucco Salvatore, Piazza Pellicciari 4; 080-326-1872; osteriacucco.it; closed Mondays. In the historic center of this small city built over a ravine (*gravina*), this is a rustically attractive, down-home sort of restaurant with a friendly staff and a menu built on local traditions like cicerchie (an ancient legume) and cardoncelli (the wild mushrooms of Puglia's Murge district).

ORSARA DI PUGLIA (FOGGIA): Nuova Sala del Paradiso, via Piano Paradiso 11; 0881-964-763; open for lunch only, except for overnight guests. Chef Pepe Zullo produces his own wine, sausages, and pasta for his restaurant and small (five suites) hotel, in the Daunia Mountains of northern Puglia. He is also a fine resource for locally crafted cheeses and heirloom apples, many of which come from a nearby orchard he has painstakingly restored.

OSTUNI (BRINDISI): Il Frantoio, SS 16, klm. 874; 0831-330-276; masseriailfrantoio.it Armando and Rosalba Balestrazzi run a beautiful agriturismo (farm-stay hotel) of great comfort and character; delicious meals are available for guests, with most of the dishes based on the farm's own products, including especially their fine olive oil.

MONOPOLI (BARI): Masseria Curatori, Cont. Cristo delle Zolle 227; 080-777-472, 338-624-2833. Another agriturismo of great character with fine food, produced on the premises by Lucrezia Contento from the products of the farm, which she owns and operates with her husband, Onofrio. The Contentos are fifth-generation farmers of this property.

MARITTIMA DI DISO (LECCE): Il Convento di Santa Maria di Costantinopoli, via Convento; information +44 (0) 7736-362-328; Lord and Lady McAlpine, Alistair and Athena, are the unlikely owners of this splendid retreat where the sumptuous meals, available for guests only, are supervised by Lady McAlpine with a local chef who sometimes consults his mother when he's stumped for a recipe. The cuisine is based on rigorously selected local products.

SPECCHIA GALONE (LECCE): Panificio Donato Caroppo, via S. Anna 34; 0836-818-519; panificiocaroppo.it. A family bakery: Mr. Caroppo makes a number of traditional Pugliese breads, including especially puccie, crisp little buns with black olives tucked inside, which he bakes in his wood-fired ovens; his wife provides lunch daily, serving a set menu of traditional dishes at a few tables laid out in a room next to the bakery; his mother, Abbondanza, tends the cash register and spins delightful tales of life as it used to be.

FOOD PRODUCTS TO LOOK FOR IN RESTAURANTS OR SHOPS

BURRATA FROM ANDRIA: Shreds of cow's-milk mozzarella, mixed with cream, are encased in a mozzarella sack to make this sumptuous cheese, which is apt to be served as an antipasto rather than at the end of the meal. It was invented in Andria in the 1930s but is now quite widespread throughout the region of Bari.

LOCALLY-MADE PASTA, produced from hard durum wheat grown on the Tavoliere, the plain of northern Puglia, especially that from Pastificio Benedetto Cavaliere in Maglie, south of Lecce. Another good local brand is Pastificio Benagiano, made in Sant'Eramo in Colle, in the Murge.

EXTRA-VIRGIN OLIVE OIL: Puglia is Italy's largest producer of olive oil by far, and much of it is high-quality extra-virgin. Look for any of Puglia's DOPs (denominations of protected origin): Collina di Brindisi, Dauno, Terra d'Otranto, and Terra di Bari. In addition, the huge and meaty green table olive Bella della Daunia, familiar in the United States as bella di Cerignola, has a protected designation.

ALTAMURA BREAD from the city of the same name in the heart of the Murge is said by many Italians to be the best bread in Italy. Made in huge loaves, sometimes weighing as much as fifteen kilos (thirty-plus pounds), using locally grown hard durum wheat, the loaves are baked in wood-fired ovens. The bread, which recently received "denomination of protected origin" status, is available in local groceries, but to see it being baked on the spot, go to Altamura itself, a charming town, and follow your nose to one of several bakeries producing these remarkable loaves.

WINES: Puglia rivals Sicily for Italy's largest wine producer, but a huge amount of what is made here is shipped out as blending wine. Still, to knowledgeable wine lovers, Puglia means some of Italy's most interesting red wines, notably big, chewy, dark-textured reds produced from native grapes negro amaro (black bitter) and primitivo, which most experts now accept as the ancestor of California's zinfandel. (Pugliese whites are less interesting—quaffing wines for hot summer days but not much more.) A surprising candidate for serious wine attention is Puglia's rosati (rosé wines), especially those from the DOC Castel del Monte, made from the native bombino nero grape. Producers to look for include Cosimo Taurino, a historic winery in the Salentino peninsula, Accademia dei Racemi for elegant zinfandel/primitivo reds, and Masseria Monaci, the estate of Puglia's top wine consultant, Severino Garofano.

COOKING SCHOOL: Silvestro Silvestori is a young Italian-American with a passion for the culinary traditions of his adopted Puglia. Throughout the year, except in the heat of summer, he runs weeklong cooking classes from his headquarters in Lecce and is also available for culinary consultation. For more information, on the school as well as on local cuisine and products, check out his website awaitingtable.com.

In Basilicata

TERRANOVA DI POLLINO (POTENZA): Luna Rossa, via Marconi, 18; 0973-93-254. In a village situated high amid the peaks of the stunning Parco Nazionale del Pollino, chef-proprietor Federico Valicenti is a passionate advocate of his local terroir and the cuisine that has evolved in this mountain fastness. After dining at La Luna Rossa, where portions are copious, you may want to stay and explore this delightful village and the surrounding terrain—there are a number of simple, comfortable hotels and pensions for hikers and mountaineers, attracted to the park that extends across the mountains of southern Basilicata and northern Calabria.

VENOSA: Ristorante Il Grifo, via delle Fornaci 21 (in the center of town, near the sixteenth-century fortress); 0972-35-188; closed Tuesdays. A bustling restaurant in the heart of this fascinating town that was, among other things, birthplace, in 65 B.C.E., of the great Roman poet

Horace (Orazio in Italian). Known for serving traditional local dishes, such as *strascinati*, a wide pasta shape, made from *farina di gran'arso*, flour ground from burnt wheat, an ancient custom.

FOOD PRODUCTS TO LOOK FOR IN RESTAURANTS OR SHOPS

SWEET CHESTNUTS, called *marrone*, from the slopes of the Vulture, the extinct volcano that dominates northern Basilicata. Chestnuts from the groves that spread along Vulture's slopes are used to make purees and other sweets, but they are delicious when fresh, simply roasted on their own.

BREAD FROM MATERA, made with locally grown hard durum wheat and baked in wood-fired ovens in big loaves, is as acclaimed as that from Altamura (see Puglia), and like Altamura bread it has a special recognition, IGP (Indicazione geografica protetta), for its quality. While in Matera, don't miss the Sassi, the incredible rock-cut houses piled one on the other that make up a UNESCO World Heritage Site.

OLIVE OIL: Basilicata doesn't yet have a DOP for olive oil, but that doesn't mean the oil isn't good. More likely, no one has yet bothered with the bureaucratic hijinks necessary to acquire DOP status. Maiatica is a major variety, along with ogliarola in the Vulture region, as well as more familiar varieties like frantoiana and coratina. The ancient olive trees of Basilicata and neighboring Calabria are often spectacular giants, as tall as elms. A single tree may be owned by several families, each family claiming a branch or two of the main tree and harvesting separately.

PECORINO CHEESES from Filiano and Moliterno, two towns widely separated but both making high-quality cheeses from the raw milk of Gentile da Puglia sheep that graze on natural mountain pastures. Up to 10% goat's milk is often added to both cheeses, because the flocks of sheep include a goat for every ten sheep, to induce the sheep to follow more adventurous goats into less accessible pasture. Pecorino di Filiano is aged for a year, canestrato di Moliterno for about eight months. The process of making the cheeses is slightly different, but both are elegant, with complex and robust nutty, lactic flavors. Two other cheeses of interest: aged caciocavallo podolico, made from the milk of native podolico cows, and casieddu, a fresh goat's milk cheese made in summer, perfumed with ferns and nepitella, a wild mint.

OTHER LOCAL PRODUCTS worth looking for include grano pestato, an ancient strain of durum wheat that is pounded to rid the grains of a thin indigestible pellicle, usually cooked as whole grains and served sauced with a ragù or mixed with nuts, pomegranate seeds, and vincotto to make a sweet pudding; Senise peppers from the Sinni and Agri River valleys, a thin-skinned pepper with a distinctive flavor, not particularly hot but sweet and satisfyingly spicy. A low water content makes these peppers good for drying, and you'll often find them sold in braids or crushed to a coarse powder.

WINES: For wine lovers, Basilicata means just one thing: aglianico del Vulture, one of Italy's greatest red wines, on a par with the great barolos and brunellos of the North. This is the same aglianico grape that goes into Taurasi from Campania and any number of other fine southern red wines, but here on the mineral-rich slopes of a spent volcano, the Vulture, in northern Basilicata, this late-maturing variety reaches its apotheosis in an intensely fragrant wine, deep ruby red in color, filled with dark fruit flavors and hints of spice and vanilla. Outside the region, aglianico del Vulture is not always easy to find, so it's worth a trip to towns like Rionero del Vulture, Melfi, and Venosa to sample this great wine. Gerardo Giuratrabochetti's Cantine del Notaio is a producer to look for, along with d'Angelo, Paternostra, Tenuta Le Querce, and others.

In Calabria

CASTROVILLARI (COSENZA): Locanda di Alia, via Jetticelle 55; 0981-46-370; alia.it. A lovely, small, chic hotel and restaurant, run by the Alia brothers, just fifteen convenient minutes off the A-3 Autostrada between Napoli and Reggio Calabria (exit Frascineto-Castrovillari) and right next to the splendid Pollino National Park. Chef Gaetano Alia produces elegant and stylish food, very imaginative but always firmly tied to local traditions and ingredients. The restaurant, which is closed on Sundays, also prepares jams, marmalades, rosolii (liqueurs), and other delectables from fruits and vegetables found in local markets and available for guests to purchase—Tropea red-onion jam, for instance, or rosolio of violets.

CIVITA (NEAR CASTROVILLARI): Ristorante Agorà, Piazza Municipio 30; 0981-73410; closed Mondays. Settled many centuries ago by Christian Albanians fleeing the Turks, Civita vaunts its Albanian (Arbëreshe in the local dialect) heritage to this day. Agorà's menu—the restaurant is famous for its abundant antipasto selection—may not be genuinely Albanian, but it is certifiably delicious, and the enchanting town, concealed in a deep mountain valley, is well worth a detour.

ALTOMONTE (COSENZA): Hotel Barbieri, via San Niccola 30; 0981-948-073. Perched on a hillside overlooking medieval Altomonte, the hotel is best known for its restaurant, a treat on any occasion but especially during the October mushroom festival, when all the many different wild mushrooms from the nearby Pollino National Park are celebrated in a variety of dishes.

Food Products to Look For in Restaurants or Shops

DRIED DOTTATO FIGS, baked in the oven and stuffed with almonds or walnuts and grated orange peel, called *crocette,* produced by the Colavolpe family in the little coastal town of Belmonte Càlabro. Giulia, Nicola, and Gerardo Colavolpe are the third generation to produce these delicacies; each of the siblings knows just a third of their grandfather's secret formula for preparing the delicious figs, ensuring family solidarity as well as continuity.

CITRUS FRUIT: Calabria is home to two odd and little-known citrus fruits—the bergamot lemon, whose musky oil gives Earl Grey tea its characteristic smoky aroma, which grows along the Ionian coast (the inner part of the toe), and the citron (*cedro* in Italian), a lemon-colored fruit cultivated along the Tyrrhenian or west coast that can grow as big as a football. Here, they tell me, rabbis come from all over the Jewish world to select the most perfect fruits for the feast of Sukkoth (the Feast of the Huts, celebrated in autumn), but the thick peel of the fruit is also candied and used to make jams and liqueurs.

HOT PEPPERS: You'll find them everywhere in Calabria, which is famous for its use of them in everything from soups to sausages. The little seaside town of Diamante, on the Tyrrhenian coast, sports the headquarters of the Accademia Italiana del Peperoncino (via Fausto Gullo 1; 0985-811-30; peperoncino.org), which enthusiastically promotes the consumption of hot chilies.

'NDUJA: A lightly smoked, soft, spreadable sausage, innocent looking when smeared on a crust of bread, but bite into it and you will be set back on your heels by the hot flavors that flood your palate. For every pound of pork in 'nduja, I'm told, 100 grams (about 3½ ounces) of chili is added. The best, they say, is from Catanzaro. Anchovies and sardines are also cured with hot chilies, and a special condiment, called *rosamarina* in some places and *mustica* in others, is a paste of baby anchovies mixed with chili and put aside to mature. It too can be spread on bread, but it's really for die-hard chili addicts.

RED ONIONS from Tropea, an appealing medieval hilltop village on the Capo Vaticano, are as sweet as Vidalias but with lots more onion flavor. They are widely available.

OLIVE OIL: Calabria has two DOPs for olive oil, Bruzio and Lamezia. As in Basilicata, Calabria's olive trees can be as large as oaks or elms. This makes them difficult to harvest except by waiting for mature fruits to drop to the ground, not the best way to produce good olive oil.

WINE: Calabria's best-known wine and major DOC is Cirò, made from the local gaglioppo grape, which some ampelographers claim is one of the oldest varieties in the world. In any case, as a variety it lacks tannins and must be fermented at low temperatures or get a boost from cabernet sauvignon, to augment color and flavor. At its best, as made by top producer Librandi, for instance, Cirò reds (white and rosé wines are also produced) can be light-colored but full-flavored, pleasantly tart, and with a nicely spicy finish that adds to their rustic charm.

Librandi's Cirò rosato is a fine example of rosé wines at their best, crisp-textured but satisfyingly full of flavor.

In Sicily

The island of Sicily, which often acts as if it were an independent country, deserves a volume of its own, so rich is it in wonderful foodstuffs, olive oils, wines, cheeses, restaurants, markets, and traditions. I have made a reluctantly slim suggestion of notable places that might otherwise be overlooked.

The following five restaurants are alike in that they are places where young chefs, all native-born Sicilians, are creating a stir with innovative reinventions of traditional dishes and sparkling presentations that would create attention even in the sophisticated atmosphere of London, Barcelona, or New York. They are also alike in that, except for La Madia, all are located in the southeastern part of the island, but that's just coincidence:

CATANIA: Ristorante Il Cuciniere in the Hotel Katane Palace, via Finocchiaro Aprile 10; 095-747-0702. Chef Carmelo Chiaramonte.

LICATA (AGRIGENTO): Ristorante La Madia, Corso Filippo Re Capriata 22; 0922-771-443; closed Tuesdays. Chef Pino Cuttaia.

MODICA (RAGUSA): Ristorante La Gazza Ladra ("The Thieving Magpie") in Hotel Palazzo Failla, upper Modica; 0952-941-059. Chef Accursio Craparo

RAGUSA: Baglio La Pergola, Contrada Selvaggio; 0932-686-430; closed Tuesdays. Chef Enzo Scrofani.

RAGUSA/IBLA: Ristorante Il Duomo, via Capitano Bocchieri 31; 0932-651-265; closed Mondays. Chef Francesco (Ciccio) Sultano.

Other restaurants of note:

CHIARAMONTE GULFI (RAGUSA): Ristorante da Maiore, via Martiri Ungheresi 12; 0932-928-019. Pork, pork, pork is the theme of this historic restaurant. Vegetarians and fish lovers should stay away, but carnivores will be in heaven.

PALERMO: Antica Focacceria San Francesco, Palermo: A good place to sample some of the delights of Palermitano street food, including an authentic pane co' la meusa, golden arancini, and deep-fried panelle served hot and crisp in a sandwich.

PORTICELLO (PALERMO): Trattoria dell'Arco, Franco u' Piscaturi, Largo Pescheria 26; 091-957-758. Located practically on the docks at Porticello, a delightful and very active fishing village about twenty minutes' drive east of Palermo, this is one of the best fish restaurants along the entire stretch of Sicilian coast. Chef Franco Crivello, a former commercial fisherman, knows what he's doing in the kitchen and the markets as well as in the fishing fleet.

TRAPANI: Cantina Siciliana, via della Giudecca 36; 0923-28-673; cantinasiciliana.it. All the seafood is exceptional here, but Chef Pino Maggiore has a particularly fine hand with traditional Trapani couscous. It's handmade on the premises and served with a substantial fish broth and your choice of fried or grilled fish to accompany it.

Food Shops, Pastry Shops, Ice Cream Shops, Etc.

NOTO (CATANIA): Caffe Sicilia, Corso Vittorio Emanuele 125; 0931-835-267; caffe.sicilia@tin.it. Corrado Assenza has inspired a whole generation of chefs (many of those mentioned earlier) and food writers, with his insistence on the importance of quality and the flavors of terroir, which you can taste immediately in his ice creams, as much as in his jams and other condiments. Unusual ingredients—bergamot lemons, pink quinces, sweet Moscato grapes from Pantelleria—but even the most ordinary flavors (vanilla, chocolate, almond) are treated with respect.

MODICA (RAGUSA): Antica Dolceria Bonajuto, Corso Umberto I 159; 0932-941-225; bonajuto.it. Established more than a century ago by the great-grandfather of the present owner, Francesco Ruta, the shop produces grainy, intensely aromatic bittersweet chocolates made according to ancient Mexican formulas and flavored with cinnamon, vanilla, or chili; another unusual and traditional sweet made here is 'mpanatigghi, baked ravioli filled with a mixture of chocolate, crushed almonds, sugar, and shredded beef.

ERICE (TRAPANI): Pasticceria Maria Grammatico, via Vittorio Emmanuele 14; 0923-869-390; mariagrammatico.it. Maria Grammatico, whose life story is told so well in her book *Bitter Almonds,* written with Mary Taylor Simeti, is an authority on Sicilian convent sweets, having spent her childhood in just such a convent. Her frutti della Martorana, lifelike miniature fruits made from almond paste (marzipan) and tinted to look like the real thing, are a small miracle, and the other sweets and pastries sold in her shop or in the nearby tea room are equally spectacular.

PALERMO: La Dispensa dei Monsù, via Principe di Villafranca 59; 091-609-0465. Francesco Guccione and Boni dell'Oglio are the proprietors of this smart shop where you can try, in a very relaxed setting, all manner of prize Sicilian wines and food products—cheeses, jams, condiments, specialty breads, salumi—before you decide in which direction to head. Both Francesco and Boni are deeply knowledgeable and full of advice and information about the remarkable gastronomic possibilities of their island.

FOOD PRODUCTS TO LOOK FOR IN RESTAURANTS OR SHOPS

PANE NERO DI CASTELVETRANO: The bread, traditionally baked in a wood-fired oven, is made from the stone-ground flour of a locally grown wheat called *tumminia.* Although it's called *nero,* it isn't a black bread at all—rather a grayish beige with a subtle nutty aroma and flavor from the wheat. Tommaso Rizzo, Piazza Matteoti 58, is a baker who has staked his reputation on this excellent bread.

CHEESE: Sicily is a repository for great cheeses, including caciocavallo made from cow's milk by the pasta filata (stretched curd) method, one of the best being ragusano, made from the milk of modicana cows and aged for up to a year in huge blocks weighing several kilos. Sheep's milk pecorino cheeses include the saffron-flavored piacentinu from Enna and the unusual vastedda del Belice, a sheep's milk cheese made by the pasta filata method. Fresh sheep's milk cheeses like tuma and primosale are often served as an antipasto, and ricotta, warm from the dairy, is considered a special breakfast treat.

BOTTARGA: Salted, dried, and pressed tuna roe is a rare delicacy still being made in many parts of the island. The best is probably that made by the Salvatore Campisi firm in Marzamemi, near Pachino, but it is widely available, a good product to take back as it costs a small fortune in the United States. The Campisi firm also makes mosciame di tonno (a sort of tuna prosciutto), top-quality canned (actually jarred) tuna and ricciola (amberjack), and many other seafood products, including dried squid ink for making risotto nero.

SALTED-PACKED CAPERS FROM THE ISLANDS OF PANTELLERIA OR SALINA: These are exquisite because of the care that is taken in handling them. They are available loose, by the etto (100 grams), in most markets.

OLIVE OIL: There's been a real increase in quality production of Sicilian olive oil in recent years, and the region has five denominations of protected origin (DOP): Monti Iblei and Monte Etna on the east side of the island and Valli Trapanesi, Val di Mazara, and Valle del Belice on the west. Some of the most interesting oils are Olio Verde from Gianfranco Becchina in Castelvetrano,

Olio Titone, much of it certified organic, from the Titone family in Marsala, and Pianogrillo from Lorenzo Piccione in the Monti Iblei near Chiaramonte Gulfi.

WINES: It's as difficult to categorize Sicily's wines as it is the cheeses and oils of the island, which, as the largest island in the Mediterranean, represents an enormously varied territory. Major producers include Planeta and Regaleali (the Tasca d'Almerita family). Planeta has vineyards in several parts of Sicily, while the Tasca d'Almeritas have stuck pretty much to their home base in the central part of the island. But both have been adventurous in experimenting with autochthonous grapes as well as with international varieties. Smaller producers have often been even more adventurous: COS in the southern territory of Vittoria has experimented with fermentation in old-fashioned terra-cotta *orce,* big amphoralike jars such as were used by ancient Greek winemakers, while Giuseppe Benanti, working on the slopes of Mount Etna with enologist Salvo Foti, has won recent acclaim for his recovery of old varietals, like the carricante that goes into his prize-winning white Pietramarina, a surprisingly intense, dry, fruit-flavored wine with an aroma of citrus blossoms.

A few special Sicilian wines deserve notice—moscato di Pantelleria and malvasia delle Lipari, sweet wines for after-dinner consumption but, when well made, without any of the cloying, syrupy characteristics that sweet wines all too often connote. And then there is Marsala, a complex wine that, at its best (and this is increasingly rare, alas), is as superb as the finest oloroso sherry. The best and most conscientious producer is Marco di Bartoli. Di Bartoli's Vecchio Samperi is marketed as vino da tavola rather than Marsala because the wine has less than the minimum of 18% alcohol required by the DOP and di Bartoli refuses to fortify it by adding alcohol. He calls it a *vino liquoroso,* but it is as close to the old-fashioned, much-loved Marsalas as you can find on the market today.

COOKING SCHOOLS

THE WORLD OF REGALEALI: Anna Tasca Lanza, of the Tasca d'Almerita winemaking family, gives cooking classes for a day, several days, or a week, at her property overlooking the vineyards of the family's huge establishment at Regaleali in the heart of Sicily, about ninety minutes from Palermo. There are also rooms and suites available for the night or longer. For more information, or to book classes, go to absoluteitalia.com.

CUCINA DEL SOLE: via Contemare 9, Viagrande (Catania); 095-789-0016; cucinadelsole.it. In her own very comfortable village home and kitchen, located about thirty minutes north of Catania on the slopes of Mount Etna, Eleonora Consoli, retired journalist and prolific food writer, gives classes (in English or Italian) in the finest Sicilian traditional home cooking. For those who wish it, she also offers bed and breakfast possibilities.

Anderson, Burton. *Vino: The Wine and Winemakers of Italy*. Boston: Little Brown, 1980.

Bastianic, Joseph, and David Lynch. *Vino Italiano: The Regional Wines of Italy*. New York: Clarkson Potter, 2002.

Belfrage, Nicolas. *Life Beyond Lambrusco: Understanding Italian Fine Wine*. London: Sidgwick & Jackson, 1985.

Benivegna, Angelo. *Il gusto della tradizione*. Trapani: Coppola Editore, 2003.

Cavalcanti, Ottavio. *La cucina della Basilicata*. Roma: Newton & Compton, 2003.

Cilento, Adele. "Presenze etniche nella Calabria medievale: testimonianze di fonti agiografiche" [A stampa in "Rivista Storica Calabrese," XVI (1995), pp. 91–117—Distribuito in formato digitale da "Reti Medievali"].

Coria, Giuseppe. *La cucina della Sicilia orientale*. Padova: Franco Muzio Ed., 1996.

———. *Profumi di Sicilia*. Palermo, Caltanisetta, and Catania: Cavollotto Ed., 1981.

Cornelison, Ann. *Women of the Shadows: Wives and Mothers of Southern Italy*. Boston: Little Brown, 1976.

Dalby, Andrew. *Siren Feasts: A History of Food and Gastronomy in Greece*. London and New York: Routledge, 1996.

Davidson, Alan. *Mediterranean Seafood: A Comprehensive Guide with Recipes*, 3rd ed. Berkeley, Calif.: Ten Speed Press, 2002.

Davidson, James. *Courtesans and Fishcakes: The Consuming Passions of Classical Athens*. New York: HarperCollins, 1999.

Douglas, Norman. *In Old Calabria*, based on the original edition, published in 1915. Evanston, Ill.: Marlboro Press, 1993.

Francesconi, Jeanne Caròli. *La Cucina napoletana*, Roma: Newton Compton, 1992.

Goethe, J. W. *Italian Journey* [1786–1788], trans. W. H. Auden and Elizabeth Mayer. London: Penguin, 1992.

Gosetti della Salda, Anna. *Le ricette regionali italiane*, 11th ed. Milano: Solares, 1967.

Gray, Patience. *Honey from a Weed*. New York: HarperCollins, 1987.

Grewe, Rudolf. "The Arrival of the Tomato in Spain and Italy." *The Journal of Gastronomy* 3, no. 2 (summer 1987).

Hazelton, Nika. *The Regional Italian Kitchen*. New York: M. Evans, 1978.

Jenkins, Nancy Harmon. *The Mediterranean Diet Cook Book*. New York: Bantam, 1994.

———. *Flavors of Puglia*. New York: Broadway, 1997.

———. *The Essential Mediterranean*. New York: HarperCollins, 2003.

di Lampedusa, Giuseppe. *The Leopard (Il Gattopardo)*. New York: Pantheon (reissue), 1991.

Lanza, Anna Tasca. *The Flavors of Sicily*. New York: Clarkson Potter, 1996.

———. *The Heart of Sicily*. New York: Clarkson Potter, 1993.

Maggio, Theresa. *Mattanza: Love and Death in the Sea of Sicily*. Cambridge, Mass.: Perseus, 2000.

Middione, Carlo. *The Food of Southern Italy*. New York: Morrow, 1987.

Noyé, Ghislaine. "Villes, économie et société dans la province de Bruttium-Lucanie du IVe au VIIe siècle," in *La storia dell'altomedioevo italiano (VI–X secolo) alla luce dell'archeologia* (Siena, 1992), a cura di R. Francovich e G. Noyé, Firenze 1994, pp. 693–733; distribuito in formato digitale da "Reti Medievali."

Phillips, Kyle, varia. italianfood.about.com.

Pieroni, Andrea, Sabine Nebel, Cassandra Quave, Harald Münz, and Michael Heinrich. "Ethnopharmacology of liakra: traditional weedy vegetables of the Arbëreshë of the Vulture area in southern Italy." *Journal of Ethnopharmacology* 81 (2002), pp. 165–85.

Simeti, Mary Taylor. *Pomp and Sustenance: Twenty-Five Centuries of Sicilian Food*. New York: Knopf, 1991.

Slow Food Editore. *Ricette di osterie di Puglia*. Bra (CN), 2000.

———. *Ricette di osterie e genti di Sicilia*. Bra (CN), 2003.

Turfa, Jean. Review of Alastair M. Small and Robert J. Buck (ed.). *The Excavations of San Giovanni di Ruoti, Volume 1: The Villas and Their Environment* (Phoenix Supplementary vol. 33. Cheektowaga: University of Toronto Press, 1994). *Bryn Mawr Classical Review* 97.11.14.

Yeadon, David. *Seasons in Basilicata: A Year in a Southern Italian Hill Village*. New York: HarperCollins, 2004.

Acknowledgments

Acknowledgments are a place for the writer to thank all the people who have been helpful in the course of writing a book, but, rather than a thank you, I want to begin with precisely an acknowledgment of a book that preceded this one by several decades and that has given me great pleasure and inspiration over the years I've been reading it and cooking from it. If I had never come across Carlo Middione's *The Food of Southern Italy* (Morrow, 1987), I might still have discovered the Mezzogiorno eventually, but it probably would have taken much longer. As it is, his book has been a stepping-stone from which I've arrived at my own, and I hope he will take my offering as an homage to his.

I'd also like to thank the many, many people of the regions of southern Italy who have been generous with advice, recipes, insights, memories, tips, and stories. That happy band includes but is not limited to Gabriela Becchina, Gianfranco Becchina, Benedetto and Claudia Cavalieri, the Colavolpe family, Eleonora Consoli, Maria Grammatico, Wences and Anna Tasca Lanza, Giuseppe Licitra, Pino Maggiore, Roberto Rubino, Mary Taylor Simeti, Rossella Speranza, Ciccio Sultano, Silvestro Silvestori, and the Titone family.

A special thanks to my former editor, Susan Friedland, and my agent, David Black, for their faith in this book, and to my present editor, Hugh van Dusen, for his patience with my vagaries.